C00 943 805X

D1758901

Spotlight on First

Student's Book

Second Edition

CANCELLED

John Hughes
Jon Naunton

NATIONAL GEOGRAPHIC LEARNING

CENGAGE Learning®

Australia • Brazil • Japan • Korea • Mexico • Singapore • Spain • United Kingdom • United States

ngl.cengage.com/eltexampreparation

PASSWORD spotlightfirs!D5#

**Spotlight on First Student's Book
(2nd Edition)**

John Hughes and Jon Naunton

Publisher: Gavin McLean

Publishing Consultant: Karen Spiller

Freelance Editor: Clare Shaw

Marketing Manager: Charlotte Ellis

Content Project Manager: Tom Relf

Manufacturing Buyer: Eyvett Davis

Head of Production: Alissa McWhinnie

Cover design: Oliver Hutton

Original page design: Keith Shaw

Additional text design: Oliver Hutton

Compositor: MPS Limited

National Geographic Liaison: Wesley Della Volla

DVD production: Tom Dick and Debbie Productions

Practice Test: Helen Chilton and Helen Tiliouine

© 2015 National Geographic Learning, as part of Cengage Learning

ALL RIGHTS RESERVED. No part of this work covered by the copyright herein may be reproduced, transmitted, stored, or used in any form or by any means graphic, electronic, or mechanical, including but not limited to photocopying, recording, scanning, digitizing, taping, Web distribution, information networks, or information storage and retrieval systems, except as permitted under Section 107 or 108 of the 1976 United States Copyright Act, without the prior written permission of the publisher.

For permission to use material from this text or product, submit all requests online at **www.cengage.com/permissions**
Further permissions questions can be emailed to
permissionrequest@cengage.com

ISBN: 978-1-285-84948-5

National Geographic Learning
Cheriton House, North Way, Andover, Hampshire, SP10 5BE
United Kingdom

Cengage Learning is a leading provider of customized learning solutions with office locations around the globe, including Singapore, the United Kingdom, Australia, Mexico, Brazil and Japan. Locate your local office at:
international.cengage.com/region

Cengage Learning products are represented in Canada by Nelson Education, Ltd.

Visit National Geographic Learning online at **ngl.cengage.com**

Visit our corporate website at **www.cengage.com**

Please note that the correct title for the National Geographic Channel video in Unit 13 is *The greenhouse effect*.

Printed in Croatia by Zrinski
Print Number: 04   Print Year: 2015

CONTENTS

DUNDEE CITY COUNCIL

LOCATION
OPPORTUNITIES ROOM

ACCESSION NUMBER
C00 943 805X

SUPPLIER   PRICE
AMAZON   £24·06

CLASS   DATE
428·24   19·11·15

Unit		Vocabulary	Grammar	Use of English	Reading
1	**Friends and family**	Family Describing relationships Key word: *like*	Present tenses	Gossip Paper 1, Part 2: Open cloze Recording phrasal verbs	*Soap operas around the world* Paper 1, Part 7: Multiple matching
2	**Jobs and work**	Jobs and work Personal qualities Key word: *as*	Making comparisons	Paper 1, Part 1: Multiple-choice cloze	*Finding a job* Paper 1, Part 5: Multiple choice
3	**Sport and free time**	Sport and free time Key word: *time*	Obligation and necessity Expressing ability	Paper 1, Part 4: Key word transformations	*Eccentric sports* Paper 1, Part 6: Gapped text
4	**Nature and animals**	Nature and animals Key word *look*	The grammar of phrasal verbs	Paper 1, Part 3: Word formation	*A dog's life* Paper 1, Part 7: Multiple matching
5	**Books and films**	Books and films Key word: *thing* Descriptive verbs	Narrative tenses		*The bangle* Paper 1, Part 5: Multiple choice
6	**Transport and travel**	Travel Travel phrasal verbs Words in context Key word: *just*	Expressing the future		*Dream holidays* Paper 1, Part 7: Multiple matching
7	**Inventions and technology**	Inventors and inventing Key word: *to* Technology	Verbs followed by the gerund or the infinitive	Paper 1, Part 4: Key word transformation	*Robot revolution* Paper 1, Part 6: Gapped text sentences
8	**Crime and social responsibility**	Crime and criminals Key word: *get*	Relative clauses	Open cloze	*Crime and punishment* Paper 1, Part 7: Multiple matching

Listening	Speaking	Writing	Video / Review
Talking about people Paper 3, Part 1: Multiple choice	Paper 4, Part 1: General conversation Asking and answering questions	An essay (1)	Video: a match made in Africa
Talking about jobs Paper 3, Part 4: Multiple choice	Paper 4, Part 3: Collaborative task	A letter	Review U1 and 2 Paper 1, Part 1: Multiple-choice cloze Paper 1, Part 2: Open cloze Paper 1, Part 3: Word formation Paper 1, Part 7: Multiple matching
Free time Paper 3, Part 3: Multiple matching *The early history of football* Paper 3, Part 2: Sentence completion		An article	Video: adventure
Animals and humans Paper 3, Part 3: Multiple matching Points of view	Points of view Paper 4, Part 2: Individual long turn	An essay (2)	Review U3 and 4 Paper 1, Part 1: Multiple-choice cloze Paper 1, Part 2: Open cloze Paper 1, Part 3: Word formation Paper 1, Part 4: Key word transformation Paper 3, Part 2: Sentence completion Paper 3, Part 4: Multiple choice
Great adaptations Paper 3, Part 4: Multiple choice Paper 3, Part 2: Sentence completion	Swapping stories	A short story	Video: Sleepy Hollow
Travel and visits Paper 3, Part 1: Multiple choice	Organising a schedule Discussing options Discussing your travels	A report	Review U5 and 6 Paper 1, Part 1: Multiple-choice cloze Paper 1, Part 2: Open cloze Paper 1, Part 3: Word formation Paper 1, Part 4: Key word transformation Paper 2, Part 2: Review Paper 4, Part 3: Collaborative task
Intelligent robots Paper 3, Part 2: Sentence completion	Suggesting and recommending Paper 4, Part 3: Collaborative task	A review	Video: solar cooking
Stopped by the police Paper 3, Part 3: Multiple matching Paper 3, Part 4: Multiple choice Social responsibility	Showing you are listening Paper 4, Parts 3 and 4: Collaborative task and discussion	An article (2)	Review U7 and 8 Paper 1, Part 1: Multiple-choice cloze Paper 1, Part 2: Open cloze Paper 1, Part 3: Word formation Paper 1, Part 4: Key word transformation Paper 2, Part 1: Essay

Unit		Vocabulary	Grammar	Use of English	Reading
9	**Food and eating out**	Food and drink Key word: *take*	Forms of *used to* and *would*	Paper 1, Part 4: Key word transformation	*All mouth* Paper 1, Part 6: Gapped sentences
10	**Shopping and money**	Shopping and consumerism Key word: *if*	Conditionals Mixed conditionals / *wish*		*Pocket money* Paper 1, Part 7: Multiple matching
11	**Colours and shapes**	Colour and decoration Key word: *seem* Describing objects	Modal verbs for guessing, speculating and deducing	Paper 1, Part 4: Key word transformations	*Crop circles* Paper 1, Part 5: Multiple choice
12	**Nature and energy**	Weather and disasters Key word: *way* Energy and the environment	Contrast and concession The definite article	Paper 1, Part 1: multiple choice cloze Paper 1, Part 2: open cloze	*Being a weather forecaster* Paper 1, Part 6: Gapped text
13	**News and media**	*In the news* Key words: *say* and *tell*	Reported speech Reporting verbs		*Social media* Paper 1, Part 5: Multiple choice
14	**Fashion and appearance**	Fashion Key word: *think*	*Have something done* The passive *Make, let* and *allow*		*The Cosplay craze* Paper 1, Part 5: Multiple choice
15	**Culture and traditions**	Culture and heritage Phrasal verbs Key word: *mind*	*So, such, too* and *enough*		*Genuine fakes* Paper 1, Part 6: Gapped text

Listening	Speaking	Writing	Video / Review
Eating out Paper 3, Part 3: Multiple matching *In the dark* Paper 3, Part 4: Multiple choice	Expressing preferences Talking about the past Paper 4, Part 3: Collaborative task	A review (2)	Video: Oaxacaa
Money habits Paper 3, Part 1: Multiple choice	Regrets and suggestions	An essay (3)	Review U9 and 10 Paper 1, Part 1: Multiple-choice cloze Paper 1, Part 3: Word formation Paper 1, Part 4: Key word transformation Paper 1, Part 6: Gapped text
Colour psychology Paper 3, Part 4: Multiple choice *Out of the blue* Paper 3, Part 2: Sentence completion	Paper 4, Part 2: Individual long turn	An email	Video: secrets of Stonehenge
Natural disasters Paper 3, Part 3: Multiple matching *Hurricanes* Paper 3, Part 2: Sentence completion	Criticising and complaining	An essay (4)	Review U11 and 12 Paper 1, Part 1: Multiple-choice cloze Paper 1, Part 2: Open cloze Paper 1, Part 3: Word formation Paper 1, Part 4: Key word transformation Paper 3, Part 3: Multiple matching
A news report Paper 3, Part 2: Sentence completion *What's on TV?* Paper 3, Part 3: Multiple matching	Reporting Discussing TV programmes	A report (2)	Video: the greenhouse effect
Crazes and fads Paper 3, Part 1: Multiple choice *School uniform* Paper 3, Part 4: Multiple choice	Challenging Paper 4, Part 3: Collaborative task Paper 4, Part 4: Discussion on a topic	A description	Review U13 and 14 Paper 1, Part 1: Multiple-choice cloze Paper 1, Part 2: Open cloze Paper 1, Part 3: Word formation Paper 1, Part 4: Key word transformation Paper 2, Part 1: Essay
Statues Paper 3, Part 3: Multiple matching *Living traditions* Paper 3, Part 4: Multiple choice Paper 3, Part 2: Sentence completion	Giving reasons Adverbs in conversation	A review, a letter or an article	Video: Songlines of the Aborigines

Overview of the exam

The *Cambridge English: First* examination is an exam at B2 level of the Common European Framework of Reference (CEFR). It consists of four papers.

Grades A, B and C represent a pass grade. Grades D and E are a fail. It is not necessary to achieve a pass grade in each of the four papers to receive a final pass grade. Candidates who pass at grade A receive a certificate that notes they have achieved C1 level. A candidate who fails with a D grade may receive a certificate that notes they have achieved B1 level.

Paper 1: Reading and Use of English

1 hour 15 minutes

This paper has seven parts. Parts 1–4 test use of English; Parts 4–7 test reading comprehension.

Use of English

Part 1: Multiple-choice cloze

This is a cloze test where you have to complete a text with eight gaps. For each gap you must choose the correct word from four options (A, B, C or D).

Part 2: Open cloze

This is a cloze test with eight gaps. You have to think of a word to fit each gap.

Part 3: Word formation

You read a text with eight gaps. At the end of each line that contains a gap you have a word stem. You must change the form of the word to fill the gap.

Nowadays in schools there is a worrying trend against playing (0) _____ games. Teachers worry that such activities encourage an unpleasant (1) _____ between children, and make some kids feel (2) _____ and humiliated. Personally, I believe that a need to compete is a strong instinct – just look at the number of willing (3) _____ who want to demonstrate their (4) _____ on quiz shows. What's more, the (5) _____ and the approval we receive can strengthen rather than damage (6) _____. Learning how to lose or to face up to a (7) _____ is as important as winning. Finally, why should teachers deny kids the (8) _____ of being the best? A system that fails to encourage winners creates a nation of losers.	COMPETE RIVAL USE CONTEST INTELLIGENT RECOGNISE FRIEND DIFFICULT SATISFY

Part 4: Key word transformation

There are six questions. Each question has a lead-in sentence followed by a key word and a second, gapped sentence. You must complete the second sentence using the key word. The second sentence must have the same meaning as the lead-in sentence.

Example: 0 I can't wait to see Martha again. FORWARD I'm really looking forward to seeing Martha again. 1 What do you think I should do? WERE What would _____ me? 2 Could you look after Rex while I'm away? CARE Could you _____ Rex while I'm away? 3 In my opinion cats make better companions than dogs. AM As far _____ cats make better pets than dogs.	4 Human beings and chimpanzees aren't very different. BETWEEN There is very _____ human beings and chimpanzees. 5 Look at that tree, it's going to fall. AS That tree _____ it's going to fall. 6 Malcolm has had a good idea for a costume. UP Malcolm has _____ a good idea for a costume.

Reading

Part 5: Multiple choice

You read a text and answer six multiple-choice questions. Each question has four options (A, B, C or D).

Part 6: Gapped text

This is a text with six sentences that have been removed. These sentences are jumbled up after the text. You have to decide which sentence belongs in each gap. There is one extra sentence you do not need to use.

Part 7: Multiple matching

This is one longer text or a number of shorter texts, with ten questions. You have to decide which section of the text (A, B, C or D) answers each question.

Paper 2: Writing

1 hour 20 minutes

The Writing paper is divided into two parts.

Part 1

This part has one compulsory question (there is no choice, you have to answer this question). You are given input in the form of an essay title with some accompanying notes to help guide your writing.

Part 2

You can choose one task from a choice of three questions.

You usually have a choice from among the following: a letter / email, an article, a review, a report.

The *First for schools* exam gives the option of writing a story or answering a question based on the set book.

Paper 3: Listening

About 40 minutes

You listen to each part twice and write your answers on an answer sheet.

Part 1: Multiple choice

You listen to a series of eight unrelated extracts. These may be monologues (just one speaker), or exchanges between interacting speakers. There is one three-option multiple-choice question for each extract. You will hear each extract twice before moving to the next.

Part 2: Sentence completion

You listen to a monologue with a sentence completion task. The task has ten questions. You will hear the whole monologue twice.

Part 3: Multiple matching

You listen to five monologues on the same topic. You have to match the speaker to the multiple-matching questions. You choose five answers from a list of eight. You will hear all the monologues once, then they will all be repeated.

Part 4: Multiple choice

You listen to an extended interview or exchange between two speakers and answer seven three-option multiple-choice questions. You will hear the recording twice.

Paper 4: Speaking

14 minutes

You take the Speaking test with another candidate. There are two examiners in the room with you: the 'interlocutor', who asks the questions and introduces the tasks, and an examiner who listens. Each candidate is assessed on his/her own performance, which is marked by both examiners.

Part 1: General conversation

2 minutes

The interlocutor asks the candidates questions on everyday, personal topics.

Part 2: Individual 'long turn'

4 minutes

Each candidate in turn is given a pair of photographs and a written question relating to the photographs. They must compare the photographs and comment on the question for about a minute. Candidates are expected to talk continuously for this time and will not be interrupted. At the end of the first candidate's turn, the interlocutor asks the second candidate a question related to the photographs or the topic. Then the second candidate compares and comments on a different pair of photographs. Finally, the first candidate is asked a question related to the second candidate's photographs.

Part 3: Collaborative task

4 minutes

Both candidates receive spoken instructions and a decision-making task based on written stimuli (for example, a spider diagram).

Candidates discuss the choices that are available for about two minutes.

The interlocutor then asks the candidates to make a choice, and the candidates negotiate their final decision for about one minute.

Part 4: Discussion

4 minutes

The interlocutor joins the conversation and asks further questions relating to the topic in Part 3. Candidates will be asked to justify their answers and to say if they agree or disagree with the other candidate's opinions.

FRIENDS AND FAMILY

EXAM SPOTLIGHT

PAPER 4, PART 1 General conversation

You will take the Speaking test with another candidate. In Part 1, the examiner will begin by asking each of you your name and where you are from, and will then ask questions on general topics, for example, likes and dislikes, family and friends, free time activities, work and learning. This part of the exam will last two minutes. The questions are likely to be familiar and will help you to relax.

1 Work in pairs. Ask and answer these questions from Part 1 of the Speaking test.

1 What's your name? Where are you from?
2 How do you like to spend your evenings? Why?
3 How much TV do you and your family watch a week? Would you prefer to watch more TV than that, or less?
4 What kinds of TV programmes do you like? Do you like the same TV programmes as the rest of your family?

2 Tell the class about the person you interviewed.

> This is Marco and he's from Mexico. He likes watching TV but he thinks that he watches too much. His favourite TV programme is …

READING family soap operas

EXAM SPOTLIGHT

PAPER 1, PART 7 Multiple matching

In Part 7 of the *First* Reading and Use of English paper, you read one text divided into short texts, or several short texts. Then you match each question to the correct text or paragraph.

3 Read the article about soap operas. For questions 1–10, choose from the soap operas (A–E). Each soap opera may be chosen more than once.

Which soap opera
1 is about families living as neighbours? _____
2 includes a character that became richer? _____
3 has the name of its town as the title? _____
4 features a mother and three brothers? _____
5 is adapted from a soap in another country? _____
6 created arguments off-screen as well as on? _____
7 has a star who is starting a new job? _____
8 has actors from different ethnic backgrounds? _____
9 is about moving from one country to another? _____
10 is written in more than one language? _____

4 Complete the sentences with your opinion. Compare your sentences with a partner.

I'd like to see … because …
… is probably the worst because …

VOCABULARY family

5 **Find words in the text to match these definitions.**

1 husband or wife _spouse_____
2 our child or children _____
3 a brother who shares just one parent with you _____
4 the daughter of your father's new wife _____
5 opposite of *nuclear family* _____
6 wives of your husband's brothers _____
7 your future husband _____
8 all the members of your family including the ones who don't live with you _____
9 two children born at the same time to the same mother _____
10 the sons and daughters of your parents' brothers and sisters _____
11 your husband or wife's mother _____
12 your brothers and sisters _____

6 **Work in pairs. Think of a family you know very well. Perhaps it's a family on TV! How many of the words from exercise 5 can you use to describe them? Tell your partner.**

> *There are five people in the family who live next door to me. There's a mother and father, twin boys and a baby …*

Soaps around the World

A POLAND

Zlotopolscy (*The Golden Poles*) is a soap based around the main members of the Zlotopolscy family. That's Barbara, her sons Marek, Waldek and Kasper, plus their wives and children. But the family is divided. Some of the relatives live in a small town and the other half live in Warsaw. *The Golden Poles* forms an important part of the Polish soap industry, which is one of the biggest in the world. Poles have a particular love for soaps and many people regularly listen to the second-longest running radio soap opera in the world called *The Matysiak Family*. It has been broadcast since 1956.

B SOUTH AFRICA

South Africa's most popular soap opera is called *Isidingo* and is set in a gold mining town of the same name. It follows the lives of the local residents and has the usual storylines of car accidents and family arguments, but unlike some soaps, *Isidingo* has a multiracial cast and is often praised because it deals with real social issues. For viewers new to *Isidingo*, one of the most interesting – and perhaps confusing – aspects of the programme is that it is multilingual. Characters speak in a variety of languages to reflect the real cultural mix of modern South Africa.

C INDIA

Apart from the fact that *Kyunki Saas Bhi Kabhi Bahu Thi* (*Because Once a Mother Was a Daughter-in-Law*) has a title which is longer than most soap operas, the basic ingredients of this Indian TV series are the same as those of every other soap opera – it's about a family! It began over 1,250 episodes ago with the heroine, Tulsi, marrying into the wealthy Virani family. Tulsi, who was poor before she joined the family, is always arguing with her mother and sisters-in-law. Recently the serial jumped 20 years forward and introduced a new generation of siblings. The latest news from the series is the real-life news that Smriti Irani, who plays Tulsi, has recently started a career in politics.

D BRAZIL

In a country which loves its soap operas, the series *América* had won 64 per cent of Brazil's TV audience every night by the time it finished. It tells the story of a tough but vulnerable girl called Sol, from Rio de Janeiro, who travels to Miami in search of 'the American dream'. She leaves behind her parents as well as her fiancé, Tião, who rides bulls at the rodeo. As well as being popular, *América* was controversial. Many people criticised the show for presenting an idealised view of the USA and for encouraging illegal immigration.

E GERMANY

Germans have been watching *Lindenstrasse* (*Linden Street*), the country's favourite soap opera, since it began over 1,000 episodes ago. Set in Munich, it isn't so much about individual characters, but more about extended families living on top of, or next door to, each other. Another German soap, *Verbotene Liebe* (*Forbidden Love*), is a version of the Australian soap *Sons and Daughters*. In it, all sorts of people, including twins, cousins, half-brothers and stepsisters, spouses and their offspring, all fall in love with people they aren't supposed to fall in love with!

KEY WORD *like*

1 **Match the answers (a–e) to the questions (1–5).**

1 What's your brother like? __b__
2 Does he look like you? _____
3 What does he like doing at the weekend? _____
4 Do you like him? _____
5 Do you think he would like to come out with us sometime? _____

a I like him a lot.
b He's quite serious and quiet when you first meet him but he relaxes when you get to know him.
c Yes, I'm sure he would.
d Yes, we're both dark-haired with blue eyes.
e He likes going to the cinema or sometimes eating out.

2 **Work in pairs. Tell your partner the name of someone you know well. Take turns to ask and answer questions 1–5 from exercise 1.**

> My sister's name is Alison.

> Does she look like you?

> Not at all. She has blue eyes and light brown hair. Does your sister look like you?

GRAMMAR present tenses

3 **Compare the use of the present simple and the present continuous in each pair of sentences, and answer the questions.**

1 a Some of the relatives live in a small town.
  b Some of the relatives are living in Warsaw for the next few months.
  1 Which sentence describes something true all the time? _____
  2 Which sentence describes a temporary situation? _____

2 a Tulsi is always arguing with her mother and sisters-in-law.
  b Tulsi often argues with her mother and sisters-in-law.
  1 Which sentence describes something that is generally true? _____
  2 Which sentence emphasises the repetition (of something negative)? _____

3 a Sol travels to Miami in search of the American dream.
  b Sol is travelling to Miami.
  1 Which sentence describes a story? _____
  2 Which sentence describes something true at the moment of speaking? _____

STATE AND DYNAMIC VERBS

Verbs such as *be, like, believe, understand* and *know* describe states. We rarely use state verbs in the continuous form.
I understand the lesson today.
NOT ~~I'm understanding the lesson today.~~

Note this exception:
a *My uncle is annoying.*
b *My uncle is being annoying.*

Sentence a describes a permanent state. Sentence b describes something true at the moment of speaking.

▶ GRAMMAR REFERENCE (SECTION 12.4) **PAGE 206**

4 **Work in pairs. Tell your partner about the following.**

• your daily routine during the week
• something you are always arguing about with members of your family or with close friends
• what you are currently studying or working on
• some of the current changes in your life or in your local area
• a book or film you have read or seen recently – describe what happens

5 **Read this email from Rona to her friend Milan. Choose the correct verb forms to complete the email.**

To: Milan Spasovski
From: Rona Kalodikis
Subject: My friend from Greece

Dear Milan,

Thanks for your email. It (1) *'s / 's being* great to hear from you again and interesting to hear that your family (2) *moves / is moving* house. I (3) *hope / 'm hoping* they'll like their new home. It's also wonderful that you (4) *start / 're starting* University.

I (5) *write / 'm writing* to ask you a favour. A friend of mine from Greece is going to Britain in three weeks. It'll be his first time and he (6) *doesn't understand / isn't understanding* much English. Would it be possible for you to meet him and let him stay at your flat for the night? He has a great sense of humour and he (7) *looks / is looking* rather like Brad Pitt!

Anyway, let me know if you (8) *don't have / aren't having* time.

Love,

Rona

6 **Compare the verb forms in each group of sentences and answer the questions.**

1 a The Indian soap began over 1,250 episodes ago.
  b The Indian soap has begun over 1,250 episodes ago.
  c Hurry up! The Indian soap has just begun.
  1 Which sentence is wrong? Why? _____
  2 Can you identify the tenses in sentences a and c?

2 a They've already watched 1,000 episodes of *Lindenstrasse*.
  b They've been watching *Lindenstrasse* since it began.
  1 Which sentence emphasises the duration of the activity? _____
  2 Which sentence emphasises a number or result? _____

3 a How long have you been watching *América*?
  b Have you ever watched *América*?
  1 Which question asks about an activity which started in the past and continues in the present? _____
  2 Which question asks about an experience which happened sometime in the past? _____

PRESENT PERFECT SIMPLE AND CONTINUOUS

With some verbs (e.g. *work*, *live*) there is little or no difference in meaning between the present perfect simple and the present perfect continuous.
I've lived there for three years. = *I've been living there for three years.*

If the action is quite recent or short in duration, the speaker is more likely to say *I've been working here for a week* rather than *I've worked here for a week*.

▶ GRAMMAR REFERENCE (SECTION 12.4) **PAGE 206**

---

7 **Read this conversation from Part 1 of the *First Speaking* test. Complete the conversation with the correct present form of the verbs.**

A: First of all I'd like to know something about you, Dorota. Where (1) _____ (you / be) from?
B: Poland. I (2) _____ (live) in a small town called Nowy Targ.
A: And how long (3) _____ (you / live) there?
B: I (4) _____ (live) there all my life, though I (5) _____ (study) English in Torun at the moment.
A: (6) _____ (you / ever / study) any other languages?
B: Yes. I (7) _____ (learn) German for two years when I was at school.
A: OK. So what (8) _____ (you and your family / enjoy) doing at home?
B: We all (9) _____ (like) skiing. My family always (10) _____ (go) skiing each winter in a place called Zakopane which is near us.
A: And what's the most exciting thing you (11) _____ (ever / do)?
B: Oh, that's a difficult question. Erm … well, currently I (12) _____ (take) a course in paragliding.

SPEAKING asking and answering questions

8 **Work in pairs.**

Student A: you are the examiner. Ask the questions from exercise 7.
Student B: you are the candidate. Answer the questions in your own words.

> First, I'd like to know something about you. Where are you from?

> I'm from Italy, I live quite close to Rome.

USE OF ENGLISH gossip

1 Work in pairs. Do you enjoy gossip and talking about other people? Have you heard any interesting gossip recently? Discuss with your partner.

2 Write down three pieces of news or recent gossip. Two items should be true and one should be untrue. Tell your partner your news. Your partner must guess which piece of news is untrue.

EXAM SPOTLIGHT

PAPER 1, PART 2 Open cloze

In Part 2 of the Reading and Use of English paper, you have to complete a text with eight missing single words.

- Read the whole text from beginning to end before you fill the gaps.
- Think about what part of speech is missing in each gap (a verb, an auxiliary verb, an article, a pronoun, etc.).
- Don't leave any gap without a word. Even if you aren't sure, then guess and write a word. It might be correct!

3 The table shows some of the types of words that are often tested in Paper 1, Part 2. Write the words from the box in the correct column.

| a | and | at | because | but | can | has | he | himself |
| in | on | or | that | the | us | who | would | |

article	auxiliary verb	preposition	pronoun	conjunction

4 Work in pairs. Read the text quickly. Why is gossip good for you, according to the article?

5 Work in pairs. Discuss what type of word is missing for each gap in the article. Then think of the word that fits best and write it in.

LISTENING talking about people

EXAM SPOTLIGHT

PAPER 3, PART 1 Multiple choice

In Part 1 of the Listening test, you listen to eight short texts lasting about 30 seconds. You will hear each one twice. There is one question for each text. Before you listen, read the whole question and underline any key words.

Read question 1 and the audioscript extract. The highlighted words give you clues to the answer. Notice that the exact words in the answer are not in the recording.

1 You hear two people talking at work. Who are they talking about?
 A a friend
 B a customer
 Ⓒ a manager

Audioscript extract:
B: *What's the problem?*
A: *I don't know how long I can put up with her.*
B: *She seems OK to me.*
A: *Do you think so?*
B: *Well, she's very friendly. The* other staff *get on with her. And she's got some good ideas. She* wants to move the office around *but that's fine. It doesn't work the way things are at present.*
A: *You don't think she's a bit* bossy*? I mean, all these changes. She's only been here a week!*

GOSSIP IS GOOD FOR YOU

We all love hearing gossip about people we know (0) _at_ work, or news about a friend or neighbour. Unfortunately, gossip often makes (1) _____ feel guilty because the stories might be untrue. But now a team of psychologists at (2) _____ University of Oklahoma believe we shouldn't feel guilty. They think (3) _____ gossip is positive because it can build closer relationships between people.

In part of their research, the psychologists asked a group of people to listen (4) _____ a recorded conversation between two fictional characters called Brad and Melissa. Then they put each person (5) _____ someone they had never met before. Each pair of strangers discussed what they (6) _____ liked or disliked about the couple in the recording. Pairs who disliked the speakers in the conversation developed a more friendly relationship (7) _____ pairs that both liked the speakers. One researcher concluded from this that 'shared, mild negative attitudes towards others can build (8) _____ stronger relationship'.

6 🔘 **1.1**   **You will hear people talking in eight different situations. You will hear each extract twice. For questions 1–8, choose the best answer (A, B or C).**

1   You hear two people talking at work.
    Who are they talking about?
    A   a friend
    B   a customer
    C   a manager

2   You hear two friends talking about another friend.
    What is Nigel to the two speakers?
    A   an old friend
    B   an acquaintance
    C   a boyfriend

3   You hear a celebrity talking on TV.
    Why is she angry?
    A   because she doesn't like being interviewed by journalists
    B   because of another celebrity called Brad
    C   because of gossip in the newspapers about her

4   You hear a man telling his friends about a family.
    Where are the family?
    A   in the house next door to his
    B   on a TV show
    C   in a book

5   You hear a voicemail message on a mobile phone.
    Why is the man calling his friend?
    A   to stay at her house in London
    B   to tell her that someone else might contact her soon
    C   to persuade her to help an old school friend of theirs

6   You hear the following conversation in the corridor at work.
    Why does the speaker want the other person to come to the interview?
    A   to meet a candidate for the job
    B   to talk about the new job
    C   to meet the new receptionist

7   You hear a woman talking to a friend on her mobile phone.
    Why is she phoning?
    A   to gossip about some visitors
    B   to cancel dinner
    C   to make an arrangement

8   You hear a woman talking about a TV programme.
    What does the woman criticise?
    A   the parents
    B   the children
    C   the TV programme

VOCABULARY describing relationships

7   **Read sentences 0–8. Replace the words in italics with the phrasal verbs from the box.**

break up	fall out	get back together	get on with
let down	look after	put up with	ran into	stand by

0   I don't know how long I can *tolerate* her.   <u>put up with</u>

1   All the staff *like her* and are friendly to her.
    _____

2   I *met* Kim *by chance* the other day. _____

3   She wants to *end the relationship* with him.
    _____

4   They *have arguments* over everything. _____

5   She always leaves him and then a week later they *start their relationship again*. _____

6   There was a mother and father on the show who still *take care of* their three grown-up children.
    _____

7   They never do anything around the house and always *disappoint* them *by not doing what they should do*. _____

8   She said she would *be loyal to* him whatever happened. _____

KEEPING A VOCABULARY NOTEBOOK

Phrasal verbs are used a lot in English, so keep a list of phrasal verbs and learn them regularly. Here are some ideas for ways of writing them to help you remember them.

Write a synonym: *put up with* = tolerate

Write it in your own sentence:
I can put up with hard work if it's useful.

Show where the object goes:
I let her down. NOT *I let down her.*

Write vocabulary in groups:

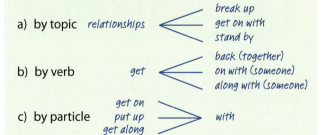

8   **Look up these phrasal verbs in a dictionary, and write them in your notebook following the suggestions above.**

make up with	take after	go along with	look up to

WRITING an essay (1)

EXAM SPOTLIGHT

In Paper 2, the Writing paper, you have to answer two questions in 80 minutes. In Part 1 there is a compulsory essay question, so you **must** answer it.

In Part 2 you write an answer to one more question. There is a choice of three or four types of writing (from an article, an email/letter, a review or a report).

In the *First for Schools* exam the writing tasks in Part 2 might also include a story or an essay about the set book. They will not include a report.

1 Read the Exam Spotlight box about Paper 2, Writing, and answer the questions.

   1 How many parts are there in this exam?
   2 How many questions do you have to answer?
   3 Can you ignore the question in Part 1?
   4 What are the different types of writing that are tested in Part 2?

2 Read the essay question from Part 1 of the Writing paper. Do you agree or disagree with the statement?

You must answer this question. Write your answer in 140–190 words in an appropriate style.

In your class you have been talking about different ways of communicating with people. Now, your English teacher has asked you to write an essay for homework.

Write your essay using all the notes and give reasons for your point of view.

It is much easier to communicate with family and friends nowadays than in our grandparents' time. Do you agree?

Notes

Things to write about:

   1 letters and emails
   2 telephones and mobile phones
   3 your own ideas

---

3 Read the essay question again and decide if statements 1–8 are true (T) or false (F).

   1 The essay question in Part 1 always appears in a context. T / F
   2 You have a statement to discuss. T / F
   3 You can write what you want. T / F
   4 You don't have to include all the notes. T / F
   5 Your own ideas are the most important. T / F
   6 An informal, 'chatty' style is OK. T / F
   7 You can write as much as you want. T / F
   8 Spelling and grammar are important. T / F

4 Read the model answer written by Lucia. Which paragraph(s):

   a introduce the topic of the essay?
   b deal with the advantages of modern methods?
   c give a conclusion?

Nowadays, we have lots of different ways to communicate thanks to new technology.

First of all, let's consider email and texting. As far as I'm concerned these are useful for sending and receiving messages quickly. In comparison, my grandparents used to send letters. These were much slower, especially if you wanted to communicate with people in other countries.

Next, modern mobile phones are excellent for talking but also for sending photos of the family to each other. According to my grandmother, in the old days, people only contacted each other or sent photos once or twice a year. I think this is sad!

Finally, the younger members of my family communicate with social media sites like Facebook and Twitter. We can share our whole lives with each in a way our grandparents never dreamed of.

In conclusion, communicating with family and friends has never been easier.

---

5 Underline the different expressions that Lucia uses to introduce opinions.

6 Complete the expressions in these sentences with the correct preposition.

   1 According _____ experts, most of us have only three or four close friends.
   2 _____ far _____ I'm concerned I'd never fall in love with someone I met on the Internet.
   3 First _____ all, we should never contact people who hide behind pseudonyms.
   4 _____ my opinion, the best way of meeting people is at school or work.
   5 _____ conclusion, we should think twice before giving personal details.

7 Read the sentences in exercise 6 again. What topic are they about?

SEQUENCING WORDS

Sequencing words are very important in an essay, but some of them can be easily confused. We use:

at first to talk about a first opinion, impression or action that is different from what comes later.

firstly / first of all to introduce the first item in a list of reasons or arguments.

afterwards / after that / next to introduce another action in a series.

secondly to introduce a second reason or argument.

finally / lastly to introduce a final opinion, reason or argument.

at last to say that something happened after a long delay.

in the end to talk about a final result, often after lot of other things have happened.

---

8 Read the information about sequencing words in the box, then choose the correct option (in italics) to complete sentences 1–5.

1 *Firstly / At first* I spent a lot of time phoning people, but nowadays I chat to them on Facebook.
2 There are several reasons for being careful on social media sites. *At first / First of all*, anything we write immediately becomes public. *Afterwards / Secondly*, we can never delete what we have written. *Finally / At last,* it leaves us open to identity theft.
3 Danny and Morag looked everywhere for their tablet. *At last / Lastly* they found it behind a cushion on the sofa.
4 They tried to repair the computer, but *at last / in the end* they had to buy a new one.
5 We had a long conversation on Skype. *Afterwards / Secondly* I sent her our latest photographs.

9 Now read this exam question. Work in pairs or groups and discuss your ideas.

> 'Thanks to the Internet there has never been a better way of making friends.' Do you agree?

Notes

Things to write about:

1 meeting new people
2 finding people with similar interests
3 your own ideas

10 Use Lucia's answer as a model and write your answer, using the ideas you discussed in exercise 9. Check your work using the checklist.

WRITING CHECKLIST

AN ESSAY

After you write your essay, check your work.
- Does it cover the two points you are given? ☐
- Does it include your own ideas? ☐
- Does it use a range of expressions for giving your opinion? ☐
- Is it between 140 and 190 words? ☐
- Have you checked your work for mistakes and punctuation? ☐

WRITING GUIDE   **PAGE 212**

GLOSSARY

orphan: a child whose parents have died (adj. orphaned)
drought: a long period when it doesn't rain and there isn't enough water for plants or animals
formula: dried milk for babies
grieve: to feel very sad after the death of someone close
breakthrough: a sudden and important development or discovery
herd: a large group of animals such as elephants or cows

VIDEO a match made in Africa

1 Look at this photograph of an elephant calf (baby elephant) and a sheep called Albert. Where do you think the photograph was taken? What is strange about it?

2 You are going to watch a documentary about the story of this unlikely friendship. While you watch, number the events a–h in the correct order 1–8.

a   The calf begins to drink water. _____
b   The elephant goes walking with Albert. _____
c   No other elephant wants to take care of him. _____
d   A baby elephant loses its mother. __1__
e   Albert the sheep arrives. _____
f   The calf is rescued. _____
g   They name the elephant *Temba*. _____
h   The elephant starts to drink milk. _____

3 Read the glossary and watch the video again. While you are watching, decide if statements 1–8 are true (T) or false (F).

1   An elephant calf needs milk for six months. T / F
2   Elephants never adopt calves without mothers. T / F
3   There was a serious shortage of water. T / F
4   The team from Shamwari drugged the calf. T / F
5   At first, the calf was too unhappy to drink water. T / F
6   Albert and the calf became instant friends. T / F
7   The calf eventually started to drink 'formula' milk. T / F
8   Albert and the calf did everything together. T / F

4 How did Albert help to save the elephant calf's life? Why do you think this was?

5 **Match the expressions in italics in 1–5 to the definitions a–e.**

1 The Shamwari team *moves in* for a rescue. _____
2 The staff was afraid that the calf would not *make it* through the rescue. _____
3 At first the elephant and Albert didn't *hit it off*. _____
4 Baby elephants are emotional, if they aren't happy everything *shuts down*. _____
5 The orphaned elephant was grieving *in a big way*. _____

a stop operating
b survive an illness or dangerous situation
c a lot / a great deal
d like each other as soon as you meet
e go closer

6 **What close relationships do you have with family or friends? Can you think of a time in your life when a friendship started off in a difficult way?**

PAPER 4, PART 1 General conversation

7 **Read the Ideas generator and start making a mindmap about you, your life and your relationships to prepare for Part 1 of Paper 4. Choose the main topics and add some details.**

8 **Work in pairs. Take turns to be the interlocutor and the candidate. Ask these questions and answer them using the useful expressions in the box.**

1 Where are you from?
2 Tell me about your home town or city.
3 What do you like doing in your free time?
4 Do you prefer to spend time on your own or with friends?
5 Do you spend more time with family or with friends?
6 Do you like animals? Tell me about your pets.
7 Do you spend much time on social media websites like Facebook? Are they a good way to make friends?

USEFUL EXPRESSIONS

TALKING ABOUT YOURSELF

I'm from / I come from …
I live in … / (It's a beautiful place with …)
I like playing … / doing … / going …
I prefer being with friends because … / I enjoy time on my own (to read a book …)
I think I probably spend more time (with friends at college / with my family) at the weekend
I love my pets. I have (a cat and a dog …)
I like meeting people online. (On Facebook I have about 200 friends.)
I don't spend much time online because …(I prefer seeing my friends.)

 IDEAS GENERATOR

MINDMAPPING A TOPIC

In Part 1 of the *First* Speaking test, you talk about different personal and general topics, such as your family and friends, pets and hobbies, where you live and your occupation. To prepare for this part of the exam, it's useful to generate ideas by making a mindmap. Here's a mindmap by a student. He begins by writing categories and then adds details. He can refer back to the mindmap and add more information later on. It will help him answer the examiner's questions.

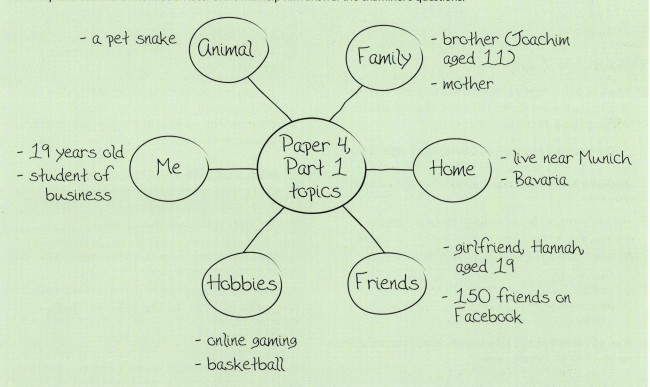

JOBS AND WORK

1 **Look at the photo and think of one advantage and one disadvantage of being:**

1 a photographer
2 an actress

VOCABULARY jobs

2 **Work in pairs. Add a suffix from B to each word in A to make the words for job titles. More than one suffix may be possible.**

A act   assist   employ   journal   music   teach   wait

B ant   ee   er   ian   ist   or   ress

3 **Add suffixes to these words to make job words.**

1 conduct_____
2 manage_____
3 art_____
4 paint_____
5 write_____
6 electric_____

4 **Can you think of any jobs which do not combine a suffix with an existing word?**

doctor, cook

5 **Play *Guess the job!***

Student A: choose a job from exercises 1–3. Answer Student B's questions but don't say what your job is.

Student B: interview Student A about his / her job and guess the job. Ask these (or similar) questions.

• What's your typical day like?
• Do you require special skills for this job?
• Which parts of your job do you dislike?
• What benefits do you have in your job? (e.g. health insurance, a company car)?

USE OF ENGLISH multiple-choice cloze

EXAM SPOTLIGHT

PAPER 1, PART 1 Multiple-choice cloze

In this part of the Reading and Use of English paper, you read a text with eight gaps and have to decide which answer (A, B, C or D) best fits each gap.

The types of words missing from the text include: present / past participles, verbs, collocations, part of a fixed expression, linkers, adjectives, a part of a phrasal verb, and adverbs.

As you complete the next exercise, identify the types of missing words. For example, the word missing in the first gap (0) is the particle of a phrasal verb.

6 For questions 1–8, read the text and decide which answer (A, B, C or D) best fits the gap. There is an example at the beginning (0).

Assistants to the stars

Los Angeles is home to the rich and famous so it's also where you come (0) _C_ the most celebrity personal assistants. But (1) _____ the highly-paid lawyers and agents who work (2) _____ the stars, personal assistants (PAs) typically (3) _____ about $56,000 a year, which isn't much by Hollywood standards. As for the job description, responsibilities include (4) _____ laundry, fetching groceries and paying bills. Rita Tateel has (5) _____ many courses for trainee assistants to the stars and describes a successful job (6) _____ . 'You must be in good health at all times, because you are in (7) _____ of a celebrity's life. You need to be flexible and you have to be a 'can-do' person. If there's one word that celebrities don't want to (8) _____ , that word is "no".'

0	A off	B over	C across	D about
1	A despite	B unlike	C however	D similarly
2	A for	B in	C at	D on
3	A lend	B do	C pay	D earn
4	A making	B doing	C having	D fixing
5	A trained	B run	C made	D taught
6	A applicant	B person	C assistant	D employee
7	A deal	B manage	C charge	D responsible
8	A say	B hear	C know	D learn

VOCABULARY jobs and work

7 Choose the correct options (in italics) to complete the sentences.

1 We read candidates' CVs and discuss which ones might be *convenient / suitable*. Then we invite them to come for an *interview / interrogation*.
2 Personal *qualities / qualifications* such as enthusiasm and motivation are just as important as formal *education / qualifications*.
3 This job *notice / advertisement* looks really interesting.
4 We have a (an) *overtime / flexitime* system at work. We all work 35 hours a week but can organise exactly when we work those hours.
5 The company *recruits / applies* six graduates on its management *employee / trainee* programme every year.
6 We were forced to *make her redundant / sack her* because she kept arriving late.
7 The Minister of Health was forced to *hand in his notice / resign* over the hospital scandal.
8 The *salary / wages* isn't great but there are lots of great *perks / pay rises,* such as health insurance and other benefits.

8 Complete the phrasal verbs in these sentences with a particle from the box.

back	down	for	in	off	on	out	with

1 If you would like to apply for the job, simply fill _____ the online application form.
2 Petra deals _____ some of our most important clients and handles their accounts.
3 He is looking _____ staff. He always takes _____ extra staff during the holiday season.
4 I sent _____ my CV and a letter of application but they never wrote _____.
5 Terrible news … the factory is laying _____ three hundred people; the jobs are going overseas.
6 They offered me the job but I turned it _____ when I found _____ the salary was too low.

LISTENING talking about jobs

9 ⦿ 2.1 **Listen to eight people talking about jobs. Which speakers (1–8) say how they got the job? Which say what the job is like?**

PAPER 3, PART 1 multiple choice texts

10 ⦿ 2.1 **Listen again, and for questions 1–8, choose the best answer (A, B or C).**

1 How did the woman find out about the job?
   A through a friend
   B from a job agency
   C from a charity
2 Why did the man choose this kind of work?
   A because his father did it
   B because he likes working on farms
   C because it was well-paid
3 Why did the speaker get the job?
   A because very few people want to work in advertising and marketing
   B because she attended an interview
   C because the interviewer was her old boss
4 What is the speaker's main responsibility?
   A attending meetings
   B writing up the sports results
   C reporting the local news
5 What does the woman think about training?
   A It's a waste of time.
   B It's useful.
   C It's more useful than learning on the job.
6 What was the woman's problem when she started?
   A Some staff didn't like her.
   B She didn't have the right skills for the job.
   C Some staff didn't believe she had the right skills.
7 What does the employee want?
   A a pay rise
   B a company car
   C overtime
8 Where does the artist work?
   A he doesn't say
   B on TV
   C from home

READING finding a job

1 Work in groups. Discuss the five ways to find a job (a–e). Which do you think are more effective? Put them in order from 1 (most effective) to 5 (least effective).

a   Use personal contacts like friends of your family.
b   Register with a job agency.
c   Read the job adverts in the newspaper or online.
d   Send your CV to every company you would like to work for.
e   Do an unpaid work placement at a company.

2 Compare the two photographs of Adam Pacitti in the article on the next page. How did he try to find a job? Do you think he was successful?

3 Read the article and match the headings (A–E) to the paragraphs (1–5).

A   A new approach to job searching
B   A new challenge
C   Looking for a job
D   An instant response
E   A big thank you

EXAM SPOTLIGHT

PAPER 1, PART 5   Multiple choice

In this part of the Reading and Use of English paper you read a text with six multiple-choice questions. There are four choices for each question. As you choose the correct answer, make sure you understand why the other three are incorrect. Usually one or two of the incorrect choices are very similar to the correct answer so it's important to check. In the exam, you can underline words and sentences in the reading text and this will help you identify reasons for your answers.

4 Read the article again. Choose the answer (A, B, C or D) which you think fits best according to the text.

1   When Adam first left university, we understand that
A   his approach to finding a job was very different from other people.
B   his approach to finding a job was the same as everyone else of his age.
C   he didn't look for a job.
D   he found a job almost immediately.

2   Adam had difficulties finding a job because
A   he wasn't qualified.
B   he needed more training.
C   there was so much competition for posts.
D   there weren't any vacancies.

3   The word *dismal* in the first sentence of paragraph him was
A   bright and cheerful.
B   unpredictable.
C   sad and without hope.
D   difficult and challenging.

4   On the same day that Adam put the billboard up
A   he got a new job.
B   there was an immediate response online.
C   he made a video CV for his website.
D   he owed £500.

5   Adam is pleased to work on a new TV series because
A   it's what he's always wanted to do.
B   now he can pay back the £500 for the billboard.
C   there are lots of new opportunities.
D   he thinks it will help people like him.

6   Adam thinks other ordinary people
A   should use billboards to find a job.
B   were the reason for his success.
C   spend a lot of time on the Internet.
D   were surprised that he got the job.

5 Find words in the article to match these definitions.

1   a job that no one is doing and is available
2   a description (usually written) of a person's education, work history and details
3   something new and original
4   an ability that lets you do a job well
5   when something becomes popular on the Internet and lots of people read or watch it
6   the money you earn for a job

VOCABULARY personal qualities

6 Match the personal qualities in the box to the comments 1–6. Two comments have two answers.

| ambitious | careful | considerate | imaginative |
| punctual | reliable | team-player | trustworthy |

1   'He wants to be a manager in the future, so I wonder if he'll stay in that job very long.'
2   'We need someone who can come up with interesting new ideas to old problems.'
3   'You could give her the key to the safe, she's completely honest and dependable.'
4   'He's always on time and I never have to worry about whether he's done the work.'
5   'She really cares about the staff and always thinks about their feelings before making a decision.'
6   'I love solving problems with large groups of people.'

7 Which of the personal qualities in exercise 6 do you think describe Adam best?

8 Work in pairs. Choose three jobs from the box and discuss the personal qualities that you would need for each one. Tell the class.

| accountant | bank clerk | computer programmer |
| graphic designer | nurse | salesman | teacher |

Graduate spends £500 on getting a job

Like lots of young people these days, 24-year-old Adam Pacitti left education and was unemployed. At first, he tried the usual ways of finding work. He searched through newspaper adverts and registered with job agencies. He estimates that he sent off around 200 CVs and applied for hundreds of jobs. Adam's qualifications were good, with a degree in media studies from the University of Westminster, but he faced the same dismal prospect as lots of other graduates: that there weren't enough vacancies for the hundreds of applicants.

After months and months looking for a job, Adam had an innovative idea. He decided to pay for a billboard in London with the message: 'I spent my last £500 on this billboard, please give me a job.' The billboard included a three-metre-high picture of Adam and a link to his website, employadam.com.

Within 24 hours, nearly 10,000 people on Twitter were talking about the billboard and there were more than 1.5 million hits on his website, from all over the world. On the website, potential employers could watch Adam's four-minute long video CV. He remembers: 'I had thousands of emails and an unbelievable amount of interest.'

Adam's skill at advertising himself had paid off. Within a few days, Adam had received over 100 job offers from companies. In the end, he took a job with the TV production company KEO. In his new position, one of Adam's first projects is to make a TV series about helping jobseekers with innovative ways to get a job. Adam says, 'I'm really looking forward to it. I'm working on so many projects, but this is the one that is most personal to me. I know how difficult finding a job is, so to be given the opportunity to help other people find employment is incredibly exciting.'

During the time of his billboard and website, Adam received lots of emails and support from ordinary people on the Internet as well as from people in business. They helped to make the story of his billboard go viral. 'Without them, I'd still be looking for work.' To show his gratitude, Adam spent his first wage packet on another billboard, reading: 'I spent my first wage packet on this billboard. Thank you for helping me.'

GRAMMAR making comparisons

1 Work in pairs. Look at the two adverts below. Which job would you prefer? Why?

RECEPTIONIST WANTED

Enthusiastic, friendly person with excellent interpersonal skills required for agency for actors.

Duties include meeting and greeting visitors, answering calls and some general secretarial responsibilities.

- Salary: €30,000 per year
- Hours: 35 hours a week minimum (9 to 5)
- 25 days' holiday per year
- Experience not necessary as full training provided
- Regular opportunities for overtime
- Company pension scheme available

PA (Personal Assistant) wanted

Experienced PA required to support busy actor. You need to be flexible and have experience in planning and organising, and be available to travel at any time – including weekends. You will work a flexible 40-hour week with a basic salary of €45,000 with pension scheme and health insurance. Bonuses and overtime are also paid. 20 days' holiday per year.

---

2 Read the job adverts again and correct any factual errors in these sentences.

1 The receptionist is much better paid than the PA.
2 The receptionist's holidays aren't as long as the PA's.
3 The PA receives the best perks and benefits.
4 As PA, the harder you work, the more likely you are to receive a bonus.
5 The PA doesn't need as much work experience.

MAKING COMPARISONS

Complete these rules using sentences 1–5 in exercise 2.

Rules for comparing

1 Add _____ or -*est* to make a comparative or superlative form of a one-syllable adjective.
2 Use *more* or _____ with adjectives of more than two syllables.
3 Use _____ + adjective + _____ to show something is similar or equal to something else.
4 Use _____ before a superlative adjective.
5 With two comparatives we often use *the* ..., *the* ... .
6 Some adjectives and adverbs are irregular: *good*, _____, *best*

---

3 🔊 **2.2** Listen to two people discussing the jobs in the adverts. Complete the conversation with words or short phrases.

A: Anything in the paper today?
B: Nothing much. Though there are a couple of jobs that might interest you.
A: Well they (0) *can't be any worse than* the others I've seen.
B: This one is for 30,000 a year which is (1) _____ your old job.
A: Well I used to do (2) _____ overtime, so actually that isn't (3) _____ much.
B: Oh, it says here 'opportunities for overtime', so it's probably (4) _____ the same.
A: Yes. It sounds OK. What is it?
B: Receptionist, and they provide training.
A: But my last job was (5) _____ responsible than that. And I know how to answer the phone and all that stuff.
B: All right. I'm just trying to help.
A: Sorry, but it's just that I don't want to do something that isn't (6) _____ skilled than what I was doing before.
B: Well here's one. 'Personal Assistant. Forty-five thousand', so it's easily (7) _____ your last job and you have plenty of experience in planning and organising. Oh, and you get to travel ...

4 The answers in exercise 3 use phrases to modify the comparisons. Write the phrases in the three categories below.

Large difference: *very much, a great deal,* _____ , _____ , _____

Small difference: *a little, slightly, not quite as,* _____ , _____

No difference/equal: *no ... than,* _____ , _____

5 Work in pairs. Ask and answer questions to find out the following information about your partner.

- size of your partner's family
- when your partner learnt to ride a bike
- your partner's height
- how many activities your partner does after school
- number of holidays your partner takes every year
- approximate distance your partner walks per day

6 Now compare your information with your partner's information, using phrases from exercise 4.

> *My family isn't quite as big as yours.*

> *That's true, my family is slightly bigger.*

▶ GRAMMAR REFERENCE (SECTION 5) **PAGE 193**

7 Complete the article with the missing words. All the words are connected with making comparisons.

AN OLDER WORKFORCE

Surveys show that more and (1) _____ young people plan to work a great (2) _____ longer than people have in the past. In fact, the majority expect to continue working beyond (3) _____ most typical retirement age of 65. The reasons are that most people's pensions won't be worth as much (4) _____ they are now, and that we are living (5) _____ longer than ever before. Some companies are also looking for (6) _____ experienced employees, so a new recruitment website in America actually targets a (7) _____ older workforce. The boss of one company using the site commented: 'This sector of the workforce is a (8) _____ easier one to employ because they already understand the needs of business and they are often (9) _____ at jobs which require greater concentration (10) _____ their younger counterparts.'

KEY WORD *as*

8 Match the sentences (1–5) to the meanings (a–e).

1 He's as tall as me.
2 I earned as much in my last job as I do now.
3 She was arriving as I left.
4 He's as happy now as he ever was.
5 She doesn't sing as well as you do.

a compares appearance _____
b compares the present with the past _____
c compares qualities or abilities _____
d compares two actions at the same time _____
e compares the past with the present _____

9 Work in pairs. Make sentences to compare the following:

• the past and the present
• your appearance and qualities.

SPEAKING comparing

EXAM SPOTLIGHT

PAPER 4, PART 3   Collaborative task

In this part of the Speaking test, you work in pairs and discuss a series of options with your partner before making a final decision. It's important to discuss and compare each option in full before making a final decision.

10 Work in pairs. Read the instructions given by the interlocutor in an exam, and look at the diagram. Follow the instructions.

I'd like you to imagine that a local countryside charity has a group of 12 volunteers aged 18–21 coming to spend a weekend doing volunteer work in your village. Here are some ideas they are thinking about. Talk to each other about why these ideas would be useful for your village.

Decide which would be the most useful project for your village.

```
put up nesting boxes        Why would these        build cycle paths
for some rare owls          ideas be useful         around the village
                            for your village?

make a skateboard        create walking trails      build a children's
park                     through the woods          playground in the park
                         near the village
```

WRITING a letter

1 Work in pairs. Imagine you are going to write these letters. Do you think they should be formal (F) or informal (I)?

1 a letter to the bank about a loan
2 a letter to a friend you haven't seen for years
3 a letter applying for a job
4 a letter asking for information about a holiday
5 a letter to complain about a product you bought

2 Read these formal expressions (1–8) from a letter of application for a job. Match them to the less formal phrases (a–h) from a letter to a close friend.

1 I am writing to … _____
2 I have recently completed … _____
3 I am particularly keen on … _____
4 In addition to this, I have always been interested in other countries and cultures … _____
5 I would be grateful if you could … _____
6 and inform me how to apply … _____
7 I look forward to hearing from you … _____
8 Yours faithfully, _____

a I've just done …
b Just a quick note to …
c Please …
d Best wishes,
e and let me know what to do next.
f What's more, I like travelling …
g Be in touch …
h I like …

EXAM SPOTLIGHT

PAPER 2, PART 2 Writing a letter

In Paper 2, the Writing paper, you have a choice of three or four types of writing. One choice might be a letter. It might be formal or less formal. You need to read the task carefully and decide on the correct level of formality.

3 Becky Raven has written an answer to this exam task. Read Becky's letter and the comments that her teacher has written. Rewrite the letter.

> **You see this advert for volunteer work in a student magazine. Read the advert and write a letter of application.**
>
> **Volunteer work in your gap year**
>
> We are looking for enthusiastic young people to spend six months doing environmental projects around the world.
>
> Write for an information pack and tell us about:
> • your current situation and interests
> • your personal qualities and reasons for doing volunteer work
> • any previous work experience.

4 Now turn to the Writing guide, page 214. Read the new version of Becky's letter. Compare it with your ideas.

5 Read the job advert about work on a summer camp. Write your letter in 140–190 words.

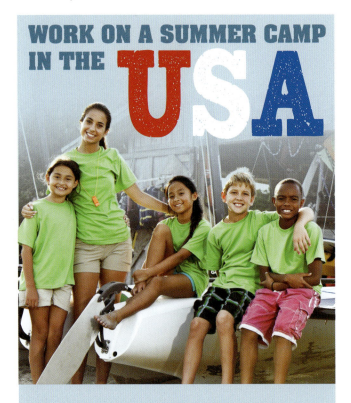

WORK ON A SUMMER CAMP IN THE USA

We are looking for enthusiastic young people to spend the summer working as volunteers on one of our many summer camps for children (aged between 8 and 16). You should be able to help organise team games and activities such as painting and pottery. The camps are in over ten different states. You receive free accommodation and a salary. At the end of your six-week placement, you will also have time to travel around the USA. Write for an information pack and tell us about yourself and why you would like to apply.

WRITING CHECKLIST

A LETTER

After you write, check your work. Check grammar and vocabulary, but also check the structure and layout.

- Does the letter have at least three paragraphs? ☐
- Does the first paragraph give the reason for writing? ☐
- Does the second paragraph tell the reader about you? ☐
- Does the third paragraph ask for some action? ☐
- Does the letter have the correct level of formality? ☐
- Does the letter have between 140 and 190 words? ☐

WRITING GUIDE **PAGE 214**

(1) Are you sure it's a man who's reading this letter? What if it's a woman?

(2) Where did you see the information? In a newspaper advert? Say where you saw it.

(3) You have used the verb 'do' three times in this paragraph. Can you use some other verbs?

(4) In formal writing, try not to use words like 'but' or 'and' at the beginning of a sentence. In this case 'However' is better.

(5) Can you give a better reason than this? It's not very convincing.

(6) Use paragraphs. The first paragraph should say why you are writing. The middle paragraphs should give more information about you and why you want to apply. The final paragraph requests some action.

(7) This is interesting and relevant. Can you give some more detail?

(8) The same as in (7). Give some more detail.

(9) Maybe your parents should go and you should stay at home! This isn't a good enough reason.

(10) This sounds like an order. Can you be more polite?

(11) This is very informal. We'd only use it in an email or a letter to a friend. What's a more formal way to end a letter?

(1)
Dear Sir,

(2)
I'm writing about your advert for Volunteer Work
(3)
because I've just done my studies at school and
(4)
will go to university in September. But I don't
want to do my degree in business studies or start
my career yet so I'd like to do a gap year to have a
(5)   (6)
good time and see the world. I like mountain biking
and sailing. This year at school I was involved
(7)
in getting money for some local children and I
(8)
also worked on the school drama festival. I enjoy
meeting people and I want to do one of your gap
(9)
year projects because my parents think it would
be good for me. So send me your information pack
(10)
and tell me how to apply.

(11)
Thanks a lot.

Becky Raven

REVIEW AND EXAM PRACTICE Units 1 and 2

1 For questions 1–8, read the text below. Use the word given in capital letters at the end of some of the lines to form a word that fits in the gap in the same line. There is an example at the beginning (0).

Volunteers needed

We are a volunteer (0) _organisation_ and every summer we   ORGANISE
offer 50 (1) _____ the chance to help us provide fun for   STUDY
many (2) _____ who could not normally have a holiday.   CHILD
No specific (3) _____ are necessary. You just need the   QUALIFY
(4) _____ to look after kids and organise activities. To apply,   ABLE
fill in our (5) _____ form online. Then we'll invite you to an   APPLY
(6) _____ weekend where you work with others.   ASSESS
Finally, if you are (7) _____ , we'll ask you to provide two   SUCCESS
(8) _____ from people who have known you well for more than   REFER
two years.

---

2 For questions 9–16, read the text below and decide which answer (A, B, C or D) best fits each gap.

Lisa Lilley is working (0) A with Ferrari's Formula One team. The most exciting (9) _____ of the job is working at the races. Last year she attended her first one at Imola. (10) _____ the famous red suit and ear defenders for the first time was an (11) _____ that left her nearly lost for words, and something she'd first seen as a career (12) _____ has become a passion. 'Now when I'm not at a race I watch it on TV.'

'The Ferrari team have (13) _____ me feel so welcome. Because I have a technical role at the track it wouldn't matter whether I was male or female; you have to gain respect for (14) _____ good at your job.' Next year Lisa will (15) _____ about 200 nights away from home with the team. 'At the moment, I'm loving it. The Ferrari team is like an extended (16) _____ ,' she says.

0	A with	B on	C at	D by
9	A way	B piece	C part	D quality
10	A Changing	B Wearing	C Buying	D Showing
11	A experience	B qualification	C application	D interest
12	A job	B chance	C opportunity	D position
13	A had	B did	C made	D were
14	A staying	B being	C applying	D wanting
15	A move	B work	C drive	D spend
16	A family	B partnership	C life	D interview

---

3 For questions 17–24, read the text below and think of the word which best fits each gap. Use only one word in each gap. There is an example at the beginning (0).

A recent study has concluded (0) _that_ close friends and solid relationships may help you (17) _____ keep healthier and live longer. Psychologists already knew that having good companions maintains mental well-being, (18) _____ this new data tells us that a strong friendship also extends (19) _____ expectancy. The researchers were particularly surprised (20) _____ their discovery because it was more true (21) _____ friends than family. Perhaps this is because we share personal problems or express (22) _____ likes and dislikes (23) _____ freely with friends. So, if you like the idea of living a few extra years, why (24) _____ ring your friends right now and invite them over?

4 You are going to read an article about four volunteers who work for an organisation. For questions 25–34, choose from the volunteer (A–D). Each volunteer may be chosen more than once.

Which person

25 already had a career before joining Raleigh International? _____
26 will begin university next year? _____
27 didn't travel abroad for her gap year? _____
28 learnt to understand other people's views? _____
29 helped to teach people? _____
30 prefers people to possessions? _____
31 communicated between volunteers and local people? _____
32 was surprised that making meals for lots of people would be a useful skill? _____
33 helped to make a place for local children? _____
34 admits missing home? _____

WORKING FOR A VOLUNTEER ORGANISATION

Raleigh International is a volunteer organisation which runs youth projects worldwide. Its aim is to develop self-confidence and leadership in young people, through their participation in adventure, scientific exploration and community service. Read about the work of four volunteers.

A Felicia, 19, from the Netherlands, joined a Raleigh International overseas programme to Costa Rica. 'I've just finished high school and next year I'm going to university. I thought Raleigh would be the best opportunity to take a gap year and see more of the world. I've learnt a lot working with people from a mix of different backgrounds. It has opened my eyes to a much bigger world than my own. People around the world have their own opinions and beliefs and that should be respected. You appreciate little things in life and realise you don't need lots of luxury objects like expensive clothes and TVs. Happiness is found in different things such as the kindness of people.'

B Rebecca was already a qualified doctor and had participated in the overseas programme to Costa Rica and Nicaragua as a programme doctor: 'Having worked as a doctor in England for three years without a break, I decided to take three months out to do something different. As a medic, my responsibilities were broad, ranging from training both staff and programme participants in health, hygiene and first aid to providing on-site medical support. I relied heavily on the medical and telephone consultation skills from my experience as a doctor in England. More generally, my experience as a parent and teacher helped in working with the young people. An ability to cook for large numbers, meanwhile, proved unexpectedly valuable.'

C Amira, 21, from Kuala Lumpur in Malaysia, took a break between completing her degree at university and finding work, to join a Raleigh programme in her own country: 'I heard about Raleigh International through the Careers Advisory Service at university. As a Malaysian, I wanted to find out more about different aspects of my country. I also wanted to see how I reacted when put in different, quite extreme, situations as well as playing different roles within a team of individuals. One of my jobs was to act as a go-between for the group and the local community, which improved my knowledge of translating and the different ways of life in my country. I also learnt the basic skills of working on a building site, and one of my most enjoyable moments included seeing the kindergarten for a local village go up.'

D Holly, 20, Canadian, took a break after her studies to join a Raleigh overseas programme: 'I was looking for volunteer work abroad and came across Raleigh International on the Internet. I didn't really know what to expect, apart from the fact that it was likely to be hard work. I hoped the programme would give me a better understanding of my strengths and weaknesses and would give me the opportunity to develop my abilities to work in a team as well as improving my leadership skills. For the first few days I found life in the programme fairly difficult. We had to adjust to the accommodation, Malaysian culture, homesickness, fatigue and various other differences. My highlight was socialising with villagers. They gave me a skirt, made me a necklace and often gave us lunch. On a personal level I feel I have improved my communication skills, and find that I now listen to others more readily before speaking.'

SPORT AND FREE TIME

1 **Work in pairs. Look at the photo. Which activities does the game combine? What do you think the rules might be?**

VOCABULARY sport and free time

2 **Which verbs are used with which activities?**

do play go	archery bowling boxing chess golf karate sailing tennis

3 **Choose the correct options (in italics) to complete the sentences.**

1 My favourite *play / game* is chess.
2 In my free time I like to play *violin / the violin*.
3 Model making is a marvellous *hobby / sport*. It helps me *pass / spend* the time.
4 Try to *hit / kick* the ball with your racket.
5 We *scored / let in* a goal in the last minute and lost.
6 Kirsten keeps on *winning / beating* me at table tennis.
7 Don't play tennis when the *pitch / court* is wet.
8 Look at the lovely trophy Justine has *gained / won*.
9 I am a big *fan / spectator* of American football.
10 Hooligans attacked rival *supporters / pitches*.
11 Chess, mahjong and backgammon are three complicated board *pastimes / games*.
12 Beckham used to play *for / against* Manchester United, but then he moved to Real Madrid.
13 We were *lost / beaten* in the semi-finals.
14 It is time for you to *practise / practice* your service.

4 **Match the words in the box to the descriptions (1–5).**

backgammon badminton ball bat chess court darts field foot pitch puck racket shuttlecock soccer tennis

1 You need a net or a goal: _____ , _____ , _____
2 You play on these: _____ , _____ , _____
3 You need a board: _____ , _____ , _____
4 You hit the ball with these: _____ , _____ , _____
5 You hit these: _____ , _____ , _____

LISTENING free time

EXAM SPOTLIGHT

PAPER 3, PART 3 Multiple matching

Read the exam question and answer these questions.

1 How many speakers do you listen to?
2 Do they speak to each other, or by themselves?
3 Is the topic for each speaker the same or different?
4 How many sentences do you have to choose from?
5 How many of the sentences **don't** you use?

Often the answer isn't directly stated on the recording; instead you have to arrive at the meaning by putting together different parts of what you've heard.

You will hear five extracts in which people are talking about sport and leisure. Choose from the list A–H what each speaker says. Use each letter only once. There are three extra letters which you do not need to use.

_____

A   There are ways of being unsporting even playing chess. _____

B   My parents wouldn't approve of what I do.

C   I achieved an ambition. _____

D   It is hard to become a professional player. _____

E   I underestimated the difficulties I would face. _____

F   Online gaming is a serious activity. _____

G   I used to play extreme sports. _____

H   I sometimes do charity work. _____

5 **Now read what Speaker 1 said. Notice the highlighted words. Which sentence in the exam question best describes what the speaker said?**

Speaker 1: *'Well, when I was a kid my hobby was collecting football stickers. You know, for the World Cup, or the league – you put them in an album and try and get all the players for all the teams. They sell them in packets – you've got half a dozen stickers in each one.* ==There were always three or four I could never find.== *One year, there was just one player I needed – Roberto Carlos, that's right. Well,* ==in the end I got him== *by swapping 15 of my spare stickers for just one of him – but* ==it was worth it. I completed the whole album== *for the first and last time. Now and again, I look at it and* ==feel the same pride.=='*

6 🔘 **3.1 Now listen to the five speakers and do the exam question.**

7 **Work in pairs. Look at the audioscript on page 221 and underline the information which helped you to identify what each speaker said.**

8 **Think of a sport or activity you have played. Write a short presentation about it. Give your presentation to the class. The class should guess what activity you are talking about.**

KEY WORD *time*

9 **Match the sentence beginnings (1–6) with the endings (a–f).**

1   The meeting was a complete waste of time; _____
2   Thanks for inviting me; _____
3   How do you spend _____
4   We see Marina from time to time; _____
5   Nowadays it's so quiet, but _____
6   I'll never forget the first time I used chopsticks; _____

a   your free time?
b   once upon a time this was the busiest port in the country.
c   I made a complete fool of myself, dropping food all over the table!
d   we talked for three hours but in the end nothing was decided.
e   I had a really good time.
f   maybe once at New Year and twice during the summer.

10 **Complete the second sentence so that it has a similar meaning to the first sentence. Include the word *time* in each sentence. You must use between two and five words.**

1   I had never been bowling before.
    It was the _____ had ever been bowling.
2   To be honest I didn't learn anything from the experience.
    The whole experience was an absolute
    _____.
3   Now and again we go to the theatre.
    We go to the theatre from _____.
4   Our local team used to be in the first division, but not any more!
    Once _____ our team was in the first division.
5   What sort of things do you do when you're not working or studying?
    How do you _____?
6   I really enjoyed myself a lot last Saturday.
    I had a _____ last Saturday.

11 **Work in groups. Tell each other about the following topics. Listen to the other students in your group and ask follow-up questions.**

*   when something you did was a total waste of time
*   the very first time you did an interesting or dangerous sport or leisure activity
*   something you do or a place you go to from time to time
*   what life in your country / region was like once upon a time
*   what you do in your free time (in the evenings or at weekends)
*   an occasion with friends or family when you had a really good time

READING eccentric sports

1 Quickly read through the text and find the names of the sports or activities shown in the photographs.

EXAM SPOTLIGHT

PAPER 1, PART 6 Gapped text

In this part of the Reading and Use of English paper, you match six sentences to the gaps in the text. There is also an extra sentence you don't have to use. To answer this question successfully you need to use logic and clues in the text.

Look at the words highlighted just before and after gap 1 in the article.

a number of: more than one
unusual sporting competitions: they are strange and interesting, so we might expect the gap sentence to give more specific details.

these events: refers back to the previous sentence. The gap sentence must give details of the events or competitions.

The correct answer is sentence G because:
Contests is a synonym for *competition*.
For instance introduces **three** specific examples of **competitions** which are **unusual** (*wife carrying, swamp soccer and endurance sauna sitting*).

2 Choose from the sentences (A–G) the one which fits each gap (1–7). The important information is highlighted to help you. There is one extra sentence which you do not need to use.

A Finland hosts one event in which success depends on creativity rather than strength.

B So the 'wife' can be one's own, or a neighbour's, or someone from even further away.

C We aren't likely to see them in the Olympics just yet.

D Some competitors have wanted to throw their own, but that's against the rules.

E For example, the wife-carrying competition has its roots buried deep in an old local tradition – the 19th-century practice of wife stealing.

F These finalists must perform a compulsory one-minute song as well as a song of their own choice.

G Contests in, for instance, wife carrying, swamp soccer and endurance sauna sitting attract hundreds of competitors every year from around the globe.

ECCENTRIC SPORTS

In the past decade or so, Finland has become host for a number of unusual sporting competitions. (1) _G_ In many of these events, the winner – or winners – will be crowned as world champions.

Common to most of these pursuits is their origins in Finnish folk heritage. (2) _____ Intelligence or social skills are not required for success but power, stamina, and courage are vital. What, then, are these strange sports? Here are a few of the most popular ones.

The Wife Carrying World Championships have been held in the small town of Sonkajärvi, central Finland, since 1992. The winners are the couple who complete the course in the shortest time. To make it more difficult, two dry and two metre-deep water obstacles have been added. Competition rules also state that men can choose any woman over the age of 16 to be their partner for the event. (3) _____ The competition is usually dominated by Estonian pairs.

GRAMMAR obligation and necessity

▶ GRAMMAR REFERENCE (SECTION 11.3 AND 11.4) **PAGE 202**

3 Match the sentence beginnings (1–7) with the endings (a–g).

1 You really **must** watch tonight's final _____
2 Jason **has to** make sure the players are fit as _____
3 I **must** buy some tickets for the match _____
4 Players **mustn't** deliberately commit fouls _____
5 You **don't have to / needn't** set the DVD recorder as I've _____
6 Fans **aren't supposed to** take drinks into the stadium _____
7 You'**d better** finish your homework quickly _____

a already set it up.
b if you want to watch the match later.
c he is the team's trainer.
d or insult each other on the pitch.
e because it's going to be the best for years!
f but a lot of people do.
g otherwise there won't be any left.

This obviously doesn't please the local Finns, who have been wife carrying for centuries.

Finland, being the home of Nokia, is the obvious place to organise the Mobile Phone Throwing World Championships. This year, a record 3,000 spectators watched the competition in Savonlinna, eastern Finland. The mobile phones used in the competition are provided by the organisers and fitted with batteries. (4) _____ And the prize for the longest throw? A new mobile phone.

(5) _____ For the past decade, the northern Finnish town of Oulu has gathered imaginary guitar heroes to the annual Air Guitar World Championships. In recent years, more than fifteen nationalities have been represented in this light-hearted competition. ('Air guitar' is the art of pretending to play along to a rock solo with nothing but an imaginary guitar and the fitting facial expressions.) Most contestants are national champions sent to Oulu by their local air guitar associations. (6) _____ Judges are looking for originality, technique, stage charisma, artistic impression and, obviously, 'airness'.

Overall, even though the Finns are sometimes described as being reserved, no nation taking itself too seriously could come up with these amazing sports!

4 Match the forms in bold in exercise 3 to these functions (1–7).

1 to say something is absolutely forbidden _____
2 to talk about a rule which may not be respected _____
3 to say that something isn't necessary _____
4 to give a threat _____
5 to give an order to yourself _____
6 to describe a responsibility which is part of someone's job _____
7 to make a strong recommendation _____

5 Rewrite each sentence twice, using the past simple and the future simple.

1 She has to sell tickets.
2 We must post that letter.
3 You don't have to come.

▶ GRAMMAR REFERENCE (SECTION 11.10) **PAGE 202**

6 Look at sentences a and b and complete rules 1 and 2 using *needn't have done*, or *didn't need to*.

a **I didn't need to** buy any equipment, so I didn't / but I did anyway.
b **I needn't have bought** any equipment. I wish I had known it wasn't necessary.

1 We use '_____' both for when we did OR didn't do something which wasn't necessary.
2 We use '_____' only for situations where we did something we later discover wasn't necessary.

7 What would you say in these two situations?

1 You took your own lunch but lunch was provided.
2 You didn't have to wear running shoes, so you didn't.

8 ⊙ 3.2 Listen to five situations and respond using expressions of obligation and necessity from exercise 3.

9 Work in groups. Read the rules of air guitar and answer the questions.

1 Which things are absolutely compulsory?
2 What are the things you have to / don't have to do?
3 What isn't permitted?

RULES OF AIR GUITAR

➤ The instrument must be invisible and must be an air guitar (not drums or another imaginary instrument).
➤ Your performance has to last one minute.
➤ You don't have to know the notes you are playing on your imaginary guitar.
➤ Back-up bands are not allowed.

'Football? It's the beautiful game.'
BRAZILIAN FOOTBALLER, PELE

'Some people think football is a matter of life and death ...
I can assure them it is much more serious than that.'
BILL SHANKLY, LIVERPOOL FOOTBALL CLUB MANAGER

LISTENING the early history of football

1 Work in pairs. Do you agree with these quotes? Do you think people care too much about winning?

PAPER 3, PART 4 Multiple choice

2 3.3 You will hear the first part of an interview with an expert on the history of football. For questions 1–7 choose the best answer (A, B or C).

1 According to Jessica,
  A football has had an uninterrupted history.
  B the Ancient Egyptians used their feet to play with balls.
  C prehistoric people played ball games.
2 The Chinese played
  A with a ball filled with feathers.
  B with a rubber ball.
  C with an inflatable ball.
3 The Chinese game
  A was the simplest version.
  B was just for pleasure.
  C had a military purpose.
4 What was tlatchi like?
  A a mixture of other sports
  B a kind of martial art
  C similar to the football we play today
5 Where was tlatchi played?
  A on an outside court
  B in front of an exclusive audience
  C before the general public
6 When a player put the ball in the basket
  A the game automatically ended.
  B there was a religious ceremony.
  C the teams changed ends.
7 Sometimes in tlatchi, the losing team
  A were sent into exile.
  B became slaves.
  C could be executed.

EXAM SPOTLIGHT

PAPER 3, PART 2 Sentence completion

In this part of the Listening test, you listen to a conversation or talk and complete some notes you are given.

Follow these steps.
- Before you listen, use the title to predict what will be said.
- Read the gapped text and guess what kind of information is missing.
- While you listen, only write the words that you hear. Never use your own words.

Remember:
- No marks will be given for wrong or incomplete answers.
- When a word is spelt out, you must write it correctly.

3 3.4 Listen to part B of the interview and correct the candidate's answers.

People played different kinds of football across Europe during (1) the Medium Ages.

Jessica tells us that the Anglo-Saxon version of football was called kicking (2) the Anglo's Head.

The Italians developed a version of the game they called (3) calcia.

Jessica says that two big differences between the Italian and English game were that the Italians wore beautiful costumes and played in proper (4) groups , whereas in England (5) no one could join in because whole villages used to take part!

4 ◉ **3.5 Now listen to part C of the interview and complete the sentences.**

The English game ended when someone kicked the ball (6) _____ of the other team's captain.

Jessica says sometimes there wasn't a winner because people were tired or it (7) _____ to continue.

Some kings of England and the Lord Mayor of London (8) _____ football.

The kings wanted people to do their (9) _____ instead.

Jessica thinks that football is just an excuse for bad behaviour; in Ancient Rome there were (10) _____ hooligans who often killed each other!

GRAMMAR expressing ability

▶ GRAMMAR REFERENCE (SECTION 11 .1 AND 11.2)   **PAGE 201**

5 **Look at sentences a and b and answer questions 1 and 2.**

a   She **could run / was able to run** for miles when she was young.

b   After weeks of practice she **was able to** complete the routine.

1   Which sentence refers to general abilities in the past? _____

2   Which sentence describes a specific occasion when a person achieved something difficult? _____

6 **Read these sentences. Underline the correct option to complete the sentences, or tick (✓) if both options are possible.**

1   We're in luck! I *could / was able to* get some tickets for the final. _____

2   They *could / were able to* pass the ball for ages without letting it fall to the ground. _____

3   I looked everywhere for my racket but I *couldn't / wasn't able* to find it. _____

4   I was delighted when finally I *could / was able to* stand up on my skis. _____

7 **These two sentences are similar in meaning, but what is the difference in their grammar?**

1   We managed to score a goal.

2   We succeeded in scoring a goal.

8 **Work in groups. Tell the others in your group about a time when you succeeded at something that was difficult. Think about the following.**

•   a sporting achievement
•   an academic success
•   learning a new and difficult skill

Last year I did a Russian course. It was really difficult, but I managed to learn a few sentences.

USE OF ENGLISH key word transformation

EXAM SPOTLIGHT

PAPER 1, PART 4 Key word transformation

In this part of the Reading and Use of English paper, you have to rephrase sentences using a key word for each sentence. You can only use between two and five words, including the key word. In all parts of the exam, contractions count as the number of words that would be written in full, e.g. *don't = do not =* two words.

Look at these examples and explanations.

1   Fans shouldn't take food into the stadium.
    SUPPOSED (the key word)
    Fans <u>aren't supposed to</u> take food into the stadium.
    Explanation: *Supposed to* is similar to *should* and is used passively.

2   Every so often we go to a Premier League match.
    TO (the key word)
    From <u>time to time</u> we go to a Premier League match.
    Explanation: *Every so often* means *occasionally* or *from time to time.*

9 **Complete the second sentence so that it has a similar meaning to the first sentence, using the word given. Do not change the word given. Use between two and five words including the word given.**

1   I took my football boots but it wasn't necessary.
    TAKEN
    I _____ my football boots.

2   If I were you, I'd take a waterproof jacket.
    HAD
    You _____ take a waterproof jacket.

3   In his free time Wayne builds model planes.
    SPENDS
    Wayne _____ model planes.

4   Smoking is prohibited in this building.
    SUPPOSED
    You _____ in here.

5   Rita knows how to walk on her hands.
    AT
    Rita _____ on her hands.

6   I found snowboarding too difficult.
    ABLE
    I _____ to snowboard.

WRITING an article

1 Work in pairs. Look at the photographs of two racing events. Where are they taking place? Would you like to go to an event like these?

EXAM SPOTLIGHT

PAPER 2, PART 2 Writing tasks

In Paper 2, the Writing paper, you have a choice of three or four types of writing. One choice might be an article. You are always given a context and an idea of the people who will read it. You need to write the article in an appropriate style.

Last year my friend Omar invited me to a camel race at the Kuwaiti racetrack. It was my first time so I didn't know what to expect. When we arrived, most people were dressed in traditional costumes and it felt very exotic. We looked at the different camels and tried to guess which ones would win. They were impressive creatures.

When I asked about their riders Omar just laughed. The jockeys are radio-controlled robots not humans! They wear caps and costumes, which is really funny. During the races the camels' owners drove their jeeps alongside the track so that they could control the robots. The races were exciting and often very close. Sometimes it was hard to see anything through the clouds of dust. People shouted louder and louder as the camels got closer to the finishing line. It was really atmospheric. There were fantastic prizes including brand new 4x4s.

Afterwards we went to Omar's uncle's tent where we drank camel milk and ate dates. My day out was an unforgettable experience! I would certainly recommend it if you ever get the chance.

2 Read the exam question and the article. Which event from exercise 1 does it describe? What is unusual or special about the event?

> **You have seen the following announcement in a travel magazine for young people.**
>
> ---
>
> **Calling all sports' enthusiasts**
>
> Write an article for our international readers about an interesting sporting event you have been to. We will publish the best articles next month.

3 In this kind of article it's important to use lots of interesting adjectives to describe the event. Circle all the adjectives in the article about camel racing.

4 Read these sentences and decide if the adjective is correct (✓) or incorrect (✗). Correct any incorrect adjectives.

                    interesting

0   We had a really ~~interested~~ night out. ☐
1   The crowds were so exciting – they couldn't stop cheering and shouting. ☐
2   The meal was very enjoyed. You should have come with us. ☐
3   I find most TV very boring. Only football is worth watching. ☐
4   My taste in sport is quite various. I tend to watch most things. ☐
5   We saw this fascinating documentary about the history of Real Madrid. ☐
6   The commentators were very fun. They made us laugh! ☐
7   I enjoyed the game but my friend wasn't impressed. ☐

5 Choose four adjectives from the box and describe the other event from exercise 1.

> atmospheric attractive colourful complicated
> exciting exotic fantastic funny huge important
> interesting loud physical varied well-designed

6 Read the extracts from two articles. Complete each extract with words from the box in exercise 5. There may be more than one possibility for each gap.

A

It was the first time I'd ever seen this type of sport so it was really (1) _____ to read about the game and find out the rules before I went. I don't think I would have understood otherwise because it's fairly (2) _____ . The players are (3) _____ and when they play it's a very (4) _____ game. I'm amazed they don't get hurt more. Even if you don't like sport, American football is still very (5) _____ with all the singing and the cheerleaders dancing.

B

I couldn't believe how (6) _____ it was. There were some enormous speakers and you could hear all the way at the back of the stadium. The good thing was that you could see the band from anywhere because the stage was so (7) _____ . I was surprised because they didn't just play all their recent hits. The songs were fairly (8) _____ with some from their early years. Anyway, they did three encores and then ended with my favourite song, so it was a / an (9) _____ night!

7 Write your own answer to the exam question in exercise 2. Include the following information.

Before
- the background to the event – when and where it took place
- before the event / preparations
- any food or costumes associated with it

During
- what happened, how it progressed, the different stages
- something special, funny or unusual about the event
- the atmosphere

After
- what happened afterwards
- how you felt / how other spectators felt
- if you would recommend it

WRITING CHECKLIST

ARTICLE

After you write, check your work. Check grammar and vocabulary, but also check the structure and layout. Use this checklist to help you.

- Does the article tells us
  - what the event is? ☐
  - what the reaction of the audience was? ☐
  - why you would recommend it? ☐
- Does the article contain at least three paragraphs? ☐
- Does it include a variety of adjectives? ☐
- Does it include no fewer than 140 and no more than 190 words? ☐

WRITING GUIDE **PAGE 218**

GLOSSARY

adrenaline: the substance that makes your heart beat faster when you are excited or are in danger
propeller: the metal object that turns quickly in the water to make the boat move along
shallow: the opposite of deep
thrill: a strong feeling of excitement

VIDEO adventure

1 Match words 1–8 to words a–h to make the names of extreme sports.

1	kite	a	climbing
2	jet	b	rafting
3	whitewater	c	gliding
4	bungee	d	boating
5	mountain	e	diving
6	free	f	jumping
7	hang	g	surfing
8	sky	h	jumping
9	base	i	running

2 Complete the table with the activities from exercise 1. Some activities may go in more than one column.

WHICH SPORTS:				
take place on water	take place in a city	take place in the air	need a lot of equipment	need an engine

3 You are going to watch a video about Queenstown in New Zealand. Why do you think it calls itself *the adventure capital of the world*?

4 Watch the video and tick the activities you see from exercise 1.

5 Watch the video again and choose the best answers (A or B).

1 The bungee jump is
   A about 440 metres high.
   B a bit less than 140 metres high.
2 What's special about jet boats?
   A They don't have a propeller.
   B They are shallow.
3 Why were jet boats invented?
   A to deal with New Zealand's rivers
   B for sport
4 If you wanted to do every activity New Zealand offers you'd have to stay
   A two months.
   B 16 days.
5 The mountain adventure takes between
   A four and five hours.
   B five and six hours.
6 The Kawarau bridge is
   A the birthplace of bungee jumping.
   B where the first money-making site for bungee jumping was set up.
7 How does the elderly lady feel about bungee jumping?
   A She can't wait to try it herself.
   B It's fun watching other people do it.
8 According to the member of the bungee jumping crew, who enjoys bungee jumping the most?
   A people who have to force themselves to do it
   B people who look forward to it

6 Why do you think people do these extreme sports? Would you like to try some of them? Why, and which ones? Why not?

7 Read the Ideas generator and do the task.

IDEAS GENERATOR

MAKING CONNECTIONS

In Part 2 of the *First* Speaking paper, you compare two photographs. To prepare for this part of the exam, it's useful to generate ideas about the similarities or connections between two photographs, and the differences between them.

Look at this photograph and the photograph on page 38 and make a list of the similarities and differences between them. In particular, consider the following:
- the people (activity, appearance and emotions, reason for being there)
- the location (outside or inside, country or city, type of country)
- the environment (weather, time of day, any buildings or other objects).

8 Work in pairs. Imagine you are doing the *First* Speaking test. Take turns to be the interlocutor (examiner) and the candidate.

Interlocutor: give your partner these instructions from the exam.

Here are your photographs. They show people who are enjoying sport in different ways. I'd like you to compare these photographs and say what you think the people are enjoying about sport in these different places.

Candidate: listen to the instructions and talk about the photographs for one minute.

USEFUL EXPRESSIONS

COMPARING PHOTOGRAPHS

Talking about similarities
The first photo shows … and so does the second.
Both of them are …
They're similar because …
In both photos the people are …

Talking about differences
They are more / less … than / aren't as … as …
In this one they are less … / but this one shows more …
This place is more … while / whereas the other place is …

4 NATURE AND ANIMALS

1 Look at the photo and discuss the questions.

1 Why did mammoths become extinct?
2 Do you think it might be possible to bring them back to life?

VOCABULARY nature and animals

2 Complete sentences 1–9 with words from the box.

> breed cage endangered extinction habitat
> instinct pet prey safari tame train wild

1 The Siberian tiger is a / an _____ species. It faces _____ within the next 20 years.
2 Some animals, such as pandas, are notoriously difficult to _____ in captivity.
3 Rachel has been asking for a / an _____ rabbit for ages, but where could we keep it?
4 Human beings depend on reason more than _____ .
5 It is better to study _____ animals in their natural _____ rather than in zoos.
6 You can _____ birds of _____ to do some amazing things.
7 Even though it looks _____ , it could attack you without warning.
8 It's cruel to keep a bird locked up in a _____ .
9 I have always wanted to go on an African _____ and visit the national parks.

3 Match each adjective (1–6) to the correct preposition from the box.

> for of on in to with

1 keen _____   4 allergic _____
2 aware _____   5 fed up _____
3 famous _____   6 interested _____

4 Use the collocations from exercise 3 in these sentences.

1 I wasn't _____ the time so I missed my riding lesson.
2 I'm really _____ our new dog; it keeps digging up the garden.
3 Australia is _____ its koalas and kangaroos.
4 Lucy has been _____ wildlife programmes since she was small.
5 I keep sneezing; I must be _____ the cat.
6 No, I don't want to hold him; I'm not very _____ snakes.

5 Write your own sentences using three of the collocations from exercise 3.

1 _____
2 _____
3 _____

LISTENING animals and humans

PAPER 3, PART 3 Multiple matching

6 ◉ **4.1** **You will hear five speakers talking about animals. Choose from the list (A–H) what each speaker is talking about. Use the letters only once. There are three letters you don't need to use.**

A insects and problem-solving
B a sporting mascot
C the death of a pet
D the habits of an ancient animal
E a badly behaved pet
F an animal hero
G the beginning of an allergy
H a particularly greedy pet

Speaker 1 _____
Speaker 2 _____
Speaker 3 _____
Speaker 4 _____
Speaker 5 _____

7 ◉ **4.1** **Work in pairs. Listen again and discuss these questions for each speaker.**

1a How did the speaker feel about the circus?
1b What were his symptoms?
2a How long have scorpions existed?
2b Where can't we find them?
3a What agreement did he make with his children and how well was it respected?
3b What happened when the first guinea pig died?
4a Who gives the orders in an ant colony?
4b How has their behaviour inspired scientists?
5a How did the owners find out that they shared Sid with other people?
5b Did Sid deserve his nickname?

GRAMMAR the grammar of phrasal verbs

8 **Look at sentences a–d and match the phrasal verbs in bold to the meanings (1–4).**

a I went into the garage and noticed one of them had **passed away**.
b They didn't want to **let** me **down** so they came over after dinner.
c You can even **come across** them between the bark of trees.
d I had really been **looking forward to** it.
1 find / discover, often by chance _____
2 die _____
3 wait with excitement, anticipate with pleasure _____
4 disappoint _____

9 **Look again at sentences a–d in exercise 8 and answer the questions.**

1 Which sentence has a pronoun between the verb and its particle? _____ (transitive separable)
2 Which phrasal verb consists of three parts followed by a pronoun? _____ (three part transitive)
3 Which sentence has a phrasal verb with no object? _____ (intransitive)
4 Which sentence has a pronoun after the second part of the phrasal verb? _____ (transitive inseparable)

▶ GRAMMAR REFERENCE (SECTION 12.3) **PAGE 205**

10 **Look at the audioscript on page 222. Find the phrasal verbs in bold that match these definitions, and complete column 2 of the table.**

	Phrasal verb	Definition	Type
1	live off	survive	transitive inseparable
2		discover information	
3		invent / have the idea for something	
4		endure / suffer an unpleasant experience	
5		perform / complete	
6		become extinct	
7		finish	
8		trick / deceive	
9		consider something as inferior	
10		be careful	

11 **Work in pairs. Look at the audioscript again. Match each phrasal verb to a type in exercise 9, and complete column 4 of the table.**

12 **Work in pairs. Look at these situations. Take turns to complete the comments using the phrasal verbs from exercises 8 and 10.**

0 You took a car to the garage to be repaired. They couldn't fix it because they didn't have the part they needed.

> *I'm really fed up. I took my car to the garage but they couldn't fix it because they didn't have the part they needed.*

1 You've discovered an old painting in your grandmother's attic.
  'You'll never guess what I …'
2 You're really excited that your friend from Australia is coming to visit you.
  'I'm so glad that he's coming to visit us. I'm really …'
3 A snobbish friend thinks his new neighbour is inferior because he doesn't have an expensive car.
  'You really shouldn't …'
4 A classmate promised to bring you back a grammar book you lent him, but he forgot.
  'I needed it to do my homework. You have really …'
5 Your friend is back from her holiday. You have some bad news about her pet rabbit.
  'I'm afraid I've got some bad news. Your …'
6 You and your friends gave money to a woman for a children's charity. You discover that she tricked you.
  'I'm afraid we …'
7 You have thought of a theme for the class party.
  'I think I've …'
8 You want to make people aware that polar bears may soon become extinct.
  'If we don't do anything about global warming …'

READING a dog's life

1 Which do you think is a better pet, a dog or a cat? Make a list of the advantages and disadvantages of each. Do a quick survey. Are there more dog lovers or cat lovers in the class?

EXAM SPOTLIGHT

PAPER 1, PART 7 Multiple matching

Read the texts all the way through for a general understanding before trying to answer the questions.

Then read the questions very carefully so you know what to look out for. Underline key information in the text that helps you to answer the questions.
Remember:
* The questions you are given paraphrase the ideas that appear in the text, they do not copy them word for word.
* Key words in the questions might seem to match more than one text, so check the whole of the question carefully before you choose. For example, two owners mention criticism of the way they treat their dogs, but only one of them is a correct match to the whole of question 4.
* There can be up to six texts in the exam.

2 Read the article about five women and their dogs. For questions 1–10, choose from dog owners A–E.

Which owner
1 values her dog more than her partner? _Lynda_
2 has a dog who's a top model? _Shelley_
3 saved her dog's life? _Karen_
4 is annoyed at the criticism she has received? _Carlotta_
5 thinks her dog could have a future on TV? _Lynda_
6 has a dog with impressive ancestors? _Shelley_
7 depends on her dog? _Bronwyn_
8 isn't keen on her dog's name? _Karen_
9 books her dog its own seat on the plane? _Lynda_
10 keeps her dog in its place? _Bronwyn_

3 Work in pairs and discuss the questions.

1 Which dog do you think leads the best life?
2 What do you think of people who dress their dogs up?
3 How much do you think the pets enjoy it?

SPEAKING points of view

4 ⊙ 4.2 Three friends are discussing the article about dogs. Listen and decide who says what. Write *T* for Terry, *C* for Charlotte or *R* for Rebecca.

Who
1 thinks that the dogs look lovely? _____
2 thinks that it's crazy to spend so much on them? _____
3 talks about hungry children? _____
4 mentions the homeless? _____
5 thinks it is immoral to spend money in this way?
   _____
6 talks about the needs of the animals? _____
7 supports the right of the owners to choose? _____

5 ⊙ 4.2 Listen again. Look at the table below and tick (✓) the expressions that you hear.

Expressions	tick
Giving opinions I think / believe (that) … As I see it … From my point of view … In my opinion … As far as I'm concerned …	
Agreeing and disagreeing I (quite / totally) agree (with) … Absolutely …	
Giving someone else's point of view Marcus says … Antonia thinks …	
Disagreeing Yes, but … I don't / can't agree … I (completely / totally) disagree …	
Acknowledging what the other person says I hear / understand what you're saying but … I understand / respect your point of view but … I can see where you're coming from, but … I see your point, but … I suppose so / I suppose (Terry) is right. That's true but …	

6 Work in pairs. Think of any other expressions you could add to the list in the table.

7 Work in groups. Discuss the following statements using the expressions from the table.

1 Animals should have the same legal rights as humans.
2 It is natural for people to be vegetarians.
3 We should never use fur and leather.
4 Experiments on animals are never justified.

A dog's Life

A Karen owns Spike the mongrel, seven years old

I wouldn't have called him that myself, but Spike has been with us for three years now. He was a rescue dog and would have been put down if we hadn't taken him. He didn't cost us anything, but we have spent a fortune on vets' bills since we have had him. He had been badly treated by his owners and was in a terrible state when we got him. It took him ages to start to trust people again. Spike is incredibly loyal and is great with kids, but we have to keep an eye on him in case he meets any other dogs.

B Lynda owns Araminta the pedigree pug, five years old

People tell me off for spoiling Araminta, and I suppose they're right. We dress her in the latest fashions from Princess Pooches and she even wears her own special fragrance. My boyfriend, Femi, gets fed up with all the fuss she gets, but he realises that I would always put Araminta before any boyfriend! She sleeps in our bedroom in her own four-poster bed, but usually when we wake up in the morning we find her snuggled under our duvet. When we go to the States we buy her a ticket in the cabin. I couldn't bear to think of her stuck in the hold. I have taught her a few tricks and I'm going to try and get us onto one of those TV talent shows – I think she'd be a real hit.

C Shelley owns Gelert the wolfhound, three years old

I know more about Gelert than I do about my own family. He has got an incredibly long pedigree and there are lots of champions in his family tree. He was very expensive to buy and he's even more expensive to feed, but he has been worth every penny. You can often see him in adverts in glossy magazines alongside top models like Griselda Jenner. Luxury brands don't want any old dog in their adverts, you see. He has been in ads for posh outdoor clothing and expensive 4x4 cars. Each time we get a fee, so he has paid for himself many times over.

D Bronwyn owns Squib the collie dog, five years old

Squib is more intelligent than most people I've met. I don't know how I would manage without him – as soon as I step out into the yard he jumps onto the quad and we're off onto the hillsides to gather all our flocks together. The herding instinct is strong in sheepdogs and he is the fourth generation we have had. People often ask me why I don't put him in for competitions, but I think he works hard every day and he deserves his rest. He sleeps in a barn most of the year, but we move his basket into the kitchen in the winter months. We don't let him into the rest of the house though. After all, a dog is still a dog.

E Carlotta the terrier, three years old

When Carlotta was two we organised a bark-mitzvah for her – you know, a coming-of-age ceremony. Two for a dog is like 14 in human years. It was a great occasion and we dressed her up in her favourite outfit. All her friends from the park came and had individual birthday cakes made of her favourite food. We hired a caterer for the human guests and a film-maker to record everything on video. People may think we were foolish, but it was a once in a lifetime thing for Carlotta, and I think that they should mind their own business. We donate a lot to charity so it is up to us how we spend what's left.

USE OF ENGLISH word formation

EXAM SPOTLIGHT

PAPER 1, PART 3 Word formation

In this part of Paper 1, you must change the part of speech of the word in capitals so that it can be used in the gap in the sentence.

Follow these four steps.

1 Read the text, without focusing on the gaps, and make sure you understand the story.
2 Identify the part of speech of each word in capitals.
3 Decide into which part of speech you need to transform the word in capitals.
4 Finally, build the necessary word.

1 Read the completed example and the explanations 1–5.

People may be able to have a close (0) relationship with large animals but be afraid of a tiny spider! On country walks we are (1) terrified in case we see a snake. Yet, apart from a few (2) exceptions, they present little real danger. European spiders are shy and (3) harmless creatures so our fears are (4) imaginary.	RELATION TERRIFY EXCEPT HARM IMAGINE

0 RELATION (personal noun) > *relationship* (concept noun). The gap comes after the article *a* and adjective *close*, so we know we need a noun. Use the noun suffix -*ship*.
1 TERRIFY (verb) > *terrified* (participial adjective). We need to follow the verb *be* with an adjective. We have a choice of two participial adjectives: *terrifying* or *terrified*.
2 EXCEPT (verb) > *exception* (noun). *Few* comes before nouns. We make the noun by adding the suffix -*ion*.
3 HARM (noun / verb) > *harmless* (adjective). -*less* is a suffix meaning *without*. We need an adjective to describe the noun *creatures* and to partner *shy*.
4 IMAGINE (verb) > *imaginary* (adjective).

2 Read the rest of the text and decide what the original word in capitals was.

Sometimes our fears can become a reality. For most of us a wasp sting is an (5) unpleasant experience. It is (6) painful for a few minutes but then it is over. However, when a friend was stung by a wasp she had an (7) extremely severe reaction which almost killed her. So even a simple sting can prove (8) deadly to some people.

3 Work in pairs. Read the text quickly and explain the story in a few words.

Chef Paul Stevens was in the kitchen of the restaurant where he worked when he was bitten on the hand by a giant spider. His first (0) reaction was to take its picture on his mobile to show his friends. However, when he started to feel ill he was taken to hospital. The doctors were (1) _____ in making a diagnosis and sent him home. When Paul felt worse he was rushed back to hospital. (2) _____ he still had his mobile with the photograph. This time doctors sent it to Bristol Zoo where they identified his (3) _____ as a Brazilian Wandering Spider – one of the world's most (4) _____ arachnids. Its venom can kill 225 mice. In humans it can provoke an (5) _____ heartbeat and high blood pressure. In some instances it can even result in (6) _____ . Happily, since the (7) _____ of an antidote nobody has died. At first nobody could explain its (8) _____ appearance, then people realised it had almost certainly hidden away in a box of bananas.

4 Now read the text again and follow the steps in the Exam Spotlight to fill in the table.

Word in CAPITALS	Part of speech of the word in CAPITALS	Part of speech of the new word needed	New word needed
0 REACT	verb	noun	reaction
1 SUCCESS			
2 LUCKY			
3 ATTACK			
4 POISON			
5 REGULAR			
6 DIE			
7 INVENT			
8 MYSTERY			

SPEAKING comparing photographs

5 ⊙ 4.3 Listen to the interlocutor's instructions in Part 2 of the Speaking test. Complete these instructions with the interlocutor's words.

In this part of the test, I'm going to give each of you two photographs. I'd like you to talk about your photographs (1) _____ for about (2) _____ , and also to answer a short question about (3) _____ .

Beate, it's your turn first. Here are your photographs. They show people and dogs interacting in different ways. I'd like you to (4) _____ , and say what you think (5) _____ is between the animals and the humans in the photographs.

6 Now look at this pair of photographs from the Speaking test. Work in pairs. List the similarities and differences between the photographs.

7 ⊙ 4.4 Beate is one of the two candidates in this Speaking test. Listen to her talking about the photographs and tick the points on your list that she mentions. Does she say anything you didn't list?

8 ⊙ 4.5 Now the interlocutor asks the second candidate a question about the photographs. Listen to Walter answering the interlocutor's question. How well do you think he answers?

EXAM SPOTLIGHT

PAPER 4, PART 2 Individual long turn

In Part 2 of the Speaking test, you have to compare two photographs for about one minute. You shouldn't describe the photographs, you should only describe things that are relevant to your comparison.

Useful expressions

- Playing for time: *Well, let me see …*
- Similarities: *Both photographs show …*
- Making a contrast: *In the first one / top one there's a …, whereas in the second one / the bottom one I can see a …*
- Referring back to the first photo: *Anyway, going back / returning to the first photo …*
- Speculating: *Perhaps / Maybe it is …*
- *It might be / could be …*

9 Work in pairs. Look at the photographs on page 238 and talk about them using some of the expressions in the Exam Spotlight box. Take it in turns to be the interlocutor (asking the questions) and the candidate (speaking for about one minute).

KEY WORD *look*

10 ⊙ 4.4 Beate uses several expressions with the word *look*. Complete these sentences with the words she uses. Then listen again and check.

1 In the first photo, there is a man … it _____ a soldier … (It's not very clear.)
2 … the dogs _____ happy.
3 It _____ they are in a race …

11 Work in pairs. What words and forms follow *look* in exercise 10?

12 Where necessary, correct these sentences.

1 The dog looks like a German Shepherd.
2 The dog looks like tired.
3 It looks as though it is going to bite.
4 It looks as like they are going to stop.
5 The photographs look as if similar.

13 Complete the phrasal verbs in these sentences. All of these verbs appear somewhere in this unit.

1 I can't find my keys. Can you help me look _____ them?
2 Looking _____ someone else's pet is always a big responsibility.
3 The police are looking _____ the problem posed by dangerous dogs.
4 I'm really looking _____ reading her new book about horses. Her last one was fascinating.
5 We shouldn't look _____ on people who live in smaller homes than we do. It's wrong.

WRITING an essay (2)

1 What is the relationship between the people and the animals in the photographs?

2 Would you rather take a child to a zoo or the circus? Give your reasons.

EXAM SPOTLIGHT

PAPER 2, PART 1 An essay

In Paper 2, Part 1, there are different ways of answering the essay question. In Unit 1 we looked at an essay giving a clear opinion on the essay question, and giving reasons for that opinion. With some essay questions, you may want to consider the arguments on both sides of the question before deciding your opinion.

What is important is that you provide a clear, well-organised answer, with a wide range of expressions and topic vocabulary. The examiner doesn't have to agree or disagree with you!

3 Read the exam question and Jorge's essay on page 47. Answer the questions.

1 Do you agree with what Jorge says? How important is this?

2 Is the essay well organised? Does Jorge use all the notes?

> In your English class you have been talking about the advantages and disadvantages of zoos. Now your teacher has asked you to write an essay.
>
> Write an essay using all the notes and give reasons for your point of view.
>
> **Is there still a place for zoos in the modern world?**
>
> **Notes**
>
> Write about:
>
> 1 conservation
> 2 education
> 3 your own ideas

4 Jorge's essay uses a four-paragraph model. Complete the essay plan.

Introduction: introduce proposition
zoos are controversial
Arguments against:
1 _____
2 _____
3 _____
Arguments for:
1 _____
2 _____
3 _____
Conclusion: summary of the writer's opinion
1 _____
2 _____

5 What words and expressions does Jorge use:

1 to introduce an additional point?
2 to put his ideas in order?

6 When we don't know or don't want to say *who* or *what* should do something, we may use the passive form. Find more examples of the active and passive form of *should* in the model essay.

Someone should take action. (active)
Action should be taken. (passive)

Zoos are controversial places. Their supporters think they are important for conservation and education, while their opponents claim they are cruel and should be closed. Let us consider some arguments from both sides.

Let's begin by considering the arguments against. Firstly, wild animals should live as nature intended. In addition, they should be free to follow their instincts even if their lives are short and dangerous. Last but not least, zoos are no longer necessary – if we really want to learn about animals there are always documentaries.

Now let's turn to arguments in favour of zoos. First of all, zoos help to save some animals from extinction with their breeding programmes. Next, they are essential for scientific research. What's more, modern zoos are safe, happy places with spacious natural habitats. Finally, zoos are educational; a visit to a zoo is an important childhood experience.

On balance, I sincerely believe that zoos are essential for protecting endangered species and for scientific research. Many important discoveries have been made in zoos. Most zoo animals are born in captivity so they would die in the wild. Finally, there is no substitute for experiencing animals close up and most of us cannot afford to go on a safari!

7 Look at these sentences and rewrite them using the passive form of *should* or *ought to*.

1 Schools ought to teach children how to look after pets.
   Children _ought to be taught_ how to look after pets.
2 We should take Emma and Anaïs to the zoo, I'm sure they would enjoy it.
   Emma and Anaïs _should be taken_ to the zoo.
3 Farmers shouldn't raise chickens in such terrible conditions.
   Chickens _shouldn't be raised_ in such terrible conditions.
4 The government ought to do more to tackle cruelty to animals.
   More _should be done_ (by the government) to tackle cruelty to animals.
5 People should only wear fur in really cold countries.
   Fur _ought to be / should to be_ in really cold countries.

8 Rewrite the sentences in exercise 7 as personal opinions by adding an introductory phrase. For example, *I sincerely believe that, in my opinion, from my point of view*.

I sincerely believe that farm animals should be treated with more respect.

9 Work in pairs or in small groups. Read the essay question about circuses and decide which points in the list could be for (+) or against (−) circuses. Add other ideas of your own.

- trainers are brave _amazing +/-_
- you can see animals up close +
- animals are well looked after +/-
- circuses can work without animals + _AGAINST_
- circuses are part of our cultural heritage + _FOR_
- circuses are entertaining and fun + _FOR_
- circuses are cruel and unnatural − _AGAINST_
- animals can be injured −
- animals develop skills + _FOR_
- animals spend hours and days in lorries −
- children enjoy watching animals perform +
- trainers use fear to train animals −
- animals often enjoy performing

Should people go to circuses that use wild animals?

Notes

Write about:

1 entertainment
2 education
3 your own ideas

10 Plan a four-paragraph essay using the ideas you chose in exercise 9, and show your plan to your teacher. When you are ready, write your essay using the useful expressions.

USEFUL EXPRESSIONS

LISTING REASONS

To begin with; First of all; Firstly
Secondly; Next
What's more; In addition
Finally; Lastly
Last but not least
(to show something is important even if you mention it last)
On balance; In conclusion

WRITING CHECKLIST

AN ESSAY

Did you:
- write a four-paragraph essay? ☐
- use all the notes? ☐
- include your own idea? ☐
- use a range of expressions for listing ideas? ☐

WRITING GUIDE **PAGE 212**

REVIEW AND EXAM PRACTICE Units 3 and 4

1 Read the text and decide which answer (A, B, C or D) best fits each gap. There is an example at the beginning (0).

An eight-year-old peacock called Mr P has fallen in love with a row of red and white pumps at a petrol station. (0) _C_ to a bird expert, peacocks are keen (1) _on_ colourful objects and always return to the same place. Lots of people come to fill up just to see him; however, (2) _many_ local residents have complained because of the awful noise he makes. His owner says the sound made by the pumps is (3) _D_ to that made by female birds looking (4) _for_ a mate. During the mating season Mr P (5) _C_ up to 18 hours a day by the pumps. Sometimes he is even away for a (6) _A_ nights. His brothers, on the other hand, remain for (7) _most_ of the mating season in their owner's garden, where they are fascinated by bright objects such (8) _as_ orange balls and kittens!

0	A For	B Further	C According	D By	5	A takes	B lasts	C spends	D allows
1	A on	B of	C by	D for	6	A few	B couple	C many	D lots
2	A lot	B amount	C number	D many	7	A nearly	B most	C every	D hardly
3	A same	B alike	C almost	D similar	8	A a	B like	C as	D lovely
4	A forward to	B for	C into	D after					

2 For questions 9–16, read the text and think of the word which best fits each gap. There is an example at the beginning (0).

Football means something different according to where you find yourself. For Europeans and Latin Americans it means the fast moving team game (0) _also_ known as soccer. For North Americans it is the contest (9) _between_ large muscular men wearing protective clothing. American football's closest European equivalent is probably rugby.

All (10) _the_ same, soccer has now really taken off in the US, where children play it as a (11) _less_ brutal alternative to American football. Soccer is also played by women, (12) _whose_ professional league has its own galaxy of stars, which explains (13) _why_ many American males regard American football (14) _as_ a more manly activity. There is some truth in this. When soccer players fall over they often roll around on the ground like children, only to get (15) _up_ just a few seconds later! When someone doesn't get up in American football it is usually (16) _because_ they have been hurt quite seriously.

(margin note: nevertheless)

3 For questions 17–24, use the word given in capitals at the end of some of the lines to form a word that fits the space in the same line. There is an example at the beginning (0).

Nowadays in schools there is a worrying trend against playing (0) _competitive_ games. Teachers worry that such activities encourage an unpleasant (17) _rivalry_ between children, and make some kids feel (18) _useless_ and humiliated. Personally, I believe that a need to compete is a strong instinct – just look at the number of willing (19) _contestants_ who want to demonstrate their (20) _intelligence_ on quiz shows. What's more, the (21) _recognition_ and the approval we receive can strengthen rather than damage (22) _friendships_. Learning how to lose or to face up to a (23) _difficulties_ is as important as winning. Finally, why should teachers deny kids the (24) _satisfaction_ of being the best? A system that fails to encourage winners creates a nation of losers.	COMPETE RIVAL = competitor USE CONTEST = participant INTELLIGENT RECOGNISE FRIEND DIFFICULT SATISFY

4 For questions 25–30, complete the second sentence so that it has a similar meaning to the first sentence, using the word given. Do not change the word given. You must use between two and five words, including the word given.

---

0 I can't wait to see Martha again.
FORWARD
I'm really <u>looking forward to seeing</u> Martha again.

25 What do you think I should do?
WERE
What would <u>you do if you</u> *were* me?

26 Could you look after Rex while I'm away?
CARE
Could you <u>take care of</u> Rex while I'm away?

27 In my opinion, cats make better companions than dogs.
AM
As far <u>as I'm</u> *concerned* cats make better pets than dogs.

28 Human beings and chimpanzees aren't very different.
BETWEEN
There is very <u>little</u> *difference between* human beings and chimpanzees.

29 Look at that tree, it's going to fall.
AS
That tree <u>looks as if</u> it's going to fall.

30 Malcolm has had a good idea for a costume.
UP
Malcolm has <u>come up</u> *with* a good idea for a costume.

---

5 🔘 4.6 You will hear part A of an interview with Professor Helena Murray, an expert on animal behaviour. For questions 1–10, complete the sentences with a word or short phrase.

Humans are mammals, but there are three things which separate us from most other animals in our group. There is (1) _____ , (2) _____ (we can think logically), and our capacity for (3) _____ . Animals don't 'think'; instead they are governed by their (4) _____ . We know if an animal recognises itself by using the (5) _____ test. Chimps, (6) _____ and elephants can recognise their reflection. A New York zoo carried out some experiments. They studied the behaviour of (7) _____ elephants. When they recognised their reflections they put (8) _____ their mouths! One of the elephants, called (9) _____ , actually removed a mark from her face. However, people who believe that cats and dogs are self-aware are (10) _____ .

---

6 🔘 4.7 You will hear part B of the interview. For questions 11–17, choose the best answer (A, B or C).

---

11 Dogs form such close relationships with humans because they
   A think like humans.
   B are pack animals.
   C can tell what humans feel.

12 How good are dogs at reading human expressions?
   A They're not as good as chimpanzees.
   B They're better than our closest relatives.
   C They're worse than dolphins.

13 What happens with the cup test?
   A Chimpanzees simply guess.
   B Chimps and dogs have similar success rates.
   C Dogs get it right most of the time.

14 What, according to Professor Murray, is the principal reason for this ability to read expressions?
   A a combination of human company and evolution
   B It is an instinct possessed by canines.
   C Any dog can quickly acquire this skill.

15 Which dogs can read human expressions?
   A dogs raised from puppies, by humans
   B wolves
   C those with a history of domestication

16 What is special about the New Guinea singing dog?
   A It had never been tamed.
   B It had once lived alongside humans.
   C It had never been used in a scientific experiment.

17 The singing dogs experiment demonstrated that the ability to read human expressions
   A could easily be re-activated.
   B was passed from generation to generation.
   C could be lost.

BOOKS AND FILMS

VOCABULARY books and films

1 **Look at the photo from a film based on the novel *Pride and Prejudice*. What do you think the book was about? What classic works of literature from your country have been turned into films?**

2 **Complete sentences 1–12 with the words from the box. Make any changes necessary.**

chapter character classic episode fiction
heroine location mythology narrator novel
novelist 2 playwright 8 plot scene scenery
script serial set 1 TV series villain

1 My favourite _TV series_ is *The Big Bang Theory*.
2 Shakespeare is England's most famous _playwright_ and poet, whose plays are performed all around the world.
3 Charles Dickens, who wrote the books *Oliver Twist* and *Bleak House*, is probably England's best-known _novelist_ .
4 When they made a _serial_ of *Oliver Twist*, it was divided into eight one-hour _episodes_ .
5 *Vanity Fair* is considered a _classic_ work of English literature, but like many books at that time it was serialised for magazines. Writers had to produce several _chapter_ each week.

6 In addition to the hero and _heroine_ there are lots of minor _characters_ who make an appearance.
7 This book has got one of the most complicated _plots_ I've ever come across. It's hard to work out who is who and what's happening!
8 The story was clever but the _script_ was poor – some of the dialogues were terrible.
9 The _narrator_ , or storyteller, has an important role in this book.
10 The most moving _scene_ in the film is when Esther meets her mother for the first time.
11 The film was shot on _location_ in Kenya; the _scenery_ is absolutely amazing.
12 I don't like the version of *Romeo and Juliet* which was _set_ in Miami.
13 Generally I prefer fact to _fiction_ but I also love a good historical _novel_ .
14 In the legend of *Robin Hood*, the _villian_ , or 'bad guy' is the Sheriff of Nottingham.
15 One of my teachers used to read us Greek _mythology_ , which I really enjoyed.

3 **Work in groups. Find out:**
- each other's favourite books and films
- what kinds of books and films the others in the group dislike and why.

LISTENING great adaptations

4 You will hear an interview with a scriptwriter who adapts books for TV and the cinema. What questions do you think the interviewer will ask? What do you think the scriptwriter will say?

EXAM SPOTLIGHT

PAPER 3, PART 4 Multiple choice

In the Listening paper, there is a pause after each part of the test, which gives you time to check your answers and to prepare for the next part.

Use this time to read all the questions. This will give you an idea of what you are going to hear, and will help you know what information you have to listen for. It may also remind you what you already know about the topic.

5 ⦿ **5.1** Listen to Part A of the interview. For questions 1–7, choose the best answers (A, B or C).

1 How did Jacinta become a specialist in adapting books for the cinema?
  A She realised she would never be a successful writer.
  B It happened by chance.
  C It had always been her ambition.

2 What does she need to know before she begins an adaptation?
  A which parts of the book she can cut
  B the medium and type of story
  C the audience she is writing for

3 Why does she prefer working on TV serials?
  A Because it's less stressful.
  B There are fewer problems with the budget.
  C The adaptation can be closer to the original work.

4 According to Jacinta, what do people expect when they go to the cinema?
  A a gripping story
  B visual excitement
  C well-known stars

5 What does she think of the ballroom scenes in the big-screen version of *Pride and Prejudice*?
  A They take time away from other parts of the story.
  B At times the attention to detail is poor.
  C People will enjoy them just as much if they watch them at home on TV.

6 Why does Jacinta prefer the TV version of *Pride and Prejudice*?
  A It pays particular attention to the ballroom scenes.
  B She likes the actor who played the hero.
  C It is old-fashioned.

7 How does Jacinta feel about changing the original story of the book she's adapting?
  A It gives adapters the chance to show their creativity.
  B She will do it if it improves the plot.
  C She's against changing the story.

PAPER 3, PART 2 Sentence completion

6 ⦿ **5.2** Now listen to Part B. Jacinta and Lorolei discuss some of the differences between literature and films, and the film adaptation of *Vanity Fair*. For questions 1–10, complete the sentences with a word or short phrase.

Jacinta thinks that sometimes film and cinema are better than the written word because film can be (1) _____ in terms of time. Sometimes descriptions in books can go on for (2) _____ and pages.

A lot depends on the filmmaker's correct choice of (3) _____.

For Jacinta, the main problem with film is that it cannot replace the (4) _____. Jacinta says it is possible to use (5) _____ from the page to tell the story but you can't do this with the narrator unless you use lots of (6) _____.

Vanity Fair tells the story of Becky Sharp and her desire to (7) _____. Becky is a terrible person. In the book the narrator observes and comments on what's (8) _____.

Jacinta admits that the film looked (9) _____ because of the fabulous scenes and breathtaking costumes. However, the overall effect was that the film was empty because the (10) _____ was missing.

KEY WORD *thing*

7 Turn to audioscript 5.1 on page 224 and find these phrases. Match the expressions in bold (1–6) to their meaning (a–f).

1 **one thing led to another** _____
2 The director **made a really big thing of** the big formal dances. _____
3 **All things considered** I'd rather adapt a classic … for the small screen. _____
4 **I've got a thing for** Colin Firth, the actor who played the hero. _____
5 If you want to **do your own thing**, that's fine, but … _____
6 Well, **the other thing of course is** that … _____

a I have strong feelings for
b do what you want, how you want
c emphasised
d we shouldn't forget
e having taken everything into account
f one opportunity created another

READING the bangle

1 Novelist Alexander McCall Smith has written a series of stories set in modern-day Botswana. The main character is Precious Ramotswe, a private detective and founder of the No. 1 Ladies Detective Agency. Read the extract and discuss which of the following would be the best title.

a   How to catch a thief
b   The last honest woman
c   A quiet cup of tea

EXAM SPOTLIGHT

PAPER 1, PART 5 Multiple choice

Follow these steps.
1   Quickly read the text all the way through to get a general idea of what it is about.
2   Carefully read the questions.
3   Never jump to immediate conclusions. Obvious answers are often traps.
4   Re-read the text and identify and mark the parts of the text which refer to each question.
5   Reject obviously wrong answers.
6   If you are not sure, use a process of elimination.
7   Always justify an answer to yourself, with supporting evidence from the passage.
8   Guess rather than leave a blank. (You will not be penalised for a wrong answer and you just might guess correctly!)

2 Work in pairs. For questions 1–6, choose the answer (A, B, C or D) which you think fits best according to the text, and say why you think the other options are wrong. Question 1 has been done as an example.

1   The woman in the market
   A   was an ordinary shopper. (wrong – she was a thief)
   B   knew someone was watching her. (wrong – she had no idea Mma had seen her)
   C   wanted to buy some sunglasses. (wrong – a trader tried to get her to buy some)
   D   distracted the stall keeper. (correct – she pointed to something at the back of the stall so that the trader would have to turn around. In other words, she distracted him.)

2   What was Mma Ramotswe's reaction to what she had seen?
   A   It contradicted her views on human nature.
   B   She was quietly amused by it.
   C   She thought the trader should be more careful.
   D   She was shocked and prepared to act.

3   How did the woman behave after she had taken the bangle?
   A   She argued noisily with the trader.
   B   She returned to the previous stall.
   C   She chatted to the trader about his wares.
   D   The woman coolly moved away.

4   How did Mma Ramotswe feel when the waitress stopped her?
   A   that anyone can make a mistake
   B   that she had done a terrible thing
   C   that the waitress had made a reasonable assumption
   D   robbed of the power of speech

5   After hearing Mma Ramotswe's explanation the waitress
   A   tried to blackmail her.
   B   realised an honest mistake had been made.
   C   laughed out loud.
   D   called the police.

6   The woman at the nearby table
   A   disapproved of Mma Ramotswe's behaviour.
   B   pretended not to notice what had happened.
   C   wasn't that honest herself.
   D   thought Mma Ramotswe was innocent of the crime.

3 Work in groups. Sometimes people are wrongly accused of doing something dishonest. Has this ever happened to you or to someone you know? Tell the group what happened and what the consequences were.

Mma Ramotswe raised her tea cup to her lips and looked over the brim. At the edge of the car park, immediately in front of the café, a small market had been set up, with traders' stalls and trays of colourful goods. She watched as a man attempted to persuade a customer to buy a pair of sunglasses. The woman tried on several pairs, but was not satisfied and moved on to the next stall. There she pointed to a small piece of silver jewellery, a bangle, and the trader, a short man wearing a wide-brimmed felt hat, passed it across to her to try on. Mma Ramotswe watched as the woman held out her wrist to be admired by the trader who nodded encouragement. But the woman seemed not to agree with his verdict, and handed the bangle back, pointing to another item at the back of the stall. And at that moment, while the trader turned round to stretch for whatever it was she had singled out, the woman quickly slipped another bangle into the pocket of the jacket she was wearing.

Mma Ramotswe gasped. This time she could not sit back and allow a crime to be committed before her very eyes. If people did nothing, then no wonder that things were getting worse. So she stood up, and began to walk firmly towards the stall where the woman had now engaged the trader in earnest discussion about the merits of the merchandise which he was showing her.

'Excuse me. Mma.'

The voice came from behind her, and Mma Ramotswe turned round to see who had addressed her. It was the waitress, a young woman whom Mma Ramotswe had not seen at the café before.

'Yes, Mma, what is it?'

The waitress pointed an accusing finger at her. 'You cannot run away like that,' she said. 'I saw you. You're trying to go away without paying the bill. I saw you.'

For a moment Mma Ramotswe was unable to speak. The accusation was a terrible one, and so unwarranted.

Of course she had not been trying to get away without paying the bill – she would never do such a thing: all she was doing was trying to stop a crime being committed before her eyes.

She recovered sufficiently to reply. 'I am not trying to go away, Mma,' she said. 'I am just trying to stop that person over there from stealing from that man. Then I would have come back to pay.'

The waitress smiled knowingly. 'They all find some excuse,' she said. 'Every day there are some people like you. They come and eat our food and then they run away and hide. You people are all the same.'

Mma Ramotswa looked over toward the stall. The woman had begun to walk away, presumably with the bangle still firmly in her pocket. It would now be too late to do anything about it, and all because of this silly young woman who had misunderstood what she was doing.

She went back to the table and sat down. 'Bring me the bill,' she said. 'I will pay it straightaway.'

The waitress stared at her. 'I will bring you the bill,' she said, 'but I shall have to add something for myself. I will have to add this if you do not want me to call the police and tell them about how you tried to run away.'

As the waitress went off to fetch the bill, Mma Ramotswe glanced around her to see if people at the neighbouring tables had witnessed the scene. At the table next to hers, a woman sat with her two children, who were sipping with great pleasure at large milkshakes. The woman smiled at Mma Ramotswe, and turned her attention back to the children. She had not seen anything, thought Mma Ramotswe, but then the woman leaned across the table and addressed a remark to her.

'Bad luck, Mma,' she said. 'They are too quick in this place. It is easier to run away at the hotels.'

VOCABULARY descriptive verbs

1 Find these verbs in the article on page 53 and decide which of the definitions (a or b) is best.

1 *gasp*
   a to breathe in with surprise
   b to make a disapproving noise
2 *stare*
   a a short quick look
   b a long fixed look
3 *glance*
   a a long look into the distance
   b a quick sideways look
4 *sip*
   a to drink greedily in large mouthfuls
   b to drink slowly, appreciating each drop

2 Read sentences 1–10 and look at the verbs in bold. Match the verbs to the categories a–e.

a ways of looking _____
b ways of drinking _____
c ways of breathing _____
d ways of walking / moving _____
e ways of laughing _____

1 He **sighed** with disappointment when he saw his examination results.
2 When they reached the top of the hill they **gasped,** and **gazed** in wonder at the beautiful valley spread out below them.
3 I wish you wouldn't **slurp** your coffee so noisily. People are **staring** at us!
4 Those girls get on my nerves. They just sit at the back and **giggle** at stupid jokes.
5 They **staggered** towards the van, carrying the heavy box between them.
6 We were so thirsty that we **gulped** down a whole bottle of water each.
7 The librarian **glared** at the children, who were making too much noise.
8 We took our time and **strolled** along the beach in the warm sunshine, looking out over the sea and throwing stones into the waves.
9 Maurice heard the boys **sniggering** nastily when he fell over on the icy road.
10 After the match, the losing team **limped** in pain back to the changing room.

3 Look again at the sentences in exercise 2. Write a short definition for each verb.

snigger: to laugh in an unpleasant and unkind way, especially at someone who looks foolish or who has hurt themselves

4 Work in pairs. Take it in turns to mime the different verbs. Be as dramatic as you like! Your partner must guess which verb you are miming.

GRAMMAR narrative tenses

5 Read this extract from the article and underline examples of the following.

a the simple past
b the past continuous
c the past perfect

> As the waitress went off to fetch the bill, Mma Ramotswe glanced around her to see if people at the neighbouring tables had witnessed the scene. At the table next to hers, a woman sat with her two children, who were sipping with great pleasure at large milkshakes. The woman smiled at Mma Ramotswe, and turned her attention back to the children. She had not seen anything, thought Mma Ramotswe, but then the woman leaned across the table and addressed a remark to her.

6 Which tense from exercise 5 is used for the following.

1 to describe an action in progress _past continuous_
2 to talk about an action further back in the past: 'past in the past' _simple past_
3 to describe a single or sequence of completed actions in the past _past simple_

▶ GRAMMAR REFERENCE (SECTION 12.1) **PAGE 203**

7 Look at sentences 1–4. Underline examples of the past continuous and circle examples of the past perfect continuous.

1 The woman stole the bangle while the trader was searching through his wares.
2 The waitress challenged Mma just as she was leaving the café.
3 Mma Ramotswe realised that the kids' mother had been following everything.
4 It was a typically busy market day. People were looking at the stalls, traders were selling their goods and Mma Ramotswe was waiting for her tea to arrive.

8 Look again at the sentences in exercise 7 and answer the questions.

a Which sentence sets the scene and gives the background for the story? _____
b Which sentence describes a single completed action which happened while something else was going on? _____
c Which sentence describes an action which started further back in the past and was still in progress at this point in the story? _____
d Which sentence describes an action which prevented an even earlier action from continuing / being completed? _____

9 Work in pairs. Complete the extract by underlining the correct narrative tense in italics.

Olivier and Isabelle (1) *were going / had been going* out ever since they (2) *were meeting / met* at university two years earlier. Olivier (3) *felt / was feeling* it was time to ask her to marry him so he (4) *bought / was buying* an engagement ring. He (5) *had been / was* determined to make a romantic proposal so he (6) *had prepared / was preparing* a delicious picnic in a surprise location. Driving his dad's Land Rover, Olivier (7) *was picking up / picked up* Isabelle who (8) *had waited / was waiting* impatiently outside her house. After they (9) *had driven / drove* for an hour Olivier (10) *was making / made* her cover her eyes with a scarf until they (11) *had been reaching / had reached* their final destination. Olivier (12) *had been driving / had driven* directly onto the sand! Boats (13) *had sailed / were sailing* across the bay as seagulls (14) *had dived / dived* beneath the waves. It (15) *had been / was* simply perfect!

10 Complete the next part of the story with suitable narrative tenses.

They (16) _____ (eat) the picnic that Olivier (17) _____ (prepare) and (18) _____ (drink) champagne. He (19) _____ (give) her the ring when he (20) _____ (notice) his bride-to-be (21) _____ (already fall asleep). He (22) _____ (yawn) sleepily too. Olivier (23) _____ (have) a wonderful dream when he (24) _____ (be woken) by Isabelle's scream. While they (25) _____ (have) their nap the tide (26) _____ (come in) and now the sea (27) _____ (surround) them.

11 Look at the pictures. Work in pairs or small groups. Write an end to the story, using a range of narrative tenses. Use the ideas in the pictures. Imagine how:
- they were rescued from the sea.
- Isabelle felt about Olivier afterwards.
- his father reacted when he saw the state of the car.

SPEAKING swapping stories

12 Work in groups. Tell the group a story about something that happened to you. Use different narrative tenses. Begin with one of these phrases.

That reminds me of the time when…

I'll never forget the time when…

WRITING a short story

EXAM SPOTLIGHT

PAPER 2, PART 2

In the *First for Schools* Writing paper, there will be a choice of writing tasks, one of which might be a short story. It may ask you to write a story which begins or ends with some words you are given. You will also be given two things or ideas that you **must** include in your story.

1 **Read the exam question and answer the questions.**

1 What two things does the story have to include? How does it have to end?
2 Read Margot's short story. How well does she answer the question?

Stories wanted

We are looking for stories for our English-language magazine for teenagers. Your story must **end** with this sentence:

I have never been so embarrassed in my life.

Your story must include:

- an invitation
- a piece of clothing.

I was very pleased to get an invitation to Jenny Hall's 16th birthday party. In fact, I was absolutely delighted as she was the most popular girl in my year at school. We had never really been friends, although we were in the same class. I told my mum, who took me shopping and bought me a lovely dress. Afterwards she did my hair.

When I rang the bell at Jenny's house, Mrs Hall answered the door. She gasped in horror as she saw me and I soon understood why. You see, Jenny was wearing exactly the same dress. What's more, we even had the same hairstyle. We looked like twins, it was creepy!

Everyone stared at us. There was a deathly silence, then Jenny's brother Tommy started to giggle nervously. I felt very embarrassed, and after that I sat quietly in the corner trying to be invisible. Anyway, after playing party games and dancing I started to feel more relaxed. I had been feeling thirsty, so I went into the kitchen for a glass of water. Unfortunately, I was going through the door just as her Dad came out with the birthday cake, which fell on the floor. Even though everyone knew it was an accident, I was absolutely mortified. After we'd cleaned up, I was ready to leave. By the time Dad came to pick me up, I was already waiting impatiently outside. I have never been so embarrassed in my life.

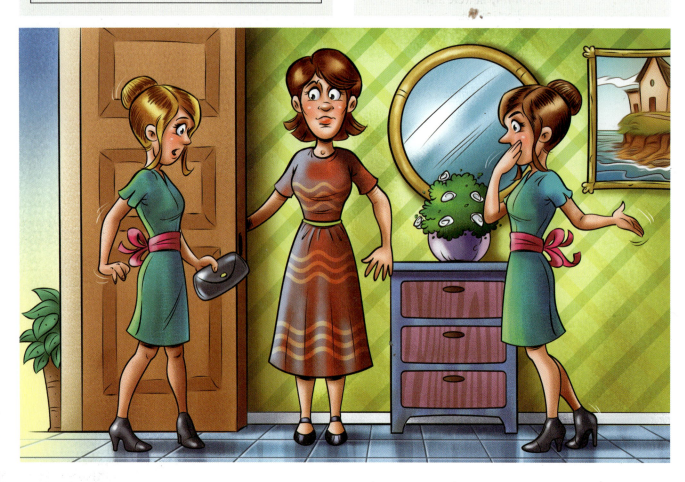

2 When we write, we should vary how we sequence events to keep our readers interested. Read the short story again and underline examples of sequencing using *then, after, after that* and *afterwards*. What verb form or tense follows each one?

3 Rewrite the short text below. Make it more interesting by using a variety of sequencing words.

Last weekend I got up late then I took the train to Barcelona, then I bought some shoes. I met my friend, Aranxa, in the shop, then I met my other friends in Catalunya Square. Everyone arrived then we had lunch, then we walked down the Ramblas to the sea. Then I bought ice creams, then we went to the movies. Then I went home.

4 Look at these sentences. What is the difference between the two adjectives in bold and how they are modified?

   a   I was **very pleased** to get an invitation to Jenny Hall's 16th birthday party.
   b   In fact, I was **absolutely delighted** as she was the most popular girl in my year.

GRADABLE AND NON-GRADABLE ADJECTIVES

Angry is a **gradable adjective**. We can modify it using *slightly, very, quite, extremely*.
I was extremely angry when I heard the news.

If we want to express stronger emotion, we can use a more extreme adjective, e.g. *furious*. *Furious* means *extremely angry* and is a **non-gradable adjective**. If we want to emphasise the adjective even more we have to use an extreme adverb, e.g. *absolutely, completely*.
I was absolutely furious when I heard the news.

▶ GRAMMAR REFERENCE (SECTION 1.3)   **PAGE 191**

---

5 Match a gradable adjective (1–9) with its non-gradable partner (a–i).

1	disappointed	a	astonished
2	pleased	b	ridiculous
3	surprised	c	devastated
4	embarrassed	d	gorgeous
5	tired	e	terrified
6	frightened	f	terrible
7	stupid	g	delighted
8	lovely	h	mortified
9	bad	i	exhausted

6 We often use non-gradable adjectives when we want to exaggerate. Work in pairs. Take turns responding to sentences 1–5 using non-gradable adjectives.

Were you tired after the match?

I was absolutely exhausted!

   1   Did you feel embarrassed when you found out who he was?
   2   She must have been disappointed with her results.
   3   What's wrong? Are you feeling ill?
   4   Were they pleased at the news?
   5   Do I look stupid in this hat?

7 Create some further exchanges of your own.

8 We can add interest to a story through our choice of vocabulary. Find further examples of the following from the short story.

   a   non-gradable adjectives e.g. *delighted*, _____
   b   descriptive verbs e.g. *gasped*, _____
   c   adverbs of manner e.g. *nervously*, _____

9 You have seen this announcement in a new English-language magazine. Write your story.

Stories wanted

We are looking for stories for our English-language magazine for teenagers. Your story must **begin** with this sentence:

Julia will never forget the time when she found a handbag on the bus.

Your story must include:

   •   a visit to the police station
   •   a reward.

WRITING CHECKLIST

SHORT STORY

Did you:

   •   use a range of narrative tenses?   ☐
   •   include some direct speech (to make the narrative come to life)?   ☐
   •   use a rich range of vocabulary, including descriptive verbs (to give the story interest)?   ☐
   •   enrich descriptions with well-chosen adjectives and adverbs?   ☐
   •   use relative pronouns to combine clauses?   ☐
   •   use a variety of ways of putting actions in sequence?   ☐
   •   begin and end the story with the words given?   ☐

WRITING GUIDE   **PAGE 219**

HEADS WILL ROLL

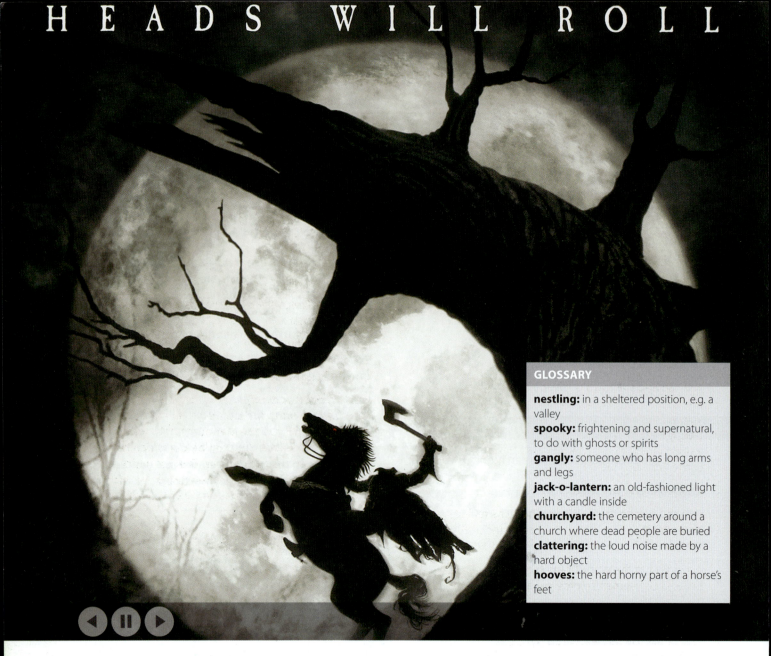

GLOSSARY

nestling: in a sheltered position, e.g. a valley
spooky: frightening and supernatural, to do with ghosts or spirits
gangly: someone who has long arms and legs
jack-o-lantern: an old-fashioned light with a candle inside
churchyard: the cemetery around a church where dead people are buried
clattering: the loud noise made by a hard object
hooves: the hard horny part of a horse's feet

VIDEO Sleepy Hollow

1 **Choose three types of films from the box and think of a film for each one. Tell the class.**

> action adventure   cartoon   documentary   drama
> fantasy   horror movie   musical   romantic comedy
> science fiction film   spy thriller   western

Skyfall *is a James Bond spy thriller.*

2 **Work in pairs. Take turns to tell your partner about a film you really like.**

3 **Look at the film poster. Discuss these questions.**

1 What type of film do you think it is?
2 Where and when do you think it is set?
3 Who do you think the main characters could be?
4 Would you like to see it? Why? Why not?

4 **Read the Ideas generator and do the task.**

ⓘ IDEAS GENERATOR

ANSWERING THE FIVE WH- QUESTIONS

In Part 1 of the Speaking paper, the interlocutor can ask you questions on different topics, for example: 'Tell us about a film you really like.'

To answer this type of question, remember to answer the following five question words:
What?   Where?   When?   Who?   Why?

Read this student's response to the examiner. How does she answer the five *wh-* questions?

'Well, one of my favourite films is Pirates of the Caribbean. *It is set in the Caribbean in the 1700s, and the main character is the pirate Jack Sparrow, who is played by Johnny Depp. It is a mixture of a fantasy, an adventure movie and a romantic comedy. I really love it because it is exciting and full of great acting and special effects.'*

5 You are going to watch a documentary about the place in the USA called Sleepy Hollow. While you watch, decide if statements 1–10 are true (T) or false (F).

1 Sleepy Hollow was named after the story. F
2 The town was originally founded by German farmers. F
3 You can learn what life was like hundreds of years ago. T
4 The town became famous because of the legend. T
5 Ichabod Crane was known as 'the headless horseman'. F
6 Irving had never been to the town before he wrote the story. F
7 Katrina van Tassel, the main female character, really existed. T
8 Crane's horse was called *Thunder*. Gun Powder F
9 They re-enact the story each Hallowe'en. T
10 Irving settled in the area when he was an adult. F

6 Watch the documentary again and complete the notes using one or two words for each gap.

You can find the town of Sleepy Hollow in the (1) _hills_ of New York's Hudson River Valley. The Dutch started to farm the land in Sleepy Hollow in the (2) _____ . At the visitors' centre you can discover what life was like in the 17th and 18th (3) _centuries_

Ichabod Crane worked as a (4) _schoolmaster_

Bill Lent likes to show visitors where the real-life characters are (5) _buried_ ; they include Katrina van Tassel.

According to the story, Crane tries to escape the headless horseman by crossing a (6) _bridge_ .

Sal Tarantino plays the headless horseman each year at the town's Hallowe'en (7) _festival_ . Sal has has to carry a lantern that weighs (8) _20 p_ pounds while riding his horse at (9) _40_ miles an hour.

According to the narrator, if we listen we can hear the (10) _clattering_ of the headless horseman's horse! _hooves_

7 Jonathon Kruk, the storyteller, uses special or old-fashioned vocabulary to make his story more dramatic and exciting. Decide which meaning, a or b, is closest to the word in bold in extracts 1–4.

1 Now **dwelling** in these parts, in a tenant house, was a certain schoolmaster …
   a working   b living
2 As the story goes, Ichabod Crane **fled** across this bridge.
   a ran away   b hurried
3 Ichabod **urged** his horse, Gunpowder, on.
   a encouraged   b rode
4 **Beware!**
   a listen   b be careful

8 Work in pairs. Are there places in your country that are famous because of their association with a writer or other kind of artist? Tell your partner.

9 From what you have learnt, would you like to see the film of *The Legend of Sleepy Hollow*? Do you think it is suitable for younger teenagers?

10 Work in pairs or groups. Imagine you are working at a summer camp for mixed groups of young teenagers, and you are planning a trip to the cinema. Look at the diagram below which has some ideas for you to discuss. Discuss which kinds of films would be suitable, then decide which one would be best. You can use some of the expressions in the box.

USEFUL EXPRESSIONS	SUGGESTIONS AND OPINIONS
	Do you think … would be suitable? Why? Why not?
	How about watching …?
	Why don't we take them to see …?
	I think this is a good film for young teenagers because …
	I think they'd prefer … because …
	But wouldn't they rather watch …?
	We could always take them to see …
	Yes, I think they'd like that type of film.

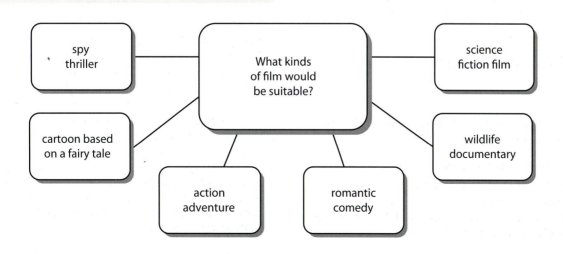

spy thriller — What kinds of film would be suitable? — science fiction film

cartoon based on a fairy tale — wildlife documentary

action adventure — romantic comedy

6 TRANSPORT AND TRAVEL

1 Look at the photo. What are the advantages and disadvantages of this type of transport for these groups of people?

- the people on the aeroplane
- the people on the beach
- local people living in the area

2 Work in pairs. List three more types of transport and discuss one advantage and disadvantage for each type.

VOCABULARY travel

3 Choose the correct word (in italics) to complete sentences 1–6.

1 They say that *travel / travels* broadens the mind, but I'm not so sure.
2 We had a fascinating conversation during the *journey / travel*.
3 He is away on a short business *journey / trip / travel*. He'll be back on Thursday.
4 How long does it *last / take / need* to get there?
5 How *long / far* is it from Stockholm to Oslo?
6 The *voyage / flight* from London to Auckland takes about 26 hours.

4 Work in groups. Discuss the differences between the following.

1 a *package holiday* and a *holiday resort*
2 a *brochure* and a *guidebook*
3 a *timetable* and an *itinerary*
4 a *commuter* and a *traveller*
5 a *souvenir* and a *reminder*
6 *heritage* and *sightseeing*
7 an *excursion* and a *trip*
8 a *tourist* and *tourism*

LISTENING travel and visits

5 ◎ 6.1 Work in pairs. Listen to eight people talking in different situations. Discuss the questions.

1 How clear are Sophie's plans?
2 What kind of job do you think Juan has?
3 How does Sharon keep her travel costs to a minimum?
4 Who do you think Professor Heron is? Why is Blanka planning his visit so carefully?
5 How do you think Seb's mother will feel as she:
   (i) steps off the train?
   (ii) walks into the sitting room?
6 Where are Kim and David?
7 Why is Dan in Krakow?
8 How adventurous is Gemma really?

EXAM SPOTLIGHT

PAPER 3, PART 1 Multiple choice

In this part of the Listening test, you are tested on more than gist. You may need to listen for detail, but you may also be asked to understand people's relationships, attitudes and feelings.

6 ⊙ **6.1 Listen again. For questions 1–8 choose the best answer (A, B or C).**

1 You will hear a young person discussing her plans for the future. Which of these statements is true?
   A She is going to university soon.
   B She has discussed her plans with her parents.
   C She is planning to spend some time abroad.

2 You will hear Juan leaving a message for a colleague. What is the purpose of his message?
   A to say he is going to be late
   B to ask for help
   C to ask for directions

3 You will hear Sharon talking about what appeals to her about travelling. What do we find out about her?
   A She enjoys the unknown.
   B She likes to visit the well-known sites.
   C She hates being uncomfortable.

4 You will hear a manager briefing her colleagues about an important visitor. What do we learn about Professor Heron?
   A He doesn't mind where he speaks.
   B He refuses to go anywhere by plane.
   C He is a demanding person.

5 You will hear Seb talking to a group of family and friends. What is he organising?
   A a train journey
   B a wedding anniversary celebration
   C a surprise party

6 You will hear a couple, Kim and David, discussing their holiday. What do we learn?
   A Kim isn't pleased with David.
   B The brochure gave inaccurate details.
   C There isn't much night life.

7 Dagmara is discussing plans with Dan, a British colleague. What do we learn about Dan?
   A He would like a quiet evening in, or near the hotel.
   B He is expected to buy presents.
   C He doesn't enjoy sightseeing.

8 Gemma is in a restaurant in Rome. What do we learn from her choices?
   A She has adventurous tastes.
   B She can be conservative about what she eats.
   C She is a vegetarian.

VOCABULARY travel phrasal verbs

7 Replace the words in bold in each sentence with one of the phrasal verbs from the box.

| check in   drop ... off   meet up (with)   phone ... back |
| pick ... up   put ... up   set off   show ... around |
| take off   take ... out   travel around   turn up |

1 There isn't anywhere to park. Is it OK if I just **leave you** in front of the hotel? _drop you off_

2 I'll go and **register** for my flight. _____

3 We need to **leave** as early as possible if we want to miss the rush hour. _____

4 I'm coming to London next week. Can you **give me a bed** for a couple of nights? _____

5 Can you **return my call** on this number? _____

6 I'll come and **collect you** at seven in front of the hotel. _____

7 When I was a student I used to **tour** the continent with a rail pass. _____

8 You can't just **arrive unexpectedly** at someone's door without phoning first. _____

9 Why don't you let me **give you a guided tour of** the old city. You'll love it. _____

10 Today we're **seeing** some old friends. _____

11 My flight should have **left the ground** an hour ago, but it has been delayed. _____

12 We'd like **you to go with us** to a restaurant this evening. _____

8 ⊙ **6.2 Work in two or three teams. Listen to the definitions and say the correct phrasal verb from this box or from exercise 7.**

| eat out   freshen up   get away   give away   go for |
| put off |

SPEAKING organising a schedule

9 In many countries, towns and cities 'twin' themselves with similar places in other countries. How common is this in your country?

10 Work in groups. As part of the 'twinning programme', you are going to look after a family of foreign visitors. Look at the information and decide how you will entertain them. Complete the programme with activities for everyone.

Mother: Sharon (age 45)
   Loves: sightseeing, clothes shopping, eating out
   Hates: fast food, sport
Father: Nick (age 47)
   Loves: sightseeing, traditional markets, eating out
   Hates: high street shopping
Daughter: Lucinda (age 17)
   Loves: shopping, the beach, dancing, fast food
   Hates: sightseeing
Son: Alex (age 14)
   Loves: swimming, watching sport, fast food
   Hates: sightseeing, eating out in restaurants

Morning	Afternoon	Evening
Friday		Arrive by bus. Welcome party.
Saturday		
Sunday		Farewell party at hotel.

GRAMMAR expressing the future

▶ GRAMMAR REFERENCE (SECTION 8) **PAGE 198**

1 **Work in pairs. Look at sentences a–d and identify the tenses in bold.**

a **I'm meeting** the visitors at three o'clock.

b His train **arrives** at four.

c **I'm going to take** a gap year.

d **I'll begin** with the artichokes and goat's cheese salad.

2 **Read the sentences in exercise 1 again and answer the questions.**

1 Which sentence describes an arrangement? _____

2 Which sentence describes a personal plan or intention? _____

3 In which sentence is a decision taken at the time of speaking? _____

4 Which sentence involves a timetable or a regular event? _____

3 **Complete these two conversations using the future simple or *going to* future.**

Conversation 1

Martin: What (1) _____ (we / do) this weekend, Phoebe?

Phoebe: I don't know. Why don't we invite Rebecca and Steven for dinner?

Martin: That's a great idea. I (2) _____ (phone) them straightaway.

Conversation 2

Carmen: What (3) _____ (we / get) Harriet for her birthday?

Miles: I know, I (4) _____ (buy) her some flowers.

Carmen: Good idea! And I (5) _____ (get) her a box of her favourite chocolates.

Five minutes later …

Paolo: Hi, everyone, have you thought about Harriet's birthday?

Carmen: Yes, Miles (6) _____ (buy) her some chocolates and I (7) _____ (get) her a box of her favourite chocolates.

4 **Read the sentences and tick (✓) the sentence in each pair that makes a prediction.**

1 a Be careful! Someone is going to get hurt. _____

b I'm going to meet him next Wednesday with Alexandra. _____

2 a You should give couch surfing a try. _____

b I should get there at around seven. _____

3 a I'll email you the website details. _____

b He'll be tired after the journey. _____

5 **Read the sentences in exercise 4 again and answer the questions.**

1 Which sentence gives advice? _____

2 Which sentence is a spontaneous offer? _____

3 Which sentence expresses an intention? _____

6 **Look at sentences a–c and answer questions 1–3.**

a Kate will be waiting at the station.

b I didn't know it was going to be like this.

c He'll have had time to freshen up.

1 Which sentence uses the future perfect? _____

2 Which sentence uses the future in the past? _____

3 Which sentence uses the future continuous? _____

7 **Read the sentences in exercise 6 again and answer the questions.**

1 Which sentence describes something that has already happened by a point in the future? _____

2 Which sentence describes an action which is in progress at a point in the future? _____

3 Which sentence describes something that hadn't been predicted? _____

8 **Complete sentences 1–8 with the future continuous (*will be doing*), future perfect (*will have done*), or future in the past (*was going to do*).**

1 If we do nothing about it very soon, in another two or three hundred years Venice _____ (sink) beneath the waves.

2 My guess is that scientists _____ (already find) an environmentally friendly alternative to oil long before it runs out.

3 It's not your fault you're late. You didn't know that the car _____ (break down).

4 This time tomorrow we _____ (eat) seafood and _____ (watch) the sun set over Cascais beach.

5 By August he _____ (have) the same car for ten years.

6 Don't worry; I _____ (wait) for you at the end of the platform.

7 That's not fair. How was I to know that the restaurant _____ (be) full?

8 Hurry up, otherwise they _____ (eat) all the food by the time we get there.

9 **Some adjectives have a future meaning. Look at the adjectives (in bold) in sentences a–c and answer the questions 1–3.**

a She's **likely to** be feeling a bit sad.

b He's **bound to** want some time to himself.

c A taxi is **due to** pick us up.

1 Which sentence means something is scheduled? _____

2 Which sentence means something is certain? _____

3 Which sentence means something is highly possible? _____

10 🔊 **6.3 Listen to information about eight situations. Decide what you would say in each situation, using an appropriate future form.**

LISTENING travel arrangements

11 You are going to hear three friends (Loïc, Tess and Marco) discussing travel arrangements from Birmingham in England to their holiday destination near La Rochelle in France. Work in groups. Look at the map. Discuss the different ways you think they could travel.

12 🔘 **6.4** Listen and decide who says what. Tick one name for each question.

Who	Loïc	Tess	Marco
1 suggests taking the tunnel?	☐	☐	☐
2 says the motorways will be expensive to drive on?	☐	☐	☐
3 thinks flying or driving will cost about the same?	☐	☐	☐
4 has never driven on the continent?	☐	☐	☐
5 is unhappy with the way someone else drives?	☐	☐	☐
6 suggests a night crossing?	☐	☐	☐
7 is going to check prices?	☐	☐	☐

13 Which travel option would you choose?

SPEAKING discussing options

14 Look at sentences a–d and answer the questions (1–4).

a We could take the tunnel.
b We could always hire a car if we need one.
c We'd better make up our minds.
d If we took a night crossing, it would give us a night's sleep.

1 Which sentence considers a condition and its consequence? _____
2 Which sentence presents a possible option? _____
3 Which sentence suggests an option of last resort / necessity? _____
4 Which sentence suggests that something should be done? _____

15 Practise saying sentences a–d in exercise 14, then answer these questions.

1 Which word is stressed in sentence b? _____
2 What is the full form of 'd in sentence c? _____

16 Compare sentences a and b, and sentences c and d. Then answer the questions.

a It's time for us to decide.
b It's time we decided.
c I'd rather get there as quickly as possible.
d I'd rather we got there as quickly as possible.

1 Which tense is used for the second verb in sentences b and d? _____
2 What happens when we use the personal pronoun (we) in sentences b and d?

17 Work in groups of three or four. Imagine that you are all going to take a short break together in a foreign city. Using questions 1–8 below as a guide, organise a trip that will have something for everyone. Remember to give your opinion and make your own preferences clear. You can refer to the audioscript on page 225.

1 Where will you go?
2 What time of year will you go? Say why.
3 How will you get there? Give reasons.
4 Where will you stay?
5 How long will you spend there?
6 What will you do when you get there?
7 What special sights will you visit?
8 What will you do about food and eating arrangements?
9 How much money will you take?
10 What will you bring back as a souvenir?

READING dream holidays

1 Work in pairs. Where do you usually go on holiday? What would be your dream holiday destination? Explain why.

2 Quickly read the article about four travel destinations. Which one would you most like to go to? Which one would you least like to go to?

PAPER 1, PART 7 Multiple matching

3 Read the article again and for questions 1–10 choose from the destinations (A–D). Each destination may be chosen more than once.

Which place or travel experience
1   has to deal with a lot of letters? _____
2   has encouraged the re-birth of a tradition? _____
3   lets us witness an annual migration? _____
4   has links with a tragic artist? _____
5   offers you a bird's-eye view of events below?
    _____
6   has atmospheric bars and clubs? _____
7   brings a children's dream to life? _____
8   offers valuable prizes? _____
9   is linked with a famous rescue mission? _____
10 has a place where you can buy presents? _____

VOCABULARY words in context

4 Find the words and expressions in the article to match these meanings.
Text A:
1   a colourful display _____
2   grassland for food _____
Text B:
3   long, difficult and exhausting _____
4   where no one lives and nothing grows
    _____
5   encourage _____
Text C:
6   filled with emotional pain _____
7   increased and decreased
    _____ and _____
8   with little light to see by _____
Text D:
9   lived there for a long time / original _____
10 friendly and cheerful _____
11 small amount of money _____

SPEAKING discussing your holiday

5 Imagine that you have just come back from a visit to one of the places in the article. In groups, ask and answer questions about your trip. Use these suggestions.
Questions
I haven't seen you for a while. Have you been away?
Oh really? Whereabouts?
What was special about it?

What exactly did you do / see?
So what was it like … (+ –ing)
How did it feel to …?
Tell me more about …
What will you remember most about your trip?
Comments
That sounds fun / scary.
Wow! Amazing!
How fascinating / interesting, etc. …
What a wonderful / frightening experience!

KEY WORD just

6 Look at the word *just* in sentences 1–6 and match each one to a meaning (a–f).
1   I arrived just as the train was leaving. _____
2   There'll be just a short delay while we wait for clearance to take off. _____
3   I'm afraid the bus has just left. _____
4   The flight is just about to board. You'd better hurry. _____
5   With all the traffic on the roads, cycling to work is just as fast as taking the car these days. _____
6   We're just leaving. Are you coming with us? _____

a   a short time ago
b   a small amount (of time)
c   exactly equal to something else
d   at this moment
e   at exactly the same time
f   very soon

7 Write the word *just* in each sentence to modify the meaning.
0   Can I have *just* a little sugar with that, please.
1   My car is as fast as yours.
2   I'm about to switch this off. Did you need to use it?
3   You've missed him I'm afraid. He'll be back at two.
4   Hold on, he's walking through the door as we speak.
5   I'll need a minute of your time, if that's OK.

8 Think of a comment using *just* for situations 1–5.
1   Your friend Stephanie went home 30 seconds ago. Someone has phoned to speak to her.
2   You want to go on an expensive holiday with a friend. Two different travel agents have given you the same price.
3   You are walking out of the door when your teacher asks to speak to you. You want to get home quickly to watch your favourite programme on TV. Politely explain to your teacher why you'd like to go home.
4   Your dinner is in the oven and will be ready in a couple of minutes. Your friend phones you. Explain and promise to phone back when you've eaten your meal.
5   Your friend has asked you to help her. You are finishing an email, then you'll be free.

Dream Holidays

A Safari: the Masai Mara, Kenya

The Masai Mara must be the most spectacular wildlife pageant on earth. Each year, when the rainy season ends in May, hundreds of thousands of wildebeests mass together. They move in search of greener pastures from the Serengeti in Tanzania north to the wide open grasslands of Kenya's Masai Mara. Along with migrating herds of zebra, antelope and gazelle, there are sometimes more than a million animals on the move at one time.

You can follow their journey on a horseback safari. Riding through the unspoiled Loita Hills and the great rolling plains of the Mara, you'll pass through the *manyattas* (villages) of the nomadic Masai people who protect the animals they believe to be 'God's cattle'. Some ascents will reach 2,500 metres, providing spectacular views and open vistas. And while you marvel at the views, the staff go on ahead to set up camp in a lovely setting and have dinner and a hot shower ready for your arrival.

B The Iditarod: Anchorage, Alaska

The Iditarod is a gruelling sled-dog race across the Alaskan wilderness, from Anchorage all the way to Nome on the coast of the Bering Sea.

Dogsledding had almost disappeared until 1973 when the first Iditarod was organised to revive the tradition and commemorate historical dogsledding events. One such historical event had taken place during the 1925 diphtheria epidemic in Nome when 20 riders (called *mushers*) and a sled team crossed the frozen landscape to fetch essential medicine for the town.

Today an average of 65 mushers and their teams come from as far away as Japan and Russia to compete for a share of the $600,000 prize money, traversing 1,149 miles – a journey which usually takes between eight and fifteen days. The Iditarod has become the largest spectator event in Alaska. Along the way, entire towns turn out to cheer on the mushers and their teams.

C Las Tanguerias de Buenos Aires

The Tango is Argentina's celebration of machismo, domination, and tormented love. This intricate and exquisite dance is the most authentic of Argentine creations. The tango's popularity has waxed and waned since the 1920s when the darkly handsome singer, Carlos Gardel, drove the country wild before dying tragically in a 1935 plane crash.

A recent revival of tangomania confirms that this indigenous popular music has survived the era of rock and roll, and some of the large dance halls, such as El Viejo Almacén and Casa Blanca, still put on an emotion-packed nightly show with the country's finest tango dancers, singers and musicians. To see tango in its natural habitat – the classic small, smoky, dimly-lit tango bar where things don't start happening until the other side of midnight – the casual Bar Sur is the place to go.

D Santa's village: Rovaniemi, Lapland, Finland

Rovaniemi, in Finland's Arctic Circle, is considered the gateway to Lapland. It is known for its indigenous, formerly nomadic, Sami people (once commonly known as 'Lapp'). Santa's village is how every child always imagines it to be – a snowy winter wonderland with a jovial Santa in attendance every day!

His busy workshops show how he keeps up with his toy-making, and the post office displays some of the 600,000 letters received every year from all over the world. About a third of these letters get answered. An irresistible gift shop provides a myriad of Yuletide presents that can be shipped back home with a Santa's village postmark, or, for a nominal fee, you can add your child's name to a list to receive a postcard from Santa.

WRITING a report

1 **Work in pairs. Make notes about these questions. Discuss your answers with your partner and compare your information.**

1 What types of public transport are there in your local area?
2 Do you often use public transport? Why? Why not?
3 Do you think your local public transport could be improved? How?

2 **Read this exam question from Paper 2, Part 2. Which information in your notes in exercise 1 would be useful for answering this question? Underline information that you could use in a report.**

> A tourist office wants information about public transport in your local area for visitors to the region. The manager has asked you to write a report.
>
> You should explain what the best types of public transport in your area are and give reasons why they are good for tourists.

3 **Read two different answers to the exam question. Which report do you think would receive a higher mark? Give your reasons.**

Public transport for tourists in the region

There are three main types of public transport in the local area which are good for tourists to the region.

Trains

Many tourists arrive at the region's main train station. This is because there isn't an airport and private cars are not allowed into the city centre.

Buses

A one-day bus ticket can be bought at the train station and there is an extensive bus network around the city and out to the surrounding countryside. A shuttle bus to the port leaves every 15 minutes for anyone travelling to the islands.

Ferries

There is a ferry terminal in the port with regular ferries to all the main islands off our coast. On board each ferry, there are dining facilities and shops. Once the ferry arrives at its destination, tourists can either explore the island or catch another ferry to one or the smaller islands in the area.

In conclusion, public transport in the region offers tourists and visitors an excellent alternative to means of transport such as private car hire.

B

We have lots of public transport in our local area so it's a good place for tourists.

For example, you can get to the city by train. You can't fly because there isn't an airport and there isn't much parking for cars in the city centre.

Also you can buy a one-day bus ticket at the train station and then the bus service around the city is pretty good. A bus to the port leaves every fifteen minutes if you want to go to the islands. You go to the ferry terminal and catch a ferry. They're great because you can eat and go shopping while you're on board. When we take the ferry to an island we often take another ferry to one of the smaller islands to get away from all the tourists. So I'd recommend our region to tourists.

4 Decide if these statements about writing a report in the *First* exam are true (T) or false (F).

1 It's a good idea to use headings and sub-headings in your report to help the organisation. T / F
2 You don't have to include an introduction, use paragraphs or give a conclusion. T / F
3 Use a friendly informal writing style. T / F

5 Read the Exam Spotlight. Then underline examples of 'neutral style' in Report A.

EXAM SPOTLIGHT

PAPER 2, PART 2 A report

In this part of the Writing paper, you write one text from a choice of three or four texts. One choice may be a report. In the exam, you have about 40 minutes to write your report. Don't use an informal or personal style. Write your report in a neutral style using these types of words and structures:

There is / There are
There are
~~We have~~ over 100 underground stations.

Passive form
Tickets are bought
~~You buy your tickets~~ from the driver.

Avoid subject pronouns such as *I, you, we, they*
Most people
~~We~~ normally take the airport shuttle bus.

Formal vocabulary and punctuation
                                    excellent
From the top of the bus, tourists can enjoy ~~great~~ views!

6 These sentences are too informal and personal for a report. Complete the more neutral second sentence with the words and phrases from the box.

there is   there are   exceptional   popular
many people   can be bought   are advised not to

0 We have an extensive underground network with regular connections to all parts of the city.
  There is an extensive underground network with regular connections to all parts of the city.
1 You can buy a visitor's city day-pass directly from the tourist information office.
  A visitor's city day-pass _____ directly from the tourist information office.
2 You can find taxis waiting outside the central station, 24 hours a day.
  _____ taxis waiting outside the central station, 24 hours a day.
3 Hiring a bicycle for the day is a great way to see Amsterdam.
  Hiring a bicycle for the day is a / an _____ way to see Amsterdam.
4 These days I prefer train travel to air travel.
  These days _____ prefer train travel to air travel.
5 In the winter, there's a cable car to the top of the mountain for a fantastic view!
  In the winter, there's a cable car to the top of the mountain for a / an _____ view.
6 I don't think you should take the subway at night.
  Tourists _____ take the subway at night.

7 Now answer this Paper 2, Part 2 exam question.

A tourist office wants information about destinations for tourists in your local area. The manager has asked you to write a report.

You should describe three good destinations for tourists to visit and say why you think they are popular.

WRITING CHECKLIST

REPORT

Check the report. Does it:
• have between 140–190 words? ☐
• have an introduction and conclusion? ☐
• use sub-headings and paragraphs? ☐
• describe three destinations? ☐
• give reasons why they are popular? ☐
• use a neutral style (not informal and personal)? ☐

WRITING GUIDE   **PAGE 217**

REVIEW AND EXAM PRACTICE Units 5 and 6

1 For questions 1–8, read the text and decide which answer (A, B, C or D) best fits each gap. There is an example at the beginning (0).

The Go-Between, by L P Hartley, is the story of a tragic love affair (0) __A__ two people divided by social class. During the long, hot summer in 1900, Leo (1) _____ a rich school classmate called Marcus at his family's magnificent country house. He immediately develops a (2) _____ crush on Marcus's elder sister, Marian. (3) _____ Marcus falls ill, Leo is bored and Marian (4) _____ him deliver love letters to a farmer called Ted. Their meetings have to be secret (5) _____ to Ted's lower social position. (6) _____, Marian is engaged to be married to a gentleman. Poor Leo is used by the couple, (7) _____ secret is finally revealed with the most tragic consequences. Not (8) _____ is the book a wonderful tale, but it was adapted into a haunting film directed by Joseph Losey.

0	A between	B over	C across	D from	5	A due	B because	C owed	D according
1	A stays	B maintains	C keeps	D visits	6	A While	B Although	C Moreover	D Yet
2	A helpless	B useless	C hopeless	D helpful	7	A whose	B which	C that	D their
3	A If	B When	C Unless	D Although	8	A all	B yet	C only	D again
4	A engages	B makes	C employs	D gets					

2 For questions 9–16, read the text below and think of the word that best fits in each gap. Use only one word in each gap. There is an example at the beginning (0).

If you're feeling tired (0) *of* the routines and pressures of daily life, why not treat (9) _____ to a short trip to Prague? (10) _____ part of the package, you can visit many tourist attractions, (11) _____ as its famous castle. We also provide a trip to the New Town (12) _____ you can visit the Charles University. In (13) _____ to the standard tour, you can opt for an art tour with visits to the famous art collections in the city. Or if you prefer something (14) _____ lively, you could try one of the city's medieval banquets. The city is also great (15) _____ shopping, and at the Christmas market in December you can really enjoy the festive atmosphere, as (16) _____ as buying some last-minute presents.

3 For questions 17–24, read the text below. Use the word given in capitals at the end of some of the lines to form a word that fits in the space in the same line. There is an example at the beginning (0).

A recent opinion poll to choose Britain's most popular novel (0) *produced* a	PRODUCE
surprising result. Rather than the latest spy (17) _____, the book with the	THRILL
most votes was written by an 18th-century (18) _____, Jane Austen. *Pride*	NOVEL
and Prejudice describes the romance between the (19) _____, Elizabeth	HERO
Bennet, and the snobbish Mr Darcy. The book is full of brilliant	
(20) _____ about the society of this period and the complex social	OBSERVE
(21) _____. However, voters' choices appear to have nothing to do	RELATION
with a love of the printed word. When asked who had read the book, very few	
people, indeed hardly anyone, had actually read the original novel. Instead, they	
remembered the film (22) _____ with its wonderful acting and beautiful	ADAPT
(23) _____. The poll seems to conclude that the British still maintain a	SCENE
nostalgia for a more (24) _____ age.	ROMANCE

4 For questions 25–30, complete the second sentence so that it has a similar meaning to the first sentence, using the word given. Do not change the word given. You must use between two and five words only, including the word given. There is an example at the beginning (0).

0   I can't wait to see Martha again.
    FORWARD
    I'm really <u>looking forward to seeing</u> Martha again.

25   I think you should find a job.
    TIME
    It's _____ a job.

26   I'll call the moment I have some news.
    SOON
    I'll call _____ I have some news.

27   I've never driven on the left before.
    EVER
    It's the first _____ on the left.

28   How long does the journey last?
    TAKE
    How _____ to get there?

29   I'd prefer us to go to the seaside.
    WE
    I'd _____ to the seaside.

22   You ought to get some travel insurance.
    BETTER
    You _____ get some travel insurance.

5 Work in pairs. Imagine you have been asked to advise a visitor to your country on the best ways to travel to different places and regions. Look at the exam task and discuss which are the best ways for tourists to travel. At the end, decide which two would be best.

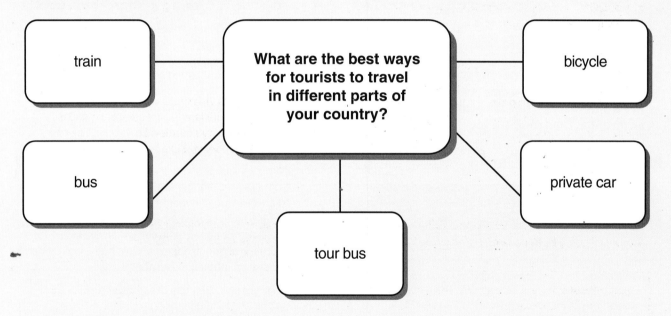

train

bus

What are the best ways for tourists to travel in different parts of your country?

tour bus

bicycle

private car

6 You have seen the following advertisement in a film magazine. Write your review in 140–190 words.

Film lovers! Can you help us?

Write a review about the best film you've ever seen.

Say briefly what the film is about, and explain why you liked it. Tell us whether or not you could recommend the film to other people. We will publish the best reviews next month. Send us your review, and you could see your name in print!

INVENTIONS AND TECHNOLOGY

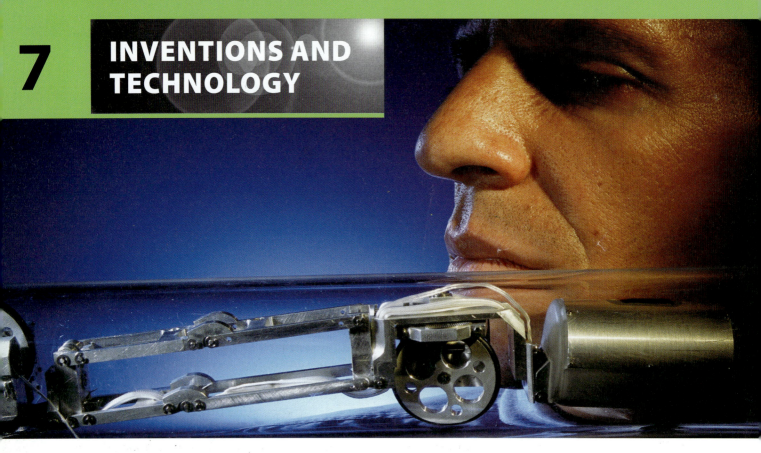

1 Work in pairs. Look at the photo of an inventor. What sort of people become inventors? Think of five words that describe the qualities and skills of an inventor. Then compare your list with the class.

READING robot revolution

EXAM SPOTLIGHT

PAPER 1, PART 6 Gapped text

In Part 6 of the Reading paper, you read a text where six sentences have been removed. The missing sentences are given after the text, in jumbled order, and you have to choose the sentence which fits each gap. There is an extra sentence you do not need to use.

Here are four pieces of advice for this exam task. Which one is bad advice? Can you rewrite it?

1 Try to predict from the title what the text will be about.
2 Pay special attention to pronouns to help you.
3 Don't read all the text before you start to fill in the gaps.
4 When you're sure, copy your answers on the answer paper.

2 You're going to read about a man who invents robots. Six sentences have been removed from the text. Choose from the sentences (A–G) the one which fits each gap (1–6). There is one extra sentence which you do not need to use.

A At that time he didn't even know the term *robot*.
B More recently, his house burnt down from his experiments.
C A newer model named Number Six is a monkey-like robot with magnetised feet which enables it to crawl slowly up metallic walls.
D He has now come up with one that will walk like a human being.
E He dreams his robots may become like the compass, gunpowder and the umbrella, all of which China pioneered the use of, before exporting them to Europe and the rest of the world.
F As for his next robot, Mr Wu is unsure.
G The inventor has already earned around £200 for a mechanical grasshopper, while a high-tech company has shown interest in Number Eight.

3 Work in groups. Discuss these questions.
1 What's your opinion of Mr Wu?
2 How would you describe Ms Dong?
3 Mr Wu believes that many good things in life could become the basis for a robot. Do you agree with him?

4 Work in groups. These items were recently voted the world's worst inventions. What order do you think they were in from 1 to 10? See page 238 for the answers.

cigarettes	☐	mobile phones	☐
car alarms	☐	TV	☐
weapons	☐	cars	☐
fast food	☐	plastic bags	☐
computers	☐	nuclear energy	☐

5 Work in groups. Make a list of the world's best ten inventions. Join with another group and decide on one invention which is the best.

MR WU'S ROBOT REVOLUTION

If you met Wu Yulu, father of two from Tongzhou, China, you'd probably just think you were meeting a farmer. He appears to be quite poor and perhaps wouldn't be regarded by many people as a success story. At 42 years of age he has destroyed his family home, been seriously burnt and ended up £5,000 in debt. But Mr Wu, who left school at 14 and has no formal technical training, is a part-time inventor who creates robots to help people reduce their time spent on doing jobs like the housework. What's even more amazing is that these 'labour-saving robots' are all created from scrap he comes across in rubbish dumps.

His brainchild, the robots, are all developed during long nights spent in his garden shed with only his imagination as a guide, including Number Five, a one-metre-tall humanoid robot capable of walking, changing light bulbs, lighting cigarettes and pouring tea. (1) _____ Like all of Mr Wu's inventions, it is made out of bits of old metal, tape and second-hand batteries.

Although a man of few words, the farmer will admit that his ultimate robot is a virtual human. 'It would have a brain that could think, and arms and legs like a real person.' Mr Wu also hopes that his creations may one day join a long list of Chinese inventions. (2) _____ With funding and support, Mr Wu believes his robots could similarly revolutionise everyday life and change the way we work.

You might doubt Mr Wu's self-belief but you certainly can't question his unstoppable enthusiasm. He started over 25 years ago. (3) _____ . Since then he thinks he has made at least 25 robots. He came up with the idea for his first robot while watching people walking and studying the motion of their bodies. Despite a number of setbacks, he has never thought of giving up. Once he went to hospital after trying out a new invention. It exploded and he still has scars on his hands and arms. (4) _____ 'I was left with nothing,' he said. With a new house costing 90,000 yuan, Mr Wu's long-suffering wife, Dong Shuyan, has started a private kindergarten in an attempt to pay off the family's loans. She describes her husband as 'child-like' in his obsession with inventions, though she is philosophical about her burden.

'When we got married, everyone warned me he would care more about his robots than about me,' she said, but Ms Dong is also optimistic about her husband's new plan to start selling the patents for his robots. (5) _____ 'He has so much talent,' said his wife, 'he should at least be able to make some money out of it.'

His latest 'robot rickshaw' took a year to build. The 1.8-metre-tall robot pulls a rickshaw and is operated by the driver operating a hand-held control. After its batteries have charged for six hours the robot can walk for eight kilometres, approximately one step every three seconds. (6) _____ 'There are so many good things in life, and any of them could become the basis for my robots.'

VOCABULARY inventors and inventing

1 Read these sentences (1–4) from the article on page 71. Match each phrasal verb in bold to the definition (a–d).

1 These 'labour-saving robots' are created from scrap he **comes across** on rubbish dumps.

2 He **came up with** the idea for his first robot while watching people walking.

3 Despite a number of setbacks, he has never thought of **giving up**.

4 Once he went to hospital after **trying out** a new invention.

a think of (something) _____

b test _____

c stop / quit _____

d find by accident _____

2 Choose the correct word (in italics) to complete these sentences about inventions and inventors. Use the article to help you.

1 Both the USA and Russia were *pioneers / prototypes* of space exploration.

2 Scientists have suffered a number of *drawbacks / setbacks* in their search for a cure.

3 The sad thing is that his *imagination / obsession* has virtually destroyed his family life.

4 This new method is a great *invention / innovation* in language learning.

5 I've had an amazing *brainwave / brainchild* – it's an idea for a new car.

6 My new robot has passed all the necessary *tests / experiments* and is ready to go on sale.

7 This is an amazing *breakthrough / breakdown* that has provided hope to millions of bald people.

3 Now complete these sentences using the other words from exercise 2.

1 One of the _____ of being married to an inventor is that they are always working.

2 The lack of progress on the project was due to a _____ in communication.

3 Before a company launches a new device, they need to make a _____ which they can test thoroughly.

4 Science is very important but I don't agree with doing _____ on animals.

5 The _____ of the compass was very important as it meant that sailors no longer had to navigate by the stars.

6 This computer game is amazing. I think the person who designed it must have had an incredible _____ .

7 His latest _____ is a baseball cap with built-in headphones.

LISTENING intelligent robots

PAPER 3, PART 2 Sentence completion

4 ⊙ 7.1 You will hear an interview about robots of the future. For questions 1–10 complete the sentences with a word or short phrase.

Old black and white science fiction films used to show robots that were dangerous and would attack (1) _____. Nowadays, you can see robots in our (2) _____.

The Japanese are developing them to look after both (3) _____. Rather than have robots around the house, the interviewer thinks most of us would rather talk to a (4) _____.

Professor Witfield doesn't agree that humans don't like talking to (5) _____. Humans might prefer robots to ordinary computers because they wouldn't have to stare at a (6) _____ .

Witfield thinks there is a problem with letting robots have (7) _____.

Unlike the past, robots in the future will be capable of making (8) _____.

Professor Witfield thinks the effect of computers now being able to think for themselves means that we need to have a (9) _____.

If robots are used in the army, we also need to think about problems of (10) _____.

5 Discuss these questions in groups.

1 Do you think the kinds of robots Professor Whitfield describes are a good idea?

2 If you designed a robot, what would you like it to do? What would it look like?

GRAMMAR verbs followed by the gerund or the infinitive

▶ GRAMMAR REFERENCE (SECTION 9) **PAGE 199**

6 🔘 **7.2 Complete these sentences from the interview with the gerund or the infinitive form of the verb. Then listen and check.**

0 We all remember _watching_ (watch) those old black and white science fiction films at the cinema with androids and robots.

0 As soon as you saw a robot you expected _to see_ (see) them go crazy.

1 Do we risk _____ (have) our day-to-day life controlled by machines that think for themselves?

2 Don't you think most people would prefer _____ (communicate) with a real person?

3 The Japanese have succeeded in _____ (develop) household robots for some time …

4 A human being isn't designed _____ (look) at a screen all day …

5 But we've also heard a lot about scientists who've managed _____ (make) robots with intelligence.

6 I would like _____ (see) a real public debate take place on how this will affect society in the future.

7 Governments should consider _____ (use) robots ethically.

7 Work in pairs. Decide which form (gerund, infinitive or both) can follow each verb in the box. Then match each verb to a category (1–5) in the grammar box.

| afford   decide   enjoy   finish   like   look forward to |
| mind   seem   try   want   would like |

VERBS + GERUND OR INFINITIVE

Remember:
1 Some verbs are always followed by the gerund (*risk having* …).
2 Some verbs are always followed by the infinitive (*expect to see* …).
3 Some verbs may be followed by either the gerund or the infinitive. With some of these verbs there is little difference in the meaning (e.g. *start attacking / start to attack*), with others there is a big difference in meaning (*remember to watch / remember watching*).
4 Verbs + preposition are always followed by an *-ing* form (*succeeded in developing*).
5 Verbs such as *like* and *prefer* can be followed by the infinitive or the *-ing* form. When we add *would* (*would like, would prefer*), they are followed by the infinitive only (*I'd like to meet at nine*).

8 The verbs in these sentences can be followed by either the gerund or the infinitive, but the meaning is different. Complete each sentence with the correct form.

1 A She always remembered _____ her medicine before she went to bed. (take)
   B She remembered _____ a drink from the glass before she fainted. (take)

2 A He stopped _____ at the map because it was out of date. (look)
   B He stopped _____ at the map because he was lost. (look)

3 A I regret _____ you that your delivery will be late. (tell)
   B I regret _____ you now because you've told everyone else. (tell)

4 A I'll never forget _____ my husband for the first time. (meet)
   B Don't forget _____ your visitors at three. (meet)

5 A I had a difficult pupil in my class who went on _____ a famous celebrity. (be)
   B I had a difficult pupil in my class who went on _____ difficult all through his life. (be)

6 A Sorry, I didn't mean _____ you from going out this evening. (stop)
   B It meant _____ her from going out with her friends every evening. (stop)

7 A I've tried _____ that window but it seems to be locked. (open)
   B I've tried _____ the window but it's still hot in here. (open)

PAPER 1, PART 4 Key word transformation

9 Complete the second sentence so that it has a similar meaning to the first sentence, using the word given. Do not change the word given. Use between two and five words, including the word given.

1 She hasn't smoked since 1996.
   STOPPED
   She _____ 1996.

2 Can I offer you a cup of tea or coffee?
   LIKE
   _____ a cup of tea or coffee?

3 You don't like to work late, do you?
   HATE
   You _____ you?

4 We've asked someone for directions but he sent us the wrong way.
   TRIED
   We've _____ but he sent us the wrong way.

5 The student got the funding with some difficulty.
   MANAGED
   The student _____ the funding, with some difficulty.

6 I shouldn't have asked him to come.
   REGRET
   I _____ to come.

KEY WORD *to*

1 **The word *to* is missing in each sentence. Decide where the word should be added.**

1 I look forward ∧*to* seeing you.
2 What are you listening?
3 That's a terrible thing say!
4 Is she old enough ride a bike?
5 Remember call me when you get there.
6 Take a coat. It's sure rain.
7 Do you have leave so soon?
8 We're afraid go out in the dark.
9 OK. Let's get down some work now.
10 I prefer talking face face than on the phone.

2 **Work in pairs. Here are five responses containing *to*. Think of five sentences that would receive these responses. Then say a sentence to your partner. Can he / she give the correct response?**

What a horrible thing to say!
In order not to be late.
To be honest, I think you're right.
But I've got too much to do.
I'm sorry to hear that.

> *Why do you have to leave so early?*

> *In order not to be late for my piano lesson.*

DICTIONARY SKILLS

Use your dictionary to help you learn verb patterns. Look at this example from the *Collins Cobuild Intermediate Dictionary*. How many verb patterns are there which contain the word *to*?

---

ask / ɑːsk, æsk / **(asks, asking, asked)** 1. V-T If you ask someone something, you say something in the form of a question because you want some information *'How is Frank?'* he asked. *I asked him his name. I wasn't the only one asking questions. She asked me if I'd already had my dinner.* 2. V-T If you ask someone to do something, you tell them that you want them to do it. If you ask to do something, you tell someone that you want to do it. *We had to ask him to leave. I asked to see the Director.* 3. V-I If you ask for something, you say that you would like it. If you ask someone

---

Look up the following verbs in your dictionary. How many have verb patterns which contain the word to?

| say | tell | manage | forget | like |

VOCABULARY technology

3 **Replace the words in bold in the sentences with the phrasal verbs in the box. Change the verb form if necessary.**

| back up | click on | hack into | log in | plug in | set up |

1 To **enter** the website you need to type your username and password.
2 The bank has said that someone **illegally accessed** their computer records.
3 Just **put the arrow here and press** this icon twice to run the program.
4 Next, you need to **insert** this cable to connect it to the printer.
5 Did you **make a copy of** these documents?
6 Have you seen the blog my class has **created**?

4 **Categorise these computer words under the correct heading in the table.**

| attachment | blog | inbox | keyboard | links | mouse |
| online | subject | touchscreen | web | YouTube |

Hardware	Email	Internet

5 **Work in pairs. Discuss the questions.**

1 What's your favourite website? Why do you like it?
2 Have you ever set up a website or blog?

6 **Work in pairs. You are going to read about a person who has been successful because of the Internet. Make notes about them in the table.**

Student A: turn to page 238.
Student B: turn to page 239.

	Rebekka	Alex
What kind of background did this person have?		
When did he / she come up with the initial idea?		
How did he / she use the Internet?		
What has happened as a result?		

7 **Now ask your partner questions about their person and complete the table.**

8 **What are the similarities between the two people? Do you know about other people in your country who have been successful because of the Internet?**

SPEAKING suggesting and recommending

9 🔘 **7.3 Listen to a web designer describing how to make a simple home page. Make notes about his recommendations using the headings below.**

- Name
- Links
- Icons
- Other features
- Contact

10 Work in pairs. Do you agree with the speaker's recommendations? What do you think makes a good website?

11 🔘 **7.3 Match the sentence beginnings (1–10) with the endings (a–j). Listen again and check.**

1 Let's _____
2 How about _____
3 Perhaps _____
4 Make sure you know _____
5 It's also important _____
6 It should be a name that's _____
7 I strongly recommend _____
8 Don't forget that _____
9 It's also worth _____
10 It's a good idea to _____

a that you include links to other sites.
b why you want a website.
c remembering that the more features you have …
d links can take the form of words that you click on.
e you could even start an e-business.
f advertising your local club?
g set up a website.
h give a contact email.
i to choose a good name.
j easy to remember.

12 Which words and phrases in exercise 11 are followed by these forms?

1 *to* infinitive: _____

_____

2 the *-ing* form: _____ How about _____

_____

3 the bare infinitive: _____ Let's … _____

13 Choose one of these topics and write three tips.

- riding a bike for the first time
  Make sure you know how to stop quickly!
- finding useful information on the Internet
- choosing a mobile phone
- memorising new English words
- designing a room in a house

14 Work in pairs. Make your suggestions and recommendations to your partner.

EXAM SPOTLIGHT

PAPER 4, PART 3 Discussing a topic

In this part of the Speaking test you have to discuss a topic with your partner and reach an agreement. It's important to respond appropriately to your partner when they make a suggestion or recommend something.

Here are some useful phrases:

- *That's a good idea.*
- *Sure.*
- *Yes, I think so too.*
- *Right.*
- *I know what you mean, but …*
- *Yes, but …*
- *And we could also …*

15 Work in pairs. Read the interlocutor's question from Part 3 and follow the instructions.

I'd like you to imagine that your local town wants to set up a website to attract visitors and tourists, with pages on different topics. Here are some ideas and a question for you to discuss. Talk to each other about why these topics would attract visitors. Decide which two topics would be best.

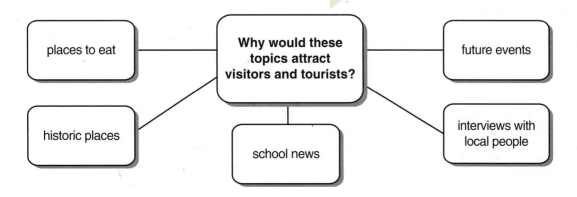

places to eat — Why would these topics attract visitors and tourists? — future events

historic places — school news — interviews with local people

WRITING a review

1 Work in pairs. Compare these pictures from two video games. What types of games are they? Why do you think people choose to play these different games?

2 How much time do you spend playing video games? Tell your partner about a game you play. What do you like about the game? Is there anything you could do to improve it?

EXAM SPOTLIGHT

PAPER 2, PART 2 A review

In the *First* Writing paper you can choose from different text types. The choice may include a review. For example, the question might ask for a review of a book, a magazine, a film, a music CD or a computer game.
Before you start writing your answer in the exam, it's a good idea to make brief notes and plan what you want to write.

3 Sarah is going to answer this question on the Writing paper. She begins by writing some notes and planning her review. Read the exam question and Sarah's notes. Does she like the game?

> **You see this advert in a magazine about computer games and video games.**
>
> ---
>
> **Reviews wanted: your latest games**
>
> Next month we are starting a new review feature. We want your reviews of any new computer and video games. Say what kind of game it is, why you like it, if there is anything you would improve and your overall opinion. Let other readers know what you are playing!
>
> ---
>
> **Write your review.**

TITLE: GOLDFINDER 3

AIM OF THE GAME
You have to find treasure - not very original

THINGS I LIKE
– The graphics are very realistic.
– The puzzles and tasks are very challenging and addictive.
– Your character can change shape and win interesting powers.

THINGS TO IMPROVE
– It all happens inside caves and mountains – needs to be more varied with jungles and cities.
– Most expensive game currently in the shops.

CONCLUSION
– Well above average.
– Better than Goldfinder 1 and 2.

4 Complete Sarah's review of Goldfinder 3 using information from her notes in exercise 3.

Recently, I've been playing a new video game called 'Goldfinder 3'. It's the third in the series but it's very different to Goldfinder 1 and 2.

As the name suggests, the main aim is to (1) _____ which isn't very (2) _____ but the graphics are (3) _____ and the tasks are all (4) _____ . Another nice feature is that your character can (5) _____ .

One thing that could be improved are the locations. More action needs to happen outside the caves and mountains. On the next edition the makers should add (6) _____ . It's also (7) _____ .

So, overall I'd recommend the game as it's (8) _____ and (9) _____ .

5 When we write reviews, we use words and phrases to describe the positive and negative points. Read extracts from four reviews and answer the questions for each review.

1 What is the writer reviewing?
2 Are the underlined phrases positive or negative?

One thing that the writer could have improved is the confusing plot, and it's also a bit slow at the start. However, halfway through the pace of the story improves and you can't wait to find out what happens.

This probably isn't worth paying to see at the cinema, but if you haven't got anything else to do at the weekend you could watch it. The special effects are impressive and the actors do their best. Unfortunately, the storyline is awful.

Track one is good and you'll sing along to the tune, but then the other nine are dismal. I recommend you download the first song and forget the rest.

One thing I really liked about the homepage is that it's easy to navigate. Some of the graphics are a bit boring and unimaginative but the links are all up to date and you can find and order products very quickly.

6 Work in pairs. Tell your partner about a book, film, music CD or website you have read, seen, heard or visited recently. Use some of the underlined phrases from exercise 5.

My favourite CD at the moment is the latest one by Jake Bugg. One thing I really like about it is the lyrics, they're so interesting.

I haven't heard that. What else do you like about it?

7 Now write your own review of a website, book, film or music CD that you like. Begin by planning your review and writing notes. Then write your review with four paragraphs. Use some of these expressions to help:

USEFUL EXPRESSIONS

A REVIEW

Introducing your review
My favourite book / film / website / CD is …
One book / film / website / CD I really like is …
An interesting book / film / website / CD I read / saw / visited / heard recently was …

Describing the main features of the website, book, film or music CD and what you like about it
One thing I really like about it is …
… is very well done / written / made.
It's worth visiting / reading / seeing / listening to because …

Describing what needs improvement
It should …
It isn't very …
One thing that could be improved is …

Conclusion
Overall, I (strongly) recommend …
(Nevertheless,) it's much better than …
To summarise, I'd say that …

WRITING CHECKLIST

A REVIEW

After you write, check your review.
Does the review:
• include between 140 and 190 words? ☐
• include three to four paragraphs? ☐
• say clearly what the subject is? (film, magazine, book, etc.) ☐
• describe what you like about it? ☐
• give suggestions for improvement? ☐
• give a conclusion? ☐

WRITING GUIDE   **PAGE 216**

VIDEO solar cooking

1 Work in groups. You are going to watch a video about the invention in the photograph. It's called a solar cooker. How do you think it might work?

2 Now watch the video and find out how the solar cooker works. Decide if the statements 1–6 are true (T) or false (F). Were any of your ideas in exercise 1 mentioned?

1 It uses electricity or gas as fuel.
2 It cooks meat, fish and vegetables.
3 You can use it anywhere in the world.
4 It burns wood and creates smoke.
5 It costs about $5 and lasts about two years.
6 It can purify water.

3 Watch the video again and complete the notes.

1 Eleanor has been using a solar cooker for _____ years.
2 It doesn't matter if it is a cold day, so long as it is _____ .
3 A lot of people use solar cooking because they care about _____ .
4 Bob Metcalf says solar energy can be used instead of _____ .
5 Two and a half billion people are running out of _____ .
6 Solar Cookers International's two main goals are:
   to stop _____
   to make life easier for _____ .
7 In the developing world, solar cookers can help prevent the _____ of millions of people every year.

4 **Complete the notes using the numbers in the box.**

two   three   five   65   6,000   22,000   2,000,000

Some women have to walk up to
(1) _____ miles a day just to collect
wood.

The 'indoor pollution' from fires kills as many
as (2) _____ women and children each
year.

SCI has taught about (3) _____ families
how to use solar cookers to prepare their
traditional food.

A solar cooker costs about (4) $ _____
and can last for (5) _____ years.

It is estimated that as many as (6) _____
people die each day from waterborne diseases.

A solar cooker can pasteurise water by heating
it to (7) _____ Celsius.

5 **In the video you see how the solar cooker can help
people living in the developing world. Work in
pairs. Imagine you are trying to sell the solar cooker
to people in your own country. Think of different
arguments to convince these people to buy one.**

- a person who likes to spend time outside in their garden
- a friend who is interested in the environment
- a local school with children aged between 11–15

6 **Work in pairs. Read the Ideas generator and do the
speaking task. Remember to consider the options
from other people's points of view as well as
your own.**

USEFUL EXPRESSIONS

SPECULATING AND EVALUATING

This might be useful for …
This one would be popular with teachers because …
I think students would probably prefer …
This is a good one for giving presentations because …
If I was a maths teacher, I'd find this useful because …

Making a final decision
On the whole I think this one is best because …
Overall, this one seems to be the best.
Taking everything into account, I'd choose …

 IDEAS GENERATOR

SEEING THINGS FROM ANOTHER PERSON'S POINT OF VIEW

In Part 3 of the *First* Speaking paper, you have to discuss a situation with different choices. To prepare for this part of the exam, it's useful to practise seeing a situation from a different point of view. For example, in this task from Part 3 you have to imagine that a school has some money to buy some new technology. You discuss each item and choose the two best options. You might have your own opinion, but also think about what other people in the school might choose. For example, a music teacher might want the recording equipment, but an English teacher might want ebook readers.

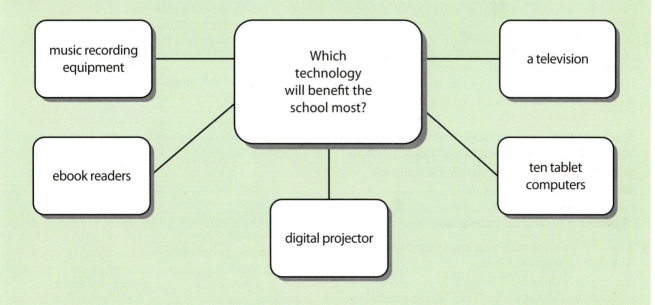

CRIME AND SOCIAL RESPONSIBILITY

VOCABULARY crime and criminals

1 **What do you think the man in the photo is doing?**

2 **Match the crimes in the box to the descriptions (1–10).**

> arson burglary forgery hacking kidnapping
> mugging murder shoplifting smuggling vandalism

1   stealing from a shop
2   attacking someone in the street for their money
3   breaking into a house to steal money and objects
4   killing another person
5   taking someone (e.g. a child) and asking for money
6   breaking into the data of a computer from another computer to steal information
7   damaging property (e.g. graffiti, breaking windows)
8   setting fire to property on purpose
9   copying something (e.g. money or products)
10   carrying and not declaring items at customs

3 **The criminal in the photo is called *a burglar*. What do we call the criminals who commit the other crimes in exercise 1?**

READING crime and punishment

4 **Read the article quickly and match the headings 1–4 to the paragraphs A–D.**

1   When is a crime not a crime?
2   A criminal whose bark was worse than his bite!
3   One way to impress your future employer
4   Lock me up – now!

PAPER 1, PART 7 Multiple matching

5 **For questions 1–10 choose from the criminals (A–D). Each criminal may be chosen more than once.**

Which criminal

1   wanted to be arrested? _____
2   benefited from the crime? _____
3   hadn't remembered something? _____
4   has the support of other people? _____
5   might encourage further crime? _____
6   wanted some new clothes? _____
7   is doing someone else's job? _____
8   hadn't expected to meet so many people? _____
9   has improved something? _____
10   tried to hurt a policeman? _____

6 **In the article the computer hacker didn't receive a punishment. Do you think this was right?**

7 **Discuss the crimes (1–6) and match them to the punishments (a–f) given in the UK. Turn to page 239 for the answers.**

1   Bank robbery
2   Hacking into school computers
3   Speeding in town
4   Mugging someone late at night
5   Shoplifting some DVDs
6   Dropping litter in the street

a   Do community service for 40 hours
b   Spend one year on probation
c   Get 18 months in prison
d   Get ten years in prison
e   Pay a fine of £100
f   Go to a police talk about dangerous driving

POLICE WATCH

Your monthly round-up of the mad, bad and not-so-dangerous crimes from around the world.

A A 14-year-old boy whose favourite pastime was hacking into the confidential computer records of banks and government organisations was finally caught by police last week. However, rather than receiving a prison sentence or fine, the child criminal has now been offered a job with a software developer specialising in anti-virus programs. The company that made the job offer said the boy had more than met their requirements, but one government minister commented that this kind of reward set a bad example for other youngsters thinking of breaking into systems. The software company defended its decision, saying the boy had shown real initiative and that this approach to the crime would be more effective than sending him to juvenile prison.

B Do you often think that your town may benefit from more green spaces? Would you prefer fewer roads and buildings and more trees and flowers instead? If your answer is 'yes', then you might be surprised to hear about the local council in the English town of Blakenthorpe, which is currently trying to arrest people for 'planting flowers'. It all began when flowers and plants started appearing at roadsides and areas around the city. The town council, which is responsible for green spaces in Blakenthorpe, has blamed 'green vandals' for doing some 'midnight gardening'. However, the council and police shouldn't expect much help from local residents, who say this is the best kind of vandalism. As one person said, 'These so-called law-breakers are just doing the job that our local council should be doing. I wish them the best of luck!'

C Many burglars are probably prepared to deal with alarms, or maybe one or two large dogs at the front door, but a burglar in Osaka, Japan, had a surprise when he broke into a house where 15 sumo wrestlers were staying the night. Shiro Morioka, 42, had broken in through the back of the house and climbed into a bedroom in the middle of the night. He was in the process of looking for something to steal when he met a 130-kilo sumo wrestler. That would have been bad enough but Mr Morioka was even more horrified to find that the whole house was full of sumo wrestlers. 'First I was caught by a massive man. When the lights went on, I was surrounded by sumo wrestlers,' Mr Morioka told reporters. He instantly surrendered himself and was relieved when the police took him away to the safety of a police cell.

D Police arrested a 76-year-old man last night for shoplifting and also accused him of attacking a police officer. The man had tried to escape by biting the officer. Unfortunately, he'd left his teeth on his bedside table at home. The pensioner, who tried to steal some trousers from a shop, sank his gums into the officer's arm – but it had no effect and the policeman was unhurt. A spokesperson for the police said, 'He had forgotten to put his false teeth in.' Journalists had arranged to have an interview with the ageing shoplifter, but it was later reported that he was unavailable for comment. However, it is believed that he may simply be incapable of answering any questions without his teeth in!

KEY WORD *get*

8 Replace the bold phrases containing *got* in these sentences with the correct form of a verb from the box.

annoy   arrest   arrive   capture   force   is
manage   meet   receive   understand

1 The police **got** him for shoplifting and attacking an officer. _____
2 He **got** ten years in prison for the crime. _____
3 I don't **get** how someone can do that to someone else. _____
4 By the time the police **got there**, the burglars were miles away. _____
5 We didn't **get around to going** to the public meeting. _____
6 What **gets** me is that the judge let him go with only a fine! _____
7 The police were determined to **get** the thieves. _____
8 Local people **got together** to discuss the problem of vandalism in the area. _____
9 He held a gun to my head and **got** me to open the safe in the bank. _____
10 Joe **got** robbed on his way to work. _____

9 Complete sentences 1–5 with these particles.

away   away with   into   out of   up to

1 The thieves climbed into a van and got _____ .
2 She got _____ the robbery because there wasn't enough evidence to convict her.
3 It's very quiet. What do you think the children are getting _____?
4 The 42-year-old got _____ such a mess with the police.
5 If I help you, what do I get _____ it? How much money do I make?

LISTENING stopped by the police

PAPER 3, PART 3 Multiple matching

1 ⊙ **8.1** You will hear five different people talking about why they were recently stopped by the police. For each speaker choose the reason from the list (A–G). Use each letter only once. There are two extra letters which you do not need to use.

A driving along the wrong street
B breaking the speed limit
C being in the area at the time of a crime
D being mistaken for someone else
E driving in the wrong direction
F taking someone else's bags
G breaking into a house

Speaker 1 _____
Speaker 2 _____
Speaker 3 _____
Speaker 4 _____
Speaker 5 _____

GRAMMAR relative clauses

RELATIVE CLAUSES

Relative clauses add information to the main clause. Read these three sentences from the article on page 81. The relative clauses are underlined:

1 A 14-year-old boy <u>whose favourite pastime was hacking into the confidential computer records of banks and government organisations</u> was finally caught by police last week.

2 The company <u>that made the job offer</u> said the boy had more than met their requirements.

3 The town council, <u>which is responsible for green spaces in Blakenthorpe</u>, has blamed 'green vandals' for doing some midnight gardening.

There are two types of relative clause:

Sentences 1 and 2 contain a defining relative clause because the information is essential. Note that you can replace the pronouns *who* or *which* with the pronoun *that*.

Sentence 3 contains a non-defining relative clause because the information isn't essential, but the writer wants to give some extra or background information. This clause is always punctuated with commas. Note that you cannot replace the pronoun *who* or *which* with the pronoun *that*.

2 There are five more sentences containing relative clauses in the article on page 81. Can you find them? Which of the clauses are defining and which are non-defining?

▶ GRAMMAR REFERENCE (SECTION 13) **PAGE 207**

3 Combine each pair of sentences using a defining relative clause. Use the words in brackets.

0 That's the policeman. He caught the burglar. (*who* or *that*).
That's the policeman that / who caught the burglar.

1 He's the one. He was seen at the scene of the crime. (*who* or *that*)

_____

2 This is the shop. We said we'd meet in this shop. (*where*)

_____

3 Do you know the reason? What was the reason he couldn't come? (*why*)

_____

4 Over there is the building. The building was destroyed by fire last night. (*which* or *that*)

_____

5 The woman is waiting for you in reception. Her car was stolen. (*whose*)

_____

6 Do you remember the time? You could walk down the streets safely at night. (*when*)

_____

4 These sentences have non-defining relative clauses. Correct the mistakes. There is at least one mistake (including punctuation) in each sentence.

1 The shoplifter, he had only been released from prison a week ago was caught on camera.

2 The house, that had a security system, has been burgled three times.

3 The town, over half a million people live, is one of the safest in the country.

4 A retired policeman, that had left the police force in 2005, was accused of forgery yesterday at the High Court.

5 The factory which employs 200 people, caught fire in strange circumstances.

INFORMALITY AND FORMALITY IN RELATIVE CLAUSES

To be more informal you can leave out the pronoun in some defining relative clauses. You can leave out *who*, *which* or *that* if it is the object of the verb in the relative clause:

The witness ~~who~~ I interviewed admitted it was her.
Do you have the money ~~which / that~~ you borrowed?

We often leave out *why* and *when* as well:

Do you know the reason ~~why~~ he left?
He'll never forget the night ~~when~~ he met a sumo wrestler.

To be more formal we replace certain pronouns with others:

who > *whom*, *where* > *in which*, *why* > *for which*, *where* > *on which*
The suspect, **whom** police questioned for over six hours, is now free.
Is this the house **in which** you grew up?

5 Add a pronoun or preposition to complete the relative clauses in sentences 1–5.

0 Where's the pen ∧ I lent you yesterday? *(which)*

0 This is the building ∧ which a famous murder took place. *(in)*

1 Which date was it we all went out to that club?

2 Do you understand the reasons which you are going to prison?

3 The neighbour I mentioned is still causing problems.

4 Do you know the reason she called?

5 The suspect says he was away on business the night which the crime was committed.

6 Read the article below about a man who was fined for dropping cigarette ash in the street. Choose the correct options to complete the article.

7 Work in pairs. Do you agree with the punishment that was given to the man in the article? Explain why or why not.

8 Read these sentences about a strange prison escape. Rewrite each pair of sentences as one sentence, using a relative clause. Use the sentences to write a news article about a prisoner.

Dragan Boskovic, who wanted to wish his girlfriend a happy birthday, escaped from a jail in Montenegro.

1a Dragan Boskovic escaped from a jail in Montenegro.
1b He wanted to wish his girlfriend a happy birthday.
2a He escaped over a wall.
2b It was over three metres high.
3a He went straight to his girlfriend's house.
3b He spent the evening there.
4a He finally explained his reasons to the police.
4b They arrested him two hours later.
5a 'I hadn't been able to call her on the prison phone to say "happy birthday".'
5b 'The phone was broken.'

9 Turn to page 239 and read the original news story. Compare it with your own. Underline the sentences that are different.

10 Now write three short sentences about a recent piece of news. Do not use relative clauses. Swap sentences with your partner and rewrite your partner's sentences as one sentence, using relative clauses.

MAN FINED OVER CIGARETTE

A man, to (1) *whose / whom* a £75 fine was given for dropping cigarette ash, has finally agreed to pay it. Richard Jones, (2) *who / that* was smoking a cigarette on his local high street, was seen by local councillor Rona Keeting. The town councillor reported the cigarette to police (3) *which / when* she described as 'dripping ash'. The local magistrate of Hemden, in Lincolnshire, the town (4) *in / on* which Mr Jones lives, ordered him to pay a penalty notice (5) *what / which* required settlement within 14 days. Mr Jones ignored the order, so was requested to appear in court. As a result he has paid the fine, but told local reporters that he can't understand the reason (6) *why / when* other people (7) *who / for which* drop chewing gum or litter don't receive similar treatment. Councillor Rona Keeting said 'Neither Hemden, (8) *who / which* has a clear policy on littering, nor the citizens of Hemden will tolerate behaviour of this kind.'

USE OF ENGLISH open cloze

1 Read this article about being a 'Freegan'. Think of the word which best fits each gap. Use only one word in each gap. There is an example at the beginning (0).

A MATTER OF CHOICE

They don't need to do this, but (0) <u>for</u> environmental and ethical reasons they choose to. They are Freegans, part of a movement (1) _____ members live off other people's rubbish. Tristram Stuart is one such member, also a Freecyler and author. He says, 'I can perfectly well afford to buy food,' and his aim isn't to save money but to (2) _____ a political point.

Researchers estimate that a quarter of all food waste that goes (3) _____ landfills is still edible. And the waste, according (4) _____ the Freegans, isn't limited only to food. They also recover things that have been thrown (5) _____ by retailers, offices, schools, homes and hotels, such (6) _____ electronics, kitchen appliances, carpets and musical instruments. The list is endless.

But before you start looking (7) _____ the bins behind your local supermarket, be careful! Freecycling isn't (8) _____ anyone with a weak stomach and it is often illegal.

2 Read the article in exercise 1 again and complete these sentences with your own ideas. Then compare and discuss your responses with your partner.

1 I found it really interesting that …
2 One thing that surprises me is that …
3 I think what they are doing is really …
4 I would / wouldn't become a Freegan because …

> I think what they are doing is really good, because we waste far too much food.

> Yes, but I wouldn't like to eat food out of rubbish bins. It's disgusting!

LISTENING social responsibility

3 ⊙ 8.2 You will hear an interview with a woman involved with 'Freecycling'. Find out one similarity and one difference between:
- Freegans and Freecyclers
- Freecyclers and recyclers.

PAPER 3, PART 4 Multiple choice

4 ⊙ 8.2 Listen to the radio interview again. For questions 1–7, choose the best answer (A, B or C).

1 Why is Connie on the radio programme?
   A in order to inform listeners about the Freecycling movement
   B because Geoff wanted to interview her
   C to find out more about recycling
2 The Freecycle Network was originally set up
   A by Connie to help her local town.
   B as an alternative to recycling.
   C to help protect a local area from waste.
3 The government
   A hasn't been involved with Freecycling.
   B tried to stop Freecycling.
   C wanted to make money from Freecycling.
4 The emphasis is on
   A using everyday items again.
   B using reuseable parts of household items.
   C selling everyday items you don't need anymore.
5 Total membership of the organisation
   A is only in the USA and Germany.
   B numbers nearly 3 million.
   C numbers over 3,000.
6 If you can't find a Freecycler near you, Connie advises you to
   A join a local group.
   B set up your own community.
   C visit the website.
7 Items for Freecycling must not
   A be for children.
   B be against the law.
   C have cost you anything to buy.

SPEAKING showing you are listening

EXAM SPOTLIGHT

PAPER 4, PART 3 AND 4 Collaborative task and discussion

You will need to talk about different topics with your partner in Part 3 of the *First* speaking paper, and with the examiner in Part 4. When you take part in these discussions, it's important to be an active listener as well as speaking effectively. Active listening means showing interest in and responding to what the other person is saying.

As well as responding verbally, remember to use body language to show your partner you are listening, e.g. look at them while they are speaking, look alert and interested, smile or frown in response to what they say.

5 🔘 8.2 **In the radio interview, the presenter uses the following expressions to show Connie he is listening. Listen again and number these expressions in the order you hear them.**

- OK. So … _____
- Right. _____
- Sure. _____
- Wow! _____
- Sounds great. _____
- I see, but … _____

6 **Work in pairs. Take turns to talk for one minute about each of the following topics. When your partner is talking, remember to be an active listener and use some of the expressions in exercise 5.**

- plans for your next holiday
- something not many people know about you
- how you get to your house
- something you would like to change about the world

7 **Work in pairs. Read the interlocutor's instructions and look at the spider diagram, then discuss the question. As you discuss each option consider:**

- its advantages
- its disadvantages
- what sort of preparation would be needed.

> *Your local college intends to have one day when students raise money for a local charity. Here are some ideas they are thinking about. Talk to each other about why these would be good ways of raising money.*

(2 minutes)

> *Decide which two you think would be best.*

(1 minute)

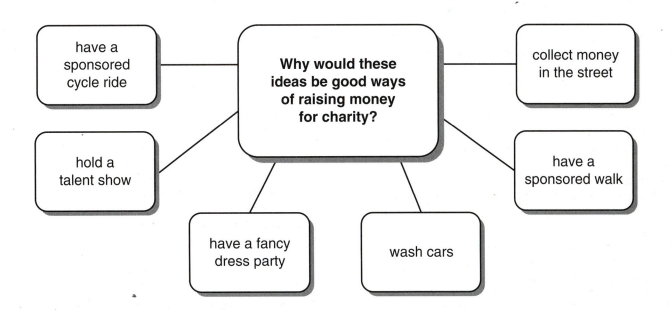

- have a sponsored cycle ride
- hold a talent show
- have a fancy dress party
- **Why would these ideas be good ways of raising money for charity?**
- wash cars
- have a sponsored walk
- collect money in the street

▲ USE OF ENGLISH open cloze ▲ LISTENING social responsibility ▲ SPEAKING showing you are listening

WRITING an article (2)

EXAM SPOTLIGHT

PAPER 2, PART 2 Article

When you write an article, it's important to:

- plan before you write
- think of a title that will attract the reader's attention
- have an opening sentence to interest the reader
- use expressions to introduce each new idea, e.g. *First … / Another way is to … .*

1 **Work in pairs. Read this exam question and then read a candidate's answer. How well do you think the candidate answers the question?**

> **You see this advertisement in a local newspaper.**
>
> _____
>
> We are looking for an article (120–180 words) that suggests three easy ways for our readers to produce less waste in their daily lives. Explain why this is an important issue and suggest three ways to help. The writer of the winning article will receive a brand new bicycle!
>
> _____
>
> **Write your article.**

Three easy ways to save you money and save the planet

Have you ever stopped to consider how much you throw away every week? Producing less waste could save you money and, more importantly, save the natural resources of the planet.

Take, for example, plastic bags. Many people put their shopping in a bag and then throw the bag away. Why not simply take the old plastic bags back to the supermarket next time you shop and use them again? A second way to produce less waste is to give your unwanted things to charity. If you have old household appliances, books, DVDs and clothes, then take them to a charity shop. They will either resell the items or give them to people in need. Finally, start recycling products like glass bottles, cans and paper. Put these items into separate bins and take them to your local recycling centre.

So, next time you are about to throw something away ask yourself: Can I re-use this? Can someone else re-use this? Can it be recycled?

It's so easy!

2 **The candidate planned the answer before writing. Below is part of the plan. Read the article again and complete the plan.**

> PLAN:
>
> Why it's important:
>
>
>
> One way to produce less waste:
>
>
>
> A second way:
>
>
>
> A third way:

3 Here are three possible titles for the article. Why do you think the candidate chose the last title? Can you think of any other possible titles?

- How we can save the planet
- Why we shouldn't throw things away
- Three easy ways to save you money and save the planet

4 It is important to have an interesting opening sentence when writing an article. These five techniques are often used. Match the techniques (a–e) to the opening sentences (1–5).

a a question _____
b a general introduction to the topic _____
c a statistic or surprising fact _____
d a point for discussion or argument _____
e a personal anecdote _____

1
> The typical household probably produces around six bags of rubbish a week.

2
> Have you ever stopped to consider how much you throw away every week?

3
> There are many ways we can reduce the amount of household waste we produce.

4
> One evening I was driving out of the city when I looked across at the sun falling behind what seemed like a giant mountain; in fact it was the city landfill.

5
> Some people still say it is too difficult to recycle products and would prefer to throw them away.

5 The candidate in exercise 1 uses these three expressions (1–3) to introduce ideas. Expressions a–h have similar meanings. Match each expression a–h to the expression 1–3 that is most similar.

1 Take, for example, …
2 A second way to produce less waste is to …
3 Finally, …

a First of all, there's _____
b And lastly … _____
c Alternatively you could _____
d You could also consider (-ing) _____
e For one thing, there's the problem of … _____
f Let's start with _____
g Thirdly, … _____
h Another easy way which takes no effort is to …

_____

6 Read this exam question. Plan the article to answer the exam question by completing the notes below.

> **You see this advertisement in a local paper.**
>
> ---
>
> We are looking for an article (140–190 words) that suggests three easy ways to improve the local community. Explain why this is an important issue and suggest three ideas to help. The winning article will receive a £50 book token!
>
> ---
>
> **Write your article.**

PLAN:

Why it's important:

One way to improve the community:

A second way:

A third way:

7 Now write the article. Write your answer in 140–190 words in an appropriate style.

WRITING CHECKLIST

ARTICLE

After writing, check your article.

- Does the title attract attention? ☐
- Is the opening sentence interesting? ☐
- Is each 'idea' introduced with an expression (*First* … etc.)? ☐
- Does the article have an introductory paragraph and a concluding paragraph? ☐

WRITING GUIDE **PAGE 218**

REVIEW AND EXAM PRACTICE Units 7 and 8

1 For questions 1–8, read the text below. Use the word in capitals at the end of some of the lines to form a word that fits in the space in the same line. There is an example at the beginning (0).

Teenage (0) <u>hackers</u> who use their computer skills to access	HACK
information (1) _____ or steal money from businesses are	LEGAL
(2) _____ likely to face a prison sentence or other serious	INCREASE
(3) _____. There have been some worrying cases recently,	PUNISH
(4) _____ that of a 15-year-old who caused a shutdown	INCLUDE
of computers at a major (5) _____ institution in the USA.	FINANCE
He received a six-month prison sentence. Many hackers, however,	
use their (6) _____ in more positive ways. Some work on	EXPERT
creating (7) _____ systems for companies. Others are simply	SECURE
curious and want to increase their (8) _____ of computer	KNOW
networks.	

2 For questions 9–16, read the text below and think of the word which best fits each gap. Use only one word in each gap. There is an example at the beginning (0).

Dancing robot copies human moves

Japanese researchers have created a dancing robot, capable (0) <u>of</u> imitating a routine with (9) _____ need for rehearsals. The robot HRP-2 can copy the moves of a human dance teacher (10) _____ video motion capture technology. For example, HRP-2 watched dance instructor Hisako Yamada performing a Japanese folk dance and accurately reproduced her performance a few minutes (11) _____. One use for such robots might be (12) _____ keep the knowledge of traditional Japanese folk dances, as fewer humans (13) _____ maintaining the skills to perform them. However, the robots are unlikely to replace ballerinas (14) _____ time soon. As one folk dancer said, 'My impression is (15) _____ there would still be a human element lacking. The robot would still look, for the want of (16) _____ better word, robotic.'

3 For questions 17–24, read the text below and decide which answer (A, B, C or D) best fits each gap. There is an example at the beginning (0).

The police have (0) <u>B</u> their crime figures for last year. Overall, the statistics show a fall in violent street crime such as (17) _____. A police spokesperson said that the number of (18) _____ for robbery has also increased. They also claimed that their work with local supermarkets and store owners had reduced cases of (19) _____.

However, (20) _____-based crime continues to rise, with twenty per cent more cases than in the previous year of hackers breaking into files to access personal data on customers. George Maynard, a software analyst specialising (21) _____ computer security, believes this trend is unlikely to change in the near future. 'Hacking is here to stay and is potentially public (22) _____ number one.'

Finally, the area attracting most attention is the increased (23) _____ to the rich and famous. The media attention given to celebrities has meant their (24) _____ have become targets for kidnappers.

0	A arrested	B released	C stopped	D judged
17	A hacking	B mugging	C blackmailing	D smuggling
18	A vandalism	B crimes	C arrests	D arson
19	A shoplifting	B police	C criminals	D forgery
20	A computer	B robber	C internationally	D password
21	A in	B with	C for	D of
22	A against	B enemy	C terrorist	D crime
23	A problem	B rise	C threat	D stealing
24	A possessions	B children	C houses	D accounts

4 For questions 25–30, complete the second sentence so that it has a similar meaning to the first sentence, using the word given. Do not change the word given. You must use between two and five words, including the word given.

(0) I can't wait to see Martha again.
FORWARD
I'm really _looking forward to_ seeing Martha again.

25 Is there a danger of having our lives taken over by technology?
RISK
Do _____ our lives taken over by technology?

26 An inventor in England has thought of a way to improve the household broom.
COME
An inventor in England has _____ to improve the household broom.

27 Why don't you have a drive in my new car and see what you think.
TRY
Do you want _____ my new car and see what you think?

28 It irritates me that criminals are released from prison early.
GETS
What _____ criminals are released from prison early.

29 The student left university and became a Nobel Prize winner in science.
WENT
The student left university and _____ a Nobel Prize winner in science.

30 One day scientists will manage to build robots that think for themselves.
SUCCEED
One day scientists will _____ robots that think for themselves.

5 You must answer this question. Write your answer in 140–190 words in an appropriate style.

In your English class you have been talking about crime and punishment. Now, your English teacher has asked you to write an essay.

Write an essay using all the notes and give reasons for your point of view.

Is prison the best punishment for criminals or are there sometimes better alternatives?

Notes

Write about:

1 paying a fine
2 doing community service
3 your own ideas

FOOD AND EATING OUT

1 **Work in pairs. Ask and answer these questions.**

1   How many foods can you identify in the photo?
2   What are your favourite foods? How healthy do you think your diet is?
3   Do you eat to live, or live to eat?
4   Do you ever count the calories of food?

LISTENING eating out

2 **Work in pairs. Discuss how often you eat out.**

3 9.1 **You are going to hear five people talking about food and eating out. Choose from the list A–H what each speaker describes. There are three extra letters which you do not need to use.**

A   a preference for ordinary, simple food
B   finding an insect in their meal
C   the production of a traditional cheese
D   a huge meal
E   an argument over a bill
F   the finishing touches for a recipe
G   dealing with a difficult waiter
H   a mealtime in the olden days

Speaker 1 _____
Speaker 2 _____
Speaker 3 _____
Speaker 4 _____
Speaker 5 _____

EXAM SPOTLIGHT

PAPER 3, PART 3 Multiple matching

Listen carefully to everything the speaker says before you make a decision.
Don't make a decision that is based on single words. An answer which looks obvious may be wrong. Read the audioscript on page 227. How could these words in A–H lead you to the wrong answer?
cheese, traditional, difficult, waiter

VOCABULARY food and drink

4 **Match each adjective (1–9) to its opposite (a–i). (Note that there are three different opposites to the word *sweet*, depending on the context.)**

1	sweet	a	bland
2	sweet	b	bitter
3	sweet	c	cooked
4	still	d	dry
5	hot	e	sour
6	rare	f	sparkling
7	spicy	g	cold
8	raw	h	mild
9	tasty	i	well-done

5 Complete the sentences using adjectives from exercise 4.

1 The bubbles go up my nose. That's why I always drink _____ water.
2 This recipe contrasts the sweetness of sugar and the _____ taste of vinegar.
3 The food in the canteen is so _____ and boring, we use lots of ketchup to add some flavour.
4 How embarrassing. I didn't realise that gazpacho was a soup that you eat _____.
5 The curry was so _____ that I thought I was going to have to call the fire brigade.
6 I can't drink black coffee without sweetening it; I find it too _____.
7 Mm, this is delicious and really _____.
8 I'd like it _____, please; I don't like it pink.
9 I'm not very keen on sweet wine. I much prefer it _____.
10 It's best to eat vegetables _____ as it preserves all the vitamins.

6 Write these verbs in the correct column of the table.

add   bake   boil   chop   fry   grate   grill   mix
peel   pour   roast   slice   sprinkle   stir

Ways of cutting	Ways of cooking	Other verbs

7 Work in pairs or groups. Think of as many words as you can for kitchen and cooking implements.

frying-pan, knife, bowl …

8 Complete the pairs of sentences using a single word which fits both gaps.

1a A three-_____ lunch only costs €12 in that restaurant.
1b Magnus is going on a three-day _____ to learn how to cook Italian food.
2a The Mediterranean _____ is one of the healthiest ways of eating in the world.
2b Goodness me, I'll have to go on a _____ if I am going to wear these trousers again.
3a Truffles are _____ because they only grow in a few special places.
3b I love steak as long as it's quite _____.

9 What is the difference in meaning between these words? Write a sentence for each word.

- a **receipt** and a **recipe**
- something **tasteful** and something **tasty**
- a **cook** and a **cooker**
- **greedy** and **ingredients**

10 Work in groups. Tell each other about your favourite recipe.

SPEAKING expressing preferences

11 *Prefer* and *would rather* are similar in meaning but have different grammar. Choose the correct word (in italics) to complete sentences 1–5.

1 I *prefer / rather* chicken to beef.
2 I'd rather *have / to have* tea than coffee.
3 What would you *rather / prefer* to do today?
4 I think I'd prefer *go / to go* to the cinema.
5 I generally *prefer / rather* coffee to tea.

12 Look at these sentences. What happens when *rather* is followed directly by a noun or pronoun?

a I'd rather go to the cinema.
b I'd rather we / all of us went to the cinema.

13 Work in groups. Look at the photos.

- Imagine that you are going to spend the evening in one of these restaurants with your group. Discuss which place you prefer and decide on a place.
- Ask each person in the group for their opinion, using *prefer* and *rather*.

READING all mouth

1 What do you think is happening in the photo? What do you think are the rules of the competition? Do you think it would be fun?

2 Read the article about a woman who takes part in eating competitions. What is surprising about her success? Does she deserve her nickname? How does she train?

EXAM SPOTLIGHT

PAPER 1, PART 6 Gapped text

Read these comments from students about how to answer this part of the Reading paper. Decide if each comment is good (G) or bad (B) advice.

1 'I never waste my time reading the text all the way through.'
2 'I always trust my instinct and go for the sentence which feels right.'
3 'I start matching sentences to gaps straight away.'
4 'I always do the answers in order.'
5 'I don't bother looking for pronouns and references.'
6 'I don't try to identify the extra sentence. At the end it's obvious.'
7 'Never guess if you don't know.'

3 Read the article about Sonya again. Six sentences have been removed from the article. Choose from the sentences (A–G) the one which fits each gap (1–6). There is one extra sentence that you do not need to use.

A However, when she started eating his confidence turned to disbelief.

B I entered the qualifying rounds of a competition and ate 18 hot dogs in five minutes.

C In geographical and cultural terms, all this is about as far away as you can get from South Korea, where Sonya was born and brought up.

D However, Sonya claims she is in good shape and that her job at a local fast-food restaurant gives her plenty of opportunity to stay fit.

E She raises one arm to acknowledge the cheers of the crowd.

F It is time that competitive eating was recognised as a serious sport alongside athletics or football.

G Today she has come to the small town of Stockton in California to take part in its deep-fried asparagus eating competition.

4 What do you think of this kind of competition? Do you think the competitors are taking risks?

5 Make nouns from the following words.

1 optimistic (adjective) → _____ (noun)
2 astonish (verb) → _____ (noun)
3 concentrate (verb) → _____ (noun)
4 appear (verb) → _____ (noun)

GRAMMAR forms of *used to* and *would*

6 Look at sentences a–c. Which sentence describes:

1 a current habit? _____
2 a developing habit? _____
3 an old habit / a situation that has changed? _____
a Her parents used to be so poor that they couldn't afford a fridge.
b She is used to running around serving the customers.
c … she gets used to consuming vast quantities by drinking a gallon and a half of cola before every meal.

7 Look at the sentences in exercise 6 again and answer the questions.

1 Which sentence uses *used* as an auxiliary? _____
2 Which sentences use *used* as an adjective? _____ and _____
3 What verb form follows *used to* in each case?
   1 _____   2 _____

8 Read the sentences with *will* and *would*. Tick the sentences that describe habits.

1 One in ten people aged 16 to 24 will use at least ten ready meals a week. _____
2 Sonya would have to fight for food with her brothers and sisters. _____
3 Steffi said she would cook dinner tonight. _____
4 She would always take the seat at the back. _____
5 Would you like to try this cake? _____

USED TO AND WOULD

We can use both *would* and *used to* to describe past habits. We **used to** / **would** have a big meal on Sundays.

We can use *used to* to talk about states in the past which have changed, but we cannot use *would*. She **used to** have long red hair.

▶ GRAMMAR REFERENCE (SECTION 15) **PAGE 209**

9 Some of these sentences are incorrect. Tick (✓) the sentence if it is correct, or write the correct sentence.

1 I would be really fat when I was younger.

   _____

2 When his mother got home she would make a cup of tea and read the newspaper.

   _____

3 That's the place where I used to going to school.

   _____

4 Are you getting used to your new job?

   _____

5 You're Jo, aren't you? I would know your mum. We used to work together for ten years. When you were young you would have blond, curly hair.

   _____

6 After five years she finally got used to live in London.

   _____

SONYA THE BLACK WIDOW

At a chicken-wing eating competition in Philadelphia, USA, Bill Simmons, a 150-kg truck driver, was confidently expecting to win the title for the fifth successive year. His optimism was in no way affected by the appearance of a 45-kg, 36-year-old South Korean woman called Sonya Thomas. (1) _____ After ten minutes Bill had managed to consume 151 chicken wings. Sonya had eaten 154.

Competitive eating used to be an entirely male affair, but Sonya has taken on the men and beaten them. Two years on, and competitive eating has taken off in a big way in the States. Now there are around 150 contests a year with the most popular being televised. Sonya has won an estimated $100,000 in prize money and a nickname to go with it. 'I'm Sonya "The Black Widow" Thomas', she announces. Then she gives a high-pitched giggle and adds 'Kill the men'.

(2) _____. As usual she has eaten sparingly in the days before the competition, but she gets used to consuming vast quantities by drinking a gallon and a half of cola before every meal. 'Because the cola is gassy, it seems to push it out that little bit more and allows you to fit in more food'. An expanded stomach, everyone agrees, is key – and the reason why thin people appear to be at an advantage. If you're fat this will produce a kind of belt around your waist, thereby stopping your stomach expanding. With no spare flesh to impede her, Sonya believes she could keep on eating until she bursts.

When the countdown begins she leans over her plate in concentration. Then as soon as the compère shouts 'Go!', she begins forcing deep-fried asparagus into her mouth. The crowd gasps in astonishment to see so much food disappear into such a tiny person. To this onlooker, it all seems like a form of mass suicide. (3) _____ She is used to running around serving the customers. Halfway through the competition the 12 competitors are still eating away. Deep-fried asparagus falls from their lips, sticks to their cheeks and piles up in little heaps on the ground. It is without doubt the most disgusting thing I have ever seen.

(4) _____ There, her parents used to be so poor that they couldn't afford a fridge and Sonya would have to fight for food with her brothers and sisters. On moving to America she was so amazed by the produce on display, she was determined to take the opportunity to eat as much of it as possible. 'When I started eating competitively I didn't mind what I ate, I just liked all the different tastes. (5) _____ A week later I did 25. Two weeks after that I was up to 37. All the time I was learning about technique; how to use your jaw strength, and also how to eat really fast, but not so fast your throat closes up'. 'Everyone stop eating,' shouts the master of ceremonies. The contestants wipe their mouths and the judges announce that Sonya has won. (6) _____.

Sonya stretches out on the grass and considers her future. 'What I want to do is make as much money from this as possible,' she says. 'And then I can achieve my dream.'

'What is your dream?', I ask.

'My dream is that one day, not too far away in the future, I will own my own fast-food restaurant.'

SPEAKING talking about the past

10 Work in groups. Talk about these topics using *used to* and *would*.

- life in your town in your grandparents' time
- your early childhood, and the people who were important to you then
- a time in your life where you found it difficult to adapt to a changing situation
- how eating habits have changed over the past two or three generations in your country
- changes in transport in your town

LISTENING in the dark

1 Look at the photo. What do you think is happening?

PAPER 3, PART 4 Multiple choice

2 9.2 You will hear a radio interview between Roddy and Katrina about a special kind of restaurant. For questions 1–7, choose the best answer (A, B or C).

1 What is the main purpose of *In the Dark*?
   A to raise money for charity
   B to improve understanding about the problems faced by the blind
   C to provide an unusual evening out

2 How successful has this restaurant concept been so far?
   A very
   B hardly
   C moderately

3 How are clients introduced to the dark?
   A They go straight through some curtains.
   B gradually
   C along a brightly-lit corridor

4 What can you take into the dining room?
   A mobile phones
   B keys
   C watches

5 How does Roddy think he would react in the restaurant?
   A He would be fine if he told himself not to panic.
   B He would only go if Katrina held his hand.
   C He couldn't stand it.

6 How did Katrina get on with the person who was sitting next to her?
   A Very well, after some initial embarrassment.
   B She never got to know him at all.
   C They recognised each other after the meal.

7 What did Katrina think of the food?
   A She'd go there again just for the food.
   B Her other senses compensated for her lack of sight.
   C It was hard to tell what she was eating.

3 What do you think of the *In the Dark* concept? Would you try one of these restaurants?

4 If you were going to open an unusual restaurant, what would it be? Work in pairs or groups. Discuss your ideas using these questions.

- What will the theme of the restaurant be?
- Where will it be? Where will people eat?
- Who will it appeal to?
- What will your speciality be?
- What music or entertainment will you have?
- What kind of atmosphere will you try to create?

KEY WORD *take*

5 **Match the sentence beginnings (a–e) with the endings (1–5).**

a If we take care of someone or something, *5*

b If we take something into account, *3*

c If we take advantage of someone or something, *2*

d If we take something for granted, *1*

e If we take the opportunity to do something, *4*

1 we only notice it when it is no longer there.

2 we exploit them to our benefit (often unfairly).

3 we include it in our consideration.

4 we take a chance which presents itself.

5 we look after them.

6 **Work in pairs. Use the expressions from exercise 5 to comment on these situations.**

1 When I lived at home, I never cooked a meal or ironed a shirt. My mum used to do everything. Now that I live on my own I really miss that!

2 Last year's holiday cost more than I had planned. I had forgotten to include the cost of petrol and motorway charges.

3 She isn't nice to her brother. She borrows money from him that she has no intention of paying back.

4 When I was in Paris on business I had an unexpected free afternoon so I visited the Louvre museum.

5 When I go away, my neighbour feeds my cat and waters the plants.

PHRASAL VERBS AND THEIR DIFFERENT MEANINGS

Often the same phrasal verb can have two or more very different meanings. Look at these examples:

*I'm afraid I can't come tomorrow. Can we **put** lunch **off** until next week?* (*put off* = postpone / delay)

*The kitchen was so dirty it **put** me **off** my food.* (*put off* = disgust)

*I played badly in the tennis match because the noise of the spectators **put** me **off**.* (*put off* = stop someone concentrating)

Remember to record new uses of phrasal verbs in your vocabulary notebook and learn them regularly.

7 **Work in pairs. Look at the pairs of sentences (1–3). Discuss the different meanings of the phrasal verbs in bold in each pair.**

1 a She **took off** her watch.

   b The idea has **taken off**.

2 a They have been able to **take on** some blind members of staff.

   b Sonya hasn't been afraid to **take on** the men at their own game.

3 a How's your new job? How are you **getting on**?

   b I couldn't **get on** the bus because it was so crowded.

USE OF ENGLISH key word transformation

EXAM SPOTLIGHT

PAPER 1, PART 4 Key word transformation

This part of Paper 1 focuses on grammar, vocabulary and collocation. Some of the areas that are commonly tested include reported speech and reporting verbs, the passive or causative *have*, gerund or infinitive, *prefer* and *rather*, sentence patterns with *too* and *enough* and prepositional phrases. Here are some examples:

1 'You should stop smoking, Rita,' her husband said.
   ADVISED
   Rita's husband <u>advised her to stop</u> smoking.

2 She managed to solve the puzzle.
   IN
   She <u>succeeded in solving</u> the puzzle.

8 **Complete the second sentence so that it has a similar meaning to the first sentence, using the word given. Do not change the word given. You must use between two and five words, including the word given.**

1 In the old days customers smoked in restaurants all the time.
   USED
   Customers always _____ in restaurants.

2 I'll never learn the art of eating with chopsticks.
   GET
   I'll _____ eating with chopsticks.

3 I think I'd prefer us to stay in and watch TV this evening.
   RATHER
   I _____ and watched TV this evening.

4 Shall we cook or shall we order a takeaway?
   RATHER
   Would you _____ ordered a takeaway?

5 They considered her age before making their final decision.
   ACCOUNT
   They _____ before making their final decision.

6 We enjoyed ourselves, even though the food was fairly awful.
   NEVERTHELESS
   The food was fairly awful; _____ good time.

7 They turned us away from the restaurant even though we had booked.
   FACT
   They turned us away _____ we had booked.

8 Don't assume that your parents will always be there for you.
   FOR
   Don't _____ granted.

WRITING a review (2)

EXAM SPOTLIGHT

PAPER 2, PART 2 Review

In Part 2 of the Writing paper you may have the chance to write a review about a place or event. You are always given a clear context, topic and purpose and an idea of the target reader. You should write your review in an appropriate style.

1 Work in pairs. What sort of places do you go to eat with your friends?

2 Lotti went to Da Guido's restaurant with her friend Giancarlo. Read her review and decide how many stars to give the restaurant for each category in the table.

* = terrible	**** = very good
** = poor	***** = excellent
*** = satisfactory	

Location	
Food	
Service	
Atmosphere	
Decoration	

Da Guido's pizzeria is hidden away in Verona's back streets. Even though it was a Tuesday evening in January there was a queue outside. Luckily, after a short wait we were at one of the long communal tables.

Not only is Guido's popular with young people, but it is also is an ideal place to experience a cosy Italian atmosphere. Another great thing is the décor: the walls are covered in autographed photographs of famous clients.

This pizzeria is famous for its thin crust pizzas cooked in a traditional oven, so I went for one with wild mushrooms and spicy sausage. It was delicious, but what I liked the best was their garlic bread.

As for the service, although it is friendly and efficient they don't like you to hang around. The desserts looked disappointing, so we decided to go somewhere else for an ice cream. No sooner had we told our waitress than she brought us the bill.

Overall I did enjoy the experience, but Guido's is not for you if you want a relaxed evening over a long meal. I'd recommend a trattoria instead.

3 **In a review, we may want to add emphasis. Find the emphatic sentences in the review that give the same information as in 1–6. Complete the sentence as in the review.**

1 It was a Tuesday evening in January but there was a queue outside.
Even though _____ .

2 It is popular with young people and a good place to experience an Italian atmosphere.
Not only _____ .

3 I liked their garlic bread the best.
What _____ .

4 The moment we told our waitress she brought us the bill.
No sooner _____ .

5 The service was friendly but they don't like you to hang around.
Although _____ .

6 I enjoyed the experience.
I _____ .

4 **What do you notice about the word order in the sentences beginning with *no sooner* and *not only*?**

▶ GRAMMAR REFERENCE (SECTION 10) **PAGE 200**

5 **Rewrite the sentences using the word in capitals.**

1 The food was ordinary. The wine was good.
ALTHOUGH
_____

2 The moment we finished the starter, the main course arrived.
NO SOONER
_____

3 It isn't cheap, but it is very good value for money.
EVEN THOUGH
_____

4 Judith told me about the restaurant.
IT WAS
_____

5 I loved the seafood.
WHAT
_____

6 I liked the location.
DID
_____

6 **Rewrite these sentences to add emphasis.**

1 They hadn't booked. They pushed their way to the front of the queue!
Although ☑, they were pushed to (handwritten)

2 Anna told me that the desserts weren't home-made.
_____

3 The second we sat down on the terrace it started to pour with rain.
_____

4 I was surprised that she didn't have any formal training as a cook.
_____

5 I enjoyed the live music.
_____

7 **Read the question from Paper 2, Part 2. Write your answer in 140–190 words. Use useful expressions from Lotti's review.**

Include the following information.
• where it is
• when you went
• what kind of people go there
• what the atmosphere is like
• what your favourite dishes are
• what the service is like
• concluding remarks

You see this announcement in your college magazine.

Reviews wanted: eating out

Do you have a favourite restaurant, or one that you would like to warn other people about?

Write a review of the restaurant, explaining what kind is it, and why you would recommend it or not recommend it to other people of your age.

The best reviews will be published in the magazine.

Write your review.

WRITING CHECKLIST

REVIEW

Did you:
• write between 140–190 words? ☐
• write about location, decoration, food, service and atmosphere? ☐ ☐
• use a range of vocabulary on the topic of restaurants? ☐
• use some of the ways of adding emphasis? ☐

WRITING GUIDE **PAGE 216**

VIDEO Oaxaca

1 **This photograph is from the Mexican state of Oaxaca. Imagine you work in the travel industry in Oaxaca. What adjectives would you use to describe this place and to convince people to visit Oaxaca?**

2 **Watch the video about Oaxaca. Tick ✓ the topics it describes.**

1 scenery ☐
2 cooking ☐
3 festivals ☐
4 architecture ☐
5 traditional dances ☐
6 theatre ☐

3 **Watch the video again and answer the questions.**

1 According to the narrator, what is a good way of keeping warm in winter?
2 What attracted Susana Trilling to Oaxaca and what does she do there?
3 How easy is it to make Oaxacan food?
4 What is the name of the sauce that accompanies most of the dishes?

5 Why is the *guelaguetza* important in Oaxacan culture?
6 What is special about some of the buildings in Oaxaca?

4 **The narrator uses lots of adjectives to say that something is 'nice' or 'good'. Complete these sentences with adjectives from the video.**

0 Oaxaca is famous for its traditions and its <u>fantastic</u> food.
1 You can enjoy its beautiful dances and its _____ streets and buildings.
2 When you come to Oaxaca, _____ colours and _____ smells are all around you.
3 They come here wanting to learn more about this _____ cuisine.
4 This _____ sauce is made from chilli peppers, spices and various other ingredients.
5 Many of the _____ buildings in the city are Mexican national treasures.
6 In the past, it was a government building. Today it has been transformed into a _____ luxury hotel.

5 Watch the video again and check your answers to exercise 4. Underline the stressed syllables in the adjectives.

6 Read the Ideas generator and do the task.

 I D E A S   G E N E R A T O R

USING A WIDE RANGE OF VOCABULARY

In the Speaking paper, you can receive higher marks for 'using a wide range of appropriate vocabulary'. This means that you need to use different ways of saying something by using synonyms.

For example, in this extract from a Speaking test, Enzo is saying what is good about his home town. Improve it by using alternative adjectives from exercise 4, or use your own ideas.

Enzo: 'Well, it is a nice town, we have lots of nice buildings and places to visit. Our food is very nice and you can have a nice time walking through the streets. The countryside is nice and you can have a nice view from the hills over the town.'

7 You work for the tourist office in your city or region. You want to convince tourists to visit. Prepare a short speech about why your city or region is a good place to visit.

8 Work in pairs. Make your speech to your partner. Sound enthusiastic and try to convince your partner by using powerful adjectives.

EXAM SPOTLIGHT

PAPER 4, PART 3 Collaborative task

In Part 3 of the Speaking test you are given a task which involves discussing and evaluating different options. At the end of the discussion, you have one minute to reach a decision. You will need to use convincing language and reach a decision through negotiation.

9 Read the Useful expressions box. Which expressions do you think are most useful for:
- asking for an opinion / suggestion?
- giving an opinion?
- acknowledging your partner's point of view?
- agreeing?
- making a decision?

USEFUL EXPRESSIONS

REACHING A DECISION THROUGH NEGOTIATION

So for our first choice, I think they should …
Do you agree?
I hear what you're saying, but …
That's a good point. I hadn't thought of that.
What do you think they should do?
Personally, I think …
I see what you mean.
OK, let's make that our first choice.
What about our second choice?
What do you think about …?
Well if … is our first choice, then this should be our second choice.
Yes I agree. I like that idea because …
Me too. So shall we go for that?
Yes, I think so.

10 Work in pairs. Read the interlocutor's instructions for Part 3 of the Speaking test and look at the spider diagram, then discuss the question.

I'd like you to imagine that your town is going to twin with another town in a different country. A group of people from that town are going to visit, and your town is organising some activities for them. Here are some ideas.

Talk to each other about why these activities would encourage the town to twin with yours.

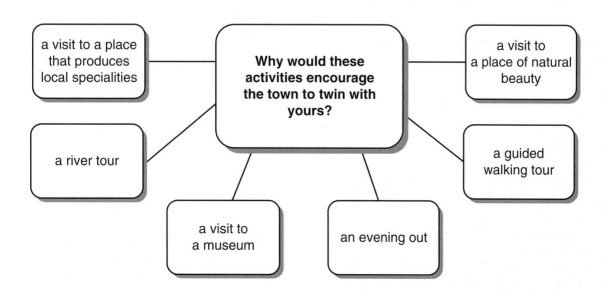

a visit to a place that produces local specialities

a river tour

Why would these activities encourage the town to twin with yours?

a visit to a museum

an evening out

a visit to a place of natural beauty

a guided walking tour

10 SHOPPING AND MONEY

1 The girls in the photo are 'window shopping'. Are you the type of person who likes window shopping? Do the quiz to find out more about your shopping habits. Compare your answers with your partner.

How well do you manage your money?

Are these statements true for you? Write 1, 2, 3, 4 or 5.
1 = disagree strongly, 2 = disagree, 3 = neither agree nor disagree, 4 = agree, 5 = agree strongly

I always decide a budget when I go shopping, and I make sure I stick to it. ☐

I always decide what I need to buy, and I don't buy anything else. ☐

I avoid buying things I don't really need just because they are a good bargain. ☐

I don't care about having the latest product as soon as it comes onto the market. ☐

I always research a product online to find out which is the best before I buy. ☐

2 Now turn to page 239 and read what your score says about your shopping habits.

VOCABULARY shopping and consumerism

3 Complete the sentences with the highlighted words from the information on page 239.

1 Look at this! If you buy two of these today you get a third one free. What a _____ !

2 She always wears the latest in designer footwear. If it hasn't got the _____ of one of the most famous _____ she isn't interested.

3 Normally I plan what I'm going to buy but yesterday I suddenly saw this, and without thinking bought it on a _____ . Now I'm not sure that I like it.

4 We have a _____ , so we know exactly how much we can spend each month and we can't go over it.

5 This was on _____ _____ for one week only. It had 50 per cent off, so I bought it!

6 He made a _____ with us that if we bought the car there and then, he'd give it a free service at the end of the first year.

7 I can give you a 10 per cent _____ if you pay for it in cash.

4 **Choose the correct word (in italics) to complete the sentences.**

1 More people than ever before are *on / in* debt.
2 I always try to stay *within / over* my weekly budget.
3 Lending money *to / from* friends often ends in tears.
4 Can I pay *by / in* cheque, or would you rather I paid *on / in* cash?
5 Excuse me, what's the *amount / price* of this shirt?
6 Do you know what he *cost / paid* for his car?
7 I'm *broken / broke*. Could you *borrow / lend* me some money until Friday?
8 How much did it *pay / cost* to have your hair done?
9 We couldn't *afford / pay* a new car, so we bought one second-hand.
10 He's so mean. He never *buys / pays* the drinks.
11 The *price / cost* of living has gone up since the euro.
12 Can you *pay for / pay* the taxi-driver? I don't have any cash.
13 He paid a high *price / cost* for his mistake.
14 They're crazy to *cost / spend* so much on their new kitchen.
15 They eventually agreed to *refund / retail* the money I had spent on the holiday.

5 **Match the sentence beginnings (1–10) with the endings (a–j).**

1 I can't be bothered to shop
2 I had lost the receipt, so they refused to take
3 They celebrated their engagement by splashing
4 You should set some money
5 When my brother left university he couldn't pay
6 When I saw what the bill came
7 If you can't afford to pay me
8 Lots of elderly people find it hard to get
9 Kids these days aren't prepared to save
10 I'd like to pay

a to, I almost fainted.
b off any of his student loan for three years.
c the dress back.
d this cheque into my account, please.
e around for the best price.
f by on a tiny pension.
g up for something they want.
h aside in case of emergencies.
i back, you shouldn't have borrowed the money.
j out on an expensive meal.

6 **Work in pairs. Ask and answer these questions.**

• Do you think it's a good idea to lend money to, or borrow money from, friends or family?
• Do you think it's important to set aside a bit of money every month? Why / Why not?

LISTENING money habits

7 🔘 **10.1 Listen to eight people talking about money and shopping and answer the questions.**

1 Which speakers are customers?
2 Which are selling something?
3 Which speaker is giving advice?

EXAM SPOTLIGHT

PAPER 3, PART 1 Multiple choice

In this part of the Listening test, you listen to eight extracts and answer a question for each. Read the tips and choose the correct options (in italics).

• Read each question and set of options carefully *before / after* you listen to each extract.
• After listening twice, if you still don't have an answer then *guess / don't guess*.
• Transfer your answers onto the answer sheet after you have heard all the extracts *once / twice*.

8 🔘 **10.1 Listen again and for questions 1–8, choose the best answer (A, B or C).**

1 You hear a woman talking about her shopping habits. What is her approach to shopping?
   A She knows exactly what she wants before she leaves the house.
   B She'll only buy something she really likes.
   C She can't leave the house without buying.
2 You hear a man talking about prices. How does he get the best bargains?
   A He looks for price information on the Internet.
   B He always uses loyalty cards and never shops around.
   C He tends to buy online rather than in a shop.
3 You hear a woman thinking of buying a second-hand car. What does she decide to do?
   A to buy it
   B to look at some other models
   C to negotiate the price with the salesman
4 You hear a sales assistant talking to some customers looking for furniture. Why can't he sell them the sofa and chairs they want?
   A They are all at another shop.
   B The manufacturer won't be producing any more until next year.
   C They don't have them in stock any longer.
5 You hear a salesperson talking to some customers. What is she explaining?
   A the policy on damaged goods
   B the policy on refunds
   C the policy on faulty goods
6 You hear a financial expert on the radio. What does he advise listeners to do?
   A Don't rush into starting a pension fund.
   B Only use your savings in a real emergency.
   C Keep setting some money aside.
7 You hear a woman talking about her holiday. What does she regret?
   A the hotel
   B the day she booked it
   C the destination
8 You hear a teenager describing his financial situation. What is he complaining about?
   A that his sister has a new bike
   B that his sister has lots of money
   C that his dad wants the money back

GRAMMAR conditionals

1 Look at these sentences from the listening exercise on page 101. Each sentence contains two clauses. What verb form is used in each clause?

1 If I suddenly **see** something I like, I either **buy** it or **come** back the following week with the money I need.
2 Maybe if he **reduced** the price, I **would be** interested.
3 If you**'d come** in last week, I **would have had** just what you were looking for.
4 If you **go** to the same shop every time, they**'ll** often **give** you a loyalty card.

2 Turn to the Grammar reference, page 195, and read the explanation of four types of conditional (zero, first, second and third). Then match the sentences in exercise 1 to the types of conditional.

Sentence 1: Conditional type _____
Sentence 2: Conditional type _____
Sentence 3: Conditional type _____
Sentence 4: Conditional type _____

3 Complete the sentences with the correct form of the verbs in brackets.

0 If you sign up today, you automatically *get* (get) the discount.
1 If you _____ (book) online, you'd probably have the ticket by Monday.
2 Would you mind if I _____ (bring) a friend with me?
3 He'll pass the exam if he _____ (revise) for it.
4 If I _____ (know) Rachel was going, I would have gone too.
5 If we continue to argue like this, we _____ (not come) to an agreement.
6 I _____ (take) it if you had sold me another at half price.
7 If I _____ (get) the house I want, I'll paint it yellow.
8 If I _____ (not hear) from you by eight o'clock, I'll assume you're coming.

4 Work in pairs. Make sentences about the things in the box using the second conditional. Start your sentences with *If we had …* or *If we didn't have …*.

> cars coffee computers free air travel
> mobile phones money satellites in space tax

> *If we didn't have cars, we wouldn't be able to travel very far.*

> *If we had more money, we could go on an exotic holiday.*

5 Look at the pictures showing events in the past. Write sentences in the third conditional.

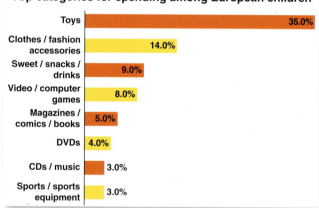

READING pocket money

6 Look at the chart and make a list of things you spend money on each week. What percentage do you spend on each thing? Compare your list with a partner.

Top categories for spending among European children

Category	Percentage
Toys	35.0%
Clothes / fashion accessories	14.0%
Sweet / snacks / drinks	9.0%
Video / computer games	8.0%
Magazines / comics / books	5.0%
DVDs	4.0%
CDs / music	3.0%
Sports / sports equipment	3.0%

PAPER 1, PART 7 Multiple matching

7 Read the article about four pocket money surveys. For questions 1–10 choose from the parts of the world (A–D).

Where in the world
1 do a lot of children receive an increase once a year? _____
2 are children increasingly making their own choices? _____
3 can you get more if you negotiate? _____
4 isn't pocket money spent straight away? _____
5 do boys have less money than girls? _____
6 might children not have the chance to spend pocket money how they like? _____
7 don't children view material items as the most important thing in their lives? _____
8 do many children not receive pocket money? _____
9 does a rise happen on a particular day? _____
10 do many children earn money by helping? _____

8 Work in pairs. Do you think children should have to earn their pocket money by doing jobs and working, or do you think they should be given it?

Pocket Money

Four different surveys into the spending habits of the young recently uncovered how attitudes to pocket money differ from country to country and continent to continent.

A INDIA

This first survey shows that almost half the children (about 49%) in India now enjoy pocket money, averaging about 132 rupees per month. Along with this increase in economic independence, the child has emerged as having a greater influence over parents in household purchases, and this increases as the child grows older. A higher percentage of older children also admitted buying items for the home and their own clothes. However, this independence need not be mistaken for growing disenchantment with family or home. Most children surveyed rated parents to be their most valued possessions, followed by toys and books at a distant second and third respectively.

B EUROPE

Six years old is the average age when a regular allowance begins in northern European countries (Belgium, Sweden, the Netherlands and Germany), and also in Spain. In the southern countries surveyed (France, Italy, Greece and Portugal), the average rises to seven years of age. Parents in northern Europe are more likely than other Europeans to buy kids the things they ask for. When given money for holidays and birthdays, most children (58%) choose to save it, though the survey found that many don't manage to keep their money for very long – 44% say they end up spending it within two months. When they part with their pocket money, kids across Europe are most likely to purchase toys and the latest electronic equipment. Clothing is next in importance, with sweets and electronic games also being important to them.

C THE UK

Teenagers in London are the pocket money winners, receiving an average of £11.71 per week, well above the UK average of £8.20, according to new research from the Halifax bank. Across the UK, girls come out on top with 12% more per week than boys. The main factor in how money is allocated comes down to age, but over three quarters of children get pocket money in return for doing jobs around the home: 31% clean the house, and 29% do the washing up. The basis for a raise in pocket money is varied but for many (39%) the increase usually occurs on a birthday. As to what the money is being spent on, nothing much has changed there from previous years – clothes, music, electronic games, mobile phones – but the biggest change has come in methods of spending, with more than half the children surveyed regularly purchasing goods online.

D CHINA AND JAPAN

Children in Japan have less money in their pockets than their counterparts in China, according to a survey by Japanese scholars. Chinese parents, it seems, are more casual in giving money to their children, though the children there have less control over the money given to them. For example, during the Chinese New Year, gifts of money from relatives to children are usually spent by their parents on education fees and textbooks. In Japan, students were found to have control over their own money while education fees were paid for by parents. Though Japanese parents are careful in giving money, they tend to give a fixed amount regularly and then don't say how it is to be spent, taking the view that children need to learn how to deal with money by themselves. In China the approach is to give money upon a child's request or wishes, but that the agreed amount is negotiated in return for parental influence over how it is eventually spent.

KEY WORD *if*

1 Work in pairs. Discuss what you think the person is thinking or saying in each picture. Use *if* in each situation.

a

b

c

d

e

f

2 Match these sentences with *if* to the six pictures.
1 I keep thinking, '**If only** I'd brought mine too'!
2 I wouldn't do that **if I were you**.
3 **I wonder if** she's ready yet?
4 **Do you mind if** he comes, too?
5 I'll buy it, **but only if** you let me have it for 9,000.
6 **What if** you tried doing it this way?

3 Match the sentences from exercise 2 to the functions (a–f).
a requesting _____
b expressing a condition _____
c suggesting _____
d expressing regret _____
e speculating _____
f giving advice _____

4 Work in pairs. Make sentences with *if* for each situation. Use the phrases in bold in exercise 2.
1 Speculate about what you might be doing in ten years' time.
2 Express regret about one thing you did when you were a child.
3 Your partner wants to go out at the weekend. Make a suggestion.
4 Your partner wants to borrow your car. Agree but express a condition.
5 Your teacher has given you lots of homework but you are really busy. Request help from your partner.
6 Give your partner a piece of advice your parents or grandparents used to give you.

5 ◉ 10.2 Sometimes you can replace *if* with other words. Listen to the recording. What do the speakers use instead of the words in bold in these sentences?
1 There's a 28-day money-back guarantee on all our products. **If** you bring it back within 28 days of purchase, that's fine. _____
2 Oh, that's also **if** you have the receipt with it, of course.
_____
3 There's short-term saving **if** you have an emergency.
_____
4 **If I had known,** I wouldn't have bought it in the first place.
_____

6 Read the sentences and decide which answer (A, B or C) best fits the gap.
1 We will give you your money back _____ you return it in good condition.
   A unless   B in case   C provided that
2 _____ you pay on time, I don't see a problem.
   A If only   B I wish   C As long as
3 _____ I seen him, I would have let him know.
   A Even if   B Had   C Should
4 _____ they arrive late, can you meet them?
   A Had   B Should   C No matter when
5 They're leaving at nine, _____ they've changed their minds since we spoke.
   A unless   B had   C only
6 Call to let me know. _____ I'll meet you at the shop.
   A Unless   B Otherwise   C Provided that

GRAMMAR mixed conditionals / *wish*

7 Look at these mixed conditional sentences. Which clause refers to the past? Which clause refers to the present situation?

   1 If I'd bought the lottery ticket, I'd be rich by now.
   2 If you had saved your money, you wouldn't be broke!

▶ GRAMMAR REFERENCE (SECTION 6.6)   **PAGE 195**

8 Look at the sentences in exercise 7 again. Which part of the sentence is from the second conditional? Which part is from the third conditional?

9 Complete these mixed conditionals with the correct form of the verbs.

   1 They would be on holiday by now, if the airport workers _____ (not / go) on strike.
   2 We _____ (be) on holiday now, if you _____ (remember) to book it!
   3 Mark would still be driving that car if he _____ (not catch) by the police for speeding.
   4 If I _____ (study) harder at school, I _____ (be) earning as much as my friends.
   5 If they'd worked for their pocket money when they were children, then they _____ (understand) the value of money.

10 Look at the sentences (a–e) and answer the questions (1–4).

   a I wish I could play the saxophone.
   b I wish I had the money for a new car.
   c I wish we hadn't bothered.
   d If only we hadn't gone on that holiday.
   e I wish you wouldn't spend all your money on toys.

   1 Which sentences refer to a situation in the present which is unlikely to change?
   2 Which sentences refer to a situation in the past which the speaker regrets?
   3 Which sentence refers to lack of ability?
   4 In sentence d, which words replace *wish*?

11 Work in pairs. Take turns reading out the first sentence and completing the second sentence so it has the same meaning.

   1 I wish I'd saved my money rather than spent it.
     If only …
   2 I wish I'd studied medicine when I was a student and become a doctor.
     If I'd studied … I would be … now.
   3 If you'd taken that job, we would have more money.
     I wish … so that …
   4 I regret not being able to speak Spanish.
     I wish …

▶ GRAMMAR REFERENCE (SECTION 18)   **PAGE 210**

SPEAKING regrets and suggestions

12 Work in pairs. Compare the two pictures below. They show people in two different situations where their travel plans have gone wrong.

   • How do they feel? What regrets do they have?
   • What suggestions would you make to help them?

USEFUL EXPRESSIONS

REGRETS

They probably wish they'd …
If only they'd …
If I were them I'd …
It'd be better if they'd …
What if they …?
If they had known …

WRITING an essay (3)

EXAM SPOTLIGHT

PAPER 2, PART 1

The Writing sections in Unit 1 on pages 16–17 and Unit 4 on pages 46–47 looked at two different ways to write the essay for Paper 2, Part 1. This writing section presents another way to plan, structure and write this kind of essay, using five paragraphs:

1 introduce the topic of the essay
2 present an argument for and against the first point
3 present an argument for and against the second point
4 present an argument for and against your own third point
5 give a conclusion with your final opinion

1 Work in pairs. Read the exam question and discuss what you would do if you needed money to start your own business.

2 There are different ways to introduce your essay. Look at these introductions from three essays. Match the techniques (a–c) to the introductions (1–3).

   a Express what many people think and explain your approach to the essay.

   b Restate the essay question.

   c Express the essay in the form of a question.

> **1** In order to set up a shop in the high street I would need quite a large amount of money. There are three good ways I could do this.

> **2** Many people think that successful shop owners must have always had a lot of money. However, many started their businesses with financial help. In this essay I am going to consider the arguments for and against the different ways to get this help.

> **3** I would like to set up my own shop in the high street but in order to do this I would need quite a large amount of money. The question is: what is the best way to get this money?

In your English class you have been talking about setting up your own business. Your teacher has asked you to write an essay for homework.

Write your essay using all the notes and give reasons for your point of view.

You want to set up a shop in your high street, but you need a large amount of money to do this. What is the best way to get the money?

Notes

Write about:

- borrowing the money from a bank
- asking family members for the money
- your own ideas

3 These sentences come from one essay. Match each sentence (1–3) with the contrasting argument (A–C) from the same paragraph.

> **1** On the one hand, a bank can lend you large amounts of money and it can give you advice on setting up a business.

> **2** The argument for taking the money from family is that the loan will be cheaper than from a bank.

> **3** One final approach might be to wait until I have saved up the money I need. The advantage is that I won't have any debt when the business starts.

> **A** The argument against is that the family might want to control part of the business, and it can be embarrassing to ask for money.

> **B** The big disadvantage is that it could take years to save the rest of the money.

> **C** On the other hand, it will charge you a lot of interest on the loan.

4 Read the extracts in exercise 3 again, and underline the useful expressions for introducing arguments for and against.

5 Here are three different conclusions to the essay question. Which opinion do you agree with? Discuss with your partner.

> **1** On balance, I think that I should borrow the money from the bank. That way I won't have family problems or have to wait. Also, they might be able to give me some useful advice.

> **2** So taking everything into consideration, I'm going to borrow the money from my family and offer to pay back the loan when I have the money. In my opinion, it's cheaper and I can trust my family.

> **3** In conclusion, I think I'm going to wait. I don't want to start a new business in debt to a bank or to a family member.

6 Read the conclusions in exercise 5 again, and underline useful language for introducing your conclusion and expressing your final opinion.

7 Read and answer the exam question. Use the structure of five paragraphs, with arguments for and against in paragraphs 2, 3 and 4.

In your English class you have been talking about different ways to pay for things. Now your teacher has asked you to write an essay.

Write an essay using all the notes and give reasons for your point of view.

Nowadays there are different ways to pay for things. What is the best way?

Notes

Write about:

- notes and coins
- credit cards
- your own ideas

WRITING CHECKLIST

ARTICLE

Does your essay:

- have five paragraphs? ☐
- have a clear introduction? ☐
- present arguments for and against in paragraphs 2, 3 and 4? ☐☐
- have a conclusion with a balanced opinion? ☐

REVIEW AND EXAM PRACTICE Units 9 and 10

1 For questions 1–8, read the text below and decide which answer (A, B, C or D) best fits each gap. There is an example at the beginning (0).

Shopping in front of a computer screen can certainly be faster and less stressful than looking for a (0) __C__ space and fighting your way through crowds of fellow shoppers. But is online shopping safer?

Some (1) _____ still seem to have some hesitation when it comes to online shopping, but authorities say it has in many ways become more secure than (2) _____ purchases at an actual store. After all, every time you use a credit card in a store you (3) _____ someone all your personal details and financial information.

Experts advise that online (4) _____ may now be better protected than traditional shoppers, especially if they follow a few useful tips. First of all, use one credit card for all (5) _____ , so if someone does use it illegally, only one card is affected.

Next, be careful that you are on the site of a real company. Some thieves have (6) _____ websites that look like the real thing just to get your information and money. The best way to check if a site is real is to (7) _____ for the 's', which stands for secure, in the 'https' part of the website address bar at the top of your browser.

The final thing you can do to (8) _____ safe while shopping online is to always make sure the computer being used has a firewall and up-to-date antivirus software.

0	A car	B large	C parking	D blank	5 A bargains	B offers	C purchases	D deliveries
1	A police	B sellers	C clients	D consumers	6 A visited	B set up	C bought	D accessed
2	A doing	B paying	C giving	D making	7 A look	B pay	C find	D click
3	A pay	B write	C give	D copy	8 A protect	B make	C have	D stay
4	A goods	B sites	C stores	D customers				

2 For questions 9–16, read the text below. Use the word in capitals at the end of some of the lines to form a word that fits in the space in the same line. There is an example at the beginning (0).

In recent years there have been lots of reports on the (0) _obesity_ epidemic affecting
many countries. Combine this with the (9) _____ increase in stress and
(10) _____ affecting the lives of workers and you have a medical time bomb.

OBESE
DRAMA
ANXIOUS

So where can we look to find effective (11) _____ to these problems? People
in the south-east Mediterranean are said to enjoy one of the (12) _____ diets
in the world. So one study set out to test this belief, with (13) _____ results.

SOLVE
HEALTH
REMARK

The researchers found that men from the island of Crete had the lowest blood
pressure and the lowest rates of cancer and heart attacks compared to men in six
other countries. Decades later, around half the Cretans were still (14) _____,
whereas there wasn't a single (15) _____ in the other countries. There may
be (16) _____ considerations to take into account, but changing to a
Mediterranean style diet could probably extend our lives.

LIVE
SURVIVE
GENE

3 For questions 17–22, complete the second sentence so that it has a similar meaning to the first sentence. Do not change the word given. Use between two and five words, including the word given. There is an example at the beginning (0).

---

0 How much money did you borrow from the bank?
LEND
How much money _did the bank lend you?_

17 I regret all the money I spent on my new car.
WISH
I _____ all that money on my new car.

18 If you change your mind, let me know.
SHOULD
Let me know _____ mind.

19 You can pay now if you have some proof of identity.
AS
You can pay now _____ proof of identity.

20 I didn't earn enough so now I'm poor.
WOULD
If I'd earned _____ rich now.

21 If they don't change their minds, we're meeting at two o'clock.
UNLESS
We're meeting at two o'clock _____ minds.

22 Is it OK if Molly joins us too?
MIND
Do _____ Molly joins us too?

---

4 You are going to read a magazine article about the type of food we might eat in the future. Six sentences have been removed from the article. Choose from the sentences A–G the one which fits each gap (23–28). There is one extra sentence which you do not need to use.

THE FUTURE OF FOOD

The World Health Organization believes that human demand for food will double in the next 40 years. The problem is that we're running out of space to grow it. The world population has risen above seven billion and more and more of us are eating meat. Most experts agree that we won't be able to produce enough meat and that we need alternatives.

One solution is to grow meat in a laboratory. Scientists have already grown a beef burger without the need to kill an animal. They can grow the meat from cells taken from a living animal. (23) _____ The real question here is whether consumers will want to eat artificial meat.

Of course, meat isn't the only option. Insects are full of protein and so offer a good alternative to beef and chicken. (24) _____ Many cultures already eat insects as part of their regular diet, but in those countries where insects are not considered 'normal food', a process of convincing people will need to begin. One research group at Wageningen University in the Netherlands is already looking into how people react to insects as food. (25) _____ In one study, nine out of ten people preferred meatballs made from insects to meatballs made from meat.

If you are a vegetarian, then you might think that the solution is obvious. Stop eating meat altogether. However, there is also a desperate need to increase the production of staple foods such as potatoes, rice and corn. There's also the danger of disease and the threat of losing entire crops. (26) _____ We'll need new varieties of crops in the future in order to prevent diseases as well as to guarantee enough food.

Lack of food is related to the lack of land space for growing, so some future projects might include using lakes and rivers. The company Aurora Algae is carrying out a water-based project in Western Australia. It's growing algae in around 40 ponds. Algae is a green plant. (27) _____ It also feeds on carbon dioxide. You can already buy green pasta with algae, and Aurora Algae is looking into more algae-based products, such as snack bars, and flour for baking.

So there's no shortage of ideas and plans for the future of food. In fact there are plenty of options. (28) _____ However, with rising populations, decreasing resources and rising costs of food, consumers may be left with little choice.

A It's an even bigger problem than scientists first thought.
B It's rich in protein, grows all year round and you can collect it every day.
C The science is at its early stages and the burger cost an estimated €250,000 to develop, but it is at least a possible option.
D The bigger problem seems to be convincing people to start eating food such as laboratory-produced meat, insects and algae.
E It has run insect tasting sessions with consumers and come up with some interesting results.
F They are also more efficient in terms of how much feed is needed to produce the same volume of protein, in comparison to chicken, for example.
G Potatoes are at particular risk.

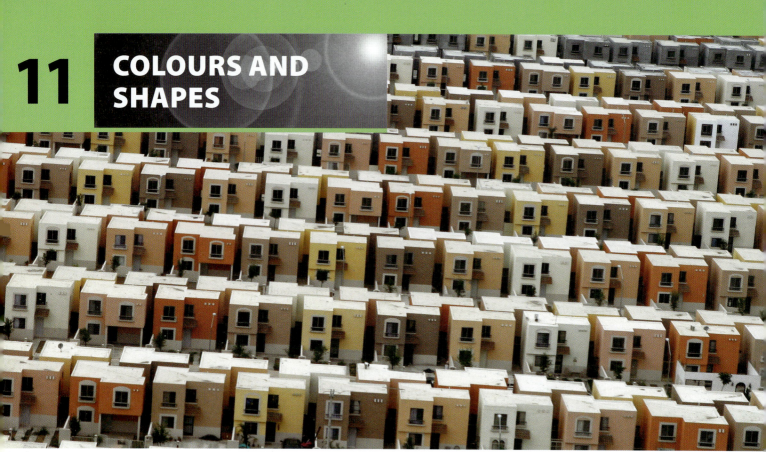

1 **Work in pairs. How would you describe the living spaces in the photo? Describe the colours, shapes and spaces you can see.**

2 **Do you think colour, shape and space affect our mood and feelings? How does the room you are in now make you feel? Tell your partner about your favourite room in your home. Why do you like it?**

LISTENING colour psychology

3 ⊙ **11.1 You will hear a TV interviewer talking to a home design expert. Complete the table. Which emotions are associated with the colours? Which rooms are they good for?**

Colour	It's good for …	because …
red		
purple		
pink		
blue		
yellow		
brown		
black		

PAPER 3, PART 4 Multiple choice

4 ⊙ **11.1 Listen again to the TV interview. For questions 1–7, choose the best answer (A, B or C).**

1 What do people usually consider first when they decorate?
   A the layout of the room
   B the contents of the room
   C the colour scheme of the room

2 What does Laurence say colour tells a visitor?
   A the mood we are in
   B the sort of person we are
   C whether they will like you

3 What does Laurence think about the choice of colours these days?
   A There aren't enough colours.
   B People still tend to prefer white or pale colours.
   C People find it hard to choose.

4 What don't people often think of when they choose a paint colour?
   A whether everything in the room will match
   B what colours are most exciting
   C that some colours are no longer fashionable

5 How do interior designers know what to do?
   A through following strict rules of design
   B through doing courses
   C through natural talent and experience

6 What kind of colours are best for rooms facing north?
   A dark   B pale   C bright

7 In order to learn more, Laurence suggests people
   A experiment with colour and do what feels right.
   B hire a decorator.
   C always follow the rules of colour.

VOCABULARY colour and decoration

5 Choose the correct word (in italics) to complete the sentences.

1 It's *a bit run down / well-cared for*, with paint falling off the walls and holes in the floor. Are you sure you want to buy it?

2 The kitchen in this London house is *north- / south*-facing, which means you get plenty of sun during the day.

3 You get more space living in a *suburban / terraced* house but I'd miss living in the city centre.

4 I love *pale / strong* colours like red and bright orange. I can't see the point of painting a room if you don't notice the colour.

5 My grandmother's house is one of those old-fashioned cottages with a *cosy / impersonal* sitting room and a fireplace.

6 That's a *cheerful / dreary*-looking room. Don't you find the dark colours a bit depressing?

7 The walls in this room are rather *bare / cluttered*. We could put some pictures up to make it feel more homely.

6 Look at the words in italics in exercise 5. Decide what they describe about a place, and write them in the correct column in the table.

Colour	Style / appearance	Type / position
pale	a bit run down	suburban

7 Add two more adjectives to each category. Compare your ideas with a partner.

8 Replace the phrasal verbs in bold in the sentences with a verb or verb phrase in the box.

> be (more) visible   combine   continue
> make light and cheerful   match   redecorate
> select   not care for (appearance)   transform

1 The dining room is looking a bit dreary and gloomy. Let's **do** it **up** with something more bright and cheerful. _____

2 This old farmhouse is a bit run down because the previous owners **let** it **go,** but with a bit of paint, it'll be fine. _____

3 That's a great job you're doing on that bathroom floor. **Keep up** the good work! _____

4 You need red and yellow and if you **mix** them **up** well, you should get a nice bright orange for the lounge that will **go with** the sofa. _____

5 Can you come with me on Saturday to **pick out** which wallpaper we're having for the hallway? _____

6 The portrait over the fireplace would probably **stand out** more if the walls weren't such a strong colour. _____

7 Do you ever watch that TV show, where they take some old shed or barn and somehow **turn** it **into** the most amazing house? _____

8 A lemon colour would probably **brighten up** the kitchen. _____

9 Work in pairs. You have just bought the apartment shown in this plan. It's very neglected, with dreary old wallpaper. Discuss each room and decide what colours you would use.

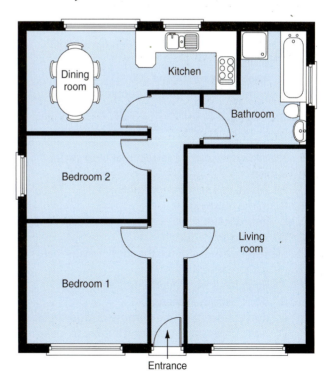

10 Now work with another pair and compare your ideas. Give reasons for your choice.

READING crop circles

1 Look at the photo of the crop circle in the article. How do you think it was made? Which of these shapes can you see in it?

circle   cross   hexagon   square   star   swirl   triangle

2 Read the article and answer the questions.

1 In the article, what are some of the reasons people have given for crop circles?
2 Do you have similar unexplained phenomena in your country?

PAPER 1, PART 5 Multiple choice

3 For questions 1–6, choose the answer (A, B, C or D) which you think fits best according to the text.

1 This is the first time that a crop circle
   A of this kind has appeared anywhere.
   B has appeared in Oxfordshire.
   C has been found in England.
   D has been made in a corn field.

2 Every time crop circles appear
   A you only find them a long way into the countryside.
   B people see an unidentified flying object in the sky.
   C people either think they are real or fake.
   D the majority of people say they are designed to deceive.

3 The new crop circle is special because
   A it has attracted more people than any previous crop circle.
   B it has an extra dimension.
   C it is only visible from the air.
   D it's the largest circle ever found in a field.

4 Crop circles
   A appeared even before 800 AD.
   B were created to protect people from evil.
   C only used to appear as triangles.
   D have appeared in many designs over the centuries.

5 Nowadays we can be certain that crop circles appear
   A where you see strange lights.
   B in the morning.
   C near ancient sites.
   D around the world.

6 Steve disagrees with the theories of many local people because they
   A don't have any evidence for their ideas.
   B don't believe in aliens.
   C don't understand the purpose of crop circles.
   D don't understand how long it takes to make a crop circle.

4 Match the words in bold in the text to these definitions.

1 a plan (or trick) to deceive someone _____
2 the distance across a circle _____
3 area where dead people were placed (from long ago) _____
4 cause the start of something _____
5 complicated, with lots of small pieces _____
6 things that are real but also especially unusual and interesting _____
7 impossible to explain by science or known fact

_____
8 rotate quickly, twisting and turning _____

5 Look at these photographs. They show three famous hoaxes. What do you think the hoax is in each case? Why do you think people believe in these kinds of unnatural phenomena?

WORLD'S FIRST 3-D CROP CIRCLE FOUND IN FIELD

The world's first three-dimensional crop circle has been discovered deep in the heart of the English countryside, near the village of Ashbury in Oxfordshire. This latest event has **sparked off** the start of the crop circle season, with enthusiasts driving all over the countryside in search of these natural – or unnatural – **phenomena**. Along with the believers at this time of year come an equal number of sceptics and people who think they are created as jokes. So, is this new crop circle another example of an artistic **hoax**, or is it really evidence of the **paranormal**? Perhaps it's a message left by aliens in a spaceship, the footprint of a giant animal or even some sort of communication from another time?

The new circle was only spotted last week by a pilot in a field in the county of Oxfordshire. From the air it was difficult to miss with it measuring over 100 metres in **diameter**. Within hours the news of the image had attracted local people, crop circle spotters and journalists from around the country. Steve Alexander, a crop circle photographer for more than 15 years, said, 'We have not seen anything like it before. It is the first of its kind and is a very, very powerful thing to look at. The crop circle community is very excited about this event.'

In the past crop circles have come in all shapes and sizes. Traditionally, there is one large circle with patterns inside such as triangles or squares, but the use of three-dimensional cubes in a corn circle has never been seen before. The first written recording of the crop circle phenomenon dates back to about 800AD, when they began appearing in fields in France. The bishop of Lyon was convinced that local people were worshipping the devil because strange circles regularly appeared in the crops, and so he tried to put a stop to the practice.

However, they have continued to reappear throughout history in many varied shapes and sizes. Early accounts describe how they always show up near to sites of historical importance such as **burial grounds** or places of worship. In the modern world, some crop circle specialists say that this is still the case, but that we no longer know where many ancient and important sites are. Others say that the appearance of similar circles made in snow and in sandy deserts suggest that the circles are not necessarily connected with the dead or the religious. Instead they would say the numerous worldwide sightings, including circles in Australia, Brazil and the USA, are the leftovers from alien spacecraft, since many circles appear the morning after a UFO sighting or when 'strange lights' have been seen at night in the sky.

Even though some local people in Ashbury reported strange noises on the night the crop circle appeared, and one person out walking their dog said they saw lights in the sky above the field, most residents are already calling their 3-D circle a hoax. A popular theory also gaining support is that a helicopter from a nearby base flew close to the ground and the **swirling** air from its rotor-blades flattened the corn. But Steve Alexander questions all these local doubts. 'How could somebody create such an **intricate** design overnight? They would have seven hours of darkness to cut it in the wheat and such a formation would be impossible to create in such a small space of time.'

KEY WORD *seem*

6 These four sentences describe the first photograph. Replace the words in bold with these words.

I'm unsure	appears	appears to be	I'm fairly certain

1 The small figure in this picture **seems** to have wings. _____
2 The girl **seems** happy. She isn't scared. _____
3 **It seems to me that** it's a clever hoax. _____
4 **I can't seem to tell** what kind of creature it is. _____

7 Work in pairs. Take turns to describe the other two pictures. Use some of the expressions with *seem*.

GRAMMAR modal verbs for guessing, speculating and deducing

1 Work in pairs. Does this photo seem real to you? What do you think it is? Have you or anyone you know ever seen anything like this?

2 Read the comments about the photo. Which comments talk about it in the present? Which in the past? Which comments in each pair are more certain?

1   a   It could be a UFO but maybe it's a cloud.
    b   That must be a cloud. It can't be an alien spaceship because they don't exist!
2   a   The photograph was taken last week so it couldn't have been a cloud. We had blue skies and sunshine all week.
    b   The photograph isn't very clear so I think it might have been a clever hoax by the photographer.

MODAL VERBS FOR SPECULATING AND DEDUCING

For speculating, guessing or discussing possibilities:

• about the present, use *could / might / may be*
• about the past, use *could / might / may have* + past participle.

For making deductions which you are very certain of:

• about the present, use *must be / can't be*
• about the past, use *must / can't / couldn't have* + past participle.

PAPER 1, PART 4   Key word transformation

3 Complete the second sentence so that it has a similar meaning to the first sentence, using the modal verb given. Do not change the words given. You must use between two and five words only.

1   I'm certain it isn't a hoax because the marks look so real.
    CAN'T
    It _____ a hoax because the marks look so real.
2   I think it's possibly my mother on the phone.
    MIGHT
    It _____ on the phone.
3   She's late – it's highly likely that's she's been delayed by the traffic.
    MUST
    She's late – _____ by the traffic.
4   Maybe the burglar used that window to get in.
    MAY
    The burglar _____ window to get in.
5   It wasn't a human because the footprint belongs to an animal.
    COULDN'T
    It _____ a human because the footprint belongs to an animal.

LISTENING out of the blue

EXAM SPOTLIGHT

PAPER 3, PART 2   Sentence completion

Before listening
• Read all ten sentences.
• Try to predict what kind of information you need to listen for.
• Note that the words in the sentences are not always the same as in the listening, BUT the missing words ARE from the listening.

While listening for the first time
• Write in the answers you can.
• Leave an answer if you don't hear it and move on to the next question. (You'll have another chance to listen.)

While listening for the second time
• Check any answers from the first listening.
• Try to fill any remaining gaps.

After listening
• Check your answers for spelling or any other mistakes.
• Transfer your answers on to the answer sheet.

4 ⊙ 11.2 **You will hear a police officer telling a story about a strange boy and a UFO. Listen twice and complete the sentences.**

The police officer was supposed to have finished (1) _____ .
She thought the odd-looking boy was no more than (2) _____ .
The boy had been found wandering down a lane about ten miles (3) _____ .
She thought that someone would come for him (4) _____ .
She was surprised because the boy was (5) _____ .
The boy's badge was made from metal and was (6) _____ in shape.
Later on she was on her way home in her police car when she thought a car was driving (7) _____ her.
The number of lights on the UFO grew and then they (8) _____ .
The base of the UFO was smooth and reflective like (9) _____ .
Then she saw the triangular shape for the (10) _____ that day.

VOCABULARY describing objects

5 **Read these sentences from the listening. Match the adjectives in bold to the categories in the table.**

a Someone brought in an **odd-looking, small** boy.

b He had a **triangular, metal** badge on his jumper.

c It had a **smooth, round** base like a mirror.

d There was a **beautiful, orange** light.

ORDER OF ADJECTIVES

opinion	size	age	texture	shape	colour	material

▶ GRAMMAR REFERENCE (SECTION 1.2) **PAGE 190**

6 **Rewrite the sentences with the adjectives in italics in the best order.**

1 We saw a *smooth / metal / long* object in the sky.

2 On the farm in winter, he would always wear a(n) *green / ancient* army overcoat that had belonged to his father, and *rubber / green* boots.

3 My uncle always used an *iron / old / enormous* frying pan.

4 They brought in a *rectangular / wooden / mysterious* box.

5 Their offices are in a *modern / glass / tall* building.

6 She turned up in a *bright / gorgeous / red* sports car.

AVOIDING TOO MANY ADJECTIVES

We can avoid having too many adjectives before a noun by transferring information elsewhere.
We saw a long, thin, silver, metal object in the sky. =
The silver object in the sky was made of metal and was sort of long and thin.

7 **What changes can you make to sentences 2–6 in exercise 6 to avoid having too many adjectives before the noun?**

8 **Write the adjectives formed from these nouns.**

1 circle _circular_

2 colour _____

3 depth _____

4 hardness _____

5 height _____

6 length _____

7 metal _____

8 softness _____

9 sphere _____

10 triangle _____

11 width _____

12 wood _____

PAPER 4, PART 2 Individual long turn

In this part of the *First* Speaking test, you need to compare two photos. If you don't know the name for an important object in the picture then you can describe what it is like, or how it is used, with phrases such as *It's a kind of / sort of …* or *It's used for … +-ing*.

9 **What objects are being described here?**

> It normally comes in a clear, round roll. It's **useful stuff for** sticking things together.

> You see them in the sky on windy days. They're **sort of** colourful, triangular shapes. You can also have **square ones.**

> It's **made of** leather and is **used in** all sorts of sports. It's usually round.

10 **Look at the photos and describe the objects. Use the words in bold in exercise 9. Do not say the name of the object. Can your partner guess which picture you are describing?**

1

2

3

4

5

6

DESCRIBING OBJECTS

It's made of …
It's kind of / sort of …
It's a thing / stuff for …+ noun or -ing verb
It's normally used for / in …+ noun or -ing verb
It's useful for …+ noun or -ing verb
It's used by (people) to (+ infinitive) / for …+ noun or -ing verb

WRITING an email

1 **Read the three emails. What is the relationship between Michelle and Yvonne? How formal is the language?**

Hi Michelle,

Hope you're well. <u>Just to let you know</u> that <u>there's a sale until the end of the week at Shoeshine</u>. It's that shop at the far end of High Street. Do you know the one? I picked up two pairs of shoes for work at half price. I couldn't resist a pair of high heels, too. <u>They're plastic, pink and the heels are 10 cm high</u> – just right for our holiday in Ibiza next month!

Anyway, <u>you should</u> get down there before they sell out.

All the best,

Yvonne

Hi Yvonne,

<u>Thanks</u> for letting me know about the sale, but I've got some good news and some bad news. <u>The good news is that</u> I've been offered a promotion. <u>The bad news is that</u> they want me to do three weeks' training next month, so <u>I'm sorry, but</u> I won't be able to go on holiday at that time.

<u>Is it OK</u> if we go the following month? Would that work for you?

Tell me what you think.

Michelle

Hi Michelle,

No problem. Don't worry. Congratulations on the new job!

<u>Why don't we</u> meet at the weekend and you can tell me all about it? <u>Would you like to</u> have dinner at my place? We can eat and talk about other possibilities for the holiday.

<u>See you soon,</u>

Yvonne

---

2 **Find the underlined expressions in the emails to match functions a–l.**

a Give reason for writing <u>*Just to let you know that*</u>
b Apologise _____
c Give good news _____
d Offer _____
e Recommend _____
f Suggest _____
g Give bad news _____
h Thank _____
i Request _____
j Say when and where _____
k Give details _____
l End email _____

3 **Match these expressions to the functions (a–l) in exercise 2.**

1 I'm afraid … _____
2 How about …? _____
3 I'm so grateful that … _____
4 I'm emailing you to … _____
5 Can you help …? _____
6 Unfortunately … _____
7 You ought to go … _____
8 There are … _____
9 It starts at 8 at the … _____
10 Look forward to seeing you. _____
11 I'm so happy because … _____
12 Can I help …? _____

4 Work in pairs. Practise writing very short informal emails to each other. Follow the flowchart below. Write your first email and swap it with your partner, then write the next email and swap again. Continue until the end of the flowchart.

Give details of something you have just bought. Recommend the shop to a friend.

Thank your friend. Suggest you meet this weekend.

Give bad news. Say sorry. Explain why you can't.

Offer to cook dinner instead next week.

Thank your friend. Offer to bring something to eat.

Request your friend brings something. Say when.

Confirm details. End email.

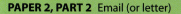

EXAM SPOTLIGHT

PAPER 2, PART 2 Email (or letter)

In Part 2 of Paper 2 you might write an email or letter. Read the context in the question carefully to help you decide on the level of formality that you need to use in your reply.

When you reply to a short email or letter from a friend you can use less formal language.

Other types of correspondence such as the letter of application on page 214 of the Writing guide use more formal language.

5 Read the exam question and write your email in 140–190 words in an appropriate style. Use the useful expressions from the box.

You have received this email from your epal Sara.

From: Sara

Subject: school project

I need your help! I'm doing a school project about life in another country and we have to write a profile of one person.

First, we have to describe the kind of place they live in. Then, we have to describe one personal object that belongs to the person and say why it's important. Can you tell me about your home and one important object?

Thanks

Sara

Write your email.

---

6 Use the checklist to check your answer.

7 Swap emails with your partner and use the checklist to comment on your partner's email.

WRITING CHECKLIST

WRITING AN EMAIL

Did you:
- use less formal language? ☐
- start and end the email appropriately? ☐
- describe the place you live? ☐
- describe a personal belonging? ☐
- use between 140-190 words? ☐

WRITING GUIDE **PAGE 215**

USEFUL EXPRESSIONS

INFORMAL EMAIL

Hi / Hello
Just to let you know that…
I'm emailing you to…
I'm afraid that…
Unfortunately…
Can I ? / Could you… ?
Is it OK if… ?
You should / ought to…
Can I / Could you…
Would you like to… ?
Why don't we… ?
How about… ?
See you soon.
Bye for now.
All the best / best wishes.

GLOSSARY

archaeologist: someone who studies ancient remains
timber: wood
bury: put something in the ground (often a body)
burial: noun from the verb *bury*
cemetery: a place where dead people are buried
cremate: burn the dead body of a person

VIDEO secrets of Stonehenge

1 Look at this photo of the ancient site Stonehenge. Have you ever heard of it? What do you think it might have been used for?

2 Over the centuries, there have been a number of different theories about Stonehenge. Here are three well-known theories. Which do you think sounds most likely? Why?

3 Watch the video. Which of the three theories does it tell us about? What evidence is given that supports the theory?

Theory 1: There were lots of burial sites around Stonehenge, so it might have been a site for people to visit with medical problems. Perhaps people believed the site had special powers and could help them.

Theory 2: Ancient people could have put the stones in circles to line them up with the movement of the sun, moon and stars during different parts of the year. So Stonehenge might be a kind of giant clock or calendar.

Theory 3: The stones might have been placed to represent the homes of the people who built Stonehenge. They would have lived in houses made of timber, but they wanted permanent homes made of stone for their dead relatives.

4 **Watch the video again. For questions 1–5, choose the best answer (A, B or C).**

1 What does the narrator say about Stonehenge in the introduction?
   A It might not be as old as people think.
   B It has hardly changed at all in its history.
   C It almost seems like Stonehenge has stood on Salisbury Plain forever.

2 What is the main starting point for Michael Parker Pearson's theory?
   A That there were other buildings in the area near Stonehenge.
   B That people built Stonehenge a long distance from their houses because of the dead.
   C That people built it as a monument to their gods.

3 What evidence does Pearson have that people lived near Stonehenge?
   A The stones at Stonehenge come from another place called Durrington Walls.
   B He found evidence of old houses made of timber in Durrington Walls.
   C There was old timber beneath the stones at Stonehenge.

4 What does Pearson think the main purpose of Stonehenge was?
   A As a site for burials and cremations.
   B As a site for celebration.
   C As a site for religious festivals.

5 How does the narrator feel about Pearson's theory in comparison to other theories about Stonehenge?
   A He is critical of it.
   B He is positive about it.
   C He doesn't say.

5 **Read the Ideas generator box. Work in pairs. Look at the Paper 4, Part 4 topics in the bullet points, and the phrases in the table. Make sentences on the topics using the phrases, and giving a reason and an example.**

• Computer games are bad for you.
• Life was easier for our grandparents.
• It's better to live in the countryside than the city.
• Schools should teach students about working life.
• Food was more natural and better for us in the past.

I (don't) think …		Take …, for instance.
I agree that …		For example …
I don't agree that …	because …	Let me give you an example.
I'm sure that …		
I'm not sure that …		

I agree that computer games are bad for you, because people spend too long sitting playing at their computer, which is very unhealthy. Take my brother, for instance. He …

IDEAS GENERATOR

GIVING SUPPORTING REASONS AND EVIDENCE FOR YOUR OPINIONS

In Parts 3 and 4 of the *First* Speaking paper, you have to give your opinion on different topics. In addition to this, you should justify your opinions by giving supporting reasons, evidence and real examples.

Remember, when your partner is talking don't 'switch off' even if it isn't your turn to speak.

Show the examiners that you are actively listening by:
– sitting forward and paying attention
– smiling and nodding
– making encouraging sounds and comments.

6 **Work in pairs. Discuss these questions from Part 4 of the *First* Speaking exam. Remember to support your opinions with reasons, evidence and real examples where possible.**

• Do you think it's important to preserve old and ancient places in our towns and cities? (Why? / Why not?)
• Is it a good idea for young people to learn about their local history at school or should they spend more time on other subjects?
• Do you think most tourists to your region are interested in visiting historical places? (Why? / Why not?)
• What are the most important attractions and activities to think about when trying to encourage tourists to visit your region?

USEFUL EXPRESSIONS

EXPRESSING AND JUSTIFYING YOUR OPINION

Expressing your opinion
In my opinion …
I tend to think that …
I'm certain that …
I'm sure / not sure that …
It seems likely that …
I agree / don't agree that …

Giving examples
I can give you a good example: …
Take … , for instance.
Let me give you an example.

Giving supporting evidence
This is supported by …
There's evidence that …
My reason for this is …

12 NATURE AND ENERGY

1 Work in pairs. Discuss the questions.

1 How does the weather in the photo make you feel?
2 How would you describe the climate in your part of the world?
3 How does the weather affect the character of people in your country?

VOCABULARY weather and disasters

2 Choose the correct word (in italics) to complete the sentences.

1 The continental *climate / weather* has typically short cold winters and long hot summers.
2 London used to be famous for its thick *fog / mist*.
3 The weather *prediction / forecast* is good, so we can go ahead with the picnic.
4 Be careful how you drive. The roads are *frozen / icy*.
5 A light *gale / breeze* provides the ideal conditions for windsurfing.
6 It's horrible when it *drizzles / dribbles* all day. I'd rather it *poured / soaked* for an hour.
7 Can you hear the *lightning / thunder*? I think there's a *storm / tempest* coming.
8 The *snow / hail* was so strong that it damaged the paintwork on our car.
9 It's *sunny / shining* today; let's go to the beach.
10 The *raining / rainy* season usually begins in May in my country.

3 Match descriptions 1–8 to the natural disasters in the box.

drought	earthquake	famine	flood
meteorite	tidal wave	tornado	volcanic eruption

1 People could see the lava flowing down the mountainside towards the town. _____
2 After eight days of constant rain, the houses near the river were under a metre of water. _____
3 We could see it twisting and turning across the plain, lifting and dropping houses and cars as if they were children's toys. _____
4 First of all, the sea went out, then we saw a huge wall of water coming towards the beach and we ran for our lives. _____
5 We were having coffee when the whole building started to shake and our cups and saucers all rattled. It was terrifying. _____
6 The harvest has failed again and people will die from starvation unless something is done to help them quickly. _____
7 It is expected to pass by the earth only three million miles away – a near miss in scientific terms. _____
8 The sight in front of us is terrible. It hasn't rained here for three years; the earth is completely dry and cracked and nothing grows. _____

4 Choose the correct word (in italics) to complete the sentences.

1 A passer-by *raised / rose* the alarm and called the fire brigade.
2 Millions of olive trees were *lost / disappeared* during the fire.
3 Sea temperatures have *raised / risen* because of greenhouse gases.
4 Comparatively few people *died / killed* in the last epidemic.
5 The island completely *lost / vanished* after the eruption.
6 More people are *killed / died* in domestic accidents than on the road.
7 This incident *rises / raises* some important issues.
8 Several new difficulties have *arisen / risen* as a result of the investigation.

▶ GRAMMAR REFERENCE (SECTION 17.2) **PAGE 210**

5 Work in pairs. Is your region or country vulnerable to natural disasters? What natural disasters has it had in the past?

> In 1755, Lisbon was destroyed by an earthquake. Nowadays, in Portugal, we have big problems with forest fires.

LISTENING natural disasters

Paper 3, Part 3 Multiple matching

6 ⦿ **12.1 You will hear five experts talking about different events in the Earth's history. Choose from the list (A–H) what each speaker talks about. There are three extra letters which you do not need to use.**

A a theory which is probably wrong
B a prediction that was incorrect
C how a region became less fertile
D the dangers of nuclear accidents
E a rare event on London's river
F people who failed to take notice of warnings
G how an island was formed
H the threat of global warming

Speaker 1 _____
Speaker 2 _____
Speaker 3 _____
Speaker 4 _____
Speaker 5 _____

7 ⦿ **12.1 Listen again and put the events described by speakers 1–5 in order, from the most recent (1) to the furthest in the past (5).**

Speaker 1 _____
Speaker 2 _____
Speaker 3 _____
Speaker 4 _____
Speaker 5 _____

8 Work in pairs. Imagine you could go back in time. Which of the events would you most like to have witnessed (from a safe distance, of course)?

SPEAKING criticising and complaining

9 Read the sentences (a–d) and the words in bold. Answer the questions (1–3).

a She **keeps on** taking my umbrella without asking!
b **Why on earth** didn't you tell me about the storm warning?
c You **should have closed** the sunroof in the car.
d He's **always complaining** about the weather, but he lives in a perfect climate.

1 Which sentences criticise someone for something they didn't do?
2 Which sentences complain about annoying behaviour?
3 Which words would be stressed?

10 Turn to audioscript 12.1 on page 229 and underline other examples of the forms used in a–d.

11 Work in pairs. Javier and Peter are flatmates, classmates and friends. Decide what they would say to each other in the following situations.

1 Peter forgot to close the window when he went out. The neighbour's cat has come into the flat and destroyed the curtains.
2 When Javier comes back from the supermarket, Peter notices that they need coffee and orange juice and Javier didn't buy any.
3 Javier is annoyed because Peter always borrows his dictionary without asking him first.
4 Peter forgot to tell Javier that they were having an English vocabulary test at school. Javier has got a very bad mark in the test.

12 Work in pairs and act out their conversation.

READING weather forecasts

1 **Look at the photos. How do these different ways of predicting the weather work? Do you know any folk methods or traditional sayings for predicting the weather?**

PAPER 1, PART 6 Gapped text

2 **You are going to read an article by a journalist who has been trying a different job every month. Six sentences have been removed from the article. Choose from the sentences (A–G) the one which fits each gap (1–6). There is one extra sentence which you do not need to use.**

A As the song says, 'You don't need a weatherman to know which way the wind blows.'

B To begin with, we practised with those old-fashioned weather maps, with shapes showing clouds and the sun and so on.

C I'd always treated the business of predicting the weather as a bit of a joke, and weather forecasters as figures of fun.

D Forecasting isn't just there to know if we should get the barbecue out, however; it has a deeply serious side too.

E Nevertheless, Francesca accepted our ignorance with good humour before swiftly de-mystifying the basics.

F I think it must have been a combination of the heat and the stress.

G Even as he stood there calling the poor man all the names he could think of, I recall thinking it was rather unfair.

3 **Work in pairs. What dream job would you like to try? Compare your ideas and discuss what you think would be the advantages and disadvantages of your dream jobs.**

GRAMMAR contrast and concession

4 **Complete these sentences from the article.**

1 _____ forecasters get it right 95 per cent of the time, it's the other 5 per cent that people remember.

2 They kept falling off, _____ the magnets on the back.

3 _____ fully prepared, the first time I tried I completely dried up.

4 _____ the studios are air-conditioned, the make-up and the lights make you feel really hot.

5 The end result wasn't too embarrassing; _____ , I did look rather jerky and wooden.

6 We started with a short quiz that showed just how little everyone knew. _____ , Francesca accepted our ignorance with good humour …

5 **Look at the sentences in exercise 4 again and answer the questions.**

1 In sentences 1–4, which words of contrast and concession are followed by:
   a a gerund?   b a noun?   c a verb phrase?

2 What is the position of the words of contrast and concession in sentences 5 and 6?

▶ GRAMMAR REFERENCE (SECTION 6.7) **PAGE 196**

6 **Rewrite each pair of sentences as one sentence, using words of concession or contrast from exercise 4. There are several possibilities for each pair.**

1 The pine cone was open. It rained heavily for the rest of the day.

2 She knew nothing about the weather. She learnt the basics quickly.

3 The weatherman had always had an excellent reputation. He lost it overnight.

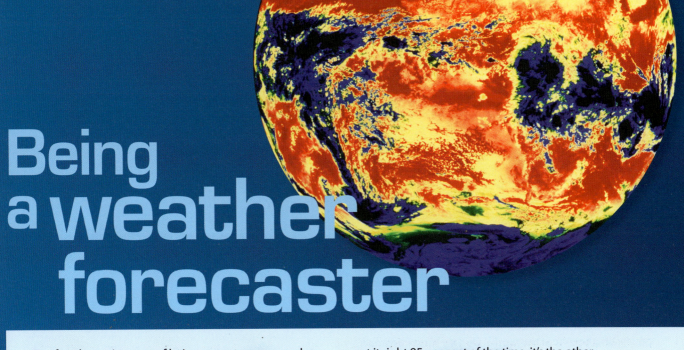

Being a weather forecaster

After the excitement of being a stuntwoman, and a DJ to hundreds of clubbers in Marbella, my latest assignment, to present the weather on TV, came as a big disappointment. (1) _____ Childhood memories include my dad examining the wreckage of our garden fence after the worst storm in decades – an event that the country's most eminent weatherman had totally failed to predict. (2) _____ After all, even if Dad had known about the coming storm, he wouldn't have been able to do anything about it.

The night before I had to show up at the weather centre, I thought I'd jot down what I knew about predicting, or 'forecasting' the weather. My list was pathetically short. It amounted to a couple of traditional sayings of the 'red skies at night and shepherds' variety, and vague primary school memories to do with pine cones and seaweed. Not exactly rocket science!

In the end, I gave up, hoping that people wouldn't be too appalled by my lack of knowledge. Francesca Cross, the head of the training centre and our course leader, proved unshockable. She had joined the weather centre having studied geography and statistics. At the centre she then learnt the secrets of forecasting. Eventually she moved over to presenting. There were half a dozen other people from local radio and TV stations. We started with a short quiz that showed just how little everyone knew. (3) _____ By the end of the morning I knew an isobar from an isotherm and could interpret one of those weather maps you find in newspapers.

The trouble with predicting Britain's weather, Francesca told us, is that we are on the edge of the Atlantic with consequently some of the most variable and unpredictable conditions on the planet. This explains the obsession the British have with the weather. Over the past few years, the extremes of weather we have witnessed have challenged the most experienced meteorologists and their sophisticated computer programs. Even though forecasters get it right 95 per cent of the time, it's the other 5 per cent that people remember.

(4) _____ Sea captains make life or death decisions based upon it. And insurance companies will seek advice before deciding whether to provide insurance cover for outdoor events like pop festivals.

Over the next couple of days, we pored over satellite images and listened in to discussions where the professionals finalised their conclusions. In the afternoon, we concentrated on turning these findings into scripts the public would understand. Reading the forecast from a carefully prepared script wasn't too hard, but it was preparing for TV that proved the greatest challenge. (5) _____ They kept falling off despite the magnets on the back. Things have come a long way since then, and today's technology is incredibly advanced. Nowadays presenters use a 'blue screen system', which means that the presenter stands in front of a clear blue screen carrying a faint image that only the presenter is able to see. The images viewers see are back-projected onto it.

The climax of the course was giving a TV forecast in studio conditions with full make-up and lighting. Despite being fully prepared, the first time I tried I completely dried up. The second time I couldn't stop giggling. (6) _____ Although the studios are air-conditioned, the make-up and the lights make you feel really hot. The third time I managed to get all the way through without a hitch. The end result wasn't too embarrassing; however, I did look rather jerky and wooden. Professional presenters have to be incredibly well co-ordinated, pointing to different parts of the screen as they read their commentary from the auto-cue. They may even have to cope with extra instructions through a hidden ear-piece while they're speaking. All in all the experience left me with a new-found respect for the professionalism and cool of the people who present it live night after night, and the invisible work that makes it possible.

LISTENING hurricanes

1 Work in pairs. Discuss these questions.

1   What do you know about hurricanes?
2   In which parts of the world are they most common?
3   How are they different from tornadoes?

EXAM SPOTLIGHT

PAPER 3, PART 2 Sentence completion

Remember, before you listen make sure that you read the notes carefully, so that you know what information you need to listen for. Reading the notes will also help you activate any previous knowledge you may have about a topic.

2 ◎ 12.2 You are going to listen to a radio interview about hurricanes with Dr Kate Jackson, a weather expert. Listen to part A of the interview and complete the notes.

The floods caused by Hurricane Katrina covered an area the size of (1) _____.
Hurricanes form over the oceans in the (2) _____ either side of the equator. They can't form over the equator itself because the spin (the earth's rotation) (3) _____.
Combined elements work together to create a (4) _____ which can result in a hurricane. Storms are called hurricanes when the winds (5) _____ 120 kph; during Katrina, winds went up to (6) _____.
A 'surge' is the sudden increase in the height of the (7) _____ caused by the hurricane. The biggest recorded surge took place in (8) _____ 100 years ago. Afterwards people found fish and (9) _____ on cliff-tops which were (10) _____ metres above sea level.

PAPER 3, PART 2 Multiple choice

3 ◎ 12.3 Listen to part B of the interview. For questions 1–7, choose the best answer (A, B or C).

1   How important does Kate think global warming is in the increase in hurricanes?
   A   It is a key factor.
   B   It has yet to be established.
   C   Warm sea currents are far more important.

2   Kate says that over the past 100 years the temperature of the oceans
   A   has hardly changed.
   B   rose, went down, then rose again.
   C   has risen steadily and consistently.

3   Kate says that drops in temperature were probably caused by
   A   a temporary reduction in greenhouse gases.
   B   an increase in volcanic activity.
   C   pollution particles.

4   She is convinced that
   A   forests will be able to absorb rises in CO_2.
   B   temperatures will eventually stabilise.
   C CO_2 is to blame for temperature rises.

5   How does the interviewer react to Kate's information about CO_2 levels?
   A   He seems to think they present a threat to humanity.
   B   He feels they are too small to be significant.
   C   He is astonished that they are so high.

6   Which aren't the same as hurricanes?
   A   typhoons
   B   twisters
   C   cyclones

7   What are the differences between hurricanes in the northern and southern hemispheres?
   A   They rotate in opposite directions.
   B   In the northern hemisphere they rotate like the hands of a watch.
   C   In the southern hemisphere they turn anti-clockwise.

KEY WORD *way*

4 **Read sentences 1–8. Replace the words in bold with an expression from the box. Make any necessary changes.**

> change your ways   to my way of thinking   by the way
> to have one's way   to come a long way   under way
> tell someone the way   to keep out of someone's way

1 You should **avoid Simon** when he is in a bad mood.
2 Can you **tell me how to get** to the medical centre?
3 Meteorologists have **made a lot of progress** in forecasting the weather.
4 If **it were my decision**, everybody would have to travel by bicycle.
5 **I almost forgot**, we need to bring the plants indoors; there's going to be a frost.
6 He **is a much better person** since he married Linda.
7 **In my opinion**, there isn't enough evidence to support global warming.
8 The report is **in the process of being written** as we speak.

GRAMMAR the definite article

5 **We use *the* to refer a specific thing or person. Match the examples (1–6) to the explanations (a–f).**

▶ GRAMMAR REFERENCE (SECTION 3.2) **PAGE 192**

1 a team of scientists has found evidence … **the** scientists believe
2 **the** British / **the** rich / **the** unemployed
3 **the** Atlantic / **the** sun
4 **the** head of **the** weather centre
5 … **the** country's most eminent forecaster
6 **the** second cause was climate change
7 **the** disappearance of the Maya perplexes scholars

a where there is only one of something
b for nationalities / classes of people
c for some titles or places that include 'of'
d the subject under discussion
e when something / someone is mentioned for the second time
f with superlatives
g with ordinal numbers

6 **Complete the article with *a*, *the* or Ø (no article).**

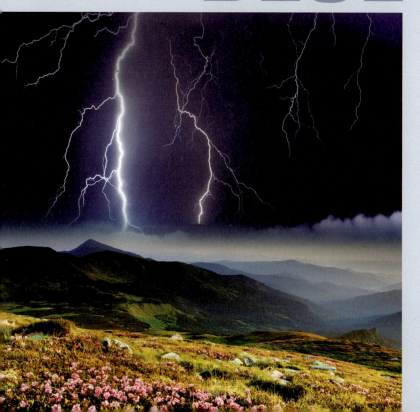

BOLTS FROM THE BLUE

Roy Cleveland Sullivan, (1) _____ forest ranger from Waynesboro, Virginia, was known as (2) _____ 'Human Lightning Rod' because he was struck by (3) _____ lightning seven times in (4) _____ course of (5) _____ 36-year-old career. (6) _____ first strike, in 1942, caused (7) _____ loss of (8) _____ big toenail. Twenty-seven years later (9) _____ second bolt burned his eyebrows off. (10) _____ following year, in 1970, (11) _____ third bolt burnt his left shoulder. After Sullivan's hair was set on fire by (12) _____ fourth strike in 1972, he began carrying (13) _____ bucket of (14) _____ water around with him in his car. In August of (15) _____ following year, (16) _____ bolt came out of (17) _____ small cloud, hit him on (18) _____ head through the hat he was wearing and set fire to his hair again. Sullivan poured (19) _____ bucket of water over his head to cool himself down. He was struck on two further occasions before his death. Two of his Ranger hats, which are burned through (20) _____ top, are on display at (21) _____ local museum. This all shows that (22) _____ lightning can strike in (23) _____ same place more than once! Sullivan must have been one of (24) _____ unluckiest people around … or perhaps, the luckiest!

WRITING an essay (4)

1 **Work in pairs. Discuss the questions.**

1 What are we drinking when we have H_2O with CO_2?
2 What are fossils? What is the problem with burning fossil fuels?
3 What is a greenhouse and what do we normally grow in one?
4 What do scientists mean when they talk about 'the greenhouse effect'?

VOCABULARY energy and the environment

2 **Make sentences by matching the beginnings (1–8) with the endings (a–h).**

1 Coal, oil and gas
2 Burning them releases
3 Increased CO_2 is a cause of
4 Water and SO_2 make
5 Huge amounts of energy
6 **Dams** and **wind-turbines** are
7 If people used public transport more,
8 Everyone should start driving

a are generated by **nuclear reactors.** 5
b there would be less **pollution.** 7
c **acid rain,** which damages the environment. 6
d the **greenhouse effect** and **global warming**. 6
e **hybrid vehicles** that use less petrol. 8
f are examples of **fossil fuels**. 2
g sources of **renewable energy**. 6
h **carbon dioxide** (CO_2) and **sulphur dioxide** (SO_2) into the atmosphere.

3 **Work in pairs. Discuss the questions.**

1 How worried are people in your country about global warming?
2 How dependent is your country on energy produced by
   a fossil fuels?
   b nuclear energy?
3 What alternative sources of energy are used in your country?

4 **Look at the three types of structure for an essay question. What are the key differences between them? Which one do you feel most confident using?**

5 **Look at the spider diagram showing useful expressions for essay questions. Match these headings to the categories of expression.**

a stating an opinion: saying what you think is morally right
b speaking generally and concluding
c giving an example
d listing reasons and arguments
e giving advantages and disadvantages
f structuring your answer
g making contrasts and balancing ideas
h giving reasons and consequences
i using questions
j adding another idea

EXAM SPOTLIGHT

PAPER 2, PART 2 Essay

We have looked at three different structures for writing an essay (units 1, 4 and 10). In the exam, you will have to decide which one to follow for your answer. Remember that you have to use all the notes and introduce your own ideas. A successful essay contains good ideas, an appropriate range of linkers, expressions and topic vocabulary.

Type one:
Essay in three paragraphs, giving an opinion

Paragraph 1
introduction: state your opinion

Paragraph 2
support your opinion, list your reasons

Paragraph 3
conclusion

Type two:
Essay in four paragraphs, considering both sides of a question

Paragraph 1
introduction: What you are going to discuss? How you are going to do it?

Paragraph 2
arguments for (i), (ii), (iii)

Paragraph 3
arguments against (i), (ii), (iii)

Paragraph 4
conclusion: your position

Type three:
Essay in five paragraphs, considering both sides of a question

Paragraph 1
introduction: What you are going to discuss? How you are going to do it?

Paragraph 2
idea 1: arguments for and against

Paragraph 3
idea 2: arguments for and against

Paragraph 4
idea 3: arguments for and against

Paragraph 5
conclusion: your position

6 Work together in pairs or groups and read the essay questions. Decide which essay structure is best for each one.

7 Choose one of the essays and write a plan to show your teacher. When you are ready, write your essay.

In your English class you have been talking about the advantages and disadvantages of nuclear energy. Now your teacher has asked you to write an essay. Write an essay using all the notes and give reasons for your point of view.

Is it a good idea to use nuclear power to satisfy our need for energy?

Notes

Write about:

1 global warming
2 shortage of fossil fuels
3 your own ideas

In your English class you have been talking about the environment and global warming. Your teacher has asked you to write an essay for homework. Write your essay using all the notes and give reasons for your point of view.

We can do very little to stop global warming. Do you agree?

Notes

Write about:

1 transportation
2 forms of energy
3 your own ideas

WRITING CHECKLIST

Did you:
- write between 140 and 190 words? ☐
- divide your essay into paragraphs? ☐
- introduce and order your main points? ☐
- use linkers to move from one idea to the next? ☐
- use different ways of contrasting and balancing ideas? ☐

WRITING GUIDE **PAGE 212**

(Personally)
I think … / I believe …
From my point of view / As I see it,
people should / everyone ought to …
As far as I'm concerned,/
According to (someone else)

To begin with / First of all /
First and foremost
Firstly / Secondly / Finally / Lastly /
Last but not least

so … / that's why … /
because … / in order to … /
as a result …

For instance / For
example …
Just look at / We only
need to look at …

What do we mean by …?
What can we do to deal
with this problem?

the essay question

On the whole … / By and large
All in all … / All things considered …
In conclusion… / To sum up …

I'd like to begin by …. /
In this essay I'd like to talk about …
Let's begin with / take / deal with /
consider / examine …
I'd now like to turn to / consider …

In addition
What's more
Moreover

One (big / important)
advantage / disadvantage /
drawback of … is …
A positive / negative point

Although / Even though /
Despite (the fact that) …
Nevertheless / However
On the one hand … on the other
hand / while …

REVIEW AND EXAM PRACTICE Units 11 and 12

1 For questions 1–8, read the text below and decide which answer (A, B, C or D) best fits each gap. There is an example (0) at the beginning.

A legend which continues to fascinate us is that of the island of Atlantis, which was lost, never to re-appear. The disappearance of the island, wiped (0) __B__ from one day to the next, would have mystified and terrified the inhabitants of the region. The story passed down from the (1) _____ Egyptians eventually reached the philosopher Plato (427–347 BC), who (2) _____ of the catastrophic disappearance of an island empire inhabited by wealthy and sophisticated people. Different locations have been (3) _____ as possible sites; the most (4) _____ candidate is the island of Santorini in the Aegean sea. 'Thera', as it was called in the Bronze Age, was a colony of the Minoan civilisation of Crete. This civilisation would have (5) _____ controlled much of the eastern Mediterranean. In 1630 BC a massive eruption and earthquake produced a tsunami which devastated the area. Part of the island (6) _____ sank beneath the sea as one plate of the Earth's crust slid underneath another. Before the disaster, Thera would have been a large circular island – which is exactly (7) _____ Plato tells us. It is impossible to imagine there being many survivors, if (8) _____ at all.

0	A off	B out	C down	D up
1	A historical	B old	C elderly	D ancient
2	A reported	B said	C told	D described
3	A risen	B arisen	C rose	D suggested
4	A alike	B likelihood	C likely	D possibility
5	A probably	B likely	C certain	D highly
6	A still	B even	C yet	D but
7	A what	B which	C that	D why
8	A none	B any	C one	D nobody

2 For questions 9–16, read the text below and think of the word which best fits each gap. Use only one word in each gap. There is an example (0) at the beginning.

In evolutionary terms, the woolly mammoth became extinct just yesterday, about 3,500 years ago, in fact. A dwarf variety existed (0) __until__ 1500 BC on Wrangel island in Russia, which was covered in its bones. Interestingly enough, the word *mammoth* originates from a Tartar language, where 'maa' means 'earth'. Mammoth remains were dug from the earth, (9) __where__ people believed that mammoths must (10) __have__ lived underground! The woolly variety known to prehistoric man dates from about 700,000 years ago. With its thick coat, it was (11) _____ to cope with the extreme cold of the ice age. Some experts claim over-hunting by man caused (12) __on__ disappearance, but the most likely cause remains the dramatic end of the ice age.

Rumours concerning mammoths hiding out in Alaska persisted until quite recently. One story from 1900 concerned a hunter who claimed he (13) __was__ killed a mammoth and donated it to a museum – the story turned (14) __up__ to be a hoax!

Even so, mammoths could perhaps (15) _____ a return; there are some scientists who believe that they can take genetic material from frozen mammoth remains and inject it into the eggs of female Indian elephants. So (16) __who__ knows, these magnificent creatures could one day roam the earth again!

3 For questions 17–24, read the text below. Use the word given in capital letters at the end of some of the lines to form a word that fits in the gap in the same line. There is an example (0) at the beginning.

Nowadays, nearly everyone agrees that global warming is happening, and that it is the biggest (0) environmental problem our generation faces. We are now in a (17) _____ position.   DANGER
(18) _____ our need for energy is growing every year, and   FORTUNATE
the production of energy contributes to global warming. Burning
fossil fuels causes the most carbon (19) _____. Nuclear   POLLUTE
energy is known for its (20) _____ and releases no carbon, but   EFFICIENT
if things go wrong the results can be (21) _____. Our best   CATASTROPHE
option is (22) _____ energy produced by the sun and the wind.   RENEW
Electric cars are also a good idea, but their (23) _____ is their   ADVANTAGE
short battery life. What's more, it makes no (24) _____ if the car   DIFFERENT
we drive is `clean', if the electricity it uses is generated by dirty means.

4 For questions 25–30 complete the second sentence so that it has a similar meaning to the first, using the word given. Do not change the word given. You must use between two and five words, including the word given.

0   Sammy can't wait for the holidays.
FORWARD
Sammy is looking forward to the holidays.

25   I think global warming is a myth.
CONCERNED
As _____ global warming is a myth.

26   Don't play with matches – you'll burn down the house!
FIRE
Don't play with matches – you'll _____ to the house.

27   Why on earth didn't you wear a coat?
SHOULD
You _____ a coat.

28   The wind certainly blew down the fence.
MUST
The wind _____ down the fence.

29   Where's the post office?
WAY
Can you tell _____ the post office?

30   The old cinema is now a bowling alley.
TURN
The old cinema has _____ a bowling alley.

5 🔊 12.4 You will hear five different people talking about a new crop circle. Choose from the list A-H what each speaker says. Use each letter only once. There are three extra letters which you do not need to use.

This speaker
A   is totally convinced aliens made it.
B   thinks the circle looks nice.
C   was involved in making it.
D   believes local people made it.
E   doesn't think people had enough time to make it.
F   criticises newspaper reporters.
G   doesn't believe in aliens.
H   doesn't mention aliens or UFOs.

Speaker 1 _____
Speaker 2 _____
Speaker 3 _____
Speaker 4 _____
Speaker 5 _____

13 NEWS AND MEDIA

VOCABULARY in the news

1 **Work in pairs. Discuss the questions.**

1   Do you always get your news from TV? Or do you prefer reading newspapers, using the Internet or listening to the radio?
2   Do you believe everything you read or hear in the news? Why / Why not?

2 **Look at these news sources. How much do you believe them? Give each source a mark from 1 to 3 (1 = very rarely, 2 = usually, 3 = all the time). Now compare your answers with the rest of the class.**

The newsreader on the TV or radio	1	2	3
Social media sites	1	2	3
Friends at school or where you work	1	2	3
News blogs	1	2	3
The daily newspaper	1	2	3

3 **Look at the sections from newspapers and news websites. Which section do you normally read first (F)? Which do you never read (N)?**

Business   Classified   Crossword   Editorial
Health   Horoscopes   News   Obituaries
Personal   Politics   Science   Showbiz
Sport   TV listings   Weather

4 **Where do you think these headlines come from? Match them to the sections in exercise 3.**

BANK BREAKS OFF TALKS WITH PARTNER

BRAZIL PULL AHEAD WITH GOAL IN FINAL MINUTE

POLITICIANS TRY TO COVER UP SCANDAL

RUMOURS OF PRESIDENT'S RESIGNATION LEAK OUT

NUMBERS ENTERING UNIVERSITY GO UP BY 3%

LEOS LIKELY TO FALL OUT WITH BOSS THIS WEEK

BRETT AND ANGELA ABOUT TO BREAK UP?

NON-GOVERNMENTAL ORGANISATIONS PULL OUT OF TALKS

5 **Match the underlined phrasal verbs in exercise 4 to the synonyms 1–8.**

1   to go in front of someone _____
2   stop doing something suddenly _____
3   disagree and argue _____
4   withdraw _____
5   increase _____
6   hide the truth _____
7   slowly become known _____
8   separate _____

6 Work in groups. Imagine you are in charge of a news programme on a local TV station. You have to select three of the following news items for the programme. Discuss which are the most important.

1 A famous Hollywood actor has been stopped by local police for speeding.
2 The weather will be windy and cold tomorrow.
3 A major supermarket has withdrawn jars of marmalade which may contain broken glass. The supermarket is advising customers to return the product.
4 Scientists have discovered that six-year-old children now prefer looking at a screen to a human face.
5 All ten passengers were unhurt as a private plane crash-landed in a field next to a major motorway. The only injury was a scratch on the pilot's hand.
6 The next James Bond movie opens in cinemas across the country this weekend.
7 Wally, the popular whale at the city's aquarium, has recovered from a serious illness and will be on show again from next week.

LISTENING a news report

EXAM SPOTLIGHT

PAPER 3, PART 2 Sentence completion

How much do you know about Part 2 of the Listening exam?
1 Will the answers be in the same order as the sentences?
2 How many words do you write in each answer?
3 Are the words in the written notes always the same as those on the recording?

7 ⊙ **13.1** Listen to a journalist reporting on a problem in education and complete the sentences.

Critics say they are the worst results for more than (1) _____ years, and one ex-(2) _____ described them as 'appalling'. Those are comments about last year's national tests, which show an increase in the number of (3) _____ errors made by 11–14-year-olds. Typical errors included the spelling of words such as *change*, *known* and (4) _____. Mistakes were made because (5) _____ had left out letters, put the wrong endings or used (6) _____. Basic punctuation mistakes included capital letters, (7) _____ and commas.
The (8) _____ for Education said she had sent a list to secondary schools of words that all children should know by the age of 14. The teachers' (9) _____ will give a statement later, but they have welcomed recent changes. Lessons begin with spelling, so sports teachers check pupils can spell words like *athlete* and (10) _____.

GRAMMAR reported speech

▶ GRAMMAR REFERENCE (SECTION 14) **PAGE 207**

8 Read these extracts from the news report. Write what the person actually said.

0 A new report on education says that the test results are the worst in over 20 years.
'They are the worst results in over 20 years.'
1 One person told me that most errors had arisen because pupils had missed out letters.
_____
2 I asked the Minister for Education what she thought the reasons were.
_____
3 She said she'd sent schools a list of 600 words all children should know.
_____
4 The teachers' union said it would be commenting later.
_____

9 Read sentences 0–4 in exercise 8 again, and complete the rules for reported speech (a–c).

a In sentences _____, _____, _____ and _____ the verb changes tense.
b The verb in sentence _____ stays the same because the reporting verb is in the present.
c In sentence _____ we report the question using the same word order as in an affirmative statement.

10 Complete the second sentence in each pair.

1 'I'm going out on Friday.'
She said that she _____ out on Friday.
2 'Can you give me a hand?'
They asked if I _____ them a hand.
3 'Don't lift that until I get home and can help you.'
He told me not to lift it until he _____ me.
4 The spokesperson said they had seen the same results five years ago.
'We _____ the same results five years ago.'
5 He asked me what I did for a living.
'What _____ for a living?'

SPEAKING reporting

11 ⊙ **13.1** Listen again and complete the notes with your own ideas.

The report reveals that …
One thing that surprised me was that …
It's amazing that …
It would be interesting to know more about …

12 Work in pairs. What is an important item of news at the moment? Where did you find out about it? Tell your partner about it.

Have you heard the news about the …

READING social media

1 **Study this infographic. What does it show? Is any of the information true for you? Do any of the figures surprise you? Tell the class.**

A survey asked a group of Americans: 'Do you normally stay online longer than you intended?'

- 8%
- 28%
- 64%

■ Yes
■ No
■ Can't say

The same people were asked: 'Do you usually lose sleep due to staying up late on the Internet?'

- 7%
- 48%
- 45%

■ Yes
■ No
■ Can't say

57% of people chat more online than they do in real life.

Since 2000, our attention span has dropped by **40%**.

65% of adults sleep with their smart phone(s).

62% of 18–34-year-olds check Facebook as soon as they wake up.

2 **Work in pairs. You are going to interview your classmates about social media and the Internet. Write three questions and use them to interview other students. Report your findings to the class.**

3 **Read the article. Which sentence is the best summary of the writer's main message?**

A Using the Internet makes you more intelligent.
B Our behaviour and brains are changing because of social media.
C Social media and the Internet is having a negative effect on human beings.

EXAM SPOTLIGHT

PAPER 1, PART 5 Multiple choice

If you don't understand a word in an exam reading text, remember that:

- you can try to guess the meaning from context
- you don't need to understand every single word in order to have a good understanding of the text and to answer each question.

4 **Read the article again. For questions 1–6, choose the answer (A, B, C or D) which you think fits best according to the text.**

1 From the first paragraph, we understand that
   A the Internet and social media might have a bigger effect on our lives than we first thought.
   B there are lots of questions about our lives that we don't know the answer to.
   C no one noticed that social media was changing our lives until recently.
   D people are spending too much time online.

2 Doctors think that, as a result of not meeting so many people face-to-face,
   A humans no longer produce a hormone that they need.
   B we are all losing our ability to socialise.
   C we have a greater chance of illness.
   D we have more time to make contact on social media sites.

3 Paragraph 2 suggests that children
   A are missing out on human contact.
   B need better education in the future.
   C are not studying enough because of video games.
   D aren't passing their exams.

4 In the test by the University of Arizona,
   A they prevented group two from using Facebook.
   B 25% of group two didn't use Facebook.
   C the scores of group one were 25% higher.
   D over-65s used social media sites more than scientists had expected.

5 Sites like Facebook might help mental ability because
   A the content on these sites is always changing and being updated.
   B they help older people to remember things.
   C there is always lots of interesting information on them.
   D they are a good way to communicate with lots of people.

6 The conclusion of the study at London University was that
   A students who use Facebook have larger brains.
   B students on Facebook do better at university.
   C greater use of Facebook can change the shape of the brain.
   D all students use Facebook and so their brains are different.

5 **Find words or phrases in the article with these meanings.**

1 not clear
2 having a natural ability or skill
3 effect that something has on decisions and opinions
4 the way we do things on a regular basis
5 how well the mind or brain works
6 ability to work and / or move quickly
7 effect or influence

6 **Work in groups. Discuss these questions.**

- What are the positive and negative effects of social media on our lives? Make two lists with your ideas.
- Which list has the strongest arguments? Are the effects of social media on our lives more positive or more negative?
- Present your conclusion about the effects of social media to other groups. Compare your ideas.

Are social media sites changing our brains?

With so many of us spending such a large part of our day (and nights) on sites like Facebook, YouTube and Twitter, it isn't surprising that people are beginning to question how this behaviour might be changing our lives forever. Have social media sites and internet
5 access made the split between work and leisure more blurred? Have our lives become less private? And it isn't only our behaviour that changes but also our mental activity. Perhaps you've noticed that you can't concentrate for long periods of time anymore. Or maybe you've become more gifted at doing quizzes and crosswords? The 24/7 media
10 influence on our lives has caused many researchers to start looking into our patterns of behaviour, both socially and at work, and also into how our brains might be physically changing.

One negative effect of social networking sites is that we are spending less time talking to each other face-to-face and more
15 time looking at screens on our own. Some doctors are concerned because when we meet people in real life (not online) the human body produces hormones which it needs to function properly. In addition to the physical risks, there is the possibility that mental performance is affected, especially in children. With so many
20 children now communicating and playing online, they are not learning certain social skills because they are not receiving regular human contact. This could even include lack of contact with a real teacher in the future as more education will be delivered online.

However, not everyone has a negative opinion about the power of
25 new social media. Some studies have shown that sites like Facebook can improve our mental performance. Take the following study from the University of Arizona: it came to the conclusion that people aged 65 who had a Facebook page did better on mental tests than people who rarely or never used social media. The researchers compared two
30 groups of people over 65: one group often used Facebook and the other group didn't. The first group did 25% better on a test of their mental skills. It's believed that this is because when you use a site like Facebook, you are constantly posting new things and reading new information.
35 As well as testing the brain for mental agility, we can also see inside the brain. Using brain scanning technology, it's possible to compare the shape of brains and the size of different areas. Recently, the brains of 125 students at the University of London were scanned in a test to assess the impact of Facebook. The study found that students with
40 larger numbers of friends on Facebook had parts of the brain which were larger. So the conclusion was that the Internet is changing our brain. However, the study wasn't able to judge if this increase in size in parts of the brain was beneficial or not. In other words, we know social media is changing us – what we don't know is whether it's for better or
45 worse. The debate continues.

SPEAKING discussing TV programmes

1A

2A

1B

2B

1 Work in pairs. Look at the photos. They show different types of TV programme. Take turns to compare the two types of programme in each pair and say why you think people enjoy watching this kind of programme.

LISTENING what's on TV?

2 🔘 13.2 Listen to five different TV programmes. What are the people talking about? Number the subjects of the programmes in the order you hear them.

_____ Economics
_____ Education
_____ Astrology
_____ Celebrities
_____ Science

PAPER 3, PART 3 Multiple matching

3 🔘 13.2 Listen again. Choose from the list (A–H) what the speaker in each TV programme is talking about. Use each letter only once. There are three extra letters which you do not need to use.

A   reporting something that might be true
B   warning people about the future
C   agreeing with the situation
D   criticising a situation
E   making recommendations
F   disagreeing with another person
G   explaining the problem and potential danger
H   predicting global events

Speaker 1 _____
Speaker 2 _____
Speaker 3 _____
Speaker 4 _____
Speaker 5 _____

KEY WORDS say and tell

4 Choose the correct word (in italics) to complete the sentences.

1   Please *say / tell* him I called.
2   The minister *said / told* they were dealing with it.
3   My parents *said / told* me to go to bed.
4   I *said / told* to him that it was a bad idea.

5 Complete these common expressions with the correct form of *say* or *tell*.

1 To _____ you the truth, I don't have any money left.
2 So what are you _____? That you can't help me?
3 I'll _____ you what. Why don't I give you a lift?
4 So, you had a good time then? You can _____ that again! It was brilliant.
5 Don't interrupt! Let her speak and then you can have your _____.
6 Only time will _____ if their relationship can survive all these problems.

GRAMMAR reporting verbs

6 Match each sentence 1–8 to a function a–h.

1 'Why don't we ask what she thinks?'
2 'There's a great new computer game you should buy.'
3 'This new law is ridiculous.'
4 'You both ought to be careful at that time of night.'
5 'If I were you, I'd accept his offer.'
6 'I'm really sorry for missing the party.'
7 'Don't forget to call me when you get there.'
8 'Would you like to come over for lunch?'

a reminding _____
b advising _____
c inviting _____
d warning _____
e recommending _____
f apologising _____
g suggesting _____
h criticising _____

REPORTING VERB PATTERNS

Say, tell, think and *ask* are examples of common reporting verbs. Other reporting verbs can summarise the main function of the original statement:
'Why don't we ask what she thinks?' > She suggested asking what he thought.
These reporting verbs can be followed by different verb patterns:
· verb + *that: suggested / recommended that*
· verb + someone + *that: reminded her that*
· verb + *to*-infinitive: *promised / offered to help*
· verb + someone + *to*-infinitive: *warned / advised her to be careful, invited me to attend*
· verb + *-ing: recommended asking*
· verb + preposition + *-ing: apologised for leaving*
· verb + someone + preposition + *-ing: criticised him for leaving*
Some verbs can be followed by more than one verb pattern: *I suggested asking him, I suggested we ask him, I suggested that we should ask him.*

7 Complete these sentences to report the speech from exercise 6.

0 She suggested <u>asking</u> her what she thought.
1 He recommended _____ the new computer game.
2 The spokesperson criticised _____.
3 His father warned _____.
4 She advised me _____.
5 Michael apologised _____ the party.
6 Mum reminded _____ her when I got there.
7 The neighbours invited _____ over for lunch.

▶ GRAMMAR REFERENCE (SECTION 14)   **PAGE 207**

8 Imagine you are a TV news reporter. You are investigating an accident that happened today. You interviewed three people. Read the notes you took at the interviews and prepare your news report. Remember to use reporting verbs.

Policeman:
'I think the car driver was going too quickly and didn't see the lorry turning into his lane. In my opinion he should have slowed down when he approached the junction. The other point was that it was a foggy morning and we always say to drivers to put your lights on in this kind of weather'.

Pedestrian:
'I was just walking along when I heard a loud bang. It was definitely the lorry driver's fault. I don't think he was looking where he was going and didn't see the car coming up the road.'

Lorry driver:
'I'm really sorry about what's happened, but to be fair I don't think the driver of the car had his lights on. He was wrong for not having them on. I didn't see him.'

9 Work in pairs. Take turns to read your news report to your partner. Compare your reports.

GRAMMAR reporting verbs ▲ KEY WORDS *say and tell* ▲ LISTENING what's on TV? ▲ SPEAKING discussing TV programmes

WRITING a report (2)

EXAM SPOTLIGHT

PAPER 2   Checking and editing

In both parts of Paper 2 you need to check your writing. Always spend five to ten minutes at the end of a writing exam looking for any mistakes. In particular, look for mistakes in grammar, spelling and punctuation.
To prepare for the Writing paper, you should read through previous writing tasks and make a list of your common mistakes. Look back at the list from time to time and remember what the mistakes were and why you made them. It's a good way to remember how to write them correctly next time.

1 Here are some of the English words that are most commonly misspelt by English people! Find the mistake in each word and write the word correctly.

0 adress   _____address_____
1 busness   _____
2 definate   _____
3 greatful   _____
4 commitee   _____
5 focussed   _____
6 recieve   _____
7 accomodation   _____
8 goverment   _____
9 advertisment   _____
10 neccessary   _____
11 wich   _____
12 seperate   _____
13 reccommend   _____

2 People often make mistakes with words that are homophones. *Homophones* are words that sound the same but have a different meaning or spelling. Find the mistake in each sentence and write the correct word.

0 This is you're book.   _____your_____
1 I need to buy some stationary from this shop.
   _____
2 Your new jacket compliments your dress.
   _____
3 Their are lots of ways to travel round our country.
   _____
4 He's the man who's brother works in our office.
   _____
5 The growing population is effecting our city.
   _____
6 They didn't loose the football match.
   _____
7 How often do you practice speaking English?
   _____

3 Work in pairs. Do you know what each of these items of punctuation is called and when to use it?

:   _____
;   _____
!   _____
'...' _____
;   _____
?   _____
,   _____

4 Correct each sentence by adding one missing punctuation item from exercise 3.
1 Its your turn I think.
2 How long have you been here
3 The boy at the bus stop, who we'd seen earlier was now crying.
4 The rabbit said to Alice, I'm late, I'm late.
5 Please bring the following items with you to the exam pens, pencils and an identity card.
6 Jesse was late as usual it had always been the case since childhood.
7 My father shouted, 'Turn that music down'
8 I look forward to hearing from you

5 Read the exam question, then look at the report written by a student (Paula). Match the numbers on the report to the notes the teacher has written.

> Your local region has a newsletter about the area. The editor wants some ideas for new articles to appear in the next few issues, in order to attract more readers of different ages.
>
> He has asked you to write a report with two or three ideas for new types of articles that readers might find interesting.
>
> Explain what they are and why people might be interested.

6 Answer the exam question in exercise 5. Write about your own region. Remember to check your writing for mistakes at the end.

WRITING CHECKLIST

A REPORT

Did you:
• use an appropriate style for the context? ☐
• use headings to organise your report? ☐
• include ideas for readers of different ages? ☐
• check your writing for spelling and grammar mistakes? ☐

WRITING GUIDE PAGE 217

Ideas for new articles in the next newsletters

There are three types of articles what [(1)] we could add to our newsletter in the next few issues. They are as follows, [(2)]

Interesting people [(3)]

People like to read about people [(4)] we should interview people [(5)] who live in the area. They could be old people who have lived here all their life. Perhaps they have interested [(6)] stories to say [(7)] about growing up in the region and can talk about how life has changed.

Historic places

The region has lots of historic villages and buildings. For example [(8)] there's an historic castle near my house that was built in the fifteenth century. It's open to visitors but very little [(9)] tourists visit it. An article in the newsletter would help to attract more people.

An interesting event

We also need something for younger people in the newsletter and one event we should write about is the summer music festival. Me and my friends always go. [(10)] Its [(11)] every August in the town park with a weekend of music by young local bands. This year we could also include some photographs. What do you think of my ideas? [(12)]

—— Colon missing

—— You need the conjunction `so´

—— Underline all headings

—— You use the same noun three times. Can you think of a synonym to avoid repetition?

—— Missing comma

—— Wrong word

—— This sentence is too informal and personal. Either change or delete.

Wrong adjective ending

—— Incorrect quantifier. The noun that follows is countable.

—— Problem with the relative pronoun

—— Missing apostrophe

—— Inappropriate style and not necessary. We don't normally ask questions in reports.

Well done, Paula. You have three really good ideas in your report and you've answered the question well. Please check your writing when you finish. There are a few mistakes and changes you could make which would improve it.

GLOSSARY

inundate (vb): flood
trigger (vb): set off, cause
catastrophic: very damaging, disastrous
blizzard: very heavy snowfall
endurance: ability to cope with difficulties
precipitation: rain or snow
vapour: particles of something (e.g. water) in the air
evaporate: turn from a liquid into a gas

VIDEO the greenhouse effect

1 Is the topic of 'climate change' often in the news in your country? Do you think people know much about it? Why? Why not?

2 Watch the first part of the video about extreme weather and climate change. It talks about four countries. Look at the table and tick the type of weather mentioned for each country.

		Australia	Russia	USA	Pakistan
a)	Cold and snow				
b)	Floods				
c)	Drought and wildfires				

3 Watch the first part of the video again. Complete the notes about the events and their results.

Event	Result
The worst floods in four decades in the state of Queensland.	An area the size of (1) _____ and (2) _____ is covered in water.
The (3) _____ summer on record in Russia.	Catastrophic wildfires have killed more than (4) _____ people.
Extreme heat in Pakistan, followed by floods that cover one (5) _____ of the country.	(6) _____ miles of road and railways are washed away.
A record winter of cold and snow in the USA.	In Chicago, the snow stopped (7) _____ dead in its tracks.
The sun heats up the oceans which creates water vapour.	Water vapour provides the source of fuel for (8) _____.
More (9) _____ means more evaporation.	More energy builds up in the (10) _____ increasing the potential for more extreme weather events.

4 The second part of the video describes a process. Number these items from 1 to 6 in the order you see them.

a a boat on the ocean 1
b the planet Earth _____
c water evaporating into the Earth's atmosphere _____
d energy in the atmosphere _____
e the sun rising over Earth _____
f clouds above the ocean _____

5 Read the sentences and look at the verbs in bold. Decide if they describe an upward trend (write ^), a downward trend (write v) or no change (write –).

1 Water vapour in the atmosphere is **building up**.
2 Summer temperatures have **stayed the same** for the last three years.
3 After a period of intense heat, things have **cooled down** now that autumn has arrived.
4 Winter was shorter this year because the planet is **heating up**.
5 Spring was very dry, so levels of water have **gone down** in the region.
6 With temperatures **remaining steady** in the last few years, some people are questioning theories on climate change.

6 Work in pairs. Can you think of six more verbs to talk about trends and changes?

7 Do you think the weather and the climate is changing where you live? What trends and changes have you noticed during each season?

8 Work in pairs. Discuss your opinions about climate change, and give reasons for your opinion. Do you strongly agree or disagree with each other, or do you have similar views?

9 Read the information in the Ideas generator.

i IDEAS GENERATOR

TAKING A POSITION

In Part 3 and Part 4 of the Speaking test, you will have a discussion with the other candidate(s). During the discussion you might need to agree or disagree, even on a subject about which you don't normally have an opinion.

For example, imagine the other candidate expressed this opinion:

'I think humans are causing climate change and so we all have a responsibility to look after our environment.'

Which of the following responses could you use? (Remember that in the exam you will need to agree or disagree in this way.)

I couldn't agree more.
I tend to agree with this view.
I think there are arguments for and against this view.
I can see your point, but …
Sorry, but I'm not sure that I agree with you.
I really don't agree.

10 Work in pairs. Express your opinions on these questions. Try to reach an agreement in each case. Use some of the expressions in the Ideas generator.

- Do you think global travel is good for people or does it cause too much environmental damage?
- Do you think there is too much news about celebrities and famous people in our media nowadays?
- Do you think young people spend too much time on the Internet nowadays?
- Do you think advertising changes the way we think, or is it a waste of money?

14 FASHION AND APPEARANCE

1 Look at the photo. Would you like to go to a fashion show like this? How important are clothes and fashion in your life?

2 Work in pairs or small groups. Ask and answer the questions.

1 How long do you spend deciding what to wear in the morning?
2 Who chooses your clothes? Who buys them?
3 How long have you had the same hairstyle?
4 What is your favourite item of clothing?
5 What are your favourite designer brands?
6 Have you ever had an argument over your choice of clothes or hairstyle?

VOCABULARY fashion

3 Choose the correct word (in italics) to complete the sentences.

1 A belt or scarf is an *extra / accessory* which can completely transform an old outfit.
2 Turn-ups on trousers are *making / doing* a comeback.
3 Oh dear, these patterns *clash / crash*; squares and stripes just don't *live / go* together.
4 She's *into / onto* weird diets, like eating nothing but grapefruit for a month.
5 An old USSR hat is the kind of *fashion / cult* object people love to wear.

6 Be honest, don't you think I look *cold / cool* in these *designer / brand* sunglasses?
7 I think my grandmother tries too hard to look young and *trendy / stylish*. It's a bit embarrassing at her age!
8 Kids hate to wear the same *names / brands* as their parents.
9 Tattoos and piercings are silly *fads / fades* which cause lasting damage.
10 A 'little black dress' is a *classic / classical* that belongs in every woman's *wardrobe / cupboard*.
11 She has got a lot of *fashion / flair*. She knows how to make herself stand out from the crowd.
12 The *craze / crazy* for 'tamagotchis' didn't last long. Kids soon got tired of them.
13 My nephew used to be obsessed by *designer / logo* jeans.
14 I absolutely love your new *suite / suit*. Is it an Armani?
15 Change out of those old clothes and wash your hair. You look too *scruffy / smart* to go for a job interview.

4 These sentences include expressions with the word *fashion*. Complete the sentences with one word.

1 Don't worry about being _____ . Just be yourself.
2 Their offices may look old - _____ , but inside they have the latest equipment.
3 Long hair simply went _____ _____ fashion in the 1980s.

5 Match the sentence beginnings (1–7) with the endings (a–g).

1 There's no need to **dress up**, _____
2 You can **try** the dress **on** _____
3 If you're hot, just _____
4 You'd better **put on** something warm because _____
5 What on earth does he **have on**; _____
6 If these trousers are too big, _____
7 I can't **do up** the buttons on this skirt; _____

a he looks really strange!
b **take off** your jacket.
c can you **let** it **out** a bit?
d just come as you are.
e we'll **take** them **in** and **turn** them **up** for free.
f it's going to be cold later on.
g to check that it fits.

6 Match the phrasal verbs in bold in exercise 5 to these meanings.

1 make bigger _____
2 make smaller _____
3 make shorter _____
4 remove _____
5 cover oneself _____
6 wear your best clothes _____
7 wear _____
8 fasten _____

7 Work in pairs. Who do you think is speaking in each sentence in exercise 5? Who are they speaking to?

LISTENING crazes and fads

PAPER 3, PART 1 Multiple choice

8 ⊙ 14.1 You will hear people talking in eight different situations. For questions 1–8, choose the best answer (A, B or C).

1 You hear a father and daughter discussing the father's clothes. What does the father decide to do?
   A He changes the shirt and tie.
   B He puts on a different jacket.
   C He changes the suit.

2 You hear a radio phone-in programme. What is the speaker giving information about?
   A a miracle way of losing weight
   B taking care of sporting injuries
   C combining diet and exercise

3 Two people are waiting for a third. How do they feel about her?
   A They think she looks terrible.
   B They think she looks lovely.
   C They are jealous.

4 You hear a radio presenter talking about how students can manage their budgets. What does he say about clothes and fashion?
   A Buy top quality which will last.
   B Don't follow the crowd – be an individual.
   C You must have one or two expensive designer items in your wardrobe.

5 You hear a sociologist talking about a new phenomenon. What does it involve?
   A creating spontaneous crowds
   B circulating as many emails as possible
   C organising short events with large numbers of people

6 You hear an elderly man talking about the objects which are special for each generation. What does he feel about this?
   A He thinks things were too expensive in the old days.
   B He thinks it is natural.
   C He doesn't understand the desire for retro fashions.

7 You hear a woman talking about fashion week. What does she think about it?
   A It's immoral.
   B It's harmless.
   C It's a waste of time.

8 An estate agent is showing some potential buyers a house. What does she say about it?
   A The house and area have a great future.
   B It is a modern family home.
   C It's in an excellent area with lots of facilities.

GRAMMAR *have something done*

▶ GRAMMAR REFERENCE (SECTION 12.2.4) **PAGE 204**

9 Look at sentences a and b and answer questions 1 and 2.

a She had her hair dyed.
b She dyed her hair.

1 In which sentence did she dye her hair herself? _____
2 In which sentence did someone else do it? _____

10 Complete the second sentence in each pair so the meaning is similar to the first. Use *have*.

1 Marcello got the garage to spray his car in his team's colours.
   Marcello _____.

2 A local firm built their new house in the mountains.
   They _____.

3 A professional photographer is going to take photos of their wedding.
   They are _____.

4 A famous dressmaker from Milan is making Helen's wedding dress.
   Helen is _____.

5 A dentist is going to whiten Kevin's teeth for the occasion.
   Kevin _____.

6 The best hairdresser in town will be doing their hair on the big day.
   They _____.

11 Make a list of the things you do for yourself, and the things that you have done by someone else. Tell your partner.

READING the *Cosplay* craze

1 Look at the photo in the article on page 143. What do you think the article is about?

2 Read the text quickly. Who or what are the following?

- *Cosplay*
- Manga and Anime
- Tamsin Harper
- the Cotswolds
- the Akihabara district
- Tomoko, Toshi and Hugo
- Dragoncon

PAPER 1, PART 5 Multiple choice

3 For questions 1–6, choose the answer (A, B, C or D) which you think fits best according to the text.

1 *Cosplay* was inspired by
   A what happens in the Akihabara district.
   B ancient myths and legends.
   C movie and comic book characters.
   D crazy US fashion.

2 What help has Tomoko's group had from its supporters?
   A They hired the hall.
   B They have given small amounts of money.
   C They have provided the lighting.
   D They have given advice.

3 Tomoko seems to believe that the traditional kimono
   A has room to move around in.
   B is an imaginative form of dress.
   C has no role to play in *Cosplay*.
   D can be modified.

4 What do Tamsin and Harriet say about their costumes?
   A They can't make everything they need.
   B They only wear them once.
   C They wish they could afford to buy them.
   D They are made by poorly-treated workers.

5 What does Tamsin think about Hugo?
   A He has authority in the group.
   B He takes himself too seriously.
   C His costume suits him.
   D He is amusing.

6 We can understand that Tamsin
   A thinks *Cosplayers* are exciting.
   B hates the idea of dressing up.
   C wouldn't mind joining in the fun.
   D has brought a costume with her just in case.

4 How popular is *Cosplay* in your country? Would you like to try it?

GRAMMAR the passive

▶ GRAMMAR REFERENCE (SECTION 12.2) **PAGE 204**

5 Look at sentences a and b and answer the questions.

a Hundreds of shiny button are being sewn onto some wings.
b Tomoko's mum is sewing on hundreds of shiny buttons.

1 Which sentence is active? _____
2 Which sentence is passive? _____

6 Look at the words in bold in each sentence. Identify the verb form. Then rewrite the sentences using the passive, beginning as shown. Use the same tense as in the original sentence.

0 **We only employ** adults in our factories.
   Form: present simple
   Only adults are employed in our factories.

1 **Young women are sewing** the labels onto designer clothes.
   Form: _____
   The labels _____

2 **They sold** 80 million pairs of trainers last year.
   Form: _____
   Eighty million _____

3 **They have taken** Japanese designs as their inspiration.
   Form: _____
   Japanese designs _____

4 **They are going to present** their new range of swimwear at the Olympic pool.
   Form: _____
   Their new range of swimwear _____

5 Our new puppy **was destroying** my favourite shoes.
   Form: _____
   My favourite shoes _____

6 **Moths had made** hundreds of holes in the clothes in the wardrobe.
   Form: _____
   Hundreds _____

7 **We will have finished** the costumes by next weekend.
   Form: _____
   The costumes _____

8 Governments **should take action** against this immoral trade.
   Form: _____
   Action _____

9 Someone **should have banned** the trade.
   Form: _____
   The trade _____

THE COSPLAY CRAZE

Cosplay is short for *costume play*, one of the latest fashion crazes. It comes from Japan where people dress up as their favourite fantasy or science-fiction characters from Manga (Japanese comic books) and Anime (Japanese animated films). Our reporter Tamsin Harper meets some of its British fans.

The Cotswolds is famous for its gorgeous countryside and rolling hills, picturesque villages and tea rooms. It is home to retired majors and old ladies in thatched cottages. You would hardly expect it to be at the heart of *Cosplay*. Yet here I am, in a town hall where a group of *Cosplay* fans are preparing for their first show. As with most new fads, *Cosplay* started in the US, with geeky guys and girls dressing up as their favourite movie superhero or comic book characters. However, it is the Japanese who have taken it over and transformed it into something a lot more ambitious.

So how did it arrive in this remote English town? Nineteen-year-old Tomoko Edwards provides the answers. 'Dad used to work in Japan, which is where he met my mum, and we lived there for quite a while. So I grew up with a foot in each culture. Like lots of kids I really got into Manga and Anime. When I was 13 I started to go into the Akihabara district of Tokyo, which is the place to go to see the latest fashions, and where there are themed cafés and people dressed in costumes. When we settled in England I decided to start my own *Cosplay* group.' Now, there are 16 serious members and another 30 or so enthusiasts.

Tomoko is now studying fashion at a local college and one day would like to have her own collection. But right now, she and her friends are getting ready for their first *Cosplay* show. 'Our teachers are really supportive', she says, 'they give us tips on how to make some of the more difficult costumes. One of our sponsors provides us with a lot of material. And luckily we haven't been asked to pay anything to use this place tonight.' As we speak, Tomoko's mother, Toshi, and another mum are frantically finishing off her costume. Hundreds of shiny buttons are being sewn onto some wings. Meanwhile, the sound system is being set up. The lighting has already been installed.

When I ask her what she thinks of that most typical Japanese garment, the kimono, there is a slight flash of annoyance. 'Well, kimonos are about tradition, *Cosplay* is about imagination and fantasy. Even so, some costumes copy kimonos, but allow you to move around,' she adds. Tomoko gestures towards two young women dressed as superheroes, leaping and twirling as they practise their elaborate sword-wielding moves.

You can, of course, buy ready-made costumes but for Tomoko and her friends at least half the fun is making your outfit yourself. Her friend Harriet chips in, 'Most of the costumes you buy over the net are rubbish and you can only wear them once. They are also produced in sweatshops where the workers are treated like slaves.' However, they admit to buying the wigs, which are difficult to make themselves, and the coloured contact lenses that can transform the *Cosplayers'* eyes.

Hugo, one of Tomoko's teachers, has joined in the fun. '*Cosplay* is part of our lifestyle, not something you just dip in and out of', he says. 'Otherwise it's just fancy dress.' Hugo is very sincere, but it's hard to take a grown-up man seriously when he is dressed as an elf. Nevertheless, as the only club member to have been to the *Dragoncon* festival in the States, he is treated with awe and respect.

Tonight Tomoko and her gang expect a couple of hundred enthusiasts will be crammed into the hall to watch the show. Followers around the world will be able to watch it live, and there will be clips and photos posted on social media sites. Perhaps it's not that weird after all to find this going on in a remote market town. With the Internet the world has shrunk. As a former weekend-only punk, I can understand the thrill of dressing up and even being someone completely different for an hour two. I wonder if they have a spare costume in my size I could slip into?

LISTENING school uniform

1 In Britain, most children have to wear a uniform to school. How common is this in your country? Do you think it is a good idea or a bad idea? Why?

2 🔘 **14.2** Three friends are talking about school uniform. For questions 1–7, choose from the speakers, Florence (*F*), Damien (*D*) or Philip (*P*).

Which speaker:
1 likes the way someone used to look? _____
2 had to wear a strange-looking hat? _____
3 thinks that school uniform is convenient? _____
4 thinks that children have the right to choose what they put on? _____
5 thinks uniform reduces social differences between pupils? _____
6 claims that uniforms only look nice for a short period? _____
7 didn't have a new uniform very often? _____

PAPER 3 PART 4 Multiple choice

3 🔘 **14.2** Listen again, and for questions 1–6 choose the best answer (A, B or C).

1 What happened when Florence wore the winter uniform?
  A She found it difficult to button up her coat.
  B People made fun of her.
  C She had to change her hairstyle.
2 What does Damien think about school uniform?
  A The problems it creates are bigger than those it solves.
  B It stops school kids from expressing themselves.
  C It is better than the alternative.
3 What happened at Philip's school during hot weather?
  A Everyone had to suffer.
  B Only the teachers were allowed to take off their jackets.
  C The children could take off their ties.

4 What does Florence believe about school uniform?
  A It teaches school children self-discipline.
  B It looks nice.
  C It soon starts to look scruffy.
5 What happened when Damien was a schoolboy?
  A His uniform was never the right size.
  B The arms of his jacket were never long enough.
  C His parents didn't have much money for uniforms.
6 According to Damien and Florence, how do parents feel about school uniform?
  A It is an unnecessary expense.
  B They are worried about the cost.
  C It means they have fewer arguments with their children over clothes.

KEY WORD *think*

4 Work in pairs. Read the sentences and replace the words in bold with phrasal verbs and expressions with *think* from the box.

> thought up   think things through   think back to
> to my way of thinking   thinking about   think so
> do you think you could   don't you think we should

1 **I'd like you to** give us your views.
2 **Wouldn't it be a good idea to** hear what she has to say?
3 We are **considering** their proposal.
4 Do you really **believe that**?
5 She has **imagined** another crazy scheme.
6 Your problem is that you never **analyse things carefully**.
7 When I **remember** the old days, things weren't any different.
8 **In my opinion**, we should ban the trade in human hair.

GRAMMAR *make, let* and *allow*

5 Look at the use of *make* in sentences a and b and answer the questions.

a She made him a sandwich for breakfast.
b She made him eat his breakfast.

1 In which sentence does it mean *force / oblige*? _____
2 In which sentence does it mean *prepare*? _____

6 Look at these sentences. Which sentence is active (A) and which is passive (P) in each pair?

1a I hated that hat, but I was made to wear it. _____
1b They made me wear that hat. _____
2a The teachers didn't allow us to take off our jackets. _____
2b We weren't allowed to take off our jackets. _____

7 Read these three sentences. Where can you use *let* instead of *allow / allowed*?

1 They **allowed us** to take off our jackets.
2 They didn't **allow us** to take off our ties.
3 We weren't **allowed to** take off our caps.

8 Work in groups. Talk about your childhood. Use a mixture of active and passive forms to discuss the following topics.

- bedtime
- TV
- music
- family
- food
- clothes
- hair
- friends

> *When I was younger I was made to practise the cello every evening.*

> *Well, when I was a teenager I wasn't allowed to go out with my friends until the weekend.*

SPEAKING challenging

9 ⊙ **14.2** Turn to audioscript 14.2 on page 232 and underline the sentences that have these introductory phrases.

1 Yes, but …
2 Don't you think …?
3 I suppose so / not …
4 What I mean is …
5 All the same, …
6 After all, …

10 Match the introductory phrases in exercise 9 to the functions a–f below.

a give more detail / expand on something you've just said _____
b disagree without saying 'No!' _____
c give a reason to explain what you have just said _____
d challenge someone to agree with you _____
e say 'nevertheless' _____
f agree (reluctantly) with what someone has said _____

EXAM SPOTLIGHT

PAPER 4, PART 3 Collaborative task

This is a two-way conversation between the two candidates. It takes about four minutes.

Remember, for the first two minutes you should discuss the different options. The examiner will stop you after this time.

You will then be asked to make a choice. You should arrive at a decision based on negotiation. The examiner will tell you stop when to stop.

USEFUL EXPRESSIONS

COLLABORATIVE TASK

Shall we start with this option?
What do you think about this option?
Which one would you go for first?
Which one do you prefer / do you think is better?
Have you got anything to add / any further ideas?
Shall we move on to the next one?
Are we ready to make a decision / our choice?
Shall we make a decision?

11 Work in groups. Read the interlocutor's instructions and look at the diagram. Discuss the question for two minutes. Then choose the best idea. Use some of the phrases from exercise 9 and the phrases from the Useful expressions box.

> *I'd like you to imagine that your school wants to organise a themed fashion show to raise money for charity. Here are some of the themes they are thinking about. Now, talk to each other about why these ideas would attract people to the fashion show.*

PAPER 4, PART 4 Discussion on a topic

12 Take turns to be the candidate and the examiner. Ask and answer these questions.

1 How important is it for you to be fashionable?
2 Do you think people worry far too much about brands and fashion?

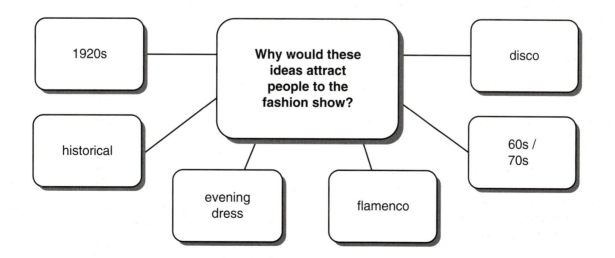

1920s

historical

Why would these ideas attract people to the fashion show?

evening dress

flamenco

disco

60s / 70s

WRITING a description

1 **In Part 2 of the Writing paper, you may have the choice of writing a story, review or article which includes a description of people or places. Read the four short descriptions and match them to the pictures (a–d).**

1

After our long walk we entered the bar which was bright and welcoming. There was a fire crackling in the fireplace and a kind-looking woman in her early forties was standing alone behind the bar. She was smallish and plump with untidy blonde hair, and when she smiled at us dimples appeared in her cheeks. It was pleasant, warm and cosy after the freezing temperatures outside.

2

I opened the door and entered what would be my room for the first year of student life. It was small and cramped with nasty wallpaper and faded floral curtains. The floor was covered in old cracked lino which was sticky underfoot. The smell of cooked cabbage was so strong you could almost taste it. Seth must have read my thoughts. 'Don't worry,' he said, as cheerful as ever, 'we'll soon brighten it up with some of your posters, and the lamps your mum lent you.' At the mention of Mum, I immediately felt desperately lonely and homesick.

3

The house stood alone at the end of a long winding lane. It had roses climbing up the walls and looked like everyone's idea of what a country cottage should be. As we got out of the car, the sweet smell of honeysuckle hit us. A wrinkled elderly lady with steel-grey hair was standing on the path leading to her door. A pretty little girl with freckles and red hair tied in pigtails stared at us as she pulled up the flowers in the flowerbed next to her.

4

The door opened before we had had time to knock, and a skinny young woman dressed in a black leather jacket covered with chains and skulls appeared. The woman, who was in her twenties, had messy, dyed hair and unhealthy pale skin covered in piercings. Behind her loomed a tall man, presumably her boyfriend, who had a tattoo of a black and red spider's web over his neck. She glared at us and through lips covered in black lipstick snapped aggressively, 'What do you want? We were just going out.'

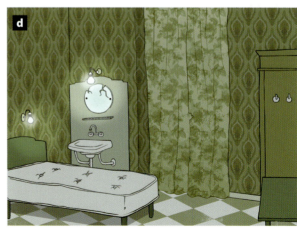

2 Work in pairs. What general impression do each of the four descriptions give? Discuss which ones feel happy or optimistic, and which ones feel sad or pessimistic.

3 Read the four descriptions again and find words which describe people. Write the words in the table under the category headings shown.

age	height / build	hair	skin

PAIRING ADJECTIVES

Two adjectives can be put together using *and*.

*The room was small **and** cramped.*

If we want to add other elements to the description we can add *with* and another noun phrase:

adjective + *and* + adjective + *with* + noun phrase

It was small and cramped with nasty wallpaper and faded floral curtains.

4 Read the information in the box about pairing adjectives. Look at the descriptions in exercise 1 again and underline examples of paired adjectives.

CONNOTATION

'Connotation' means an additional, emotive meaning that words sometimes have. For example, the literal meaning of *skinny* is 'very thin'. However, *skinny* has the additional, negative connotation of being, in the view of the speaker or writer, unattractively thin.

5 Read the box about *Connotation*. The words in the box below all have a strong connotation. Look them up in a good English dictionary and try to think of a more neutral word for each one.

skinny = <u>thin</u>

cosy	cramped	elderly	glare	loomed	messy
nasty	pretty	plump	snap	stare	

6 Match the words from exercise 5 to their connotations a–e. Some words could match more than one connotation.

a affectionate / sympathetic: <u>elderly</u>
b welcoming / comforting:
c negative / unattractive:
d menacing / aggressive:
e attractive / pleasant:

7 Sometimes we may want to convey meanings which relate to our senses. Look at the four descriptions in exercise 1 again, and find words which refer to smell, sight, taste, touch and hearing.

- smell _____
- sight _____
- taste _____
- touch _____
- hearing _____

8 Choose one of these exam questions and write an answer. Remember, the short story question is in the *First for schools* exam only.

Your school has organised a creative writing competition. Write a story of a memorable event in your life, or in the life of a fictional character, which includes a description of people and places. Begin your story with this phrase:

I'll never forget the time we …

Your story must include:

- a house
- a surprise.

Your school is asking for articles for the school magazine. Write an article about a memorable event in your life. What happened? Who was there? Include detailed descriptions of the people and places.

WRITING CHECKLIST

A DESCRIPTION

Did you:
- position your description (say when and where it happened)? ☐
- use a variety of narrative tenses? ☐
- give a full physical description of the person or place? ☐
- use adjectives and verbs which carry connotation? ☐
- use words that relate to the senses? ☐

REVIEW AND EXAM PRACTICE Units 13 and 14

1 **Read the text below and decide which answer (A, B, C or D) best fits each gap. There is an example (0) at the beginning.**

Newspaper circulation has been declining (0) _B_ decades, so where are the readers going? Some people get their news from TV channels that provide regular (1) _____ each hour. This (2) _____ that newspaper editors have had to shift their focus from 'new news' to analysis of yesterday's news. We have journalists whose role it is to comment (3) _____ events and tell us what they think. (4) _____, while sales have gone down, newspaper width has increased. There are now more sections than (5) _____ – book reviews, TV guides, travel, health and nutrition, comic books – there's no (6) _____ to what newspapers will do to win older readers back. As for the younger readers, they went online a (7) _____ time ago. Automated email will even fill you in on the latest gossip, so why go looking (8) _____ your news when it will find you wherever you are?

0 A from	B for	C since	D before	
1 A updates	B downloads	C outlooks	D input	
2 A suggests	B tells	C involves	D means	
3 A on	B by	C into	D over	
4 A Due	B Furthermore	C Because	D Although	

5 A never	B once	C ever	D ago
6 A finish	B end	C way	D stop
7 A long	B many	C previous	D very
8 A into	B over	C after	D for

2 **For questions 9–16, read the text below and think of the word which best fits each gap. Use only one word in each gap. There is an example (0) at the beginning.**

Flashmobbing is the latest craze to hit Europe from the United States. Crowds (0) _are_ created by calling people via the Internet or smart phone to do something unexpected, such (9) _____ lying down on the floor in a public place, and then disappearing as quickly as they arrived. Europe's first flashmob took (10) _____ in Rome when people went to a shop and asked staff (11) _____ books that did not exist. The latest New York flashmob caused panic (12) _____ flash mobsters gathered in a toy store. Participants (13) _____ told to stare at the store's giant animatronic dinosaur for three minutes and to react to (14) _____ roars by moaning for four minutes. Staff quickly turned off the dinosaur and called the police. Since June flashmobs have appeared (15) _____ over the world. Some people hope (16) _____ this silly craze will die out as quickly as it started.

3 **For questions 17–24, read the text below. Use the word given in capitals at the end of some of the lines to form a word that fits in the gap in the same line. There is an example (0) at the beginning.**

The world can be a terribly unfair place. While many millions	
live in (0) _misery_ and families hardly know how to satisfy the	MISERABLE
(17) _____ of their children, other people will go to ridiculous	HUNGRY
(18) _____ to follow the latest trend, and starve themselves	LONG
to look thin. It is an insult to millions of poor people that in rich	
countries it is (19) _____ to wear jeans which have been	FASHION
deliberately aged and torn, while millions of others have no	
(20) _____ other than to dress in rags. The gap between	CHOOSE
the rich and poor is (21) _____ all the time. Moreover the	WIDE
(22) _____ of cotton farmers by powerful importers of	EXPLOIT
this raw material means they get a fraction of the price of a pair of	
(23) _____ denims. Franco-Italian fashion producers Rica-Lewis	DESIGN
have made the (24) _____ brave decision to lift farmers out	ETHIC
of poverty by using their more expensive Fair Trade cotton.	

4 **Complete the second sentence so that it has a similar meaning to the first sentence, using the word given. You must use between two and five words, including the word given. There is an example (0) at the beginning.**

0 People make this product in China.
MANUFACTURED
This <u>product is manufactured</u> in China

25 Her parents would not let Sue have a nose ring.
ALLOWED
Sue _____ a nose ring by her parents.

26 I used a professional to decorate the kitchen.
BY
The _____ a professional.

27 When Tim joined the army he had to have a haircut.
MADE
Tim _____ a haircut when he joined the army.

28 Fashion magazines are encouraging young women to be unhealthily skinny.
BEING
Young women _____ to be unhealthily skinny by fashion magazines.

29 My dad finds this new fashion quite shocking.
IS
My dad _____ this new fashion.

30 They used a laser to remove Eddie's tattoo.
REMOVED
Eddie _____ with a laser.

5 **Write your answer in 140–190 words in an appropriate style.**

In your English class you have been talking about the fashion industry. Now, your teacher has asked you to write an essay.

Write an essay using all the notes and give reasons for your point of view.

Magazines and TV often have articles about the latest fashions. Do you think people should be less concerned with fashion and their appearance?

Notes

Write about:

1 the importance of fashion
2 the negative impact of fashion
3 your own ideas

CULTURE AND TRADITIONS

1 Look at the photo of a famous statue. Do you know who it is, or where it is? Do you like it?

2 What are some national symbols in your country? Think about the following categories.

> a national hero an artist a scientist a national dish

LISTENING statues

PAPER 3, PART 3 Multiple matching

3 ⊙ **15.1** **You will hear five speakers. Choose from the list (A–H) what each speaker talks about. Use each letter only once. There are three extra letters which you do not need.**

A a monument that reminds us of a famous event
B models used for comedy
C an angry crowd destroying a statue
D people who made an expensive mistake
E a technique used by experts
F an event commemorated every year
G someone who imitated a statue
H plans to erect a new statue

Speaker 1	_____
Speaker 2	_____
Speaker 3	_____
Speaker 4	_____
Speaker 5	_____

4 What materials do the speakers mention?

_____

_____

5 ⊙ **15.1** **Listen again, and decide if the following statements are true (T) or false (F).**

1 Wendel entered the museum in disguise. T / F
2 The warriors have just had their one thousandth birthday. T / F
3 Wendel stayed still as the guards removed him. T / F
4 Guy Fawkes was a kind of terrorist. T / F
5 Children buy their guys from toyshops. T / F
6 Children expect more than a penny. T / F
7 Stalingrad used to be called Volgograd. T / F
8 The statue is in the centre of Volgograd. T / F
9 It was the most moving thing the speaker saw on his trip. T / F
10 The show isn't on British TV any more. T / F
11 The puppets were easily recognisable. T / F
12 She thinks it was fair to make fun of the monarchy. T / F
13 Our first impression is often the right impression. T / F
14 The ability to make fast, accurate decisions is the result of long experience. T / F
15 The museum escaped being tricked. T / F

SPEAKING giving reasons

6 **Work in pairs. You want to erect a statue of your personal hero in the main square of your town or capital city. Follow these steps.**

- Decide who you would choose.
- Write down as many reasons as you can for why your choice is best. Why is this person important?
- Think about how the statue should show the person, for example, holding a sword, playing a musical instrument.

7 **Make a presentation to the class, telling them who you have chosen and why. Use these expressions to help you. Vote for the person who you think has made the best argument. You <u>can't</u> vote for yourself!**

Who   *The person we have chosen is …*
Why   *We think he/she deserves a statue because …*
What   *Our statue would show …*
Where   *We would like to put our statue …*
          Thank you for listening.

VOCABULARY culture and heritage

8 **Choose the correct word (in italics) to complete the sentences.**

1 There are some wonderful paintings at her *exhibition / expedition*.
2 This street is home to several expensive art *museums / galleries* and antique shops.
3 This peaceful-looking bay was once the *site / sight* of a terrible sea battle.

4 It is a *habit / tradition* for people to exchange presents at this time of year.
5 These castles and forests are part of our national *heritage / heirloom*.
6 At the top of the steps there is a *monumental / statue* of the emperor on his horse.
7 I am fascinated by *old-fashioned / ancient* history.
8 The fall of the Berlin Wall was an emotional and *historical / historic* occasion.
9 In the centre of the village there is a war *memorial / souvenir* with the names of the soldiers who gave their lives.
10 The study of the Japanese tea *ceremony / event* can often take many years.
11 The boat-race between Oxford and Cambridge takes *part / place* each spring.
12 He is one of the most *notorious / famous* murderers of the last century.
13 It is a wonderful *landscape / portrait* of a country scene.
14 An ancient *customer / custom* is to collect wild flowers for Mother's Day.
15 The Battle of the Bridge is a famous *festival / first of all* held in Pisa each year.
16 The statue the museum bought turned out to be a *priceless / worthless* fake.
17 A good guidebook with quality colour photographs is always a / an *invaluable / worthwhile* companion.
18 During the *middle-aged / middle ages*, it was a / an *infamous / well-known* prison where some terrible events took place.

9 **Work in pairs. Write five sentences using some of the incorrect word choices from exercise 1.**

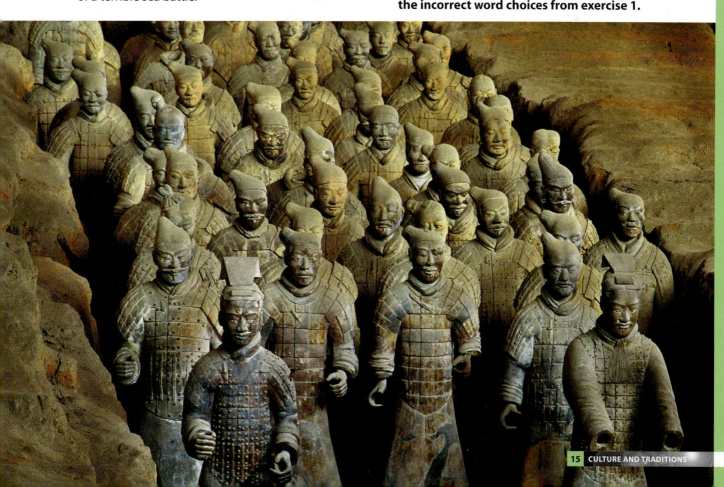

READING genuine fakes

1 **Work in groups. You are going to read an article about John Myatt, an artist with a difference. Look at the title. Discuss what you think the article will be about.**

2 **Read the article quickly and check if your predictions were correct.**

> **EXAM SPOTLIGHT**
>
> **PAPER 1, PART 6** Gapped text
>
> • Read the gapped text all the way through to get an overall idea of meaning.
> • Try to put each of the sentences in each of the gaps before making your choice.
> • Exploit reference words such as pronouns to help you match the sentences.

3 **Read the article again. Six sentences have been removed from the article. Choose from the sentences A–H the one which fits each gap (1–6). There are two extra sentences which you do not need to use.**

A It said that Myatt had made up his mind to end their partnership.

B Myatt has turned his back on a life of crime.

C Whenever he tried to produce portraits or landscapes, the results were invariably dull.

D This was followed by a commission from a member of the prosecution team.

E An eminent auction house had offered Drewe double the sum for the painting.

F He also produced the paperwork which supplied each work with a convincing history.

G He immerses himself in books and surrounds himself with examples of the artist's work.

H He needed it to pay for the painting.

4 **Work in pairs. What do you think of Myatt?**

Genuine Fakes

The artist John Myatt was responsible for one of the biggest art frauds of the last century and paid for it by spending time in prison. Over eight years he turned out more than two hundred works by surrealists, cubists and impressionists. He passed them off as originals with the aid of an accomplice. This person, John Drewe, handled the business side, dealing with auction houses and museums. (1) __F__ Provenance, knowing who has owned a work before, and in which catalogues it has appeared, is essential in proving the authenticity of a work of art.

Myatt didn't set out to become a forger. As a student, he wasn't talented enough to establish his own style. (2) _____ Instead, he taught evening classes and sold the occasional fake to friends and colleagues. Eventually he decided to put an advertisement in the satirical magazine *Private Eye*, offering copies of 19th- and 20th-century paintings from £150. Myatt soon started getting commissions from Drewe, who passed himself off as an atomic scientist and art lover. At first, he produced a Matisse and some Dutch-style portraits, but then Drewe asked him to produce a painting in the style of a German cubist. He then received a call from Drewe asking him how he would like £12,500 in a brown envelope. (3) _____ The offer was too attractive for him to turn down. He had been going through family trouble and he didn't have enough money to look after his two children. He wanted a job he could do from home, and the money was as much as he made in a year from his teaching.

Before he tries to paint anything in the style of an artist, he tries to find out as much as he can about the artist and their life. (4) _____ Even so, he is amazed that his paintings managed to take in so many experts. Drewe, in the meantime, dedicated himself to creating false provenances. He collected old receipts from galleries and forged museum records. The partnership was so successful that Myatt's paintings are in museums around the world. In the end, the whole thing collapsed when Drewe's wife went to the police. When they turned up at Myatt's house he at first denied everything. Then officers made an important discovery: an un-posted letter to Drewe. (5) _____ It was such damaging evidence that Myatt made a full confession.

Myatt survived prison by doing portraits of fellow inmates, earning himself the nickname 'Picasso'. When he was released he said the last thing he wanted to do was pick up another paintbrush. Soon after he left jail, he got a phone call which made him change his mind. It was from the policeman who had arrested him, asking for a portrait of his family. (6) _____ Myatt had made such a good impression that everyone wanted his work.

Myatt was soon back painting fakes in earnest. Now they are being sold from prestigious art galleries. He doesn't try to pass them off as the real thing – the back of each canvas carries a computer chip and the words 'genuine fake' written in indelible ink. Ironically, Myatt has been copied too.

GRAMMAR *so, such, too* and *enough*

5 Look at sentences a–c, then choose the correct options to complete rule 1.

a The offer was **too attractive** (for him) to turn down.

b … he wasn't **talented enough** to establish his own style.

c … he didn't have **enough money** to look after his two children.

> 1 We use *too* before / after an adjective and *enough* before / after an adjective and before / after a noun.

6 Look at sentences d–f, then choose the correct options to complete rule 2.

d The partnership was **so successful** that Myatt's paintings are in museums around the world.

e Myatt had made **such a good impression** that everyone wanted his work.

f It was **such damaging evidence** that Myatt made a full confession.

> 2 We use *so* before / after an adjective and *such* before / after a noun or an adjective + noun. If the noun is countable *such* comes before / after a / an.

▶ GRAMMAR REFERENCE (SECTION 16) PAGE 209

7 Now look at these sentences which rewrite the information from a–f in exercises 5 and 6. Complete the sentences using *so, such, too* or *enough*. Add any other words you may need.

1 It was _____ attractive offer he couldn't turn it down.

2 He didn't _____ talent to establish his own style.

3 He wasn't _____ to look after his children.

4 It was _____ partnership that Myatt's paintings are in museums around the world.

5 Everyone was _____ with his work that they wanted one of his pictures.

6 The evidence _____ damaging for Myatt to stick to his story.

8 Write sentences about yourself and your experiences using *so, such, too* and *enough*.

When I was younger I went to a theme park. I waited ages to go on a scary ride, but when it was my turn, they said I wasn't tall enough. I was so disappointed that it spoilt the whole day.

VOCABULARY phrasal verbs

9 Find these phrasal verbs in the article, then match them to the definitions 1–10.

find out	go through	look after	pass off	set out
take in	take off	turn down	turn out	turn up

1 take care of _____
2 begin with the intention of doing something _____
3 produce _____
4 arrive (unexpectedly) _____
5 trick / deceive _____
6 discover _____
7 present something false as the 'real thing' _____
8 experience something difficult _____
9 imitate someone _____
10 refuse _____

10 Work in pairs. Look at these groups of sentences. They show how the same phrasal verb can be used to express different meanings. Rewrite each sentence to show the meaning of the phrasal verb.

1a She **took** us **in** with her lies.
   She managed to make us believe her lies

1b When her parents died, her aunt **took** her **in**.

1c It took me a minute to **take in** the news.

2a The factory **turns out** a car every ten months.

2b We eventually discovered what had happened to the parcel: it **turned out** it had been delivered to the wrong address.

2c They **turned** everyone **out** of the nightclub.

3a He **turned up** at my house at three o'clock in the morning.

3b Can you **turn** the volume **up**? I can't hear a thing.

3c These jeans are too long. Could you **turn** them **up** for me?

DIFFERENT MEANINGS OF PHRASAL VERBS

A phrasal verb of the same form may have two or more very different meanings.

take off

The plane took off. (Type 1) = leave the ground

She was taking her teacher off when he suddenly came back into the classroom. (Type 2) = imitate someone

It was hot in the office so he took off his jacket and tie. (Type 2) = remove clothing

When you record a phrasal verb in your notebook, make sure that you put it in a context so that its meaning is apparent, and be sure to note its type.

▶ GRAMMAR REFERENCE (SECTION 12.3) **PAGE 205**

LISTENING living traditions

1 Look at the photo and read about Kelly Foster and her unusual hobby. Do you have any similar organisations in your country?

2 Work in pairs. What questions do you think the interviewer will ask Kelly?

PAPER 3, PART 4 Multiple choice

3 🔘 **15.2** You will hear part A of an interview with a woman who re-enacts the battles of the English Civil War. For questions 1–7, choose the best answer (A, B or C).

1 Why did Kelly become involved in the re-enactment society?
   A She was a bit lonely.
   B Some friends encouraged her to join.
   C as part of her job

2 Why did Kelly wait before making a decision to join?
   A She couldn't make a full commitment.
   B She thought the people might be strange.
   C from shyness

3 What made Kelly join her 'regiment'?
   A her love of history
   B There wasn't a Roundhead regiment in the area.
   C There was a strong connection to her town.

4 Why are the 'Roundheads' considered less appealing than the 'Cavaliers'?
   A They were more fun.
   B They had better uniforms.
   C They were too serious.

5 What happens during battles?
   A The outcome is not decided until the day itself.
   B The result of the battle is already agreed well in advance.
   C The people watching the battle already know which side will win.

6 How many soldiers does each side have?
   A around 1,000
   B a few hundred
   C thousands

7 Where do the society's events take place?
   A in the same place as the original conflict
   B on specially constructed stages and scenes
   C wherever they can find a sympathetic farmer

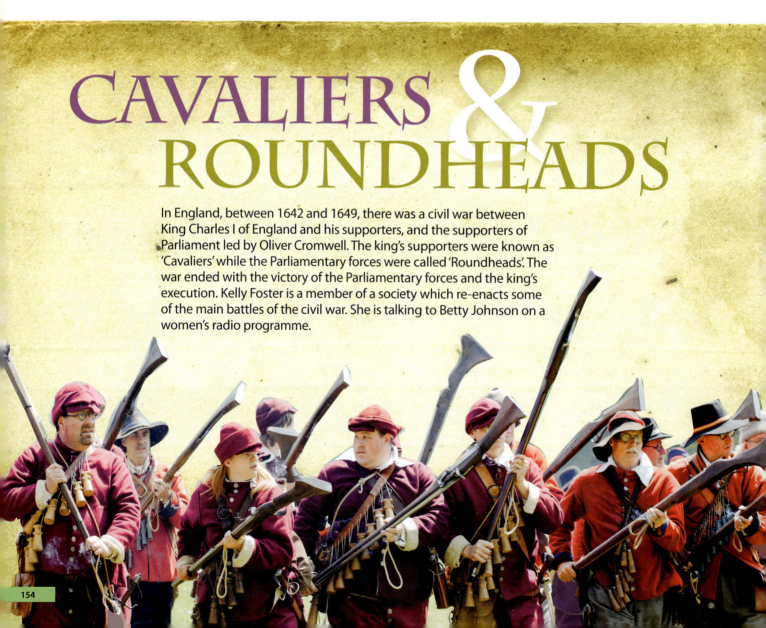

CAVALIERS & ROUNDHEADS

In England, between 1642 and 1649, there was a civil war between King Charles I of England and his supporters, and the supporters of Parliament led by Oliver Cromwell. The king's supporters were known as 'Cavaliers' while the Parliamentary forces were called 'Roundheads'. The war ended with the victory of the Parliamentary forces and the king's execution. Kelly Foster is a member of a society which re-enacts some of the main battles of the civil war. She is talking to Betty Johnson on a women's radio programme.

4 🔘 **15.3   Listen to part B of the interview and complete the notes with a word or short phrase.**

Living traditions

Before she became a 'soldier' Kelly was a
(1) _____ .
She changed role because the soldiers have
(2) _____ .
Women who want to play soldiers have to (3)
_____ as a man.

Women's military roles

In the re-enactment society it's possible for women to use a sword, fire a gun, join the cavalry, or even be a (4) _____ .

Difficulties

Women can't easily handle the spears called
(5) _____ . (They are
(6) _____ long and very heavy.)

Dangers

There aren't any serious risks, and people don't usually hurt themselves badly, but you do have to be careful of (7) _____ standing on your feet!

Other activities

The social activities are (8) _____ .
There are big meals (9) (_____)
and dances.
Every year there is a trip to London in memory of the king's (10) _____ in 1649.

KEY WORD *mind*

5 **These sentences all use a word or expression with *mind*. Complete the sentences.**

1 _____ your head! The door is very low.
2 I wish he would make a final decision; he keeps on _____ mind.
3 Sorry, I forgot to go. It totally _____ mind.
4 Her mum's crazy. She's completely _____ mind.
5 It's time to make a decision. You need to _____ your mind.
6 Most people feel more comfortable with _____-_____ people who share the same opinions and attitudes.
7 I haven't paid the phone bill; they have sent me a _____ .

6 **Use the prompts to write sentences using *mind*.**

1 I hope / you / mind / my / mention / this / but / you / wear / different-coloured socks!
   _____

2 Do / you / mind / close / window / terribly / cold / here.
   _____

3 you / mind / if / I take / a photo / you / your uniform?
   _____

SPEAKING   adverbs in conversation

BASICALLY, *ACTUALLY* AND *ANYWAY*

- We use *basically* to introduce a simplified explanation for something.
  A: *What does your job involve?*
  B: *Well, **basically** I am in charge of student registrations.*

- We use *actually* to politely contradict.
  A: *You're French, aren't you?*
  B: *Well, **actually** I'm Swiss.*

- We use *anyway* to:
  1 show we have finished with a topic / are moving to a new topic
  I'm glad you had such a lovely holiday. Anyway, I think we need to start thinking about the new project.
  (The speaker wants to bring everyone's attention back to the subject of the meeting.)

  2 summarise / avoid unnecessary detail
  I tried everywhere for a copy of the book. Anyway, I eventually found one in a second-hand bookshop.
  (The speaker doesn't tell us about all the different bookshops they visited.)

7 **Read the information in the box. Turn to the audioscript on page 233 and underline sentences that use *basically*, *actually* and *anyway*.**

8 **Work in pairs.**

- Make statements you know your partner will contradict using *actually*.
- Tell each other the essential reason why you are studying English using *basically*.
- Tell each other how you managed to do something difficult, without giving all the details, using *anyway*.

You come from Madrid, don't you?

No, actually I'm from Rome, I'm Italian.

WRITING a review, a letter or an article

EXAM SPOTLIGHT

In Part 2 of the Writing paper you may have the opportunity to write a review, a letter or an article. Make sure that you answer the question in an appropriate style for the task and that you keep the kind of reader in mind.

1 Read the exam questions 1–3 and match them to three candidates' answers A–C on page 157.

---

1 This is part of a letter you have received from your Canadian friend Jim.

Hi,

I am planning to come to your country. I would like to spend some time travelling and to see a cultural event or festival. Can you give me some advice on when to come and what to see?

Write your reply to Jim.

---

2 You see this announcement in an English Language magazine called *Teen Traveller*.

Reviews wanted: Events and festivals

Have you been to an event or festival that you would like to tell readers about?

Write a review, describing the event and saying what you enjoyed about it. Say why you would / wouldn't recommend the event to other people of your age.

Write your review.

---

3 You see this announcement in a cultural magazine.

We need your help!

Write an article about a memorable event or festival that you have attended. Send us your article and we will choose the best ones to publish in our next edition. You could win a book of amazing photographs!

Write your article.

---

2 Work in pairs or groups. Read the answers A–C again, and decide how well each candidate answers the question. Complete the table with scores for each category.

✓✓ = very good   ✓ = good / OK   X = poor
? = unsure / don't know

	A	B	C
CONTENT			
Task completion			
Relevance to question			
Length			
COMMUNICATIVE ACHIEVEMENT			
Appropriate style for reader			
Communicates ideas clearly			
ORGANISATION			
Layout			
Paragraphs			
Use of linkers			
LANGUAGE			
Vocabulary range			
Grammar / accuracy			
Spelling			

3 Work in pairs. Choose one of the three candidates' answers. Look at the scores in the table and discuss what needs to be improved. Rewrite the answer so it has ✓✓ for all the categories. Then work with another pair and compare your answers.

4 Choose one of the exam questions and write your own article, review or letter.

WRITING CHECKLIST

WRITING FOR AN AUDIENCE

Did you:
- complete the task? ☐
- use a good range of vocabulary and linkers? ☐
- write your answer in an appropriate style? ☐
- check it for mistakes? ☐
- think about who your piece of writing is aimed at? ☐

A

Last winter I have been to the Winter Wonderland in Hyde Park. It is an absolutely big fun fair and has other things. There were some rides exciting and two circuses wich was nice.

One lovely thing was ice palace. I suggest you to go there if you can. It is nice for children, they can sit in a carriage made from ice with an unicorn.

The food was quiet nice but there wasn't space enough to relax yourself.

The ice-skating looked funny but we didn't not try it because there were many persons.

I would visit it again for to go on the rides, but it was too much expensive. You hadn't to pay to go in, but everything else costed a lot.

We were enjoyed ourselves a lot, but it is not convenient for young children. If you want to take your family I suggest you that the afternoon is better. I would recommend you but it is better for teenager than youngs.

B

Dear Mr. Jim,
Further to your letter I can help you. The best time for coming is in september or early October for The Trung Thu festival. It is a celebration for the moon. The exact date it depends by the moon. It is a special time for children. Children wear masks, the most popular ones are pigs, demons and the moon. In addition we also eat moon cakes. We also carry lights, with candles inside. These are in a star shape. Furthermore, we burn money (pretend) for good luck and we also remember different generations. Please find attached some photos from last year's festival. It would be great to see you. If you accept to come and stay we will be very happy. I can show you some interesting places in Vietnam. I look forward to your reply.

Yours faithfully,

Nguyen Troc

C

I want to say you about the Day of the Dead. I was in Mexico with some relatives. This feast goes back to the ancient Aztecs. These days, it is like the day 'All Saints' Day'. First of all I thought it would be sad and even a bit scared, but in fact it was a happy occasion. In the days before, families look after the graves. They are decorating them with flowers brightly-coloured and sweets. They look like skulls and crosses. Sometimes they leave the person favourite food, and glasses of alcool! Everywhere you could see people dressed up as Catrina – the 'lady of the dead'. On the big day we put on our best clothes. We said some prayers, and fired candles. It was a really moving. An uncle said some funny poetry about the died relative, I was a bit shocking, but apparently this is a tradition. According to me, the cemetery and candles was the nicest place I have visited. It left me with some wonderful memories and no bad dreams!

GLOSSARY

ancestors: our relatives from very long ago
clan: a large group of families that are closely connected to each other
cradle: where a baby sleeps / the place where something important started
outback: the uninhabited areas of inland Australia
remote: far away from where most people live
ritual: the actions that form part of an important or religious ceremony
vital: extremely important / essential

VIDEO Songlines of the Aborigines

1 **How much do you know about your country's history? Tick one answer.**

I know a lot about history and traditions. ☐
I know the basic facts about our history. ☐
I'm not very interested in history. ☐

2 **How important is tradition in your country and culture? Where did you learn about your traditions?**

3 **Read about the modern history of Australia. Replace the verbs in bold with words and expressions from the box.**

> believed to be   died   decreased over time
> encouraged   extended across
> grew and were successful   made certain   took place

Australia was discovered by Dutch explorers in the 1606 but English colonisation (1) **occurred** in the early nineteenth century. From tiny settlements, the colonies eventually (2) **spanned** the entire continent. At that time, there weren't enough people willing to go such a long distance, so convicts from England's jails were sent there! Some of them (3) **perished** on the long sea voyage, and for those who arrived, life was hard. They were (4) **considered** little better than slaves. However, some of them (5) **thrived** and became successful citizens. The number of convicts coming to the country (6) **dwindled**, and eventually stopped in 1868. In the 1950s, the Australian government (7) **urged** new immigrants to come with the promise of a better life. You could even go all the way to Australia for just £10. Nowadays, strict regulations (8) **ensure** that only people with the right skills and qualifications can get a visa.

4 Watch a video about the original inhabitants of Australia, the Aborigines. Number these three aspects of their history and traditions (a–c) in the order you hear about them.

a the importance of the land _____
b their early history and the arrival of the Europeans _____
c the importance of songs _____

5 Watch the first half of the video again. Choose the correct option (a or b) to complete the sentences.

1 The Aborigines arrived in Australia around _____ years ago.
a 50,000   b 1,500
2 Their culture thrived for _____ thousands of years.
a a few   b many
3 The main immigration of Europeans occurred in _____ century.
a the 19th   b the 18th
4 The early European settlers considered the Aborigines as _____ .
a sophisticated people   b savages
5 The Aborigine population _____ over the following 150 years.
a dwindled   b thrived
6 Over _____ per cent of the population had perished by the mid-twentieth century.
a 19   b 90
7 The Aborigines were _____ to move to communities like Ramingining.
a urged   b forced

6 Watch the second half of the video again. Complete the notes about the Aborigines and the Songlines. Use one word from the video in each gap.

Aborigine beliefs are connected to the (1) _____ . Their (2) _____ involve walking long distances and following the routes that were taken by their (3) _____ . These routes, known as Songlines, form a (4) _____ across the continent. Some of the lines are a few miles long, while others (5) _____ hundreds of miles. The Songlines are also extremely important for (6) _____ as they show different geographical features, and they map the borders between (7) _____ . However, they also have another purpose: they are a (8) _____ journey. They recall the mythical time when the world was created: 'the (9) _____ '. As the Aborigines walk and sing, they (10) _____ that the world is re-created.

7 Read and complete the Ideas generator.

FINDING OUT MORE ABOUT A TOPIC

In the Speaking test, you might have to talk about a topic you don't have much personal experience of, or don't feel confident about.

Look at this list and write a number (1–3) for each topic:
1 = I know about this topic and I can talk about it for a long time.
2 = I know a bit about it, I can talk about it for two minutes.
3 = I don't know anything about it and I can't talk about it.

Tourism and travel	_____
History and traditions	_____
Learning and education	_____
Work and employment	_____
Media and the Internet	_____
Special occasions	_____
Entertainment and sport	_____
Fashion and current trends	_____
Shopping and consumerism	_____
Food and healthy living	_____

Look back at the topics that you marked 2 or 3. Where can you find more information about them? On the news? From friends? In a book or magazine? On the Internet? Find out more information and make lists of words to help you.

7 Work in pairs. Take turns to choose a topic from the Ideas generator box to talk about for 60 seconds. Your partner will time you!

USEFUL EXPRESSIONS

PLAYING FOR TIME

Let me think about that for a moment.
May I think for a moment?
That's an interesting topic.
I'm glad you have asked me about this.
Well, I don't know much about X but I do know about Y.
Well, let me see, …
I'm not sure about this, perhaps …

Speaking video worksheet

1 Look at the flowchart and read the sentences taken from a *First* Speaking test. Which part of the exam does each sentence come from? Who said it – the interlocutor (I) or a candidate (C)?

First Speaking test, Paper 4

Part 1

Conversation between the interlocutor and each candidate
(2 minutes)

↓

Part 2

Each candidate talks about two pictures.
(4 minutes)

↓

Part 3

The two candidates collaborate to complete a task by discussing written prompts.
(4 minutes)

↓

Part 4

The interlocutor and the two candidates discuss questions about topics related to Part 3.
(4 minutes)

1 First of all we'd like to know something about you. **Part** _1_ (I)

2 In the first picture you can see four people skiing … **Part** _2_ (C)

3 I'm from Colombia. **Part** _1_ (___)

4 I would prefer to spend my free time skiing as in this picture … **Part** ___ (___)

5 And what do you like about living in Colombia? **Part** _1_ (___)

6 Now, I'd like you to talk about something together for about two minutes. **Part** ___ (___)

7 Maybe you could have a dinner in the evening and then later have a little party. **Part** ___ (___)

8 Do you prefer spending time at home or do you like to go out in your free time? **Part** ___ (___)

9 As many people can work from home with computers, do you think more of us will move away from cities in the future? **Part** ___

10 In this part of the test, I'm going to give each of you two photographs. **Part** ___ (___)

11 I'd like you to compare the photographs … **Part** ___ (___)

12 What do you think is important, when choosing where to live? **Part** ___ (___)

13 That's right. And the last activity we can choose might be the firework display. **Part** ___ (___)

14 I'd like you to imagine that your local town is 500 years old and is planning events to celebrate the anniversary. **Part** ___ (___)

15 Well, I think at the moment with all the opportunities and technical advances it is very easy to work away from the office. **Part** ___(___)

16 Can you tell me about a day that you've enjoyed recently? **Part** ___ (___)

2 ⊙ Watch a *First* Speaking test with two real students. As you watch, look at the material that the interlocutor uses and the material that the candidates are given.

Part 1

Good morning / afternoon / evening. My name is … and this is my colleague …

And your names are?

Can I have your mark sheets please?

Thank you.

Where are you from, (Candidate A) ?

And you, (Candidate B), ?

First we'd like to know something about you.

Select one or more questions from the following.

- **What do you like about living in …?**
- **What do you like doing with your friends?**
- **Do you prefer spending time on your own or with friends? Why?**
- **What sort of holidays do you go on?**
- **Do you normally go on your own or with friends?**
- **Tell me about a holiday you really enjoyed.**
- **Do you like cooking?**
- **What sort of things do you cook?**
- **What's your favourite food?**
- **Do you like eating at home or eating out? Why?**

Part 2

In this part of the test, I'm going to give each of you two photographs. I'd like you to talk about your photographs on your own for about a minute, and also to answer a question about your partner's photographs.

(Candidate A), it's your turn first. Here are your photographs.

They show people living in different types of homes. I'd like you to compare the photographs, and say why you think people choose to live in these types of homes.

Thank you. Now, *(Candidate B)*, here are your photographs.

They show people spending their free time in the countryside. I'd like you to compare the photographs, and say which you think is the best way to enjoy the countryside, and why.

(Candidate A speaks for about 1 minute.)

Thank you.

(Candidate B), which of these types of homes would you like to live in? Why?

(Candidate B speaks for about 30 seconds.)

(Candidate B speaks for about 1 minute.)

Thank you.

(Candidate A), which of these types of activities would you prefer to do? Why?

(Candidate A speaks for about 30 seconds.)

Part 3

Now, I'd like you to talk about something together for two minutes.

I'd like you to imagine that your local town is 500 years old and everybody is planning events to celebrate the anniversary. Here are some ideas they're thinking about and a question for you to discuss. First, you have some time to look at the task.

Give the candidates the task. Allow 15 seconds to study the question and ideas.

Now, talk to each other about how the town could celebrate its anniversary.

(Candidates A and B speak for 2 minutes.)

Thank you.

Now you have about a minute to decide which idea would be best for the town.

(Candidates A and B speak for 1 minute.)

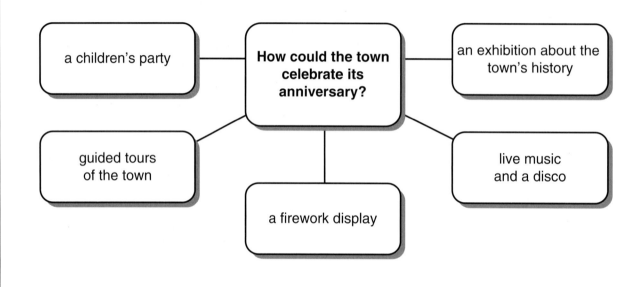

Part 4

Use the following questions, in order, as appropriate.

- **Do you celebrate events in your town?**
- **What do you think is important when choosing where you're going to live?**
- **Because lots of people work from home nowadays, do you think more of us will move away from the city to the countryside?**
- **Would you prefer to work from home or go out to work? Why?**
- **What are the most important things to consider when you choose a new job?**
- **What are some of the advantages of working in another country?**

> *Select any of the following prompts, as appropriate:*
>
> - **What do you think?**
> - **Do you agree?**
> - **And you?**

Thank you. That is the end of the test.

3 ⊙ **Look at the advice in the table. Watch the Speaking test again and score how well the two students followed the advice.**

> 1 = They did this very well.
> 2 = They did this quite well.
> 3 = They need to improve this part of the exam.

Part 1	Score
talk about general topics	1 2 3
make sure you answer the examiner's questions	1 2 3
give full answers with reasons	1 2 3
speak naturally and fluently	1 2 3
Part 2	
compare and contrast the two photographs	1 2 3
answer the question with reference to the two photographs	1 2 3
answer the examiner's supplementary question	1 2 3
give reasons for your answers and opinions	1 2 3
Part 3	
discuss the advantages and disadvantages of each suggestion	1 2 3
compare and contrast some of the suggestions	1 2 3
choose the best idea	1 2 3
ask for your partner's opinion	1 2 3
show you are listening to your partner	1 2 3
use polite phrases for agreeing and disagreeing	1 2 3
Part 4	
answer the examiner's questions	1 2 3
give opinions	1 2 3
give reasons for your opinions	1 2 3
use a wide range of language and structures	1 2 3

4 **Work in groups of three. Practise the Speaking test using the exam extracts on pages 161–162.**

Students A and B: you are the candidates. Answer the interlocuter's questions.

Student C: you are the interlocutor (examiner). Ask the questions for Speaking test Parts 1 to 4. Time each part of the test and stop the candidates when they have spoken for the correct time.

Change roles and repeat the exam.

EXAM SPOTLIGHT

PAPER 4 Speaking test

In the *First* Speaking test, the two examiners mark the following areas of your speaking performance.

Grammar and vocabulary

The examiner wants to hear a wide range of grammatical forms and vocabulary used correctly.

Discourse management

The examiner will give marks for good organisation of ideas and well-structured responses.

Pronunciation

The examiner needs to understand everything you say and wants to hear how you express meaning with your pronunciation.

Interactive communication

You can also receive marks if you interact easily with the other candidate and the examiner.

Practice test answer sheet: Paper 1

CAMBRIDGE ENGLISH
Language Assessment
Part of the University of Cambridge

Do not write in this box

Candidate Name
If not already printed, write name in CAPITALS and complete the Candidate No. grid (in pencil).

Candidate Signature

Examination Title

Centre

Supervisor:
If the candidate is ABSENT or has WITHDRAWN shade here

Centre No.

Candidate No.

Examination Details

Candidate Answer Sheet

Instructions

Use a PENCIL (B or HB).

Rub out any answer you wish to change using an eraser.

Parts 1, 5, 6 and **7**:
Mark ONE letter for each question.

For example, if you think **B** is the right answer to the question, mark your answer sheet like this:

0 A B C D

Parts 2, 3 and **4**:
Write your answer clearly in CAPITAL LETTERS.

For Parts 2 and 3 write one letter in each box. For example:

0 EXAMPLE

Part 1

1	A	B	C	D
2	A	B	C	D
3	A	B	C	D
4	A	B	C	D
5	A	B	C	D
6	A	B	C	D
7	A	B	C	D
8	A	B	C	D

Part 2

Do not write below here

9												9 1 0 u
10												10 1 0 u
11												11 1 0 u
12												12 1 0 u
13												13 1 0 u
14												14 1 0 u
15												15 1 0 u
16												16 1 0 u

Continues over ➡

FCE R

DP802

© National Geographic Learning 2015 PHOTOCOPIABLE

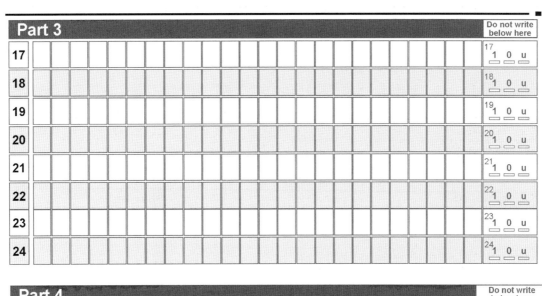

Part 3

			Do not write below here
17			17 1 0 u
18			18 1 0 u
19			19 1 0 u
20			20 1 0 u
21			21 1 0 u
22			22 1 0 u
23			23 1 0 u
24			24 1 0 u

Part 4

		Do not write below here
25		25 2 1 0 u
26		26 2 1 0 u
27		27 2 1 0 u
28		28 2 1 0 u
29		29 2 1 0 u
30		30 2 1 0 u

Part 5

	A	B	C	D
31	A	B	C	D
32	A	B	C	D
33	A	B	C	D
34	A	B	C	D
35	A	B	C	D
36	A	B	C	D

Part 6

	A	B	C	D	E	F	G
37	A	B	C	D	E	F	G
38	A	B	C	D	E	F	G
39	A	B	C	D	E	F	G
40	A	B	C	D	E	F	G
41	A	B	C	D	E	F	G
42	A	B	C	D	E	F	G

Part 7

	A	B	C	D	E	F
43	A	B	C	D	E	F
44	A	B	C	D	E	F
45	A	B	C	D	E	F
46	A	B	C	D	E	F
47	A	B	C	D	E	F
48	A	B	C	D	E	F
49	A	B	C	D	E	F
50	A	B	C	D	E	F
51	A	B	C	D	E	F
52	A	B	C	D	E	F

denote Print Limited 0121 520 5100

© National Geographic Learning 2015 PHOTOCOPIABLE

Practice test answer sheet: Paper 3

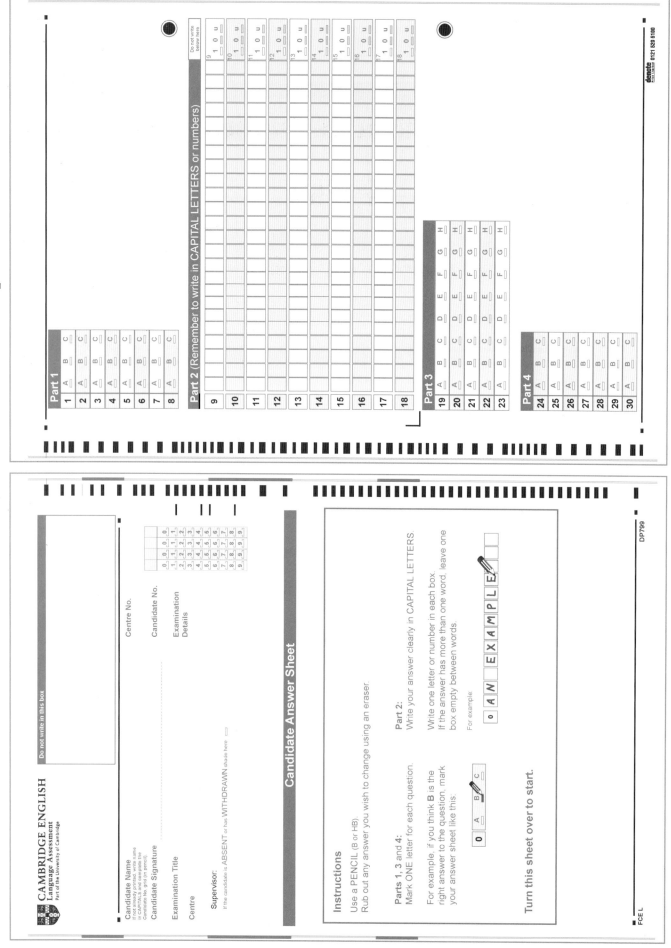

© National Geographic Learning 2015 PHOTOCOPIABLE

Cambridge English

First

Practice test

Paper 1: Reading and Use of English

Part 1

For questions **1 – 8**, read the text below and decide which answer (**A, B, C or D**) best fits each gap. There is an example at the beginning (0).

Mark your answers **on the separate answer sheet.**

Example:

0 **A** accounts for **B** counts on **C** brings out **D** clears up

0	A	B	C	D
	<u>A</u>	<u>B</u>	<u>C</u>	<u>D</u>

Non-verbal communication

Non-verbal communication, including body language and facial expression, **(0)** .... an enormous part of the way we convey our feelings to other people. This is **(1)** .... from the words we say. A smile communicates happiness, a frown the opposite. We may say one thing, but our face can **(2)** .... that we feel quite differently. Fear, anger, disgust, surprise, and a whole **(3)** .... of other expressions have been found by scientists to be **(4)** .... in the way they show on our faces. In other words, they're the same the world over.

'The eyes are the window to the soul' they say. We can tell a great **(5)** .... about how someone feels through eye **(6)** .... alone. When someone looks directly into our eyes during a conversation, we know they're interested in what we're saying; if they frequently look away, we understand they're distracted or **(7)** .... If a person's mouth is turned downwards, they're sad or **(8)** .... ; if it's turned upwards we know they're feeling positive.

1	**A**	alone	**B**	distant	**C**	far	**D**	aside
2	**A**	inform	**B**	tell	**C**	reveal	**D**	exhibit
3	**A**	range	**B**	extent	**C**	level	**D**	area
4	**A**	universal	**B**	comprehensive	**C**	widespread	**D**	general
5	**A**	load	**B**	deal	**C**	degree	**D**	ton
6	**A**	look	**B**	meeting	**C**	contact	**D**	connection
7	**A**	disagreeable	**B**	uncomfortable	**C**	painful	**D**	difficult
8	**A**	disapproving	**B**	distrusting	**C**	disturbing	**D**	disliking

Part 2

For questions **9 – 16**, read the text below and think of the word which best fits each gap. Use only **one** word in each gap. There is an example at the beginning (**0**).

Write your answers **IN CAPITAL LETTERS on the separate answer sheet.**

Example: | 0 | T | O | | | | | | | | | | | | | | | | |

World's biggest dinosaur walks again

Giant steps taken by the biggest dinosaur ever (**0**) .... walk on Earth have been reconstructed by scientists.

Argentinosaurus, from South America, was able to walk and run (**9**) .... the first time in more than 94 million

years – in virtual reality. Argentinosaurus was an 80-ton, 38-metre-long plant eater that stood as tall as a three-

storey building. Its movements were modelled (**10**) .... experts, who used a laser to scan a skeleton of the

animal in an Argentine museum.

This is science, (**11**) .... just animation, say the researchers. They claim the best way to work out (**12**) ....

dinosaurs walked is to use computer simulation, as it is the only way (**13**) .... bringing together all the different

strands of information available.

Some people say that estimates of the dinosaur's weight must (**14**) .... exaggerated, doubting that (**15**) ....

a heavy animal could have walked on land. Others say the study demonstrates it was more than capable of walking

about in (**16**) .... is now Patagonia, South America.

Part 3

For questions **17 – 24**, read the text below. Use the word given in capitals at the end of some of the lines to form a word that fits in the space **in the same line**. There is an example at the beginning (**0**).

Write your answers **IN CAPITAL LETTERS on the separate answer sheet.**

Example: | 0 | A | P | P | E | A | R | A | N | C | E | | | | | | |

The green-eyed tree frog

The green-eyed tree frog has adapted its **(0)** .... to blend in with   **APPEAR**

the moss-covered rainforests of Queensland, Australia. The frogs' exact

colouration and markings depend on their **(17)** .... habitat, but the   **SPECIFY**

colours on their bodies are usually a good **(18)** .... of the rocks and   **IMITATE**

plants of their immediate **(19)** ....   **SURROUND**

The species gets its name from the line of brilliant green along its brow,

and it is also distinguishable by an unusual skin pattern which looks like

the edge of a knife. Female frogs are **(20)** .... larger than the males   **SIGNIFY**

and grow to about seven centimetres, in **(21)** .... with the males'   **COMPARE**

five centimetres.

Green-eyed tree frogs are abundant in the wet tropics of Queensland, and

their population in the region's lower areas is **(22)** .... Unfortunately,   **HEALTH**

scientists believe that in higher-altitude areas, they may have disappeared

completely, although the reasons for this remain **(23)** .... Despite   **KNOW**

serious decline in the past, however, these handsome frogs are not

currently **(24)** ....   **THREAT**

Part 4

For questions **25 – 30**, complete the second sentence so that it has a similar meaning to the first sentence, using the word given. **Do not change the word given**. You must use between **two** and **five** words, including the word given. Here is an example **(0)**.

Example:

0   It's a pity I can't remember exactly what he said.

   COULD

   I .... exactly what he said.

The gap can be filled by the words 'wish I could remember', so you write:

Example: | **0** | | WISH I COULD REMEMBER |

Write **only** the missing words **IN CAPITAL LETTERS on the separate answer sheet.**

___

25   I'm happy to cook provided someone else clears up after me.

   AS

   I don't mind .... someone else clears up after me.

26   Lucy plays the guitar well, and she also sings beautifully.

   PLAY

   Not .... the guitar well, but she also sings beautifully.

27   Bring a hat because the sun might come out later.

   CASE

   Bring a hat .... sunny later.

28   You can solve the problem any way you like, but you must show us how you worked it out.

   MATTER

   It .... you solve the problem, but you must show us how you worked it out.

29   The lecture is likely to have finished before it gets dark.

   PROBABLY

   The lecture .... over before it gets dark.

30   John said he was sorry that he had eaten all the biscuits.

   APOLOGISED

   John .... all the biscuits.

Part 5

You are going to read an extract from an article about a pianist called Louis Lortie. For questions **31 – 36**, choose the answer (**A, B, C** or **D**) which you think fits best according to the text.

Mark your answers **on the separate answer sheet.**

Listening to a virtuoso recital of classical piano music in a concert hall isn't so different from watching an acrobat walk high up in the air between two tall buildings along a metal rope. The audience sits there in breathless silence, thinking 'will he slip or won't he?', as the pianist battles with torrents of notes, often almost impossible to play. But the risk must appeal to pianists too. Otherwise why would they put themselves through the suffering?

It's a question that's particularly relevant to the marvellous French-Canadian pianist Louis Lortie. He has recorded all of the piano Études by Chopin (a 19th-century Polish composer) – twice. An *étude* is a piece that thoroughly tests one aspect of piano technique, and the 24 Études that Chopin wrote take this idea to a level of difficulty that's rarely

line 8   been equalled by any other composer. Lortie overcame this with what sounded like triumphant ease when he first recorded them over 20 years ago.

So why put himself through it all again? 'Well, I've been playing them all the time ever since and I think they are more mature now,' says Lortie. He admits to feeling the pressure of living up to his first recording. 'A big part of the challenge is to keep one's physical freshness. That's a modern obsession, isn't it? People go to the gym and try to stay in perfect shape. In the past, people were playing lots of wrong notes, they were not so concerned with perfection. Now technique has become a matter of playing very fast and very correctly. But we have to go beyond that.'

Which brings us to Chopin, because if there was ever a composer who turned physical brilliance to genuinely poetic ends it was him. 'A genius like Chopin didn't have any interest in developing something just for technique's sake,' says Lortie. 'There was always a poetical idea, or often a completely abstract musical idea.' Does he have any examples of Chopin's finger-twisting difficulties which are 'poetic' in effect? 'Well, Chopin is very demanding on the right hand because he was obsessed with making the piano sing. He was very influenced by Italian opera composers. Quite often the pianist's right hand has to be like an opera singer singing the high notes, or sometimes even sound like two people singing together.'

This takes us more towards the Chopin many people know and love. The most popular Études are the ones with picturesque titles: The Waterfall, The Butterfly. But Lortie resists the idea that the titles are any clue to the music's meaning. 'These were added later by publishers who thought it would help to sell the music. I think the music itself goes beyond these images. Someone once asked Chopin what he had in mind when he wrote one of his most famous pieces. He brushed off the query by saying, 'it's all about a stomach ache'.

'You know, the really hard thing about Chopin is keeping the mood under control. As soon as you become too extrovert you lose the style.'

As Lortie points out, Chopin's reserve isn't reflected in contemporary behaviour. 'I look at the way young pianists play Chopin on online videos, and I see how the fast movements get faster and the slow ones get constantly slower. Chopin himself changed the instructions he wrote on one of his pieces just to discourage people from playing it too fast. We forget that classical ideals of balance and not going to extremes were very important for him. There's this idea now that spreading out and being extreme is a way of showing how deep you are, but when you do that the music loses its natural quality.'

What a strange idea, that anyone could be 'natural' when playing some of the most unnaturally difficult pieces ever written. But Lortie is one of those rare pianists who can bring it off.

31 What does the writer suggest about the audience at a piano recital?

    A They focus too much on the pianist's mistakes.
    B They are determined not to make any noise.
    C They find the pianist's struggle entertaining.
    D They demand a great deal from the performer.

32 What does 'this' refer to in line 8?

    A an aspect of piano technique
    B the idea
    C the level of difficulty
    D another composer

33 Why is Lortie recording the pieces again?

    A He understands them better than he once did.
    B He wants to prove that he is not too old to do so.
    C He is disappointed with the music he produced before.
    D He is trying to play them more accurately than he used to.

34 What does Lortie say about Chopin in the fourth paragraph?

    A He was rarely affected by technical developments in music.
    B He hoped some of his tunes might eventually be used in operas.
    C He intended his music to create a specific impression.
    D He preferred the sound of people singing to that of the piano.

35 According to Lortie, the titles of Chopin's Études

    A were intended to make the music more attractive to the public.
    B were invented by the composer to satisfy publishers.
    C are a starting point to help people interpret the music.
    D are a way of gaining an insight into the composer's life.

36 How does Lortie feel about the way Chopin's music is played nowadays?

    A impressed by the emotional depth of young pianists
    B concerned that the music is being played in the wrong way
    C anxious that some pianists may come across as old-fashioned
    D happy that the music is being played by the best pianists

Part 6

You are going to read an article about life forms living on waste plastic in the ocean. Six sentences have been removed from the article. Choose from the sentences **A – G** the one which fills each gap (**37 – 42**). There is one extra sentence which you do not need to use.

Mark your answers **on the separate answer sheet.**

Tiny new ecosystems in the ocean

Scientists have discovered new species living on small pieces of plastic in the world's oceans.

It is estimated that up to 10 million tons of plastic is dumped in the world's oceans every year. Much of this is broken down into small fragments and floats on the surface, while some of it sinks. Scientists have even found plastic bags while exploring some of the deepest parts of the ocean, and a recent study estimated that around 600,000 tonnes of plastic cover the bed of the North Sea alone.

Plastic fragments smaller than a grain of rice and synthetic fibres from clothes now make up a significant part of the 'sand' found on beaches around the world. And in the open ocean there are five large patches of floating rubbish that have formed in areas known as 'gyres', where rotating ocean currents concentrate the debris. **37**

In order to discover more about the plastic in our oceans, scientists collected minute floating plastic fragments from a number of locations in the North Atlantic. **38** At least 1,000 different types of bacteria – very tiny organisms, some of which can cause diseases – were detected. Many of the bacteria are thought to be new species previously unknown to science.

The scientists who conducted the study say the fragments of plastic are creating very small floating habitats they have named 'plastispheres'. They found evidence that the bacteria on these plastispheres may even be feeding off the plastic itself: tiny holes in the surface of the plastic suggested the bacteria had eaten into it. **39** One of the most significant would be that the bacteria could be used to break down plastics at rubbish tips.

The researchers identified several types of bacteria that can cause the hydrocarbons in plastics to split up, which makes it likely that they could play a role in breaking down plastic debris in the ocean. **40** They became even more so when the bacteria showed up on multiple pieces of plastic of different types.

In addition to the bacteria, there were also plants and algae colonising the plastic, along with plankton-like creatures that fed on them. Some of the species on the plastispheres appeared to be feeding on the plastic itself. Others produced their own food using sunlight. Further species were feeding on the bacteria, and there were also microscopic predators feeding on these in their turn. **41** They found that the organisms inhabiting the plastisphere were different from those in surrounding seawater, indicating that plastic debris acts as artificial 'microbial reefs', just as rocks can act as natural ones.

42 This assumption that they are new ecosystems is reasonable, given that the amount of plastic in the oceans has only become so significant over the last few decades. On a different scale, larger rafts of plastic and other debris are also known to provide shelter to fish and other marine creatures in the vast expanse of the ocean. Recently, for example, floating debris from Japan has allowed Asian species of shellfish and seaweed to spread around the world.

A They then analysed them in an attempt to identify any species living on them.

B This variety of life forms suggests the plastic is creating a unique ecosystem in the oceans, according to the scientists.

C It would seem unlikely that other environments could provide this.

D The biggest of these is thought to be in the North Pacific, and is said to be as large as the US state of Texas.

E When they first saw these, they were very excited.

F And it seems that these tiny habitats came into being relatively recently.

G Should this be the case, the potential benefits would be enormous.

Part 7

You are going to read an article about people who work in a hospital. For questions **43 – 52**, choose from the people (**A – D**). Each person may be chosen more than once.
Mark your answers **on the separate answer sheet.**

Which person

enjoys a specific mental challenge involved in his work? **43**

believes he is different to what people expect? **44**

says he performs best in a demanding environment? **45**

compares part of his job to working somewhere else? **46**

believes it is important to develop relationships with patients quickly? **47**

points out that some people would not be suitable for the role he performs? **48**

appreciates the opportunity to be involved in projects outside of the hospital? **49**

mentions his desire to help people feel informed and relaxed? **50**

comments on how lucky he is to be surrounded by encouraging colleagues? **51**

never ceases to be amazed by one aspect of his job? **52**

Working in a hospital

We asked four people who work in a hospital to tell us about their roles.

A John: doctor

'I couldn't work as a general doctor in a surgery where people come in with the same old aches and pains – I'd find it monotonous. I thrive under pressure and there's plenty of that in a hospital where patients are coming in all the time. Teamwork's essential, and I'm fortunate to work with a fantastic team who are really supportive of one another and communicate well – a key element to success in this line of work. Making my daily round of the patients in my care is without doubt the most rewarding thing for me – I love the interaction with them and I'm pretty good at establishing immediate bonds with people. That's vital if people are to trust you. The shifts can be long and I often arrive home exhausted, but I can't imagine having a more satisfying role.'

B Mike: pharmacist

'I'm based in the hospital pharmacy, which gets very busy. There are two halves to the job – looking after medicines, and looking after patients. I haven't reached a conclusion as to which I like best. Coming from a scientific background, I'm fascinated by medicine, but I'm a real 'people person', too. Ensuring that medicines are stored in the right conditions is essential and I enjoy making contributions to external research when the occasion arises. In addition, I collect information from patients about their drug history and I help to make decisions regarding which medicines are appropriate for which individuals. It's a responsible role, but I'm confident in what I'm doing and I'm not alone. People tend to see pharmacists as serious people working behind the scenes, and when they meet me they're surprised by my outgoing nature.'

C Theo: nurse

'The difference in focus between the work of a hospital nurse and a doctor is that a nurse is the first point of contact for a patient, so we often know more about patients' individual needs than the doctors. We don't focus so much on a person's condition or illness, but on making sure people are comfortable and carrying out continuity of care – by which I mean implementing and maintaining care procedures. It isn't just the patients you have to think about – you've got to support their relatives, too. You have to be prepared to answer a million questions, and deal with complaints and concerns, and it can be tiring trying to recall all the details of a patient off the top of your head. It's part of the job, though, and I like the fact it keeps my mind sharp! Nursing is not a job for people who don't like people!'

D Tim: radiographer

'It's my job to use imaging such as x-rays and scans to find out the extent of injuries. I'm a real 'techie' and all the machines I deal with on a daily basis provide a never-ending source of fascination. It's incredible what we can do for patients with the aid of technology, isn't it? It's almost like working in a physics lab with all the whirring, clicking machines around me. Part of my role is to assist in creating treatment plans for individuals, so I have a close relationship with other healthcare professionals at the hospital. Quite often I'm called upon to reassure patients of the safety of the machinery we're using and I've perfected my 'speech' on this over the years. I also inject a bit of humour – it's important to put people at ease. Radiography is an immensely varied role and it's never dull!'

Paper 2: Writing

Part 1

You **must** answer this question. Write your answer in **140 – 190** words in an appropriate style on the separate answer sheet.

---

1 In your English class you have been talking about why people do sport. Now, your English teacher has asked you to write an essay.

Write your essay using **all** the notes and give reasons for your point of view.

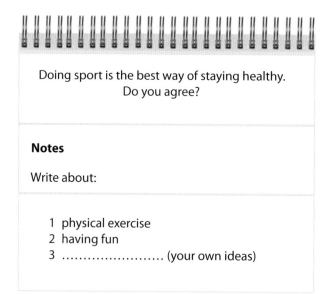

Doing sport is the best way of staying healthy.
Do you agree?

Notes

Write about:

1 physical exercise
2 having fun
3 .... (your own ideas)

Part 2

Write an answer to **one** of the questions **2 – 4** in this part. Write your answer in **140 – 190** words in an appropriate style on the separate answer sheet. Put the question number in the box at the top of the answer sheet.

---

2   You see the following announcement in an English-language magazine.

> **Articles wanted!**
>
> **An essential object**
>
> Is there something you own that you couldn't live without?
>
> If so, write an article telling us what it is, and why it is so important to you.

Write your **article**.

3   This is part of an email you have received from your English-speaking friend Mel.

> **From:** Mel
>
> **Subject:** Trip
>
> My family and I are planning a trip to your area next year. Where would you recommend that we stay, and are there any historical sights that you think we should definitely see? When is the best time of year to visit? I hope we can see you while we're there.
>
> Write soon,
>
> Mel

Write your **email**.

4   You see this notice on an English-language website.

> **Reviews of language-learning websites wanted!**
>
> Do you know a website designed to help people learn a language? If you do, write a review telling us all about it and saying whether you would recommend it to other people your age.
>
> The best reviews will appear on our website next month.

Write your **review**.

Paper 3: Listening

Part 1

You will hear people talking in eight different situations. For questions **1 – 8**, choose the best answer (**A, B** or **C**).

---

1 You hear two friends talking about the Icelandic language.

   The girl thinks that it must be difficult to

   A memorise new vocabulary.

   B learn to speak Icelandic.

   C invent words.

2 You hear two friends talking about ballet dancing.

   What does the woman say about ballet dancers?

   A She hasn't experienced the difficulties they face.

   B It's tempting to believe they have natural balance.

   C They find it harder than it looks to overcome dizziness.

3 You hear a teacher talking to her class about the subject of maths.

   What is she doing?

   A reassuring the students that they will overcome difficulties

   B explaining the value of what the students are studying

   C suggesting ways in which students can improve their work

4 You hear two friends talking about a programme they have seen.

   What does the boy say about the idea of rats helping to solve crimes?

   A He believes it's cost-effective.

   B He is doubtful of its success rate.

   C He thinks rats are suitable for the work.

5 You hear a photographer talking about working in the Arctic.

   What is he doing?

   A highlighting why he enjoys his work so much

   B explaining how to overcome certain problems

   C complaining about the difficulties of working in the cold

6 You hear a science teacher telling her class about photographic memory.

What does she say about it?

   A It isn't as helpful as it sounds.

   B It can affect how we feel about events.

   C It is something many people want to have.

7 You hear two students talking about a lecture they have attended.

What do they agree about advertising?

   A how unaware many people can be of its effects

   B how unaffected they both are by advertising

   C how immoral advertising companies are

8 You hear a man talking about a concert he has been to.

As he was listening to the music, he felt

   A annoyed that he was being taken advantage of.

   B surprised by the effects that the piece had on him.

   C inspired to create something similar himself.

Part 2

You will hear a woman called Julie Smith talking to students at a college careers day about her experience of being a photographer's assistant. For questions **9–18**, complete the sentence with a word or short phrase.

Julie says she decided to become a photographer after seeing some good photographs of

(9) .... at an exhibition.

Julie's **(10)** .... suggested that she should contact a local photographer.

At Julie's interview, she showed the photographer some of her pictures of a beautiful

(11) ....

On Julie's first day as a photographer's assistant, she was asked to buy some **(12)** ....

for the photographer.

The first assignment Julie helped on was for a local **(13)** .... centre.

Julie will always remember watching some **(14)** .... prepare to be photographed.

Julie hadn't expected to learn so much about **(15)** .... as a photographer's assistant.

The photographer told Julie that **(16)** .... are a good source of inspiration.

Julie says it's worth spending time getting the **(17)** .... right in the studio.

In the future, Julie would like to photograph **(18)** ....

Part 3

You will hear five short extracts in which people are talking about having studied linguistics. For questions **19 – 23**, choose from the list (**A – H**) what each person says they found difficult about studying linguistics. Use each letter only once. There are three extra letters which you do not need to use.

A understanding some of the subject's scientific elements

B conducting interviews for research purposes

C thinking about language in a new way

D studying a wide range of topics

E defining linguistics to other people

F dealing with complex theories

G having to learn grammar

H coping with a lot of new subject-related terms

Speaker 1   [   ] **19**

Speaker 2   [   ] **20**

Speaker 3   [   ] **21**

Speaker 4   [   ] **22**

Speaker 5   [   ] **23**

Part 4

You will hear part of a radio interview with a man called James Grant who has recently finished a training course for tour guides. For questions **24 – 30**, choose the best answer (**A, B** or **C**).

24 Why did James decide to become a tour guide?

    A   He had always been keen to travel.

    B   He knew tour guides who loved their jobs.

    C   He wanted to be able to choose when he worked.

25 How did James feel when he started the course?

    A   anxious to prove that he could manage it

    B   nervous about having to deal with difficult situations

    C   concerned that he might not be able to complete it

26 What does James say about his fellow students?

    A   They had more money to spend than he had.

    B   They were less determined to succeed than he was.

    C   They initially knew more about the topics covered than he did.

27 James says the course tutors

    A   came from the local area.

    B   were experienced teachers.

    C   set essays on interesting topics.

28 What did James enjoy most while he was on the course?

    A   practising what he'd say to tourists

    B   visiting places at unusual times

    C   experiencing being a student

29 What did James find surprising while he was on the course?

    A   how attractive familiar places could suddenly appear

    B   how much energy people on the tours seemed to have

    C   how many details he had never noticed before

30 What does James say about his language skills?

    A   He needs to improve them.

    B   They were useful on the course.

    C   Tourists have admired his vocabulary.

Paper 4: Speaking

Part 1
2 minutes (3 minutes for groups of three)

The examiner (interlocutor) will introduce him or herself, ask you your names and where you are from. He or she will then ask each of you to speak briefly in turn and to give personal information about yourselves. You can expect a variety of questions, such as:

- **Do you live in a city, a town or a village?**
- **What do you like about living there? (Why?)**
- **How do people of your age spend their free time where you live?**
- **Is there anything you would like to change about where you live? (Why?)**

Part 2
4 minutes (6 minutes for groups of three)

You will each be asked to talk for a minute without interruption. You will each be given two different photographs in turn to talk about. After your partner has finished speaking, you will be asked a brief question connected with your partner's photographs.

Interlocutor	In this part of the test, I'm going to give each of you two photographs. I'd like you to talk about your photographs on your own for about a minute, and also to answer a question about your partner's photographs.
	(*Candidate A*), it's your turn first. Here are your photographs. They show **people celebrating special occasions in different ways**.
	I'd like you to compare the photographs, and say why you think the people have chosen to celebrate special occasions in these ways.
	All right?
Candidate A (*1 minute*)	....
Interlocutor	Thank you.
	(*Candidate B*), **how do you like to celebrate special occasions? ...... (Why?)**
Candidate B (*approximately 30 seconds*)	....
	Thank you.
	Now, (*Candidate B*), here are your photographs. They show **different styles of homes**.
	I'd like you to compare the photographs, and say **why you think people choose these different styles for their homes**.
	All right?
Candidate B (*1 minute*)	....
Interlocutor	Thank you.
	(*Candidate A*), **which place would you prefer to live in? ...... (Why?)**
Candidate A (*approximately 30 seconds*)	....
Interlocutor	Thank you.

Why do you think people choose these different styles for their homes?

Being healthy
Part 3
4 minutes (5 minutes for groups of three)

The interlocutor will ask you to discuss something together with your partner. You will have a page of prompts (pictures or words) and questions to help you. The interlocutor will not take part in the conversation.

Interlocutor	Now, I'd like you to talk about something together for two minutes.
	I'd like you to imagine that your teacher has asked you to create a poster to encourage students to be healthier. Here are some ideas your class is thinking about and a question for you to discuss.
	You now have some time to look at the task.
	Give the candidates the task. Allow 15 seconds to study the question and ideas.
	Now, talk to each other about **why these ideas would be useful in encouraging students to be healthier.**
Candidates *2 minutes* *(3 minutes for groups of three)*	………………………………………
Interlocutor	Thank you.
	Now you have about a minute to decide **which two of the ideas you should choose to include on your poster.**
Candidates *1 minute*	………………………………………
Interlocutor	Thank you.

Part 4
4 minutes (6 minutes for groups of three)

The interlocutor will ask you some questions related to the Part 3 task. You should discuss these with your partner. The interlocutor will not take part in the conversation, other than to ask you the questions.

These are some examples of the kinds of questions you may be asked:

- **Why do you think eating fresh food is necessary?**
- **Do you think it's important to spend time outdoors? (Why / Why not?)**
- **Do you think spending too much time at the computer can be harmful? (Why / Why not?)**
- **Which do you think are the best forms of exercise? Why?**
- **What do you think are the benefits of getting enough sleep?**
- **How can governments encourage people to be healthier?**

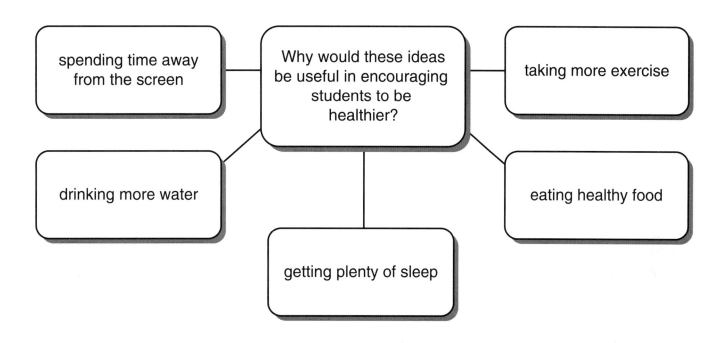

spending time away from the screen

Why would these ideas be useful in encouraging students to be healthier?

taking more exercise

drinking more water

getting plenty of sleep

eating healthy food

Grammar reference

Index

1 Adjectives

We use adjectives to classify or describe the qualities of something or someone. We use adjectives:

1 after the verb *'to be'.*
    He *is old*.
    Form: to be + adjective
2 after 'linking' verbs such as *look, seem, become* and *feel*.
    'Are you OK? You **look tired.** *' 'No, I* **feel fine.** *'*
    Form: verb + adjective
3 before nouns and pronouns.
    Her **new** coat is beautiful.
    Form: adjective + noun

REMEMBER:

i)   Adjectives do not change according to the number or gender of the thing they describe.
    There were some ~~youngs~~ young boys in the street.
ii) Adjectives come **after** the to describe a class or group of people.
    the rich, the unemployed, the homeless
iii) Colour adjectives come **before** the noun.
    She was wearing a red dress. NOT ~~a dress red.~~
iv) Some adjectives such as *asleep, alive, afraid* can only be used **after** a linking verb.
    The boy who was hiding in the cellar **looked afraid**.
    There was ~~an afraid boy~~ hiding in the cellar. ✗
    There was a frightened boy hiding in the cellar. ✓

Which one of the following sentences is correct? Correct the other sentences.
1 There were four greens cars in front of their house.
2 That watch looks like expensive.
3 You look a lovely today.
4 He was feeling sad yesterday.
5 The government should look after the poors.
6 There was an asleep baby lying in its pram.

1.1 Participial adjectives

Many adjectives are formed from the present particle (-*ing* form) and past participles (-*ed* form) of verbs.
For example: *to interest > interested, interesting.*

1 Adjectives ending in -*ing* tell us a quality of the person or thing being described. They also have an active sense. They show the effect someone or something has on someone or something else.
    It's an **interesting** *book.* = It makes me feel interested.
2 Adjectives ending in -*ed* have a passive sense and describe what has happened to the person or thing it describes. They describe states and feelings.
    The grammar class was **boring**. =The class actively had that effect.
    Nikki was **bored**. = That's what happened to Nikki.

Choose the correct form of adjective in the sentences below.
1 We were **worrying / worried** about the news from Canada.
2 Am I **boring / bored,** Maria? People don't listen to my stories anymore.
3 What's the most **embarrassing / embarrassed** experience you've ever had?
4 We are **exhausting / exhausted,** baby Oliver kept us awake all night.
5 I've never eaten anything quite so **disgusted / disgusting**.
6 I enjoy watching sumo wrestling, I think it's a **fascinated / fascinating** sport.

1.2 Adjective order

1 When we use two or more adjectives before a noun then we generally follow this order: **opinion – dimension – age – texture – shape – colour – material – purpose**.
2 If we want to use more than two adjectives we will usually try to place some of them after the noun.
    She had short curly dark hair.
    Better: *Her* **dark** *hair was* **short and curly**.
    He carried a worn old leather briefcase.
    Better: *He carried a worn old briefcase* **made of leather**.
3 Opinion adjectives, where we give our point of view, usually come before adjectives which give more factual information. Examples of opinion adjectives are *beautiful, lovely, nice, pretty, awful, ugly, horrible*.
    She wore a **beautiful blue** *dress, made of silk.*

Which one of these sentences is correct? Correct the others by putting the adjectives in the right order.
1 She put a **plastic black long** snake on her teacher's chair.
2 He was a given a / an **diver's expensive Swiss** watch for his eighteenth birthday.
3 She was wearing a **shiny Japanese lovely** dressing-gown **silk.**
4 He has bought a **wonderful new graphite tennis** racket.
5 They have a **grey big fat gorgeous** cat **Siamese.**
6 Last night I watched a **Swedish new fascinating** documentary on TV.

1.3 Gradable and non-gradable adjectives

1 Gradable adjectives
Many adjectives and adverbs describe qualities which are gradable. In other words, they can have more or less of the quality in question. We can modify, or grade ordinary adjectives using: *a little, fairly, slightly, rather, quite, very, extremely,* etc.
> *We were **fairly tired** after a long day of shopping.*
However, we **can't** use *absolutely, completely, totally,* or *utterly* to modify gradable adjectives:
I was absolutely angry when I heard the news.

2 Non-gradable adjectives
Non-gradable adjectives describe qualities that are already at their limit, e.g. *exhausted.*
We can modify them to emphasise the degree of completeness with *absolutely, completely, totally,* or *utterly.*
> *We were **absolutely exhausted** after a long day's shopping.*
We **can't** use *a little, fairly, slightly, rather, quite, very, extremely,* etc. with non-gradable adjectives:
> *We were a little exhausted after a long day of shopping.*

3 Gradable adjectives like *tired* or *angry* may have one or more non-gradable counterparts.
> *good = marvellous, wonderful, fantastic…*

Gradable

Modifiers	Adjectives	Example
a little, fairly, slightly, rather, quite, very, extremely	tired, hungry, bad, angry, pretty, embarrassed, disappointed	I was very angry when I heard the news.

Non-gradable

Modifiers	Adjectives	Example
absolutely, completely, utterly, totally	terrible, awful, dreadful, exhausted, furious, gorgeous, starving, mortified, devastated	We were utterly exhausted after a long day's shopping.

Complete the responses to these exchanges using non-gradable adjectives.
1 A: Were you pleased with your results?
   B: Pleased? No! I was completely _____.
2 A: You must have been angry when you heard the news.
   B: Angry? I was absolutely _____.
3 A: She looked lovely in her wedding dress.
   B: Lovely? She looked absolutely _____.
4 A: I heard that the play was bad.
   B: Bad? It was utterly _____.
5 A: Were you tired and hungry after the walk?
   B: Tired and hungry? We were absolutely _____ and _____.
6 A: Were they disappointed to lose the match?
   B: Disappointed? They were totally _____.

2 Adverbs

2.1 Adverbs of frequency

1 We use adverbs of frequency to say how often we do something.
> *I **sometimes** go to the cinema at the weekend.*
These are some of the most common adverbs of frequency.
> *never – seldom – rarely – hardly ever – occasionally – sometimes – often – usually – always*

2 Word order: adverbs of frequency follow 'to be'.
> *She never is on time. She is never on time.*
Otherwise, they usually come before the main verb, and between modal auxiliaries and the main verb.
> *We **occasionally eat** out.*
> *We **don't usually watch** TV.*
> *Customers will often arrive just before we close.*
Notice that we can replace *sometimes* or *occasionally* with expressions such as *from time to time, once in a while, every so often.* These either come at the beginning or the end of a sentence.
> ***Once in a while** we go to the cinema.*
> *We go to the cinema **once in a while**.*

> **REMEMBER:**
> i) We can use *always* with the present or past continuous to show annoyance or disapproval:
> *She's **always** borrowing my dictionary without asking me.* (I wish she would stop.)
> ii) When we want to emphasise something, we may begin the sentences with an adjective of 'negative force' e.g. *never, seldom.* (See Section 10 **Inversion** for more information on this.)

Put the parts of the sentences in italics into the correct order.
1 We **always take nearly** the train between Brussels and Paris.
2 Tess and Jerry go to **cinema time the to time from**.
3 Why don't we go to a restaurant? We **seem these eat hardly to days out**.
4 I'm really fed up, **clothes he borrowing is my always** without asking.
5 They **used on to tennis mornings always play Sunday** but since the baby **time ever they hardly have**.
6 Since I moved to Chicago **I see my while only a once parents in**.

2.2 Adverbs of manner

Adverbs of manner are used to describe how an action is performed.
> *She plays the piano **beautifully**.*
We generally form them by adding *-ly* to adjectives.
> *Slow* → *slowly.*
We transform adjectives ending in *-y* with *-ily* in the adverb.
> *Angry* → *angrily.*

2.3 Irregular adverbs

Adjective	Adverb
fast	fast
hard	hard
good	well

*She is a good singer, she sings **well**.*
(For comparative adverbs see Section 5.)

Complete the sentences by transforming the adjectives into adverbs. Make any other necessary changes.
1   He's a very good chess player.
    He plays chess _____.
2   Greta is a very hard worker.
    Greta works _____.
3   The way April sang that piece was beautiful.
    April sang that piece _____.
4   Be careful how you handle that vase.
    Handle that vase _____.
5   I'm happy to do that for you.
    I'll _____.
6   He is an extremely persuasive speaker.
    He speaks _____.

2.4 Introductory adverbs

Many adverbs can be used at the beginning of sentences to comment on what comes next.
Basically / Essentially, students have to sit down and learn their irregular verbs. (= *this is my main point.*)
Obviously, I need to improve my computer skills. (= *it's obvious that…*)
Unfortunately / Sadly, Hamish failed the entrance exam for medical school. (= *I regret to give you this news*.)
Hopefully everything will be ready for the next time you come. (= *if there are no problems*)

2.5 Meaning shifts from adjectives to adverbs

Adverbs generally retain the meaning of the adjectives from which they are formed. However, sometimes there is an important change of meaning.
Late = *not on time*; **lately** = *recently*.
Short = *not tall*; **shortly** = *soon*.
Hardly is an adverb meaning *almost not*, or *only a little*.
His handwriting was so messy I could hardly read what he had written.

Replace the words in bold with a one-word adverb.
1   Oh dear, the poor dog is **only just** breathing.
2   I haven't seen Malcolm **for a while,** has he gone on holiday?
3   **If everything goes according to plan** we'll be at your place by six o'clock.
4   **It's a pity, but** we won't be able to fix your car.
5   Would you mind waiting? I'll be with you **in just a couple of minutes**.
6   **There's no question about it,** we have to have the roof mended.
7   Well, **what I want to say is** you should eat five pieces of fruit a day.

3 Articles

Articles precede and modify nouns.
a / an = indefinite article
the = definite article

3.1 Indefinite article use

We use the indefinite article *a / an* in front of singular countable [C] nouns, when we use them in a general sense.
*They gave us **a** table for two.*

3.2 Definite article use

We use the definite article *the* with all types of noun, for things which are specific:
1   when we want to refer to a particular thing.
    *Where's **the** key? (The specific key that opens this door.)*
2   when mentioning something for the second time.
    *They gave us a table for two. Unfortunately **the** table was right next to the door.*
3   with superlatives.
    *It's **the best** film I've ever seen.*
4   with things which are unique.
    the world, the Earth, the universe
5   with some geographical names.
    the Himalayas, the Channel
6   with some names of organisations and titles, particularly those with 'of' or the idea of 'of'.
    the Head Teacher, the International Olympic Committee, the President (of France)
7   with adjectives to describe a class or group of people.
    the unemployed, the elderly
8   for places and amenities known to everyone.
    *I need to post this letter, I'm going to **the post office**. They took her to **the hospital**.*
9   when referring to something specific.
    *I love wild animals, but **the animals I saw at the zoo** seemed tired and depressed. (Plural countable noun.)*
    *I hardly drink coffee, but **the coffee you gave me this morning** was exceptional. (Uncountable noun.)*
    *It was a terrible secret. She found **the knowledge** too hard to bear.*
    ***The money he earned over the summer** allowed him to go on holiday.*
10   with ordinal numbers.
    *The next meeting is planned for **the ninth** of January.*
11   with musical instruments.
    *She plays **the violin** and **the flute**.*

REMEMBER:

Some countable nouns are used without articles in certain situations, such as seasons, institutions, meals, diseases and time of day:

i) ~~I'm going to the home.~~ I'm going home.
ii) ~~I'm going to eat the dinner.~~ I'm going to eat dinner.
iii) ~~The spring is a good time to clean.~~ Spring is a good time to clean.
iv) ~~He is sick with the pneumonia.~~ He is sick with pneumonia.

3.3 Zero article Ø

We **don't** use articles:

1 with plural countable nouns used in in a general sense.
   I love animals.
2 with uncountable, and abstract nouns.
   Money makes the world go around.
   Knowledge is power.

Complete the sentences with **a**, **the** or Ø (no article).

1 _____ two biggest problems we face are _____ global warming and _____ pollution.
2 She bought _____ violin for her daughter who said she wanted to learn _____ guitar.
3 There's no doubt about it, _____ rich are getting richer and _____ poor are getting poorer. _____ government should do something about this and help _____ homeless and _____ unemployed.
4 _____ famous author once said that _____ past was _____ foreign country.
5 Last month I bought _____ pair of trousers for £80 then _____ minutes later I saw exactly _____ same ones for £50!
6 They say _____ little knowledge is _____ dangerous thing. I discovered _____ truth of this when I tried to fix _____ car. In _____ end I had to call _____ mechanic from _____ nearest garage to repair it.
7 _____ cost of _____ materials like _____ oil, _____ copper and _____ rubber keeps going up. _____ last time I filled up my car I almost fainted when I saw _____ price on _____ pump.
8 _____ money can't buy you _____ happiness or _____ love, but I'd rather be _____ miserable rich person than _____ miserable poor one.
9 She is _____ third woman to be _____ Minister of _____ Education.
10 _____ fear of _____ snakes is much more common than you might think.

4 Cleft sentences

Cleft sentences let us focus on what is important in a sentence. They are particularly common in spoken English and can add extra emphasis.

1 Sentences a–c all carry a similar message, although the emphasis of b and c is the year of the fire, rather than the fire itself.
   a *The Great Fire of London took place in 1666.*
   b *It was in 1666 that the Great Fire of London took place.*
   c *What happened in 1666 was the Great Fire of London.*

Notice that cleft sentences often begin with *what* and *it* and need the introduction of the verb *to be*.

2 a *You should look for last minute flights on the Internet.*
   b ***What** you should do **is** look for last minute flights on the Internet.*
3 a *She took all of the money from her boyfriend's account.*
   b ***What** she did **was** take all of the money from her boyfriend's account.*
4 a *The thing that worries me is …*
   b ***What** worries me **is** that …*

Complete the second sentence so it means the same as the first.

1 Her last concert began at nine o'clock in the evening.
   It was _____.
2 They took the legs off the piano and carried it through the window.
   What they did _____.
3 She slipped on the ice and broke her arm.
   What happened _____.
4 I think you ought to try a dating agency.
   What you _____.
5 I find loud music in restaurants annoying.
   What annoys _____.
6 They broke into our car while we were at the beach.
   What happened was _____.

5 Making comparisons

5.1 Comparatives

We form comparative adjectives by adding *-er* to one-syllable adjectives. For example:

   soft ➔ *softer, cheap* ➔ *cheaper, sweet* ➔ *sweeter, short* ➔ *shorter*

REMEMBER:

Spelling
i One-syllable adjectives:
   • If a one-syllable adjective ends in a single vowel letter followed by a single consonant letter, the consonant letter is doubled.
     thin ➔ *thinner, big* ➔ *bigger, sad* ➔ *sadder, slim* ➔ *slimmer, fat* ➔ *fatter*
   • If an adjective ends in *-e*, this is removed when adding *-er*.
     wide ➔ *wider, rude* ➔ *ruder, brave* ➔ *braver*
   • If an adjective ends in a consonant followed by *-y*, *-y* is replaced by *-i* when adding *-er*.
     dry ➔ *drier*

ii Two-syllable adjectives:
- Two-syllable adjectives ending in -ed, -ing, -ful, or -less always form the comparative with *more or less*.
  worried ➜ *more worried, boring* ➜ *more boring, careful* ➜ *more careful, useless* ➜ *more useless*
- However with two-syllable adjectives ending in -y, we use -ier instead of *more*.
  pretty ➜ *prettier, happy* ➜ *happier, healthy* ➜ *healthier*
- With some other two-syllable adjectives we can either precede them with *more* **or** add -er to the adjective.
  clever ➜ *cleverer / more clever, quiet* ➜ *quieter / more quiet, polite* ➜ *politer / more polite*

iii Three-syllable adjectives:
- Three-syllable adjectives take *more or less*.
  ~~*expensiver*~~ ➜ *more expensive, dangerous* ➜ *more dangerous, difficult* ➜ *less difficult*
- The only exceptions are some three-syllable words which have been formed using the prefix -un.
  unhappy ➜ *more unhappy / unhappier*

Notice: *As* may be used to compare the way two things are similar or different.
Form: *as* + adjective + ***as***
  *She is **as old as** her husband.*
  *This one isn't **as valuable / well-made as** the other one.*

Other uses of the comparative:
1 to show that actions and results are connected in a progressive way.
  *The **older** he gets **the more stubborn** he becomes.*
2 instead of the superlative (see below).
  *There **isn't a more expensive** hotel in the town.* (It's the most expensive hotel in town.)

5.2 Superlatives

Most superlatives are formed by adding -est to adjectives which are short (one or two syllables); and using *the most / least* before longer adjectives (three or more syllables).
  *She's **my youngest** student and also **the most** intelligent.*
We use the superlative:
1 to compare something with the whole group to which it belongs.
  *I think that Use of English is **the most difficult** part of the exam.*
2 to compare an experience or event with all the others in a period of time, e.g. a lifetime.
  *It's **the most frightening** ride I have ever been on.*
  Form: superlative + present perfect

5.3 Comparative adverbs

We use comparative adverbs when we want to contrast how actions are performed.
1 If we want to make adverbs comparative we use *more* or *less*.
  She has been working more conscientiously this term.
2 We don't use -er or -est.

There are important exceptions, as shown in the table.

Adjective	Comparative adverb	Superlative	Adverb
good / well	better	best	well
bad / badly	worse	worst	badly
hard / hard	harder	hardest	hard
fast / fast	faster	fastest	fast

1 Complete the sentences using a comparative or superlative form of the word in brackets.
  1 It was a wonderful meal, in fact it was _____ (delicious) I had ever eaten.
  2 Last term her English was excellent and she was the _____ (good) in the class, but this term she's the _____ (bad), I wonder what has happened.
  3 Gordon is much _____ (happy) than Harry and Russell, but Gerald is the _____ (successful) and _____ (rich) of all of them.
  4 Why is it that people who live the _____ (close) to their work always arrive late?
  5 I feel much _____ (good) this morning so I'll go to school.
  6 The exam wasn't as _____ (easy) I had imagined.
  7 His brother doesn't speak _____ (good) than him.
  8 Cristiano plays football more _____ (beautiful) than any other player.
  9 Felicia swims _____ (fast) than Samantha but not _____ (quick) as Ana.
  10 Nobody works as _____ (hard) Xu, he has learned all the irregular verbs, even the _____ (hard).

2 Complete the second sentence so that it has a similar meaning to the first.
  1 I have never felt so tired.
    This _____ ever felt.
  2 Nobody knew him better than Amanda.
    Nobody knew him as _____ Amanda.
  3 I have never had such a bad flight.
    It was the _____ ever had.
  4 Her car goes faster than mine.
    My car doesn't _____ hers.
  5 Do you have a more recent version of this song?
    Is this the _____ this song?
  6 Each book I read adds to my understanding.
    The more I _____ I understand.

6 Conditionals

Conditional sentences typically contain two clauses – a condition clause and a result clause.

They allow us to talk about possible and impossible / unreal situations and their consequences.

6.1 Zero conditional

We use the zero conditional:
1   to describe a straightforward cause and effect.
    *If you **open** that door, it **makes** a terrible noise.*
2   to write a scientific truth.
    *If you **mix** oil and water the oil **floats**.*

6.2 First conditional

We use the first conditional:
1   when we believe that something is likely to happen.
    *If I **have** the money, I **will buy** the car.*
2   for promises or threats.
    *If you **pass** your exam (condition), **I'll buy** everyone a coffee (result).*
    *If you **don't do** your homework, **I'll have** to phone your Mum and Dad.*
3   We use *when* and *as soon as* when the first action is sure to happen.
    *I'll call you **when / as soon as** I get the results.*

Form: *If* + present simple / *will* + infinitive (without '*to*')

6.3 Second conditional

We use the second conditional:
1   when we think that the outcome of a future event is not very likely to happen.
    *If the students **were** more serious, they **would have** a better chance in the exam.*
2   for unreal or imaginary situations in the present or the future.
    *If I **ran** Cambridge Examinations, I'**d make the exam easier** (but I'm just a candidate).*
3   for polite requests.
    *Would you mind **if I borrowed** these DVDs?*

> **REMEMBER:**
>
> *Can, could, might, should* and *ought to* can replace *would* in second conditional sentences.

Form: *If* + simple past / *would* / *could* / *might* + infinitive (without '*to*')

6.4 Third conditional

We use the third conditional to describe imaginary or 'unreal' situations in the past and to express regrets.
    *If I **had known** he would be upset, **I wouldn't have said** it (but I **did** say it and he **was** upset).*
    (See ***Wish*** for more information on expressing regrets.)
    Form: *If* + past perfect / *would* / *could* / *might* + have + past participle

6.5 Alternatives to '*if*'

1   *Unless* and *otherwise*
    We use *unless* meaning 'if … not' in the condition clause, and *otherwise* before the likely result.
    *You will lose marks **unless** you improve your spelling.*
    *We'd better hurry up. **Otherwise** we'll miss the start of the film.*
2   *As long as / provided / on condition that*
    We use *provided / as long as / on the condition that* when we want to make the condition stricter.
    *I'll lend you my dictionary **provided / as long as / on the condition that** you promise to bring it back.*
3   Using inversion:
    ***If** I had known he would be upset, I wouldn't have said anything.*
    ***Had I known** he would be upset, I wouldn't have said anything.*

6.6 Mixed conditional

The mixed conditional combines the third conditional in the condition clause with the second conditional in the result clause. We use it to describe a past action which has a consequence in the present.
    *If I **hadn't eaten** that seafood, I **wouldn't feel** so awful now.*

1   Change the verbs in brackets to form conditional sentences.
    1   I (take) _____ her to the station if she (do) _____ my French homework!
    2   I know it's just a dream, but what (you do) _____ if we (win) _____ the lottery?
    3   If (you say) _____ that again, I (tell) _____ your father.
    4   She was lucky. If she (not miss) _____ the flight she (not be) _____ with us today.
    5   I don't believe he'll ever stop, but if he _____ (give up) smoking his health _____ (improve).
    6   When our guests (arrive) _____, Lucy, (you call me) _____ immediately?
    7   (you give) _____ him the money if you (know) _____ how he was going to spend it?
    8   If I (be) _____ in charge I (make) _____ some big changes, but I'm just a temporary worker.
    9   If Hannah (know) _____ the truth about Duncan she (think twice) _____ before marrying him.
    10 I'm so stupid; if I (remember) _____ lock up my bike, it (not be stolen) _____.

2 Rephrase these sentences using the words in **bold**.

1 We'll miss the beginning of the film if you don't hurry up. **unless**

_____

2 If you leave your car there you'll get a parking ticket. **you'd better not / otherwise**

_____

3 You can borrow my car on condition that you fill it up afterwards. **provided**

_____

4 I'll tell your sister what you did unless you give me a sweet. **if**

_____

5 Unless you promise to take care of it I won't lend you my ipod. **I'll / as long as**

_____

6 If he doesn't drive more carefully he'll have an accident. **unless**

_____

6.7 Contrasting ideas

1 Consequence

He felt ill. He stayed at home.

In this pair of sentences there is not a contrast between the two ideas. After all, if we feel ill it is logical to stay at home. We can join these ideas with *so*.

*He felt ill **so** he stayed at home.*

2 Contrast

He felt ill. He went to school.

In this pair, there is a contrast between the ideas.

a We can show the contrast between these ideas with *but*.

*He felt ill **but** he went to school.*

b We can show the contrast between these ideas with *however / nevertheless*.

He felt ill. However / Nevertheless, he went to school.

Notice: like *but*, *however* and *nevertheless* come after the original proposition, and introduce the contrast, that is, they are placed **between** the contrasting ideas.

3 Other ways of expressing contrast:

a *although / even though*

Although he felt ill, he went to school.

Even though he felt ill, he went to school / He went to school even though he felt ill.

b *in spite of / despite* + **gerund**

In spite of / despite feeling ill / the fact he felt ill, he went to school.

c *in spite of / despite* + **noun**

In spite of / Despite of his illness he went to school.

d *Despite the fact* (*that*) + **tense**

Despite the fact that he felt ill, he went to school.

Notice: These ways of expressing contrast introduce the original proposition, not the contrast.

Even though he was unhappy he was rich.

Even though he was rich, he was unhappy.

1 Decide if the sentences are correct (✓) or incorrect (✗).

1 It was a perfect day although we had a wonderful time. ☐

2 Nevertheless we were late, we managed to see the film. ☐

3 Even though she had slept, she was tired. ☐

4 Despite it was a long journey we enjoyed the trip. ☐

2 Beginning with the word in **bold**, put the rest of the sentence in the right order.

1 **Even** – she – came – minister – poor – though – from – a – family – she – became – prime.

2 **In** – tired – of – the – time – didn't – spite – we – feel – too.

3 **The** – was – rough – managed – sea – the – port – sailors – nevertheless – reach – the – to.

4 **We** – a – raining – had – lovely – evening – fact – that – the – despite – it – was.

3 Rephrase the sentences using the words in **bold**.

1 She has lots of money but she never spends it. **despite**

2 He refused to wear a coat. It was cold. **nevertheless**

3 She had hurt her foot but she still won the race. **fact**

4 He felt tired but he still drove through the night. **even**

7 Countable and uncountable nouns and their determiners

7.1 Countable nouns

A countable noun is a separate unit which can be counted. When there is more than one, the noun can be made plural: *tables, chairs, students, cats, ideas, people, children.*

7.2 Uncountable nouns

Uncountable nouns are things or ideas which cannot be counted (or only counted with difficulty), or abstract nouns and ideas. They include liquids, mass, abstract nouns and things such as *water, oil, butter, sand, information, happiness, hair, spaghetti.*

REMEMBER:

In some languages uncountable nouns such as *hair*, *information*, *news* and *advice* are countable.

7.3 Determiners

Determiners come **before** nouns. Which one we choose depends on whether the noun it introduces is countable or uncountable.

We can make uncountable nouns countable by adding a container, a quantity / weight / its length, or *a piece of* before it.

A bottle of water, a jar of instant coffee, a slice of cake, a tin of soup, a packet of biscuits, 200 grams of butter, a grain of sand, a piece of information, etc.

7.4 Determiners with countable and uncountable nouns

1 We use *all*:
   a before **plural** countable nouns [C] and uncountable nouns [U] to express the idea of 'all the ones'.
   > ***All** the students left early.* [C]

2 We use *every*:
   a before **single** countable nouns and uncountable nouns to express the idea of 'every one' (we drop the use of *a / the*).
   > ***Every** student left early.* [C]

3 We use *some*:
   a before plural countable nouns and uncountable nouns.
   > *She met **some** interesting people while she was on holiday.* [C]
   > *I asked for ~~an information~~.*
   > *I asked for **some** information about language courses.* [U]
   b in requests and offers, particularly when we expect the answer to be 'yes'.
   > *Could you give me **some** advice about which wallpaper to choose?* [U]
   > *Would you pass me **some** more coffee, please?* [C]
   > *Is there **some** of that lovely cake left?* [C]

4 We use *any*:
   a before plural countable nouns and uncountable nouns to express the idea of 'all or nothing'.
   > ***Any** child can use this computer programme.* = all children. [C]
   > *You can come and see me **any** time.* = there is no limit. [U]
   > *Oh dear, there isn't **any** sugar left.* = none at all. [U]

REMEMBER:
i We place *not* **before** *any* to express the idea of *no*.
We use *not any / no* before plural countable nouns and uncountable nouns.
> *There weren't any students in the classroom / There were no students in the classroom.* [C]

ii We place *hardly* **before** *any* to express the idea of 'not a lot'.
> *There were **hardly any** customers in the shop.* [C]

iii We place *have* **before** *any* to ask about the existence or availability of something.
> *Do we **have any** milk?* [U]

iv *Some / any / no + one / body / where / thing*
Add *some / any / no* **before** *one / body / where / thing* to create indefinite pronouns.
These follow the same rules of form as *some* and *any*.
> *There is someone outside.*
> *Really! I can't see anyone / anybody.*
> *There was nowhere to park.*
> *We couldn't find anywhere to park.*

Complete the sentences with *a*, *some* or *any*.

1 Would you like _____ cup of tea and _____ biscuit, or perhaps _____ piece of cake?

2 You don't need to ask, you can sit _____ where you want.

3 We've got _____ eggs and _____ cheese, but we don't seem to have _____ milk.

4 Could I have _____ more tea, please, and is there _____ more cake?

5 Ring me _____ time you need _____ advice, here's _____ card with my number.

6 I can't get _____ reply, there isn't _____ one there after five o'clock.

7 Oh dear, there aren't _____ rubbish-bags, can you get _____ more the next time you go shopping.

8 She won't do _____ thing without first checking with her boss.

9 Do you fancy _____ coffee? There's _____ new jar in the cupboard.

10 There isn't _____ thing _____ one can say or do – it's hopeless!

5 *Much* and *many*; *a lot of* and *lots of*
   a We use *many* with countable nouns, and *much* with uncountable nouns.
   > ***Many** students leave their revision to the last minute.*
   > *The changes to the exam have encouraged **much** discussion.*
   b However, *a lot of / lots of* are used with both countable and uncountable nouns. We tend to use them instead of *much* and *many* in positive statements.
   > ***A lot of / lots of** students use bi-lingual dictionaries.*
   > *Harry wasted **a lot of / lots of** time trying to mend the PlayStation.*

REMEMBER:
i *Lots of, loads of, plenty of* are considered to be less formal than *a lot of*.
> *Don't worry about me, I've got **lots / loads / plenty** of friends.*

ii *Much* and *many* are generally reserved for negative statements and questions.
> *How **much** time do we have before we need to leave?*
> *We don't have **much** money left.*
> *How **many** people have you invited?*
> *We weren't expecting so **many** people at the open-day.*

6   *Few* and *a few*, *little* and *a little*
    We use *few / a few* with countable nouns and *little / a little* with uncountable nouns. *A few* and *a little* mean 'some', while *few* and *little* mean 'not much / many', or 'less than normal or what we would usually expect.

    > ***A few*** (= some) *students know how to pronounce 'th' properly.*
    > ***Few*** (= not very many) *students carry on to take the Proficiency exam.*
    > *There's **a little** (= some) bit of coffee left, who would like to finish it?*
    > *There's **little** (= not much) point in trying to learn anything now.*

7   *Several*
    Several is used with countable plural nouns. It has a similar meaning to *a few* (e.g. three or four).

    > *There were **several** people waiting in the doctor's surgery.*

8   *A great (large) number (amount) of / great (good) deal of*
    a   We use *a great / large number of* with plural countable nouns.

    > ***A great number of*** *tourists were affected by the strike.*
    > Not: *A great deal of tourists…*

    b   We use *a great / good deal of* with uncountable nouns to mean 'many' or 'much'.

    > *The strike caused **a great deal of** inconvenience.*
    > Not: ~~The strike caused a large number of inconvenience.~~

Choose the correct word (in italics) to complete the sentences.

1   How ***many / much*** butter and how ***many / much*** raisins do we need for this recipe?
2   It doesn't matter how ***much / many*** times you tell her, she never remembers.
3   Her ex-boyfriend is giving her a great ***number / deal*** of trouble.
4   There's ***little / a little*** advantage in changing Internet service providers.
5   The police found the fingerprints of ***few / several*** different suspects.
6   Were there ***much / lots*** of people at the procession on Sunday?
7   Not really, there weren't ***much / many*** at all. Just ***a few / few*** regulars.
8   She's lucky – she's got ***a lots of / loads*** of money and a big house.
9   She has got very ***little / few*** friends, she stays in her room watching TV all day.
10 Our advertisement received a great ***deal / number*** of replies.
11 There doesn't seem to be ***many / much*** choice, let's try the other place.
12 I called him ***loads / several*** of times but only got his answering machine.

8 Future

There are different ways of expressing the future. The form we use depends on the circumstances and how we view the future event.

1   We use the **present continuous** to talk about future personal arrangements and plans, especially when we mention the time and place.

    > *We're **leaving** for Athens on Saturday.*

2   We use the **present simple** when we refer to timetables or programmes.

    > *The next train to Brusssels **departs** in 15 minutes.*

3   We use **be going to**:
    a   to talk about things we have already decided to do.

    > *I'**m going to take** part in the Erasmus programme next year.*

    b   to make predictions based on what we can see right now.

    > *Oh my goodness, look at that child. She'**s going to fall** off her bike and hurt herself.*

8.1 The future simple (*will*)

We use *will* (the future simple):
1   for facts and predictions.

    > *Anika **will be** three years old on Friday.*
    > *Next season **will be** a good one for our team's supporters.*

2   for decisions made at the time of speaking.

    > *Don't take the bus, I'**ll drive** you home.*

3   to predict what is about to happen, or has just happened.

    > *There's someone at the door.*
    > *That **will be** the post woman (she always comes at this time).*
    > *You're right, she's carrying a parcel.*
    > *That **will be** the books I ordered. (They always come by mail and I ordered them last week.)*

> **REMEMBER:**
> We can also use *should* to make predictions based on experience and expected behaviour.
> *What time do we get to Amersham?*
> *Well, we should be there at six o'clock* (that's the time the train usually arrives there).

8.2 Future continuous

We use the future continuous (*will be* + *-ing*) to talk about actions which will be in progress at a time in the future.

> *Hi, Jen, it's me. Just to say I'**ll be arriving** at 17.15. Can you pick me up?*
> *Sure, I'**ll be waiting** outside the station.*

8.3 Future perfect

We use the future perfect to express the idea that something will happen before a specific time in the future.

> *We'**ll have** taken our exam by July.*
> *Don't worry about us, we'**ll have** already eaten.*

8.4 Future perfect continuous

We use the future perfect continuous to describe activities which began before a point in the future and which are still in progress at that point in time.

> By next September, she'**ll have been studying** German for two years.
>
> In six months' time we'**ll have been living** in this house for ten years.

8.5 *Was going to* (the future in the past)

1 *Was going to* is used talk about something that, in the past, was thought would happen in the future.

> Don't blame me, I didn't know he **was going to react** so badly to to the news.
>
> We **were going to go** camping, but then it rained so we decided against it.

2 *Be to …*

We use the verb ***to be* + infinitive** to make announcements.

> The student exchange programme **is to begin** in the autumn.

8.6 Adjectives with a future meaning

1 *Bound / likely* and *due to* + infinitive are adjectives with an implicit future meaning.

We use *bound to* when we are sure that a future event will happen.

> The plane **is bound to land** late because of the fog.

We use *likely to* when we think it is highly probable that something will happen.

> She **is likely to be** disappointed with her results.

We use *due to* when something which has been planned is expected to happen.

> The reception **is due to** begin at six o'clock this evening.

1 Read the conversations carefully and complete the sentences with **will** or **going to**.

1 'You look nice, what's the special occasion?'
'Thanks. I _____ (visit) my boyfriend's parents.'

2 'Come back to my place for dinner.'
'That's kind, I _____ (bring) some wine.'

3 'Have you made up my mind about your studies next year?'
'Yes, I've finally decided. I _____ (study) hotel management.'

4 'I'm in the bath! Can you pick up the phone?'
'Sure, I_____ (answer) it.'

5 Have you heard? Max Bremner _____ (play) for Chelsea next season.

6 'Is that the time! Where can I get a taxi?'
'Don't worry. I (give you) a lift _____!'

2 Complete the conversation by choosing between the words in *italics*.

Jenny: (1) ***Are you doing anything / Do you do*** anything nice next weekend?

Katie: Yes, actually, (2) ***I'm going / I go to*** Bordeaux with Vincent.

Jenny: Lucky you! How (3) ***are you getting / do you get*** there?

Katie: Well, we (4) ***will take / are going to take*** the plane. There's a flight that (5) ***leaves / will leave*** at eight. It (6) ***is taking / is going to take*** just over an hour.

Jenny: Marvellous. Who (7) ***looks after / is going to look after*** your dog, Toffee?

Katie: Now there's a problem, Maryse (8) ***was going to / would*** look after the dog but now she says she can't.

Jenny: Don't worry, (9) ***I'll / going to*** take care of her if you like. When (10) ***will you come / are you coming*** back?

Katie: We (11) ***should / due*** be back on Sunday evening, by nine o'clock. I (12) ***am going to / will*** pick her up then.

Jenny: No, don't bother. You (13) ***are feeling / are going to be*** tired after your trip. (14) ***I'll drop / I'm going to drop*** her off at your place on my way to work.

Katie: That's really kind, (15) ***I'm waiting / I'll be waiting*** for you outside.

9 Gerund and infinitive

9.1 The gerund

The gerund is the noun form of the verb. We form it by adding *-ing* to the verb. Be careful not to confuse the gerund with the present participle.

> ***Smoking*** is bad for you. = gerund
>
> He is **smoking** his pipe. = present participle

We use the gerund:

1 after verbs such as *involve*, *avoid*, *consider*, *mind* and *risk*.

> Do you **mind telling** me what you are doing in my room?

2 after many verbs which express likes and dislikes, such as *hate*, *love*, *loathe*, *enjoy*.

> I **love cooking** but I **loathe doing** the washing-up.

3 as a subject or object.

> ***Eating*** is not permitted on the premises.

4 after prepositions, phrasal verbs and expressions ending in a preposition.

> He burned the letter **after reading** it.
>
> She **took up studying** Ancient Greek in her spare time.
>
> I'm **tired of listening** to your excuses.

REMEMBER:

i *Despite* and *in spite of* are prepositions / prepositional phrases. As such they are followed by the gerund or another noun:

> She played tennis **despite feeling** tired.
>
> She played tennis **despite her tiredness**.

Form: *used to* + *doing* / *look forward to* + *doing*

ii Although *to* is part of the 'full infinitive', it can also be a preposition and be followed by the gerund:

> I'm used to ~~get up~~ **getting up** early in the morning. (*used* = adjective made from the past participle.)
>
> I'm looking forward to ~~see~~ **seeing** the latest film with Julia Roberts.

iii We can follow *need* with the gerund to lend it a passive sense:

> These windows **need cleaning** = Someone needs to clean these windows.

9.2 The infinitive

1   We use the bare infinitive (infinitive without *to*):
    a   after modal verbs.
        *We **should listen** to what she says.*
    b   after *make* and *let*.
        *They **made me wear** school uniform.*
        *They wouldn't **let me play**.*
2   We use the full infinitive (with *to*):
    a   to express a reason or purpose.
        *He enrolled in evening classes **to improve** his German.* (to achieve an outcome)
        *She took off her shoes **so as not to** wake up the baby.* (to avoid an outcome)
    b   after certain verbs such as *appear, manage, seem, want, would like* and *prefer*.
    c   with the 'lexical future': *intend, plan, decide*.
        *We intend **to stay** there for three nights.*
    d   with some verbs which have two objects: *encourage, request, advise, recommend, tell* and *ask*.
        *His mother **encouraged** him **to apply** for the course.*

9.3 Gerund or infinitive

Some verbs take both the infinitive or the gerund with little change in meaning, e.g. *like, try*. Others have an important change in meaning, e.g. *stop, remember,* and *hate*.

1   A small change in meaning:
    *I **like to go** to the dentist every six months.* (It's a habit.)
    *I **like going** for long country walks.* (It gives me pleasure.)
    *I **tried to open** the door.* (This was my aim.)
    *I **tried turning** the key in the lock and **pushing** it.* (This is how I tried to do it.)
2   An important change in meaning:
    *We **stopped to look** at the map.* (We stopped in order to look at the map.)
    *We **stopped looking** at the map and continued our journey.* (We finished studying the map, then we continued our journey.)
    *I **remembered to pay** the bill.* (I remembered I had to pay it, so I did.)
    *I **remembered leaving** my bag on the bus.* (I left my bag on the bus, later on I remembered.)
    *We **hated telling** him the awful news.* (We told him even though it was a painful and difficult task.)
    *I **hate to tell** you this.* (I am about to tell you something you won't like.)
    *I **meant** to post the letter but I forgot.* (I intended to post the letter.)
    *When we discovered the problem **it meant starting** from the beginning.* (It involved starting from the beginning.)

1   Choose the correct form (in italics) to complete the sentence.
    1   We tried **to open / opening** the door but it was locked from the other side.
    2   I didn't enjoy **to play / playing** rugby when I was at school.
    3   I hate **to tell / telling** you this but smoke is coming out of the engine.

4   Would you mind **to check / checking** this form I have filled in?
5   Are you looking forward **to go / going** to college next year?
6   I know it's difficult, but have you tried **to tell / telling** her the truth?
7   Mildred likes **to keep / keeping** empty egg-boxes, it's a strange habit of hers.
8   The child stopped **to cry / crying** when we gave him an ice cream.
9   Greg keeps on **to phone / phoning** Sarah – it's really annoying.
10 Did you remember **to post / posting** that letter I gave you this morning?
11 Would you like **to come round / coming round** for dinner tonight?
12 That's not true, I don't remember **to say / saying** that!
13 She didn't mean **to upset / upsetting** him by what she said.
14 They were tired after **to climb / climbing** the hill, so they stopped **to have / having** a rest.
15 Could you remind me **to take / taking** the car to the garage?
16 We got so lost, it meant **to go back / going** back the way we had come.

2   Complete the second sentence so that it has a similar meaning to the first. Use the 'key word' in capital letters.
    1   I forgot to take my passport. **REMEMBER**
        I _____ .
    2   Remind me to record that programme. **FORGET**
        Don't let _____ .
    3   I can't wait to go to Canada next summer. **FORWARD**
        I'm _____ next summer.
    4   Do you think you could close the window, please? **MIND**
        Would _____ .
    5   He was overweight so he went on a diet. **ORDER**
        He went on a diet _____ weight.
    6   How about going to a restaurant tonight? **LIKE**
        Would _____ to a restaurant tonight?
    7   Even though he didn't have a ticket he travelled to Athens to watch the match. **SPITE**
        He travelled to Athens to see the match _____ a ticket.

10 Inversion

Sometimes, we may invert the verb and subject of a phrase.
1   Inversion is used with *so* and *neither* in short answers to agree with something someone has just said.
    A: *I really enjoyed the play.*
    B: *So did I.* Not: *So I did.*
Notice: you use *so* for answering a positive structure. You use *neither* to provide a short answer with a negative structure.
    'I don't have any money left / I haven't got any money left.'
    'Neither do I.' or *'I don't either.'*
    'Neither have I.' or *'I haven't either.'*

REMEMBER:

The short reply must use the right auxiliary. We can find this out by turning the original statement into a 'yes / no' question:
'She ate pasta for lunch.' → (Did she eat pasta for lunch?)
'So **did** I.'

2   Inversion is used with adverbs of negative force to express surprise or emphasis. This use is common in more formal or literary writing.

> **Not only did they steal** the kitchen equipment but also the food from the fridge / the food from the fridge too.
> **Hardly had I opened** the door than I noticed a strange smell.
> **No sooner had they left** the flat than Mary rang to say she couldn't come.
> **Never / Rarely / Seldom had we witnessed** such a terrible scene.

3   Inversion is used with the third conditional.

> **If we had known** about his past, we wouldn't have gone to the police.
> **Had we known** about his past, we wouldn't have gone to the police.

1   Match the statements with short replies which agree with what has been said.
   1   I laughed all the way through the film.
   2   We don't often eat out.
   3   I am going to Italy this summer.
   4   We didn't mean to upset her.
   5   I can't ski very well.
   6   They had planned to leave after lunch.

   ___ a Neither can I.
   ___ b So are we.
   ___ c I did too.
   ___ d So had we.
   ___ e We didn't either.
   ___ f Neither do we.

2   Beginning with the word in **bold**, rephrase the sentences.
   1   The moment he finished one job his boss gave him another.
      Hardly _____
   2   The second I got the exam results I phoned my parents.
      No _____
   3   I have never seen such an untidy bedroom!
      Never _____
   4   She speaks Italian, Chinese and Japanese too.
      Not _____
   5   I would have told him if I'd seen him.
      Had _____

11 Modals

Modal auxiliary verbs such as *can*, *must* and *will* allow us to express concepts such as 'ability' and 'obligation'. We also use them to allow us to perform a wide range of functional tasks, such as making requests or speculating. The context in which modal verbs appear is important as each modal has a number of different uses.
Some modals **do not** have a future or past form.
We can't use two modals together.

11.1 *Can* (infinitive *to be able*)

We use *can*:
1   to talk about abilities.
      She **can** skate beautifully.
2   to ask for permission.
      Can I borrow your dictionary?
3   for requests.
      Can you lend me £10?

REMEMBER:

i   The infinitive form of *can* is *to be able to*:
      I may **be able to** attend.
ii   The simple past of *can* is *could* or *was / were able to*:
      He **could** drive before the accident / He **was able to** drive before the accident.

11.2 *Could*

As well as being the past form of *can* we use *could*:
1   to discuss alternatives and options.
      We **could** invite everyone to a restaurant, or else we **could** have a picnic on the beach.
2   to make more polite requests.
      Could you bring me the bill, please?
      Could you speak a little more slowly, please?
3   for speculating, guessing and discussing possibilities.
      The weather **could** be better tomorrow (it's possible).
4   to talk about general past abilities.
      He **could** run for miles and miles when he was younger.
However, if we want to say we succeeded in doing something on a particular occasion, or after a lot of difficulty we use *be able to*.
      I drove around for 40 minutes, finally I **was able to** find somewhere to park.

11.3 *Must*

We use *must*:
1 for orders we give to ourselves.
> I **must** pay the phone bill, otherwise they will cut me off.
2 to prohibit something (used in mainly written rules and regulations).
> You **mustn't** speak on your mobile while you're driving.

REMEMBER:
Non-native speakers can over-use *must*. It can sound rude or aggressive. To give orders, or to describe duties use *have to* instead. Make polite requests with *could you?* instead.

3 for a strong recommendation.
> You **must** see the new James Bond film, it's wonderful.
4 for making intelligent guesses and deductions.
> She **must** be Melanie's twin sister. They are almost identical.
5 for deductions in the past we use *must have been / can't have been*.
> He **must have been** disappointed not to pass. His teacher **can't have been** pleased either.

For negative deductions we use *can't be*, not ~~mustn't be~~.
*My parents want me to revise all weekend – they **can't be** serious!* (Not: *They mustn't be serious.*)

11.4 *Have to*

We use *have to*:
1 to talk about our duties or obligations.
> I **have to** deal with phone calls and enquiries and give advice to students.
2 to show that something isn't obligatory or necessary.
> You **don't have to** bring a dictionary to school, we have one in every classroom.

11.5 *May*

We use *may*:
1 to talk about possibility.
> It **may** rain this afternoon.
2 to ask for permission.
> **May** I use your phone?

REMEMBER:
'May I' is generally considered more polite than 'Can I'.

11.6 *Might*

We use *might*:
1 to express a more remote possibility than *may*, and to speculate.
> It **might** be difficult to get a babysitter.
2 as a very polite or formal way of asking for permission, or making a request.
> **Might** I say something here?
> **Might** I borrow your phone book for a minute?

11.7 *Will*

We use *will*:
1 for making predictions and talking about the future. (See **Future** for more information.)
2 when we make offers or decisions as we speak.
> Leave the washing up, **I'll** do it later.
> Q: Can someone answer the door?
> A: **I'll** go.
3 to talk about habitual actions.
> Most days, **I'll** normally take the 7:42 train to Marylebone.
4 to make requests or give orders.
> **Will** you drop me off in front of the bus station, please?

REMEMBER:
Shall can sometimes be used instead of *will*.
In formal, or more old-fashioned English, when the subject of the modal is *I* or *we*, we can use *shall*, although this is quite rare.
> I **shall** give you my decision in the morning.
Shall is more commonly used with *I* and *we* for offers, or to ask for suggestions.
> **Shall** I answer the phone?
> What **shall** we do tonight? **Shall** we go to the cinema?

11.8 *Would*

We use *would*:
1 to make polite requests.
> **Would** you look after my bag for a few minutes?
2 in conditional sentences. (See **Conditionals**.)
3 in reported speech as the reported form of *will*.
> He said he **would** help me, but he didn't.
4 to talk about past habits.
> When we were young we **would** sit on that old bench in the park. (See **Will, would** and **used to**.)

11.9 *Should* and *ought to*

We use *should* and *ought to*:
1 to give advice.
> You **should / ought to** be more careful about what you say in front of her, she repeats everything.
2 to say what we think is morally right.
> Rich countries **should** help developing countries.
3 to criticise a past action.
> You **should have** made sure you had the money.
> You **shouldn't have** been so greedy.
> We tend not to use *oughtn't to / oughtn't to have* as it is too hard to say.
4 to make predictions based on previous experience, or what is expected.
> Don't panic, there **should** be a bus in a minute.

11.10 *Need*

1 We use *need* to say when something is necessary or unnecessary.
> We **need to** enrol for the exam before the deadline.
2 We use *needn't to* (*don't need*) to say that something is not necessary.
> You **needn't** buy / **don't need to** buy uniforms and equipment, everything is included in the fees.

REMEMBER:

Need can be used both as a modal auxiliary, and as a full verb with an auxiliary. This can be used to make an important distinction of meaning in the past.

***Need* as a modal:** *I needn't have worn a suit because everyone else was dressed casually.* = I wore a suit, but it wasn't necessary.

***Need* as a full verb:** *I didn't need to* wear a suit, so I just dressed casually like everyone else.

***Need* as a modal:** *I needn't have bought the tools because the company supplied everything.* = I bought the tools but it wasn't necessary.

***Need* as a full verb:** *I didn't need to buy any tools because the company provided everything.* = It wasn't necessary to buy any tools so I didn't.

1   Choose the correct modal verb.
   1   According to the law, you **have to / must** pay your taxes by January 1st.
   2   You **needn't have bought / didn't need to buy** this. We already have one. Take it back.
   3   A: I need someone to help me with this.
       B: I have nothing to do. I **'ll / 'd** help you.
   4   They **must / might** be late. Julie rang earlier and said it's possible because Ray has to work late.
   5   A: What **shall / will** we do tonight?
       B: We could go to the cinema.
       A: Good idea.
   6   You **would / ought to** invite them too or they'll be insulted.
   7   **Are you able to / could** you give me the bill, please?

2   Complete the second sentence so it has a similar meaning to the first sentence.
   1   **Do you** always say the first thing that pops into your head?
       _____ you think before you speak?
   2   You **should go** tonight.
       You _____ to go tonight.
   3   Your father **must have** been angry about your exam results.
       Your father _____ happy about your exam results.
   4   We weren't **able to** find somewhere to park.
       We _____ find a place to park.
   5   There's no **need to** help.
       You don't _____ to help.
   6   **Maybe** they left earlier.
       They might _____ .

12 Narrative tenses

12.1 Past tenses

1   Simple past
   We use the simple past:
   a   to talk about single past actions or a clear sequence of past actions.

REMEMBER:

We don't have to repeat the subject if it doesn't change.
She opened the envelope, (she) took out the letter and smiled.

   b   to talk about past states.
       *I **taught** in that school for 13 years.*
2   Past continuous
   We use the past continuous:
   a   to describe past actions which were in progress at a given time or period in the past.
   b   at the beginning of a narrative to set the scene.
       *The lawyers **were looking** through their papers, **preparing** their arguments for the trial to come.*
   c   to show an action was in progress when another action took place.
       *We **were watching** TV when we heard a loud bang from the street below.*
   d   to show that different actions were in progress at the same time.
       *While we **were lying** on the beach someone was **going** through our things in the hotel room.*

REMEMBER:

We can often leave out *was / were* and use the present participle on its own. As in the simple past, we don't have to repeat the subject if it doesn't change:
*Shoppers **were crowding** round the counter, (they were) **snatching** bargains from under each other's noses.*

3   Past perfect
   We use the past perfect to show that an action happened earlier than a later action:
   *By the time we got there, the film **had already** started.*

REMEMBER:

The past perfect is also used in the condition clause of the third conditional, and to express past regrets with *wish*. (See the **Third conditional** and / or **Wish** for more information on this.)

4   Past perfect continuous
   We use the past perfect continuous:
   a   to show that an action had started and was still in progress when another action took place.
       *We **had been standing** there for ages when the night bus finally turned up.*
   b   for repeated actions up to a point in the past.
       *I **had been ringing** her all morning but I couldn't get a reply.*

Complete the story by changing the verbs in brackets into a suitable narrative tense.

A few months (1) _____ (go by) since the disaster at the beach so Olivier (2) _____ (decide) to try his luck with Isabelle again. He (3) _____ (try) to ring her, but each time she (4) _____ (hear) his voice she (5) _____ (hang up). This time, however, Olivier (6) _____ (have) a secret weapon! He (7) _____ (receive) an invitation to a smart party in a country château, and many stars (8)_____ (going to) be there. Isabelle (9) _____ (not able) to resist. This time Olivier (10) _____ (borrow) his mother's new BMW. Isabelle (11)_____ (wear) a silk evening dress and pearls – she (12) _____ (never look) so wonderful. They (13) _____ (drive) through the forest to the château, when suddenly a wild boar (14) _____ (appear). Olivier (15) _____ (can not) avoid it and the car (16) _____ (drive) into it with a tremendous bang – killing the creature! Fortunately the boar (17) _____ (not do) too much damage, but Olivier (18) _____ (know) his mother would never believe what (19) _____ (happen) without seeing the evidence. With Isabelle's help, he (20) _____ (push) the boar into the back. Unfortunately while they (21) _____ (do) this, Isabelle's necklace (22) _____ (break) so they (23) _____ (have to) spend ten minutes picking up the pearls. Once they (24) _____ (finish) they (25) _____ (be) were ready to continue on their journey when they (26) _____ (hear) a loud cry from the back – the boar was not dead and (27) _____ (wake up)! They (28) _____ (jump) out of the car and (29) _____ (watch) in horror as the angry creature (30) _____ (destroy) the interior. When the police (31) _____ (arrive) they (32) _____ (have to) fire fifty shots into the car to kill it. Needless to say, they never (33) _____ (get) to the party!

12.2 Passive voice

The active voice emphasises the actions performed by people or things. The passive voice focuses on what happens to people or things as the result of the actions they experience.

Active:

a   *Debbie ate all the cakes.* = We are more interested in what Debbie did.

Passive:

b   *All the cakes were eaten by Debbie.* = We are more interested in the cakes and what happened to them.

In the first sentence, Debbie is the subject of the sentence and the cakes the object. In the second sentence, the cakes are the subject and Debbie the agent (i.e. the performer of the action); there is no object.

We use the passive:

1   when the agent (the person who performed the action) is assumed, unimportant, or unknown.
> *The poor old gentleman **was taken** directly to hospital.* (probably by ambulance, but this isn't important)
> *My bag **has been** stolen.* (by an unknown person)

2   when the action, event, and process is seen as more important than the agent. This is often the case in formal or scientific writing.
> *The formula **was checked** carefully.*

3   to put new information later in the sentence.
> *Pride and Prejudice **was written** by Jane Austen.*

REMEMBER:

The passive voice is *not* a tense.
It **always** includes a form of the verb 'to be' and a past participle. The main changes are:
Present simple: *She eats the cake / s.*
  The cake / s is / are eaten.
Present continuous: *She is eating the cake / s.*
  The cake / s is / are being eaten.
Simple past: *She ate the cake / s.*
  The cake / s was / were eaten.
Past continuous: *She was eating the cake / s.*
  The cake / s was / were being eaten.
Present perfect: *She has eaten the cake / s.*
  The cake / s has / have been eaten.
Past perfect: *She had eaten the cake / s.*
  The cake / s had been eaten.
Going to future: *She is going to eat the cake / s.*
  The cake / s is / are going to be eaten.
Modals in present: *She can / should / will eat the cake / s.*
  The cake / s can / should / will be eaten.
Future perfect: *She will have eaten the cake / s.*
  The cake / s will have been eaten.

4   The causative *have* (*have something done*)
  We use the causative *have*:
  a   to talk about services others perform for us.
> *She **had** her teeth **whitened** by a famous dentist.* (She didn't whiten them herself, the dentist did it for her.)
  Form: *have + something + past participle*
  b   to describe unfortunate incidents and accidents.
> *She **had** her handbag **stolen** from under the seat in the cinema.*

REMEMBER:

The present and past perfect continuous do not have a passive form (except for rare examples). Intransitive verbs do not have a passive form.

5   a   *Get*

Get can be used in a similar way to the causative *have*:
> We **got** *(had)* our car **repaired** *at that garage.*

Get is also used with adjectives like *married* and *hurt*:
> *Luckily nobody* **got hurt** *in the crash.*

Get also has a passive sense:
> *I thought we had bought too much food, but in the end all of it* **got eaten**.

REMEMBER:

Let does not have a passive form. We use *allowed to* in the passive:
> *She doesn't* **let** *us talk on the phone. We* **aren't allowed** *to talk on the phone.*

   b   *Need*

Need can be used with a passive sense.
We use *need* when something has to be done without saying who should do it.
> *We need to freeze the vegetables.* (active sense)
> *The vegetables* **need freezing**. (passive sense – gerund)
> *The vegetables* **need to be frozen**. (passive infinitive)

6   Passive with *say, know* and *believe*

We use reporting verbs such as *say*, *know* and *believe* in the passive when we want to report widely-held views, or opinions which are common knowledge. It is also used to distance the speaker from the information, which is why it is commonly used in news broadcasts.
> *The victim* **was known to have** *a large number of enemies in the underworld.*
> *Chinese silk* **is said to be** *the best in the world.*
> *He* **was believed to have** *a fortune in gold hidden in his house.*

7   Agent or instrument?

With an instrument we use *with* rather than *by*.
> *The cakes were eaten* **by** *Debbie.* (by + the agent)
> *They broke into his desk* **with** */ by means of a paper knife.* (with + the instrument)

Complete the second sentence so that it has a similar meaning to the first sentence.

1   Architects have turned the building into luxury apartments.
The building _____ by architects.

2   The mayor is going to open the new leisure centre.
The new leisure centre _____ the mayor.

3   Someone should show Sally what to do.
Sally should _____ what to do.

4   A journalist was writing the story as we waited.
The story _____ as we waited.

5   A photographer is going to take my photograph tomorrow.
Tomorrow, I'm _____.

6   We need to hide Melanie's present before she sees it.
Melanie's present needs to _____.

7   Thieves broke into their apartment while they were on holiday.
They had their _____ while they were on holiday.

8   We used a large screwdriver to open the car window.
The car window _____ large screwdriver.

9   A lot of people say *Le Cheval Blanc* is the best restaurant in the region.
Le Cheval Blanc is _____ in the region.

10 His parents didn't let him watch the match.
He wasn't _____ watch the match.

12.3 Phrasal verbs

Phrasal verbs consist of the verb and one or two prepositional or adverbial particles. When combined in this way their meaning can be idiomatic.
Compare:
> He **turned up** *the street* (this just tells us where he turned, he could have turned down the street).
> He **turned up** *three hours late* (= He arrived three hours late. Here *up* is part of the phrasal verb *turn up*, meaning to arrive).

There are four principal types of phrasal verb. To fully appreciate the differences, we need to understand the differences between transitive and intransitive verbs (see Section 17).

Type 1: intransitive no object, e.g. *get on* (= to progress / have a relationship).
> *How are you* **getting on**?

Intransitive phrasal verbs do not have an object. We can follow them with an adverbial or prepositional phrase:
> *How are you* **getting on with** *your new flatmate?*

Type 2: transitive separable, e.g. *let down*.
Transitive separable phrasal verbs have to take an object.
If an object pronoun is used it **must** come between the verb and the particle. The pronoun can't come after the particle:
> He **let** *Sally* **down**. He **let** *her* **down**.
> (*Not:* He let ~~down Sally / her.~~)

Type 3: transitive inseparable, e.g. *break into*.
The direct object and object pronoun cannot come between the verb and the particle. They must always follow the particle.
> *They* **broke into** *my flat while I was on holiday.*
> (Not: ~~They broke my flat into while I was on holiday.~~)

Type 4: three-part transitive (phrasal prepositional), e.g. *look forward to*.
Here, the object always comes after the phrasal verb. Three-part phrasal verbs are always inseparable.
> *I'm really* **looking forward to** *seeing Ian again.*
> (Not: *I'm* ~~looking forward really to~~ *seeing Ian again.*)

REMEMBER:

1   The same phrasal verb can have a different meaning and a different grammar.
She turned up late = She arrived late. (Type 1 intransitive.)
His trousers were too long so he turned them up.
= He altered the trousers. (Type 2 transitive separable.)

Decide if these sentences with phrasal verbs are correct (✓) or incorrect (✗).

1 She finally found out the truth about her real parents. ☐
2 We got into the car and set off. ☐
3 She can't turn up it at this time, class starts at half past eight. ☐
4 A lot of lemonade was drunk at the children's party. ☐
5 Can you look after while I go to the shops? ☐
6 I have always looked up to my father. ☐
7 Don't worry about the lights, I switched off them before we left. ☐
8 Guess what! I bumped her mother into at the supermarket. ☐
9 Sorry I am late, the bus had been broken down. ☐
10 They are really looking their holiday forward to. ☐
11 My car was broken into while I was at the cinema. ☐
12 Her illness was got over in five days. ☐

12.4 Present tenses

1 Present simple
   We use the present simple:
   a to talk about facts, routines and with adverbs of frequency.
      *She **comes** from the north of Brazil.*
      *I **go** to English classes three times a week.*
      *We usually **order** a pizza on Friday nights.*
      *They often **take** on extra staff at Christmas.*
   b with 'state verbs'. These include:
      – verbs which deal with likes and dislikes: *like, love, prefer, hate, detest, dislike*
      – verbs which deal with states: *be, seem, looks*
      – verbs of cognition: *think, know, understand, believe, remember, mean*
      – verbs of perception: *see, taste, hear, smell*
      – verbs of possession: *own, belong*
      – other verbs: *need, want, cost.*

REMEMBER:
Some of these verbs can also be dynamic, with a change in meaning:
   to be (state) = natural state.
   to be (dynamic) = to act / behave.
Dynamic verbs can be used in the present continuous to show the temporary nature of the action.
   *What **do** you **think** about global warning?*
   (= What's your general opinion – state sense.)
   *Is everything OK? What **are** you **thinking** about?*
   (right now – dynamic sense.)
   *She **is** lazy.* (it is her natural state.)
   *She **is being** lazy.* (at the moment.)
   *She **is smelling** the flowers. The flowers smell nice.*
   Not: The flowers smell ~~are smelling nice~~.
   *She **is tasting** the soup. The soup **tastes** good.*
   Not: The soup ~~is tasting good~~.

2 Present continuous
   We use the present continuous:
   a to talk about activities which are in progress.
      Q: *Hey, what **are** you **doing** in my room?*
      A: *I**'m looking** for the CD I lent you.*
   b to talk about ongoing activities. In other words, activities that began in the past, are going on now and into the future.
      *Justine studies at Bordeaux University; at the moment she **is spending** a term in Oxford.*
   c to talk about trends or a changing situation.
      *Unemployment **is** still **going up** by 1% a month.*
   d to express a future meaning (See **Future forms**).
   e with *always* to add expression.
      *She**'s** always **taking** my things* (to express annoyance).

3 Present perfect simple
   We use the present perfect simple:
   a to talk about something which started in the past and continues into the present.
      *We **have lived** in this house for 30 years.*
   b to talk about past events when no specific time is given or suggested.
      ***Have** you ever **eaten** oysters?*
      *Mandy **has been** to Argentina.*
   c to talk about recent events where the result is still visible.
      *This room looks different. **Have** you **painted** it?*
   d with adverbs such as *yet, just* and *already* (especially in British English).
      ***Have** you **written** your composition yet?*
   e to talk about quantities, a number of repeated, completed actions.
      *She **has done** more than 50 parachute jumps.*

4 Present perfect continuous
   We use the present perfect continuous:
   a to talk about continuous activities which started in the past and continue into the present (with an emphasis placed on the duration of the activity).
      *Your father **has been working** in the garden since eight o'clock this morning.*
   b to talk about repeated actions up to the present.
      *I**'ve been trying** to call the box-office all day, but I just can't get through.*
   c to emphasise an activity rather than a quantity / result.
      *She **has been writing** short stories for ten years* (activity), *she has written more than 50* (result).
   d to talk about a recent activity where a result is still visible.
      Q: *Why are you all red?*
      A: *I've been sunbathing.*

REMEMBER:

Rather is not a verb. Not: ~~I rather the cinema~~ than the theatre but *I prefer the cinema to the theatre. = I'd (would) rather go to the theatre than the cinema.*
If we want to include a noun or pronoun within the sentence then we have to use the simple past:
> *I'd rather go to the cinema.*
> *I'd rather we went to the cinema. (See **Time**.)*

Choose the correct form.

1 They regularly *leave / are leaving* this early in the morning.
2 A: Where is she? We need to go.
B: She *be / is being* difficult. She won't come out of her room.
3 A: What *do you do / are you doing* here?
B: I work in the production department.
4 The price of oil *actually falls / is actually falling* around the world at the moment.
5 A: How's the cheese?
B: It *tastes / is tasting* good!
6 They *are working / have worked* here for over ten years.
7 She's *been revising / revised* for over three hours. It's time she took a break.
8 The phone *hasn't stopped / been stopping* ringing all day.
9 This room looks nice. Have you *redecorated / been redecorating* it?
10 This room is looking nice. How long have you *painted / been painting* it?

13 Relative clauses

Relative clauses give us more information about the subject or object of a sentence. They link two ideas within the same sentence and can be defining, or non-defining.

13.1 Defining relative clauses

1 Use defining relative clauses to complete sentences with essential information.
Defining relative clauses often begin with the pronouns:
who / that for people
> *There's the man **who** / **that** helped me.*
which / that for objects and animals
> *This is the computer **that** / **which** broke down.*
where for place
> *This is the restaurant **where** we first met.*
whose for possession
> *That's the stupid woman **whose** dog bit me.*
when for time
> *Do you remember the time **when** Mary and Jack came to stay?*
whom (In more formal written or spoken English *whom* is used as the object pronoun.)
> *Here is the man **whom** we told you about.*
why for reason
> *He gave no reason **why** he couldn't come.*

2 In writing and more formal speech we may use prepositions with a pronoun.
> *on which* = when
> e.g. *This is the day **on which** we got married.*
> *in which* = where
> *for which* = why
> *to whom* = who … to

REMEMBER:

In defining relative clauses, *who, which* and *that* can be left out when they refer to the object of the verb in the relative clause.
> *Do you want to watch the DVD (**which** / **that**) I got for my birthday?*
> *The person (**who** / **that**) I spoke to yesterday said it would be free.*
> *Sam bought the jeans (**which** / **that**) she'd seen last week.*

13.2 Non-defining relative clauses

Non-defining relative clauses give extra information which is not absolutely essential for the main meaning of the sentence. In written English we separate them from the main clause by commas. In speech, the speaker will generally pause an instant before continuing with the extra information.
> *The Colossus of Rhodes, **which** / **that** stood by the harbour, was destroyed by an earthquake.*

Notice: We can't use *that* in non-defining relative clauses.
> *Vincent, ~~that~~ **who** had never eaten mangoes before, developed dark red patches all over his body.*

Correct the pronouns in each sentence.
1 Jurga is the man whose gave me my first job.
2 This is my lodger, that I was telling you about.
3 India, where is the place I first visited in 1980, is a country I'd like to return to.
4 Christmas is a time in some countries that family and friends get together.
5 The reason when I didn't call you was because my phone battery ran out of charge.
6 My only sister, that lives in Toronto, is coming to visit next month.
7 The church on which we got married is no longer here.
8 My car, that I left at home, had a flat tyre yesterday.

14 Reported speech and reporting verbs

We use reported speech to say what someone else has said. We usually take one step further back in the past when we report. This is called 'backshift'.
> Jenny: *I am going to see Barry.*
> → *Jenny said she was going to see Barry.*
> **Form: present continuous + past continuous**
1 *Say* and *tell* to **report statements**
> Steve: *I've got a headache, Malcolm.*
> → *Steve said that he had a headache.*
> *Steve said to Malcolm that he had a headache.*
> → *Steve told Malcolm / him (that) he had a headache.*
> **Not**: ~~Steve told to Malcolm / him~~ or
> ~~Steve said Malcolm.~~
> **Form: verb (+ *that*) + clause**

2   *Tell* is generally used to **report instructions and orders.**
Mum: *Tidy up your bedroom, Felix.*
➜ *Felix's mum told him to tidy up his room.*
Form: verb + object + infinitive with *to*

3   a   Reported *wh-* questions:
Use *ask* and *want to know* to **report *wh-* questions**.
Katia: *Where does Günther live, Rita?*
➜ *Katia asked (Rita) where Günther lived.*
Katia wanted to know where Günther lived. (if we don't know who Katia asked)
Form: The *wh-* word is followed by a statement word order (subject followed by verb)

   b   Reported *yes / no* questions:
Use *if* and *whether* to report *yes / no* questions.
Katia: *Do you know where Günther lives?*
➜ *Katia wanted to know if / whether we knew where Günther lived.*
Form: verb + *if / whether* + word order is the same as reported statements

4   a   *Suggest*:
Terry: *Let's go for a bike ride.*
➜ *Terry suggested going for a bike ride.*
➜*Terry suggested that we go for a bike ride.*
➜*Terry suggested our going for a bike ride.* (more formal)
➜ *Terry suggested that we should go for a bike ride.*
Form: *suggest* + *-ing*; *suggest* + *that* + simple past; *suggest* + *that* + (*should*) + infinitive without *to*

   b   *Advise*:
Dr Morris: *You ought to go on a diet.*
➜ *Dr Morris advised Henry to go on a diet.*

REMEMBER:
Some reporting verbs contain the sentiment of the original statement. It is important that the correct forms and word pattern follow the reporting verbs in question.
Form: verb + *to* + infinitive (*offer, refuse, threaten, promise, agree*)
verb + object + *to* + infinitive (*convince, persuade, tell, advise, encourage, remind, warn*)
verb + gerund (*suggest, propose, recommend, deny, admit, mention*)

Cindy: *I'm sorry about breaking the vase.*
Cindy **apologised** for breaking the vase.
Paul: *Don't touch that switch, Ben.*
Paul **warned** Ben not to touch the switch.
Steffi: *Don't forget to keep the receipt, Martyn.*
Steffi **reminded** Martyn to keep the receipt.
Rees: *I think you should see a doctor, Milton.*
Rees **advised / encouraged** Milton to see a doctor.
Katie: *You must go and see Borat, it's hilarious.*
Katie **recommended** seeing Borat.
or Katie **recommended** that we see Borat.
John: *You were stupid to leave your car unlocked, Martha.*
John **criticised** Martha for leaving her car unlocked.

---

5   Changes to place and time
Remember that using reported speech may involve making changes to references to place and time.
Now ➜ then,
Today ➜ that day
Before ➜ earlier
The day before yesterday ➜ two days earlier
This evening ➜ that evening
Last night ➜ the previous night / the night before
The next day ➜ the following day

6   No change to the verb
You can leave the verb as it is (without backshift) when:
The verb refers to a fact or ongoing state: '*We have a problem.*' ➜ *She said they have / had a problem.*
The information is still happening or still true: '*I won't agree to the proposal.*' ➜ *He said he won't / wouldn't agree to the proposal.*

1   Correct the sentences.
1   Paul said me to call this number.
2   Melinda told she felt tired.
3   Marissa told to Kevin to be careful.
4   He told to me the story.
5   She asked what time did the train leave?
6   Howard wanted to know from where we had bought the flowers.

2   Complete the reported speech sentences about the direct speech in the first line. Make any other necessary changes to the words in **bold**.
1   Lionel: You really should apply for the job, Romain.
Lionel encouraged _____ .
2   Sam: I wouldn't visit **this** area after dark, Derek.
Sam warned _____ .
3   Joan: Let's visit the ruins **tomorrow**.
Joan suggested that _____ .
4   Lori: I'm sorry I was late **the day before yesterday,** Kim.
Lori apologised to _____ .
5   Patrick: Don't forget to collect **my** prescription from the chemist's, Charlene.
Patrick reminded Charlene _____ .
6   Paul: I didn't call you **last night**, Sarah, because I couldn't find your new number.
Paul explained to Sarah why _____ .
7   Doctor: You should try to go to bed earlier, Mr Rossi.
The doctor advised _____ .
8   Penny: You shouldn't have brought the subject up, Nick.
Penny criticised _____ .

15 *Will / would* and *used to*

15.1 *Will* and *would*

1   *Will* is used to talk about expected behaviour.
    The cat scratched me when I tried to pick him up.
    *Ah yes, he **will do** that with strangers.* (He has done this with other people.)

2   *Would* is used to describe past habits and repeated actions.
    *When mother came home from working in the shop all day long she **would sit** in the armchair and put her aching legs up.*
    Would **can't** be used to talk about past states:
    He ~~would be~~ fat when he was a child.

3   *Used to* is used:

a   as an auxiliary.
    Used to + infinitive without *to* can be used to describe discontinued past habits and states.
        *She **used to be** skinny when she was a teenager* (= a state).
        *I **used to play** tennis every Saturday morning* (= a habit).
    Form: used to + infinitive without to

> **REMEMBER:**
> If we give precise information about how long a state or habit lasted then we use the simple past.
>   Not: *I used to smoke ~~for ten years~~*; but: *I smoked for ten years.*
>   Q: *Do you smoke, Martin?*
>   A: *Not any more, but I used to.* (Notice the short reply).

b   as an adjective.
    We use *be used to* + gerund or *get used to* + gerund to express the idea of being, or becoming, accustomed to / familiar with something.
    *Sally **is used to getting** up early.* (She is accustomed to getting up early, it's not a problem for her.)
    Form: be used to + gerund
    *When Sam went to university he missed his family a lot, but now things are better, he **is getting used to living** away from home.* (Being away from home is more familiar and not so difficult.)
    Form: get used to + gerund

    Complete these sentences with ***will***, ***would***, ***was*** or ***used to***.

1   Nigel _____ do that when he's tired, I'm afraid.

2   We _____ always walk this way home when we were children.

3   She _____ have black hair, didn't she?

4   They _____ always be late – even when they were children.

16 *So* and *such*; *too* and *enough*

1   Use *so* and *such* clauses to show a relationship of cause and effect between clauses. *So* and *such* appear in the cause clause.
        The lesson was boring. I fell asleep.
        cause   effect
        *The lesson was **so boring** that I fell asleep.*
    Form: so + adjective
        *It was **such a boring lesson** that I fell asleep.*
    Form: such + (adjective) + noun
    A less usual variation is:
        *It was **so boring a lesson** that I fell asleep at my desk.*
    Form: so + adjective + a (indefinite article)

2   Use *too* and *enough* to show that too much or too little of something prevented something else from happening. *Too* and *enough* provide an explanation for what happened or didn't happen:
        Julian wanted to join the army. He was only 15.
        *He was **too young to join** the army.*
    Form: too + adjective + infinitive
        *He wasn't **old enough to join** the army.*
    Form: not + adjective + enough + infinitive

> **REMEMBER:**
> We put *enough* **before** nouns, but **after** adjectives.
> *She didn't have **enough money** to rent a flat.*
> **Form: enough + noun**
> *She wasn't **rich enough** to rent a flat.*
> **Form: adjective + enough**

1   Beginning with the words in **bold**, put the sentences into the right order.

    1   **She** – have – finish – enough – didn't – time – exam – the – to.
    2   **The film** – was – all – made – me – that – so – laugh – it – day – funny.
    3   **They** – too – holiday – children – were – poor – take – to – their – on.
    4   **He cried** – because – day – he – sad – all – so – was.
    5   **Rupert was** – such – that – a – in – mood – to – refused – bad – me – he – to – speak.
    6   **Unfortunately** – to – fit – Lucy – enough – in – wasn't – final – play – the.

2   Complete the second sentence so that it has a similar meaning to the first sentence.

    1   We were so tired after the journey that we went straight to bed.
        It was _____.
    2   She is too young to travel on her own.
        She isn't _____.
    3   His exam results were such a disappointment for his parents.
        His parents _____.
    4   There isn't enough space for an extra suitcase.
        The suitcase _____.

17 Transitive and intransitive verbs

17.1 Intransitive verbs

Intransitive verbs (I) only concern the subject (the person who performs the action) and the verb (the action). There is no direct object. Examples of intransitive verbs are: *arrive, go, come, sleep, watch, move, vanish* and *disappear*.

> The bus **came**.
> The boat **disappeared**.

We can introduce another person or thing with an adverbial phrase or a prepositional phrase.

> *Melinda finally arrived* **20 minutes late**.
> *The boat disappeared* **in the storm**.

Form: subject + verb

17.2 Transitive verbs

Transitive verbs (T) concern or affect another person or thing (the object) as well as the subject.

1 They cannot stand alone and must take an object. Transitive verbs include *see, do, make* and *own*.
> ~~I found.~~ = incomplete
> *I found her watch.* = complete

Form: subject + verb + object

2 Transitive verbs, unlike intransitive verbs, can be made passive.
> *Her watch* **was found** *under the sofa.*

3 Many transitive verbs can be used intransitively.
> Q: *What did you do this morning, children?*
> A: *We played.* (I)
> A: *We played tennis.* (T)

> **REMEMBER:**
> Do not confuse intransitive verbs and their transitive equivalents.
> die (I) kill (T); rise (I) raise (T); vanish / disappear (I) lose (T)

Are these sentences correct or incorrect? Write ✓ or ✗. Then decide if the verb in the sentence is transitive (T) or intransitive (I).

1 She slept.
2 I own.
3 We played golf.
4 We play.
5 Three hundred people died.
6 Three hundred people were died.
7 Magically, the wizard vanished.
8 What have you found?

18 Wish

We use *wish*:

1 to express our hopes for what we want to happen or not to happen in the future.
> *I* **wish I knew** *the answer.* (= but I don't.)

Form: subject + simple past
> *I* **wish I could** *speak Arabic.* (= but I can't.)

Form: subject + *wish* + *could* / *was able to* + infinitive (without *to*)

2 For present / future situations you would like to change we use *wish + would*.
> *I* **wish** *he* **would** *stop whistling.* (but I don't think he will.)

Form: *wish* + *would* + infinitive (without *to*)

3 For regrets about things which happened entirely in the past and which we are unable to change we use *wish* + past perfect:
> *I* **wish I hadn't said** *anything.*

Form: *wish* + past perfect (*had* + past participle)

> **REMEMBER:**
> To express regrets, wishes and lost opportunities in the past we can substitute *if only* for *wish*:
> If only I hadn't said anything.

Match the two halves of the sentences.

1 I wish I could _____.
2 I wish I was able _____.
3 I wish he _____.
4 I wish I had visited _____.
5 I wish I spoke _____.
6 If only _____.

a would stop interrupting.
b German.
c to speak Chinese.
d I spoke German and Chinese.
e speak Chinese.
f Germany last year.

19 Verb groups

Irregular verbs can be organised into groups which behave in a similar way.

19.1 No pattern

Some verbs, including some of the most common, do not follow a pattern.

be	was / were	done
do	did	eaten
eat	ate	gone / been
go	went	seen
see	saw	won
win	won	

19.2 Simple past and past participle the same

Ending in -ought or -aught

catch	caught	caught
bring	brought	brought
buy	bought	bought
seek	sought	sought
think	thought	thought

Ending in -eep, -ept

keep	kept	kept
sleep	slept	slept

Ending in t or d

get	got	got / gotten (US)
learn	learnt	learnt
mean	meant	meant
meet	met	met
sit	sat	sat
find	found	found
have	had	had
hear	heard	heard
hold	held	held
make	made	made
stand	stood	stood
understand	understood	understood
lend	lent	lent
send	sent	sent
spend	spent	spent
sell	sold	sold
tell	told	told
pay	paid	paid
say	said	said

19.3 Other patterns

Present and past participle the same

become	became	become
come	came	come
run	ran	run

Change from -i to -a to -u

begin	began	begun
ring	rang	rung
swim	swam	swum

Change from -ear to -ore to -orn

bear	bore	born
wear	wore	worn

Change from -ow or -y to -ew to -own or -awn

fly	flew	flown
grow	grew	grown
know	knew	known
draw	drew	drawn

No change

cost	cost	cost
cut	cut	cut
forecast	forecast	forecast
hit	hit	hit
put	put	put
read	read	read

Past participle in -en

beat	beat	beaten
break	broke	broken
choose	chose	chosen
fall	fell	fallen
forget	forgot	forgotten
freeze	froze	frozen
give	gave	given
hide	hid	hidden
rise	rose	risen
speak	spoke	spoken
take	took	taken
write	wrote	written

Writing guide

PAPER 2, PART 1 an essay

In Part 1 of Paper 2, you must write an essay in 140–190 words in an appropriate style. There are three ways you can structure your essay question. Here are two exam questions and three different types of answer.

Question 1

In your English class you have been talking about young people and money. Now, your teacher has asked you to write an essay. Write an essay using all the notes and give your reasons for your point of view.

Is it better to give children pocket money or should they earn their money by working?

Notes

Write about:

1 which is good for the parents
2 which is good for the child in the future
3 your own ideas

Question 2

In your English class you have been talking about the importance of learning other languages. Now, your teacher has asked you to write an essay. Write an essay using all the notes and give your reasons for your point of view.

In some countries, learning another language is compulsory at school. Do you agree with this?

Notes

Write about:

1 needing languages for work
2 increasing knowledge of the world
3 your own ideas

Answer to question 1

From the moment we leave school to the time we retire, most of us will have to work in order to earn money during our life. So the question is whether we should have to work before this time as children or wait until we become adults.

Restate the question in the introduction.

In my opinion, children should have to work in order to earn pocket money. By that, I don't mean that they should have full-time jobs, but that there are plenty of things they can do around the house to help their parents, such as the washing-up or gardening.

State your opinion on note 1 and give reasons.

In addition to helping at home, working for money gives children a greater sense of responsibility. What's more, parents who simply give children money are not preparing them for the adult world.

State your opinion on note 2 and give reasons.

Finally, you could also argue that when a child buys something with money that they have earned from working, it will mean so much more.

Introduce your own idea.

So, to sum up, I believe that children learn from the experience of earning money and find out that nothing in life is for free.

Conclude with your overall opinion.

Answer to question 2: version 1

For many children, school is the obvious place to learn another language. However, there are so many other important subjects such as mathematics or history that not all pupils have enough time to study everything.

One argument for making language lessons compulsory is that more and more professions need people with language skills. So schools need to prepare children for their future careers. On the other hand not everyone will have an 'international job' so it might never be useful to them.

It's also true that learning a language introduces you to other cultures and helps your understanding of other people. Nevertheless, many other subjects such as geography also provide knowledge of the world.

Some people also argue that learning a language helps young children become more intelligent and helps them learn other subjects. However, if you teach children another language too early, it may also confuse them.

So, to sum up, although I believe that learning another language at school has some advantages, I do not agree that it should be compulsory. Students should be able to choose the subjects that are important for what they want to do in life.

Restate the question in the introduction.

Contrast an argument for and against in each paragraph.

Conclude with your own overall opinion.

Answer to question 2: version 2

For many children, school is the obvious place to learn another language. However, there are so many other important subjects, such as mathematics or history, that pupils do not have enough time to study everything.

One argument for making language lessons compulsory is that a child's future profession may need language skills. Another reason is that learning a language introduces you to other cultures and helps your understanding of other people. Thirdly, some people believe that it helps young children become more intelligent.

On the other hand we also have to remember that not everyone will have an 'international job' so language learning might never be useful to them. In addition to that, there are many other subjects such as geography which also provide knowledge of the world. Finally, some people believe that it may not be good for children to learn another language too early in life.

On balance, I believe that learning another language at school is important for a child and will give them an advantage later in life as well as being more enjoyable than many other subjects.

Restate the question in the introduction.

Use paragraph 2 to state 2 or 3 arguments for.

Use paragraph 3 to state 2 or 3 arguments against.

Conclude with your own overall opinion.

USEFUL EXPRESSIONS

ESSAY

Introduction
Some people claim / believe / say that …
It is sometimes said that …
The question is …
We often read / hear that …

Contrasting views for and against
On the one hand / side … on the other …
While it's true that …
You could also argue that …
Nevertheless, … / However, …
One advantage / Another disadvantage is that …
Even though …

Stating your opinion
In my opinion, …
As I see it, …
From my point of view …

Making extra points
What's more …
In addition …
Furthermore … Firstly / Secondly …

Introducing a contradictory point
Although / Even though …
Despite + noun / gerund
Despite the fact that …
However …

Concluding and summarising
On balance …
I feel / believe that …
In my opinion …
To sum up / In conclusion, …

In Part 2 of Paper 2, you might choose to write an email or letter in 140–190 words in an appropriate style. The email / letter might be more formal or less formal. Here are two answers with different levels of formality. The first answer is a model response to the essay question on page 26 in Unit 2.

A formal letter or email

Dear Sir or Madam

I'm writing about your advert for volunteer work in the June edition of the Student Times.

I've just completed my studies at school and have a place at university. However, I don't want to do my degree in business studies or start my career yet, so I'd like to do a gap year in order to increase my experience of the world.

My interests include mountain biking and sailing. This year at school I was involved in raising money for a local charity and I was also responsible for helping to organise a school drama festival.

I enjoy meeting people and I feel that being involved in one of your gap-year projects would help me to improve my communication and teamwork skills.

I would be grateful if you could send me information about your organisation and details of how to apply.

Yours faithfully

Becky Raven

USEFUL EXPRESSIONS

FORMAL LETTER

Opening salutation
Dear Sir or Madam
Dear Mr Rylands
Dear Martin

Closing salutation
Yours faithfully
Yours sincerely / Best regards
Best wishes

Reason for writing
I am writing to request / complain about / inform you …
in response to …
in connection to …

Referring to previous contact
Thank you for your letter / email …
With regard to …
Further to your letter dated …

Give good / bad news
I would be delighted to …
We would be happy to …
Unfortunately …

Refer to future contact
I look forward to hearing from you.
If you have any further questions / require any further information, please do not hesitate to contact me.

A less formal letter or email

You have received this email from your English-speaking friend Marie.

From: Marie
Subject: Help!

I need your help! I'm doing a school project on different ways that people like learning new words in English. Can you tell what techniques you use and why they work for you?

Thanks
M.

Write your email.

Hi Marie

Great to hear from you again! It's been a long time. Your project sounds interesting for me because I have an English exam soon so I need to learn and remember lots of new vocabulary for it.

One way is to carry a set of blank cards with me and when I read a new word, I write it on the card. Then when I'm sitting on the bus to college, I can test myself.

Recently, I've started using my mobile phone as well. There are lots of really good apps you can download. You click on a new word and you can listen to the pronunciation. But if I'm on the bus I need to wear headphones, otherwise people think I'm mad!

Oh, and one other thing is that I'm a visual learner, so I like lots of pictures. Watching videos in English is also useful – and fun.

Well, I hope that helps with your project. If I think of anything else, I'll email again.

Bye for now

USEFUL EXPRESSIONS

INFORMAL LETTER

Opening
Dear … Hi Hello

Give reason for writing
Just to let you know that …
I'm emailing you to …

Give good news / bad news
I'm so happy because …
The good / bad news is that …
Unfortunately …

Apologise
I really sorry but …
I'm afraid that …

Say when and where / Give details
There is / are…
It's at / starts at …
You can get there by …

Offer / Request
Would you like to … ?
Can I…? / Could you … ?
Would you mind if … ?

Thank
Thanks for …
I'm really grateful for …

Recommend and suggest
You should / ought to …
Why don't you … ?
How about … ?

End
Look forward to seeing you. / See you soon.
Bye for now.
All the best / Best wishes.

In Part 2 of Paper 2, you might choose to write a review in 140–190 words in an appropriate style.

You see this announcement in your college magazine.

FILM REVIEWS WANTED

Do you agree or disagree with the reviews on this page? If you've seen a film recently and would like to give your opinion, why not write your own review? Tell us whether or not you would recommend the film to readers. We'll send two free cinema tickets for any reviews we publish.

Write your review.

My favourite film of the last few months was the latest James Bond film. Usually we know what's going to happen in a Bond film but this one is very different from all the rest in the series.

Introduce your subject for review.

The first thing you notice about the film is that Bond is younger and more aggressive. The female character is also a spy and more interesting than the usual 'Bond girl'. In addition, it's worth seeing because it's much more realistic.

Review some of the positive points.

One problem with the film is that it happens in lots of locations and the plot is a bit too complicated. It also needs to be about 30 minutes shorter. Nevertheless, the scenes in the casino have lots of tension and the criminal characters are particularly evil and interesting.

Mention some weaker points.

So overall I'd recommend the film as it's a new kind of Bond movie and not the usual predictable mix of fancy cars and stupid gadgets. It's certainly a good choice if you want to watch a DVD next Friday night.

Conclude with your overall opinion.

USEFUL EXPRESSIONS

REVIEW

Introducing your review
The aim / purpose of this review is to …
My favourite … is …
The first thing you notice is …

Describing positive feature
One thing I really like about it is …
It's worth seeing because …
A really good part is when …

Describing weaknesses
One problem is …
It isn't very …
One thing that could be improved is …
It also needs more …

Final comments
Overall, I (strongly) recommend …
It's certainly a good …
(Nevertheless) it's much better than …

PAPER 2, PART 2 a report

In Part 2 of Paper 2, you might choose to write a report in 140–190 words in an appropriate style.

> Your school is going to have an 'eco-week' to raise awareness about the environment. The principal of your school has asked your class to think of ideas for the week. Write a report with your ideas.

Ideas for the school 'eco-day'

The aim of this report is to present Class 5's ideas for events at the school during 'eco-week'.

Poster competition

Our first idea is to run a poster competition. Each student could design a poster about the environment. For example, it might show how to recycle or suggest switching the standby switch off on the TV.

No cars

We could ask all students to walk or cycle to school during the week. The only problem would be that some students live too far from the school. However, they could ask their parents to share car journeys with others and save petrol.

Display

Our final plan is to have a display in the main hall of all the objects you can recycle. For example, we could show how plastic bottles can be made into coats.

To sum up, everyone was very enthusiastic about the 'eco-week'. Next, we would like to advertise the events during the week by sending a letter to all teachers to give to their students.

Always include a title. You could also say who the report is for.

State the purpose of the report.

Sub-headings are a good idea and help the reader.

Give examples to help explain.

Contrast and add information where necessary.

Don't forget to summarise. You might also want to say what needs to happen as a result of the report.

USEFUL EXPRESSIONS

REPORT

Introducing the report
The following report outlines …
The aim of this report is to …
The report is based on …

Giving reasons / Recommending
As result of … we think …
This is a good idea because …
We recommend this because …

Introducing ideas
The first / Another idea is to …
One possibility is to …
Our final idea / plan / suggestion is to …

Contrasting and alternatives
On the one hand … on the other …
One problem is … / However …
In contrast …

Proposing and suggesting
We should / could…
We would like to …
If possible, we …
It might be a good idea to …
One suggestion is to …

Generalising
In general …
On the whole …

Concluding and summing up
In conclusion …
To sum up …
Our final recommendation is that …

PAPER 2, PART 2 an article

In Part 2 of Paper 2, you might choose to write an article in 140–190 words in an appropriate style.

You have seen this announcement in a magazine about the natural world.

NATURE LOVERS! CAN YOU HELP US?

Next month, the magazine is about the climate and saving energy. We are running a competition for readers. Write and send us an article about how to save energy around the house. You could see your name in print !

Write your **article**.

Three ways to save energy around the home

In a time when the world is trying to save its natural resources, it's easy for many of us to help by using less energy in our houses.

Take, for example, standby switches on TVs. Many people don't realise that when you aren't watching it, you might still be using electricity. All you have to do is switch it off at the plug when you go to bed and you've already reduced your electricity bill.

A second way to use less energy is to fit special light bulbs which last longer than normal light bulbs and use less energy. They cost a little more but in the long run, they save you money.

Finally, put a sweater on! When it gets cold, many people turn up the heating. But if they just put a sweater on they would quickly get warmer without using fuel.

So next time you are about to switch it on or turn it up, ask yourself if you really need to, and save yourself some money at the same time!

Include a title.

Introduce the subject by restating the question.

Use clear paragraphs for each part of your article.

Don't forget a conclusion. Sometimes you can include a message to the reader.

USEFUL EXPRESSIONS

ARTICLE

Interesting adjectives
Positive: *fantastic, tremendous, amazing, wonderful*
Negative: *awful, dreadful, appalling, dire*
Appearance: *colourful, attractive, good-looking, visually stunning, well-designed*
Size: *huge, massive, monstrous, tiny, minute*
Noise: *loud, noisy, deafening, silent*
Surface: *smooth, rough, flat, bumpy*

Sequencers and additions
Firstly, Secondly, Thirdly, Finally
A second way is to …
Another idea is to …
In addition to that …

Examples
Take …
For example, …
One example is …
… is a good example of …

PAPER 2, PART 2 a short story

On Paper 2 Part 2 of the *First for schools* exam you might choose to write a story in 140–190 words in an appropriate style.

You see this announcement in an international magazine for schools.

STORIES WANTED

We are looking for stories for our new English-language magazine for teenagers. Your story must begin with the sentence:

Carl's family had an important reason for leaving the house at two in the morning.

Your story must include:

- a chase
- a journey.

Write your **short story**.

Carl's family had an important reason for leaving the house at two in the morning. In fact Carl had been so excited about flying for the first time he could hardly sleep. When he finally managed to fall asleep, he dreamt he saw his mother, the twins and himself all running down the airport runway chasing the plane as it took off. He was screaming, 'Wait! Wait!' Suddenly, he woke to a voice saying, 'Wake up Carl. Get dressed! We're late!'

After a one-hour journey down the motorway they finally arrived at the airport. 'Your flight is boarding now,' said the person at check-in. 'If you run you might catch it.' As they ran through the airport and reached the gate the plane was moving off. Carl shouted to his family, 'Quick, follow me!' He raced ahead out onto the runway. 'Wait! Wait!' he shouted.

Just then, he woke. Carl's alarm clock was ringing and his mother smiled at him. 'It's time to get up Carl. We don't want to miss the plane.'

USEFUL EXPRESSIONS

SHORT STORY

Background and atmosphere
It was raining with flashes of lightning outside …
The house was quiet and I sat all alone …
It all began on a day when I had been …
We were very tired and had been travelling all day …

Contrasting time and events
After …
As soon as I …
By the time …
At the same time …
While I was …-ing, they were …
Meanwhile …
A second later …

The climax / ending
Just then …
In the end …
Eventually …
Finally, I realised …
That was the last time I'd ever …

Audioscripts

Listening 1.1

One
A: What's the problem?
B: I don't know how long I can put up with her.
A: She seems OK to me.
B: Do you think so?
A: Well, she's very friendly. The other staff get on with her. And she's got some good ideas. She wants to move the office around but that's fine. It doesn't work the way things are at present.
B: You don't think she's a bit bossy? I mean, all these changes. She's only been here a week!

Two
A: I ran into Michelle's boyfriend, Nigel, the other day.
B: Really?
A: I didn't know he lives down the road from me. He was at the bus stop. How well do *you* know him?
B: Not very. I've met him a couple of times. I heard she wants to break up with him again.
A: Oh, that's a pity.
B: Don't worry. They always fall out over something, then she leaves him and then a week later they get back together again!

Three
Yes, it really annoys me because I read stories in the newspapers which aren't true. Take the story about me and Brad. I mean, I've never met him and I've never met the journalist who wrote the story. Do these people just make everything up? I know I should just ignore this kind of thing because it goes with the job, but it's hard when it's all lies.

Four
Yes, it's true. You know how he told his brother he would stand by him whatever happened? Well, not last night he didn't! He just walked out and said he didn't want to see him ever again. I can't wait to see what happens next week!

Five
Hi, it's me. Sorry I missed you. I meant to call earlier. Just to let you know that you might get a call from an old university friend of ours. Do you remember Alex? He studied science and lived in our house for a while. Anyway, he's coming to London and wants somewhere to stay. It's all very strange because why can't he stay at a hotel? Maybe he doesn't have any money. Anyway, I said I didn't have any space at mine. I thought I'd warn you in case he tries to stay at yours.

Six
A: Hi, are you free tomorrow? We're interviewing for the post of receptionist and I wondered if you could come to the interview. I'd like your opinion about one of the applicants.
B: Err, I'm quite busy, but I'm free at 12. What's the problem?
A: Well this person is a friend of a friend and the friend asked me to interview her. I don't know her, but because she knows my other friend I feel a bit uncomfortable about it all. It would be good to have another person's opinion.

Seven
Hi there. I got your message about dinner with the visitors from KLC. If you can't make Thursday then let's have dinner with them on Friday. Maybe at eight? Have you thought about where we can take them? I was thinking about the restaurant round the corner from the office. It does international food and as this is our first meeting I think we should go somewhere which serves something for everyone.

Eight
I've been watching this TV show for a few weeks now. It was one of those shows where people are really angry all the time and talk about their problems at home. It's stupid really, but good fun to watch. So, anyway, this morning there was this mother and father who still look after their three children but these children are all in their thirties! Anyway, the mother and father were saying the 'kids' never do anything around the house and constantly let them down. Unbelievable! I couldn't understand why they just didn't ask them to go and find their own place!

Listening 2.1

Speaker 1: Actually, a friend from university who had gone straight into their graduate training programme originally told me that they were looking for people. But at the time I was working for a charity and I really wanted to finish the project I was working on. It was unpaid but I was getting good experience. Anyway, a few months later I noticed in the newspaper they were looking for someone, so I called my friend again. She said I had a good chance of getting the position, so I applied.

Speaker 2: I grew up on a farm, so it's always been in my family. We had dogs and cats and of course lots of animals. The vets used to come out when there was a problem so I knew what they did, so it made sense I did something related to the countryside. I suppose my parents had hoped I'd follow in their footsteps, but farmers work hard and the money isn't anything like as much as a vet can earn. So I guess that was what convinced me in the end.

Speaker 3: I normally hate people asking me questions, but at my last interview I was quite calm for a change. Actually, I didn't really want the job that much, but I thought I'd go along for the practice. There were two people interviewing and they were both very nice and asked me lots of questions about my other work and why I wanted to leave my current job. It turned out one of the interviewers knew my boss, but he was OK about it. Advertising and marketing is a small world and everyone knows everybody else. In the end I was short-listed and finally they offered me the job, so I took it.

Speaker 4: A lot of people think being a journalist is quite a glamorous profession. They think we must all be meeting celebrities and interviewing world leaders every day of the week! Actually, I deal with stuff from all the towns and villages in the area most of the time, like finding out which village team won the football, or going to council meetings at the town hall. It really can be quite dull. It would be nice to report on something more interesting for a change!

Speaker 5: When people ask me about working in the police force I always say you need to have some experience of people and life – so don't join straight from school. Do something else for a few years first. They give you training before you start on the job, with dealing with difficult people and so on, which is great, but it isn't quite the same as being out there with the public. Of course when you do start in the job you have to learn quickly, and the first two years of the job is walking round the streets and dealing with the public.

Speaker 6: Being the daughter of the owner was a bit difficult at first. Obviously, it made it easier to get the job here, but even though I'd been to university and got a degree in business studies, I think some of the employees didn't think I could be a manager at first. They just thought I was in charge because it was my family's firm. Anyway, I'm responsible for administration and things are going really well now. I've built a good atmosphere in my office with a strong team. I always look forward to going in every morning.

Speaker 7: I know the company is going through a hard time – they've even laid some people off – so I do understand … but I've been here for two years now and I've never been sick. Last year was OK because there was plenty of extra work and I was able to work on Saturdays, so that helped earn me a bit extra. But I haven't had any way to make more money in the last few months, so I think it's about time I got one really.

Speaker 8: Lots of people say it must be great not to go out to work. And in general I do like it, but I think they imagine you're sitting in front of the TV all day. Actually, being an artist means long periods of being on your own and really hard work. If I don't finish the painting, I only have myself to blame. And if I don't paint, I don't eat, or can't pay the rent. It can be hard.

Listening 2.2

A: Anything in the paper today?
B: Nothing much. Though there are a couple of jobs that might interest you.
A: Well, they can't be any worse than the others I've seen.
B: This one is for 30,000 a year, which is a bit more than your old job.
A: Well, I used to do a lot more overtime, so actually that isn't anything like as much.
B: Oh it says here, 'opportunities for overtime', so it's probably almost the same.
A: Yes. It sounds OK. What is it?
B: Receptionist, and they provide training.
A: But my last job was far more responsible than that. And I know how to answer the phone and all that stuff.
B: Alright. I'm just trying to help.
A: Sorry, but it's just that I don't want to do something that isn't any more skilled than what I was doing before.
B: Well here's one … Personal Assistant, so it's easily as good as your last job and you have plenty of experience in planning and organising. Oh, and you get to travel …

Listening 3.1

Speaker 1: Well, when I was a kid my hobby was collecting football stickers. You know, for the World Cup, or the league – you put them in an album and try and get all the players for all the teams. They sell them in packets – you've got half a dozen stickers in each one. There were always three or four I could never find. One year, there was just one player I needed – err… Roberto Carlos, that's right. Well, in the end I got him by swapping 15 of my spare stickers for just one of him – but it was worth it. I completed the whole album for the first and last time. Now and again, I look at it and feel the same pride.

Speaker 2: Once upon a time, I used to play for fun, but now I take it very seriously and there is a lot of rivalry. At a top level you have to give the game 100%, the same as a physical sport. You have to be determined to win and can never show your opponent mercy. You must look calm and in control at all times. However, although players may *look* calm, under the surface their hearts are beating as fast as any athlete's! And of course, one bad move can mean you lose the game. There are things you mustn't do, like knocking over the board if you're losing; but believe me, there are ways your opponent can use to put you off – they can smile in a superior way, sigh impatiently, hum or tap the table. None of this is fair play, but I've seen it all in competitions.

Speaker 3: My family takes a lot of looking after. I don't get the chance for much exercise. All the same, I go to a keep-fit class once a week. My husband Jeremy leaves early on Thursdays so he can take care of the children when they get home from school. That will have to do for the time being. And from time to time, when we can get a babysitter, we go to the theatre, or have a nice meal somewhere. I play the piano for a few minutes each day; it helps me to relax. The only other thing I do, I suppose, is every so often I help out with the homeless and serve meals and stuff, not that it makes me a saint or anything.

Speaker 4: Before you go, you should have some lessons on a dry slope. I thought I didn't need to, but when I got there I was hopeless. I wasn't even able to stand up without falling over. There were all these kids, three- and four-year-olds, whizzing past me. After a couple of tries I decided it wasn't for me. Never again! I needn't have bought *any* equipment … the school supplied everything. Now I'll have to sell it all! It would have been a complete waste of time and money if someone hadn't told me about rackets, you know the kind you wear on your feet. In the end I just went off on my own and wandered through the forests – it was quite magical really – I had a great time.

Speaker 5: Most of the time I go up to my room and go online. My parents think that I am doing my homework. I like to download the latest music, surf the net, and email my friends. I also like chat rooms. I've met some really great people and formed some good friendships. You'd better not say anything to my mum and dad, though. They'll be furious if they find out!

Listening 3.2

One You are supervising an important examination. Tell the candidates that it is absolutely forbidden to whisper the answers to each other.
Two Tell your friend, Heidi, that she's going to have an accident if she doesn't drive more slowly.
Three You regret bringing towels and sandals to the spa, because everything is provided.
Four Someone is smoking in the changing room. If the coach catches them he will be furious. Warn them!
Five One of the rules of the tennis club is that you can only wear white shirts and shorts. Tell a new member, but add that not everybody always respects this regulation!

Listening 3.3

Part A
Marcus: So, Jessica. How old is the game of football, then?
Jessica: Well, throughout history people have played games using their feet and a ball, but that doesn't mean that football has had a continuous history.
Marcus: What are some of the earliest versions of the game, then?
Jessica: Well, there is evidence that the ancient Egyptians had a pastime which involved kicking a ball around. And the Chinese had a sophisticated game where players scored by kicking a ball filled with feathers into a basket. Tsu Chu, I think it was called, and it was part of a training exercise for soldiers.
Marcus: Wow! And I seem to remember hearing something about the Aztecs, who played a kind of football. Is that right?
Jessica: Well, yes. It was, if you like, a mixture of volleyball, football and basketball. It was quite a complicated game. It was called tlatchi.
Marcus: Goodness, what a strange name! And how was it played?
Jessica: In an indoor court, away from the public. The only spectators were members of the nobility. Players kicked a heavy rubber ball from side to side – without letting it drop to the floor. It could travel at high speed and players wore protective clothing and helmets. The aim was to get it through a hoop, you know, like a basket at the other end of the court. Few players were capable of doing this, and the game ended the moment someone was able to do it, which could be bad luck for the team that had been beaten.
Marcus: Why's that?
Jessica: Well, sometimes the losers were killed … you know … sacrificed to the gods.
Marcus: Wow! At least the worst you can get nowadays is a red card. And what happened to the winners? Were they rewarded, or did they get some kind of trophy?
Jessica: Well, the player who scored could claim all the clothes and jewellery of the spectators. So they were rich and famous.
Marcus: Just like today's soccer players!

Listening 3.4

Part B

Marcus: Just like today's soccer players! So, Jessica, you've told us something about some very early versions of football, but what are the roots of the game we know today?

Jessica: Well, in various forms it was played across Europe from the Middle Ages onwards. In Anglo-Saxon England in the tenth and eleventh centuries there was a game like football which was called 'Kicking the Dane's Head'. This would presumably have been the head of an invading Danish prince!

Marcus: Delightful!

Jessica: And a few hundred years later, football became very popular because of the Italians. Florence had developed its version of the game called 'calcio'. That's C-A-L-C-I-O, which is what it's still called today, in fact.

Marcus: What were the differences between 'calcio' and the English version?

Jessica: Well, it was more organised than the English game. There were proper teams, and the players wore lovely costumes. In England it was far more disorganised. There were huge matches where entire villages used to play; anyone could join in.

Marcus: Gosh.

Listening 3.5

Part C

Marcus: Gosh.

Jessica: There were no rules about how many people could play and no time limit. It only ended when the ball was kicked into the house of the opposing team's captain. Sometimes, it ended in a draw because everyone was so exhausted or it was too dark to continue. It used to get so violent that sometimes people were killed, and there are various periods in British history when the game of football was banned altogether. In the middle of the twelfth century, King Henry the Second and the Lord Mayor of London became worried that his subjects were neglecting their compulsory archery practice. So, it was banned! The ban lasted for 400 years!

Marcus: I see! There always seems to have been violence associated with the sport. Some of the behaviour of these so-called supporters or fans is really shocking.

Jessica: Yes, you're right. But this has nothing to do with the sport itself – the sport's just a focus. Where there's rivalry you'll always find this. In Ancient Rome you had chariot-race hooligans who fought and actually killed each other in large numbers.

Listening 4.1

Speaker 1: Well, I suppose we first noticed when I was about four. My mum and dad took me to the circus. I had really been **looking forward to** it. There were going to be lion-tamers, clowns and, best of all, horses. My parents knew that I was slightly allergic to dust, but they didn't want to **let me down** so off we went. Anyway, shortly after the show started, in came the horses, you know, with riders and acrobats, they came into the ring and started galloping around. And within a couple of minutes my eyes had gone red and I had started sneezing badly. When I started having trouble breathing, Mum got really anxious about me and we had to go. So it was then that we discovered that although I was crazy about horses, they couldn't stand me!

Speaker 2: People **look down on** scorpions, but human beings have no need to feel superior. We are likely to become extinct, you know, to **die out**, well before the scorpion. Scorpions have hardly changed in the past 350 million years. You can find them everywhere except Antarctica – so they are hardly an endangered species. Their habitat can be under rocks and in rainforests. You can even **come across** them between the bark of trees, so **watch out**! They can **live off** one meal for up to a year, and their favourite snack is another scorpion! It has such strong pincers that it doesn't need to use its sting that often. It breaks its victim into little pieces and then spits its digestive juices onto the bits. Then, when these are nice and soft, it'll suck them up. Bon appetit!

Speaker 3: I've never been very keen on guinea pigs – I mean they don't do much, do they? Anyway, we finally agreed to get a pair on condition that the girls looked after them, although I was usually the one who **ended up** taking care of them. I got really fed up with doing it. But then one morning, a few months after we'd had them, I went into the garage and one of them had **passed away**. Now you can imagine what a drama that was! We had to have a funeral for it – we buried it in a shoe box, I remember, – and the girls were terribly upset. And then we had to **go through** the same thing a couple of months later for the other one. Never again!

Speaker 4: The study of ants or bees can really give us an insight into the collective intelligence they use to complete tasks. Many species can achieve a common goal without a leader. Each insect simply reacts to its immediate environment. Together they can achieve enormous results. Just think of beehives and ant heaps! Scientists who have **carried out** research into insect behaviour have realised that they can teach us some valuable lessons. They've **come up with** programmes which imitate this behaviour, which can, in turn, be used to understand big problems like traffic jams, and how to control crowds and so on.

Speaker 5: So this cat, Sid, had six, yes six different owners, and six different names! None of the owners was aware of anyone else. And in each place he lived he was given something to eat every night. That's why this story is called 'Six Dinner Sid'. Sid **took everyone in**; each person believed he or she was his one and only owner. Just look at how fat he got! But one day he got a cough, and all of those people took him to the vet. In the end the vet said to himself, '**Hold on**, I've seen this fat fellow with a cough already today.' So he phoned around to all the owners and they each **found out** that they weren't the only one to think they 'owned' him! So, they started taking turns to give him a dinner once a week … one owner for each day! But, Sid was a six-dinner-a-day cat, so he moved to a new street and started again with six new owners!

Listening 4.2

Rebecca: Charlotte, did you see that article, the one about the owners who spend a fortune on their dogs?

Charlotte: Mm, yes. They look so lovely don't they, all clean and beautiful, their owners must be so proud of them.

Terry: Come on, Charlotte. Alright, so they look nice, but in my opinion they could spend their money far better … you know … in a much more sensible way.

Rebecca: I hear what you're saying, Terry. I know, for instance, that there are a lot of kids out there who don't have anything to eat, but that doesn't mean that you can't give love to a pet either.

Charlotte: Yeah, I agree with you, Rebecca. But, we don't know what else the owners do, do we? I mean they could be helping the homeless too for all we know.

Terry: I suppose so, but as far as I'm concerned it just goes completely against decent behaviour to spend so much on dogs – I'm sorry, Charlotte, but that's the way I feel.

Charlotte: I can see where you're coming from, but they aren't doing anything wrong as such, are they? It's not as if they were being cruel to animals or anything.

Rebecca: Mm, but I suppose Terry is right, Charlotte, it is rather unhealthy to be so obsessed with a pet, don't you think? And I'm not even sure that they are treating the dogs that kindly. As I see it, dogs just want to be dogs and run around and enjoy themselves. I'm sure if they could speak they'd say how awful it was having to be dressed up and shown off all the time.

Charlotte: I see your point, but as far as I'm concerned it's up to the owners to choose. And if taking care of a pet is what pleases them, who are we to argue?

Listening 4.3

Interlocutor: In this part of the test, I'm going to give each of you two photographs. I'd like you to talk about your photographs on your own for about a minute, and also to answer a short question about your partner's photographs. Beate, it's your turn first. Here are your photographs. They show people and dogs interacting in different ways. I'd like you to compare the photographs, and say what you think the relationship is between the animals and the humans in the photographs.

Listening 4.4

Beate: Well, let me see. Both photographs show people working together with dogs. In the first photo there is a man … hmm … it *looks* like a soldier … who is with a dog; it looks like a German Shepherd, I think. Whereas in the second photo, the bottom one, there are two dogs, huskies I think, and these dogs are pulling a sledge. It looks as though they are in a race, or maybe they are getting ready for the race. They are going through a forest, the sun is shining and the person in the sledge looks happy. The dogs look happy too. Anyway, going back to the first picture, I think that the man is trying to train the dog, you know, to be an army dog. Perhaps he is teaching it how to jump over things, and fences, yes? I think it takes a long time to train a dog to do this. The dogs in the other picture of course they must already be trained, but all they have to do is run and follow their leader. I imagine that this kind of dog is much wilder than the one in the first picture.

Listening 4.5

Interlocutor: Thank you, Beate. Walter, which of the dogs do you think is happier?

Walter: Which is happier? Well, I guess the … huskies, they are in the open air and they can run and act more like dogs together, with other dogs like in nature, while the army dog … I don't know if I would be satisfied with its life because it is going to be a bit like a slave for a human being, isn't it, and it will be lonely without other dogs.

Interlocutor: Thank you, Walter. Now, here are your photographs. They show …

Listening 4.6

Part A

Interviewer: The distinction between human beings and other animals is an artificial one isn't it? We live and breathe and take care of our young in a similar way, don't we?

Professor: Mm, well, yes, you're right, biologically there's little difference between us and chimpanzees, but there are a number of key distinctions which separate us from other mammals. There's language; then there's intelligence: the ability to think about things, if you like. Animals are driven by their instincts and how they react to sensation. And another important distinction is our capacity for self-awareness.

Interviewer: Self-awareness?

Professor: Mm, yes. You know, if we see ourselves in the mirror, we know that it is us we are looking at.

Interviewer: But how can you know whether an animal is self-aware?

Professor: Quite simply by placing it in front of a mirror and seeing how it reacts. Hardly any animals are capable of recognising themselves, but there are a few exceptions to this. A small number of creatures including chimps, dolphins and elephants can do this.

Interviewer: Elephants! Really?

Professor: Yes. After some research at a zoo in New York, we can now add elephants to this group. Three elephants which were given the mirror test behaved in a way which showed that they understood the animal in the reflection was them.

Interviewer: So how did they react, then?

Professor: Well, they did several things like putting their trunks in their mouths and watching themselves in the mirror, which show they're interested in themselves. One of the three, Happy, I think it was, tried to remove a spot she was ashamed of, you know, a mark which the researchers had put on her face.

Interviewer: Oh I see. And what about cats and dogs? Many people believe that they have an almost human intelligence too.

Professor: Mm, yes. But I'm afraid dogs and cats show no self-awareness at all. They are incapable of recognising themselves. People who pretend otherwise are just fooling themselves.

Listening 4.7

Part B

Interviewer: If that's the case, how come dogs have such close relationships with human beings. They couldn't do that if they weren't self-aware, could they?

Professor: Well actually, this has nothing to do with self-awareness. Basically it's all because dogs are brilliant at reading human expressions and gestures, and interpreting them. They are much better at this even than chimpanzees who are our closest relatives.

Interviewer: There is scientific proof of this, is there? Has anyone looked into this area?

Professor: Yes. There's been a great deal of research, so scientists have gathered a large amount of evidence. There's another simple experiment where there are two cups; one has food underneath it, and the other is empty. Well, with dogs, if someone touches the cup, or even just glances at it, then a dog will pick up the signal and choose the one with the food every time. Chimps, would you believe, simply guess.

Interviewer: I see, and how did this come about … the dog's ability to do this?

Professor: Good question. The most likely explanation is that it is a result of evolution. In domesticated dogs, you know, dogs which have been tamed and in human contact generation after generation, well, this ability to recognise human emotions and gestures has evolved.

Interviewer: So it wouldn't be developed in wild dogs, then?

Professor: Absolutely not. No … wolves and so on, they're different from domesticated dogs.

Interviewer: Hold on, though, how can we be sure of that? You know … that this ability to recognise human emotions is as a result of evolution?

Professor: Well, in another piece of research one scientist did the two cup experiment on a breed of dog called the New Guinea singing dog.

Interviewer: New Guinea singing dog? Weird.

Professor: It's called that because it's famous for its funny bark. When it howls, it sounds like a cross between a wolf and a whale.

Interviewer: Bizarre.

Professor: Anyway. What is special about this breed is that once upon a time, many generations ago, it had been domesticated, you know, tamed and trained how to live with humans. But then it returned to the wild and had no more human contact. This made it ideal to test the evolution theory.

Interviewer: So what happened when they carried out the experiment? How much importance does evolution really have?

Professor: Well, to cut a long story short, when they performed the cup test with these dogs, none of them were able to pick the cup with the food under it. They couldn't read human expressions or gestures any more. Any ability which had once evolved had been lost.

Interviewer: Fascinating.

Listening 5.1

Part A

Lorolei: So, Jacinta, how did you get into adapting books for the cinema?

Jacinta: Well, by accident really. I started off editing scripts for radio plays, then I had the chance to join a team writing for a TV series – a soap opera, if you like. Then one day I was asked if I'd be interested in adapting a book by Thomas Hardy for the radio, and one thing led to another.

Lorolei: So tell me, how do you begin adapting a book, or a piece of literature for the screen? What do you need to know before you begin?

Jacinta: Well, there are two main things really. First of all, what the story is, you know, if it's a long novel with hundreds of chapters, or a short story or play. And the second thing is the medium – is it going to be for the big screen, you know a movie for the cinema, or for TV.

Lorolei: And I know you've done both … adapt for both TV and the cinema … but which do you prefer?

Jacinta: Well, it may seem strange, but all things considered, I'd rather adapt a classic, say a novel by Dickens, for the small screen.

Lorolei: Why is that, then?

Jacinta: Well, even though the budget is smaller, you have more time to do justice to the original. For instance, instead of two hours to tell your tale, you may have six, ten, or even 12 one-hour episodes. In a long serial you can take it at a slower pace, and focus much more on the development of the personalities of the characters. Another thing is, you can include some of the smaller characters and sub-plots which you would just have to cut for a film.

Lorolei: Is it just a question of time, or is there anything else?

Jacinta: Well, the other thing of course is that for most films, if you are making something for the cinema, you know for the big screen, which has to appeal to a large audience, you have to introduce an element of spectacle.

Lorolei: Spectacle?

Jacinta: Yes, you know, breathtaking scenery, battle scenes, chariot races – the sort of thing which is going to fill the cinema screen. Something to make the audience say 'Wow!' I don't know if you've seen the big screen adaptation of *Pride and Prejudice*?

Lorolei: The one with Keira Knightley as the heroine, Elizabeth Bennet?

Jacinta: Yes, that's the one. Well, essentially the novel itself is a domestic drama, not the subject of a typical big budget movie. But the director made a really big thing of the big formal dances, the balls. And of course it looked magnificent and the attention to period detail was fabulous. You could only really appreciate it at a big cinema, but, of course, it took up a lot of time which could have been dedicated to other aspects of the story. I prefer the adaptation the BBC did a few years ago, but that's probably because I've got a thing for Colin Firth, the actor who played the hero, Mr Darcy.

Lorolei: I know what you mean! So, how free do you feel to change the story?

Jacinta: Well, I know some people take enormous liberties when they are adapting a book – you know, they'll mess around with the plot or change the ending. Personally, I try to be as faithful to the original book as I can. In my view, if you want to do your own thing, that's fine, but then you should create something original.

Listening 5.2

Part B

Lorolei: But can film, and here I'm talking about TV as well as the cinema, can it ever be superior to the written word?

Jacinta: Mm, yes. It is much more economical in terms of time, you know, setting a scene and so on. With just a couple of seconds of camera work, you can set a scene which, in a classic novel, would take pages and pages of description. If you choose the right location, go to where the book was set, with the right scenery, the effect is immediate.

Lorolei: So a picture is worth a thousand words. And is there anything that film or TV can't do?

Jacinta: Oh yes, lots. For me the biggest thing is the narrator, you know, the storyteller's voice, if you like. Although it's easy to use dialogue straight from the page it's very difficult to do that with the narrator's voice, unless, that is, you are going to have voice-overs every few minutes.

Lorolei: Can you give me an example of that?

Jacinta: Well, the one which immediately comes to mind is *Vanity Fair*. Now *Vanity Fair* is a story about a young woman called Becky Sharp, who will do anything to rise in society.

Lorolei: Yes, she's the ultimate social climber.

Jacinta: Absolutely – she is a terrible, heartless, ruthless young woman. Now in the original book by Thackeray, the narrator is always looking down on the action, you know, making comments on what's going on. This, in my opinion, is what makes the book. But when *Vanity Fair* was turned into a blockbuster, well this was missing. OK, it was wonderful to look at. There were some fabulous scenes and the costumes were breathtaking. Yet, the thing is, despite having a huge budget, despite its cast of stars, there was something missing from the film, which made it rather empty, in my view.

Lorolei: And that 'thing' which was missing was the narrator's voice.

Jacinta: Exactly.

Listening 6.1

One

Harry: Hi, Sophie. Nice to see you. You're going to university this autumn, aren't you?

Sophie: Hi, Uncle Harry. Well, actually, I've decided not to go this year. I'm going to take a gap year and travel around the States. I'm planning to get a job as a nanny or waitress or something like that. Apparently, even if you just turn up you can find something quite quickly. Otherwise, I might try and join a voluntary organisation, you know, do some work in Africa. Don't say anything to Mum and Dad though, will you, Uncle Harry? I haven't told them yet!

Two

Mark: Hello. This is Mark Wilson. I'm afraid I'm not able to take your call right now, but please leave a message after the beep.

Juan: Mark, hi, it's Juan. Just to say that I am setting off at three o'clock. The journey takes about three and a half to four hours, which means I should get to the exhibition centre at around seven. Hope that's not too late. Anyway, will you, or somebody else from the office be able to come and help me unload the van? There's a lot of stuff and I won't be able to do it on my own. Can you call me back on my mobile?

Three

Sharon: I hate the whole thing of organised holidays and excursions. I'm really into couch surfing. That's where you meet someone on the Internet who will then put you up for a couple of days on their sofa and show you around. It's great, honest, for a short trip somewhere … who cares if it's a bit uncomfortable? I've just come back from Prague where I spent two nights on this guy's sofa. He showed me around places you'd never find in a guide book. It was brilliant. I've had some fascinating and unexpected experiences on my travels. You should give couch surfing a try, I'll email you the website details.

Four

Blanka: Now, listen please … Professor Heron's flight takes off at three and lands at 4.15; I'm going to meet him with Marika. A taxi is due to pick us up at the airport and drop us off at his hotel. Marika will help Professor Heron check in and make sure he knows the arrangements. Now, he'll be tired after the journey, so he's bound to need some time to himself. If we plan to meet at around eight, he'll have had time to freshen up and relax. We'll take him to the conference centre and show him where he's giving his talks. Remember, he likes everything to be perfectly organised so it's very, very important that *everything* goes smoothly. Afterwards we'll take him out for dinner at the new restaurant at the Hilton.

Five

Seb: Listen, everyone. Kate will be waiting at the station. She'll call as soon as Mum has left the station to say that she's on her way home. She's likely to be feeling a bit sad. Now, the lights are going to be off, and I want everyone to hide in the kitchen with the food and drink. The kids can go behind the sofa – *not a sound*, OK? So when Mum opens the door and walks into the sitting room, everyone will shout 'Happy retirement!' She really deserves it after 25 years of commuting backwards and forwards to London.

Six

Kim: It's not a hotel, it's a building site! And we have to cross a main road to get to the beach. Someone is going to get hurt, I can see it happening. I wouldn't come here again if they were *giving* holidays away.

David: Well don't blame me! I didn't know it was going to be like this. It was supposed to be a package holiday in a luxury resort!

Kim: Well, you should have chosen a holiday from a *real* brochure, from a proper travel agent – not a so-called last-minute bargain off the Internet. Next time we go away I'm in charge!

Seven

Dagmara: This evening, we could go and visit the old town. We're very proud of our heritage here. There are some lovely squares and monuments and I could show you around a bit. What do you think? Later on we can meet up with some of the others from head office and eat out in a nice restaurant in the old town.

Dan: That sounds brilliant. I'd like to do a bit of sightseeing and maybe get a couple of souvenirs … you know … the kids always expect me to buy them something when I'm away!

Eight

Waiter: Welcome, signora. Are you ready to order?

Gemma: Yes, I think so. I'd like to try some of the local specialities. I'll begin with the artichokes and parma ham.

Waiter: Yes madam, and for your main course?

Gemma: Can you tell me what the special is?

Waiter: Ah yes, it's baby cow, cooked in the milk of the mother.

Gemma: Mm, no thanks. That's enough to turn you into a vegetarian. I think I'll have the spaghetti bolognese, if that's OK.

Listening 6.2

One To present yourself and register at a hotel or airport.
Two To give somebody somewhere to sleep for the night.
Three To choose.
Four To entertain another person by taking them to, say, a bar or restaurant.
Five To leave on a trip or a journey.
Six To have a wash and change your clothes after a journey.
Seven To move from place to place.
Eight To take someone in your car and let them out at the destination.
Nine To arrive or present yourself somewhere – often late or without warning.
Ten To have a meal in a restaurant.
Eleven To give someone a guided tour of somewhere.
Twelve To have a rendezvous.
Thirteen To collect someone in your car.
Fourteen To give something free of charge.
Fifteen To take a break.
Sixteen To delay something until a later date.

Listening 6.3

One Tell each other about your plans for next weekend or your next major holiday.
Two You want to know the time of the next coach from Oxford to Cambridge. You would also like to know the journey time.
Three Make some predictions about the results of the next elections or your country's performance in the world cup or Olympic Games.
Four A neighbour has telephoned to find out if your friend has had her baby. Promise to phone the moment you have some news.
Five You are phoning a friend to tell him or her about your travel plans. You are planning to leave your home in half an hour. Even though the traffic is heavy, you believe that you can be there by five o'clock if everything goes to plan.
Six You are in a job interview. One of the interviewers asks how you see yourself in five years' time. Make some predictions about your position in five years, and some of your achievements between now and then.
Seven You have just left the cinema. The film was awful and the people you are with are criticising you for having suggested it. Defend yourself!
Eight The roads are icy and you're starting to get worried. You expected your friend, Marina, to arrive half an hour ago. What do you say to yourself?

Listening 6.4

Tess: It's time we decided about our travel arrangements. I mean, if we leave it too late the prices will have rocketed.

Loïc: We'd better make up our minds then. I suppose we could take the tunnel and then drive all the way down.

Tess: What do you think, Marco?

Marco: It's a long way and the motorway charges will be high.

Loïc: Mm, I know what you mean, and we shouldn't forget the petrol.

Tess: We could fly, you know, take one of these low-cost flights and then we could always hire a car if we need one when we get there. We should be able to afford that.

Loïc: But wouldn't that end up just as expensive as driving?

Marco: Yes, but driving down could be part of the holiday, couldn't it? I don't mind spending a few days stopping off at different places.

Tess: OK, but personally I'd rather we got there as quickly as possible. We only have two weeks, I don't really want to spend a lot of time just getting there.

Loïc: I was just about to say the say the same thing. I just want to lie on a beach and relax.

Tess: I've got to say, too, I am a bit nervous about driving. I've never driven on the continent before.

Loïc: That doesn't bother me. I don't mind doing the driving.

Marco: And I could share it with you.

Tess: Not the way you drive, Marco! I tell you what, why don't I take the plane and meet you down there!

Loïc: Very funny. Hold on, I've just had an idea. There is another option. What if we took the ferry from Portsmouth, across to Brittany? It would make the journey at the other end a lot shorter.

Marco: And if we took a night crossing, it would give us a night's sleep and then we could get down there by the middle of the afternoon. We'll have gained an extra day.

Tess: The ferry. Mm, I like that idea. But before I look at prices, does anyone suffer from sea-sickness?!

Listening 7.1

Interviewer: We all remember watching those old black and white science fiction films at the cinema, with androids and robots. As soon as you saw a robot you expected to see them go crazy, and then they started attacking people. In reality there has never been a real case of robots attacking humans and robots have been used in manufacturing, especially car production, for years. And now robots are becoming part of our home life. In Japan for example, scientists are working on robots to be companions for elderly people. You might also have seen robot toys which children can control with their voices. Well, some manufacturers are looking at ways for such toys to look after children while their parents are at work. So, should we be worried? Do we risk having our day-to-day life controlled by machines that think for themselves? To discuss these questions I have Noel Witfield with me in the studio today. He's a professor of electronic engineering and is also a specialist in robot ethics. Professor Witfield, first of all, isn't all this talk of robots in the house a bit scary? Don't you think most people would prefer to communicate with a real person?

Professor: That's possibly true, but you mentioned the work being done in Japan for example. The Japanese have succeeded in developing household robots for some time, because they have an aging population. If they don't have robots, there won't be the people to take care of the elderly. Also, I don't agree with your comment that we don't want to talk to machines. After all, we spend hours a day on our mobile phones and computers. But in fact, a human being isn't designed to look at a screen all day. I'm actually better suited to communicate with a computer which has a human-like appearance – which is of course what a robot is. A computer with a face.

Interviewer: But we've also heard a lot about scientists who've managed to make robots with intelligence.

Professor: Well, there I do think there's a potential problem with this, and we do need to look at this.

Interviewer: In what way?

Professor: Well, when we talk about intelligence, we're really talking about the fact that robots in the future will be able to make their own decisions. In the past robots have always been controlled by humans, but we are giving them the abilities to make decisions and have some free will.

Interviewer: So do you think we should stop moving in this direction?

Professor: No, I wouldn't say stop it altogether, but I would like to see a real public debate take place on how this will affect society in the future. And there's also the issue of safety and reliability. After all, some of the major work that is being done into robots is for military purposes. Governments should consider using robots ethically.

Listening 7.2

One We all remember watching those old black and white science fiction films at the cinema, with androids and robots.

Two As soon as you saw a robot you expected to see them go crazy.

Three Do we risk having our day-to-day life controlled by machines that think for themselves?

Four Don't you think most people would prefer to communicate with a real person?

Five The Japanese have succeeded in developing household robots for some time.

Six A human being isn't designed to look at a screen all day …

Seven But we've also heard a lot about scientists who've managed to make robots with intelligence.

Eight I would like to see a real public debate take place on how this will affect society.

Nine Governments should consider using robots ethically.

Listening 7.3

Because it's so easy to use the Internet these days, virtually anyone can think to themselves, 'let's set up a website'. Maybe you want a home page for friends to look at, or how about advertising your local club? Perhaps you could even start an e-business and become a dot com millionaire. Before you begin, make sure you know why you want a website and what it's going to be for. It's also important to choose a good name early on and get an address for the web page. It should be a name that's easy to remember, and the best ones are generally those which say what the site does or which get your attention.

Take the site www.milliondollarhomepage.com. Alex Tew, the student who came up with it, chose a name that said what it was about, and it was also interesting because most people want to know about anything that mentions money. Another reason people visit sites is because they want information. So I strongly recommend that you include links to other sites. These need to be up-to-date and useful.

You might think that links to other sites will send people away, but in fact if you can help users they will keep coming back to yours. Also, don't forget that links can take the form of words that you click on or they can be icons which are more visual and make the site colourful.

People also often ask me about things like having pictures and music. That's OK, but it's also worth remembering that the more features and effects you have, the harder it will be to find what you want, and it may take a long time to load the site. Visitors will get bored if they have to wait every time they click on another page. It's a good idea to give a contact email so you can get feedback from visitors to the site.

Listening 8.1

Speaker 1: I really don't know what we would have done if he hadn't arrived. We'd been driving round the same part of the city for at least an hour and I must have asked about five different people where to go. And it was all rather dark and scary. I even drove the wrong way down a one way street! That was when, suddenly, out of nowhere this policeman stopped us! Well, once I'd explained that I was completely lost, he told us the way and we were able to …

Speaker 2: Have you seen that poster they're showing everyone? It has a man's face – he has a beard but he still looks like any number of other people. Anyway, there were about three police officers asking people in the High Street if they saw anything strange outside the local supermarket last Thursday night at 8 o'clock. I suppose they spoke to me because I always walk past at that time of night, and, well, actually, when I started to think back it occurred to me that I had seen a couple of suspicious people in that street that goes down the side of the shops, who perhaps …

Speaker 3: Believe me! I wouldn't want to be the actual attacker. I mean, the way they spoke to me was really scary! I even felt like a criminal by the time I left the police station. Even once they'd realised my name was spelt differently and I've never even known anyone called Rita, I still never got an apology. I couldn't believe it. I mean, you'd think that if …

Speaker 4: The shopping bags were both sitting there and they were identical. I just grabbed them and put them in the trolley, and I'd only gone halfway across the car park before a security guard was running and using his radio. The next thing I know is the police arrive to question me. I think they realised I'd just made a mistake and taken the wrong ones, but that security guard was determined to get me! He really fancied himself as one of those detectives you see on TV! You know the ones …

Speaker 5: It was just my luck, wasn't it? I mean, I normally go through that area quite carefully because I know they wait there. But, well, I was in a rush that day to pick up Lionel from work and I wasn't thinking. Within seconds I saw the lights flashing and they'd pulled me over. The young man was very nice about it, but it didn't stop him from giving me a fine! It just wasn't my day …

Listening 8.2

Presenter: Today, we've got Connie Wicher on the phone and Connie has rung in to let listeners know about her new idea to recycle things in your home. Is that right, Connie?

Connie: That's right Geoff, though it isn't really *my* idea. It's part of something called, 'Freecycling'.

Presenter: OK. So, tell us about it, Connie.

Connie: Well, the Freecycle network, or 'Freecycling', began in 2003. There was a group of people who wanted to save the landscape around their town from having more landfills and being used for dumping trash – which you guys would call 'rubbish'. So they set about finding ways of helping the town reduce its waste.

Presenter: I see, but didn't it cost them money to do something like that?

Connie: Well, no, it was absolutely free. It wasn't a government thing or anything like that … just a bunch of people getting together and doing something about all the stuff being thrown away. It's all done in people's spare time.

Presenter: It sounds great. Now, people listening will be wondering how this is different to recycling.

Connie: It isn't *quite* the same as recycling because everything is just reused rather than taking it away for recycling. So, for example, if I have a fridge I don't want, I advertise to my local Freecycling community and someone can have it for nothing. It's as simple as that.

Presenter: OK – I see. I had a look at the website earlier, Connie, and there are over 3,000 of these communities around the world! That's a *lot* of people.

Connie: Yes … I think the most recent number is 3,719, with close to three million members in places all over the world, in countries including the USA and Germany … all sharing their unwanted things.

Presenter: Wow! So tell our listeners how they can become Freecyclers.

Connie: Just go to the website www.freecycle.com and find your local group. You click 'join' and then you get an email telling you what to do. If you can't find a Freecycler nearby then you can start your own in your local area.

Presenter: And what can people give away?

Connie: Literally anything. Chairs, fax machines, pianos. You name it! I gave away a door last week.

Presenter: Right. So pretty much everything, then!

Connie: Sure, as long as it's legal and free, you can freecycle it.

Presenter: Well thanks, Connie. And if you want to get in touch here's the website again. It's www.freecycle.com …

Listening 9.1

Speaker 1: I used to go there a lot, but the last time I ordered a steak, it was hardly cooked at all. Anyway, when I asked one of the staff if I could, you know, have it cooked a bit more he said that I'd asked for it rare – you know as though it was my fault. I told him it was more like raw than rare. Of course he took his revenge – when he brought it back it was so well-done I could hardly cut it. I won't be going there again.

Speaker 2: It's often a problem when I go out because I'm not used to eating hot, spicy food. I prefer, you know, plain home cooking – if it's too spicy, well, it upsets my stomach. A Chinese takeaway, you know, sweet and sour, that's OK, but on the whole I'd rather have something plain and bland … you know … quite unadventurous. So, as I was telling you … we went to this Indian restaurant and I ordered the mildest curry on the menu but it was still far too hot for me. I couldn't eat it!

Speaker 3: Well, I don't like to give away my secrets, but it's quite simple really. I prefer to use low-fat cream for this. So what you do is … when the pasta is cooked, you mix in the egg and cream mix – it'll cook on its own without going back on the heat. Stir in the chopped up bacon pieces … like so. And then sprinkle on some fresh basil to decorate it. Food has got to look good too – tasty and tasteful – that's what I always say. We eat with our eyes as much as with our mouths! If you don't have basil you can use parsley – only use the leaves though because the rest is bitter.

Speaker 4: Well, in those days they would work in the fields harvesting the corn by hand, and then they'd come in for a simple meal at lunchtime. It was a tradition that the farmer and workers ate together. The farmer used to sit here, at the end of this long table. Meals were quick because they had to get back to work. Usually, there would be soup and bread and cheese. Anyway, once the farmer closed up his knife, well, that was the end of the meal. Everybody had to get up and get back to work – even if they hadn't finished eating! There were no arguments about that back then.

Speaker 5: To begin with the waiter brought us a tasty salad, with locally produced cheese. Then there was fish and a fabulous stew. There was a different wine for each course – dry white with the fish, red with the meat. I drank lots of water. I always drink still – sparkling makes me too full. Finally, there was a delicious dessert with a sweet white wine. At the end I felt like, you know, one of those snakes which can swallow a whole sheep! All the same, I could get used to eating like that!

Listening 9.2

Roddy: So here in the studio we have Katrina, our food and restaurant critic. Now Katrina, what have you been up to since we last spoke?

Katrina: Well, I have had the most extraordinary eating-out experience at a restaurant called In the Dark.

Roddy: In the Dark?

Katrina: Yes, it's precisely that – you eat in a pitch-dark restaurant where you can't see a thing.

Roddy: Well, OK, but what's the point of that?

Katrina: Well, first of all, I should say it is run for the blind.

Roddy: Oh really? It's a kind of charity then is it?

Katrina: Mm, more than that. The idea is to give us, that is sighted people – those of us who can see – the sensation of what it must be like to be blind. It also provides work for blind people who are taken on as staff, and some of the money, it is true, is donated to charities for the blind.

Roddy: So mainly it raises awareness among sighted people and provides jobs. And is it popular, as a concept I mean?

Katrina: Oh yes, it has really taken off – there are restaurants like it in major European cities, from Paris to Moscow. Anyway, the next thing is, once you've ordered your food from the menu and your drinks, blind serving staff lead you down the corridor towards the dining room. They took really good care of us.

Roddy: What, straight into the dark? That's scary.

Katrina: Not really, they let you get used to it bit by bit. There are a few red lights and then it gets darker and darker and you go through heavy drapes, you know … thick curtains … into the dining area where they help you sit down.

Roddy: How do they get it to be so dark – I mean in most situations a bit of light normally manages to penetrate the room, doesn't it?

Katrina: Mm, that's true. You have to leave things like matches and cigarette lighters with your stuff, and you aren't even allowed to take a mobile phone in with you, 'cos that could act as a source of light. Oh, and another thing – you have to take off your watches as well – those which have a face which glows in the dark.

Roddy: I've got to say, I wouldn't be able to cope with it at all. I'm claustrophobic and I panic if I can't see anything. I always have to have a light on somewhere.

Katrina: So you wouldn't come with me? Not even if I held your hand?

Roddy: Not even. And what about the meal, how did you get on with that?

Katrina: Well, the practical aspects were quite difficult. You have to grope for everything – your knife and fork and so on, and your wine glass. So I found myself knocking into my neighbour's and drinking his wine.

Roddy: Oh no!

Katrina: Yeah, but he took his revenge by pouring wine over my arm – so in the end we were even! At first everyone was nervous and giggly at the beginning, but pouring wine over each other is a real ice-breaker. After that, we got on really well. He had a lovely voice, although I never got to see his face.

Roddy: Shame. And how easy was it to eat?

Katrina: Well, let's say that good table manners go out of the window too. But you can take advantage of the dark to eat with your fingers.

Roddy: Gross! And how did you know what you were eating, then?

Katrina: Well, we had opted for the surprise menu so we had no idea what would be landing on our plates. I think we had meat.

Roddy: You think!

Katrina: Well, OK, we could tell it was meat, but not what type. The same goes for most of the vegetables.

Roddy: So would you recommend it?

Katrina: Well, the food wasn't bad, but it was the overall experience, of course, which is memorable. So basically, yeah, I'd recommend it – I would. But if you do go, make sure you don't wear your best clothes.

Roddy: And what else did you get out of it – apart from, of course, an evening out?

Katrina: Well, it made me much more aware of what it must be like to be blind. Like most of us I've always taken my eyesight for granted – it made me realise how hard it must be to get by without one of your major senses.

Listening 10.1

Speaker 1: Well, I'd say that I'm fairly good at staying within my budget. I mean I won't just buy stuff for the sake of it – like on a whim or anything. I go out with a certain amount of money in my purse and I won't go over that amount. Most of my friends have credit cards, but they're always in debt, so I just carry cash. That way, if I suddenly see something I like, I either buy it or come back the following week with the money I need. And then if it's gone, it's gone, but usually you find it's still there.

Speaker 2: I'm a bit of a bargain hunter. If I see something on special offer, I'll buy it, but I'll never pay full price for anything. I don't go from shop to shop, but what I will do is look it up on the Internet and compare prices of things. There are some great websites that will actually show you how much you can save depending on where you go. And besides, if you go to the same shop every time, they'll often give you a loyalty card so you save money when you shop there. And that's on top of any discounts.

Speaker 3: I just can't make my mind up. It looks in good working order. It only has about 30,000 kilometres on it and he says the last owner was an old couple who only drove it at weekends, but he probably says that about every one in the showroom. I don't know. It's not like I've even looked at any others. Maybe if he reduced the price, I would be interested. After all, it's only two years old. It seems like a good deal. Let's see what he says.

Speaker 4: Well, it's funny you're asking for that 'cause if you had come in last week, I would have had just what you were looking for. It was a green sofa and chairs that would have matched your wallpaper. I'd order you another but I'm pretty sure it was the last in that line. They said they'll be sending us the new catalogue for next year in the next couple of days, and then I can tell you. Otherwise, all we have is what you can see here. Though one thing I can do is ring our other branch and see if they have any left in stock. Don't go away. I'll give them a call right now.

Speaker 5: You don't have to decide now. If you want to take it home and see how it looks once you get it home, that's fine. There's a 28-day money-back guarantee on all our products. So long as you bring it back within 28 days of purchase, that's fine. Oh, that's also provided that you have the receipt with it of course. So you could take it today with absolutely no obligation. All we ask is that you return it in the same condition as you bought it. You'd be amazed to see what some people bring back …

Speaker 6: At the end of the day, I think the main thing to remember is that whether you earn a lot or a little, it's really important to make sure you've got some left over for a rainy day. So there are three ways you can do this. There's short-term saving, in case you have an emergency. Then there's medium-term saving, which means money that you might need to use in about five or ten years' time. And finally, there are long-term things like pensions, and the rule on that is you start paying into it as soon as you can. The younger the better, in fact.

Speaker 7: You know, I really wish we hadn't bothered. For one thing it's caused so much stress worrying about how much it's all going to cost and then they've changed the hotel twice. It isn't the one in the brochure anymore so I hope it's decent. Of course, I didn't want to go in the first place, but Graham was with me and we went into the travel agent and the next thing I know, he's writing the cheque.

Speaker 8: I wish I could afford it, but I can't borrow any more from my mum and dad. I already owe them money for my new bike. In fact, it's a bit unfair because my sister got a bike for her birthday and so she has some money she's saving. But for me, my dad wants to know when I'm going to pay him back. Had I known, I wouldn't have bought it in the first place.

Listening 10.2

One There's a 28-day money-back guarantee on all our products. So long as you bring it back within 28 days of purchase, that's fine.

Two Oh, that's also provided that you have the receipt with it of course.

Three There's short-term saving, in case you have an emergency.

Four Had I known, I wouldn't have bought it in the first place.

Listening 11.1

Presenter: Good morning, and this week on 'Home help' we're looking at colour in the home. Now, for many of us, when we think of decorating, the first thing we think about is things like curtains, paintings and furniture and quite often the colour of the walls comes after, but in fact colour should be the starting point. And joining us this week is the design expert Laurence Cooper-Stafford to tell us why.

Laurence: Good morning.

Presenter: So Laurence, tell us why colour is so important.

Laurence: Basically, it makes a statement about who we are to anyone coming into the house. It also says what the purpose of a room is.

Presenter: How do you mean?

Laurence: Well, I don't think people realise how much colour can affect our mood or how comfortable a visitor might feel.

Presenter: I see. So, imagine I've bought a new house and I'm getting ready to make it a home. Where do I start with colour?

Laurence: Well, one of the most exciting things about decorating any room is that moment when you first take the lid off the tin and start to paint. And the days when the choice was either white or something neutral are well over. These days people almost can't decide what colour to use because of the *huge* range available nowadays. But what happens as a result is that people cover their walls, and then they realise it won't match the shade of their furniture, or they find that bright red in the bedroom actually stops them from sleeping. So planning all your colours is crucial.

Presenter: But how do you know? I mean, most of us will find it quite difficult to imagine how it will look.

Laurence: It's true that interior designers often seem to have a built-in instinct for what goes with what, but actually a great deal of their skill comes from years of working with different colours and learning to follow some basic principles.

Presenter: I see. Like what, for example?

Laurence: Well, for example, red looks great in dining rooms because it makes people feel social and stimulates an appetite. On the other hand, you wouldn't use it in a nursery or baby's room.

Presenter: What colour would you use?

Laurence: Pink is restful, though boys may find this a bit 'girlie', so blue is probably a better choice. They also say it prevents nightmares.

Presenter: Isn't blue a cold colour though? Not very welcoming.

Laurence: True, but you can find warm tones of blue. Actually, bedrooms are somewhere where purple can also work well. Downstairs you might choose yellows or something bright for the kitchen. These types of colours also help make north-facing rooms more cheerful. Brown is another very practical colour for kitchens or living rooms where you spend a lot of time during the day.

Presenter: And I guess black is a real no-no.

Laurence: In moderation black's OK. It can create a sense of drama if that's what you're looking for. But often it's the sort of thing you might see in a teenager's bedroom. But having said all that about rules and principles, people should also rely on their own instincts and playing around with colour is one of the best ways of learning …

Listening 11.2

It was ten o'clock and I was supposed to have finished for the night. But then someone brought in an odd-looking, small boy. He couldn't have been much more than nine or ten. They said he'd been wandering down a lane about ten miles south of town. But he couldn't say a word – in *any* language. Anyway, we made him a bed in one of the cells at the station. Maybe someone would show up in the morning looking for him. He seemed surprisingly calm – not worried at all. There was nothing on him to say where he was from. The only thing that was strange was a triangular, blue metal badge on his jacket. It was a deep blue colour. It must have been special to him, 'cos when I reached out to touch it he got kind of angry. I tried asking him about it but he didn't answer. His eyes just got big and more angry.

Anyway, I had kids of my own waiting at home, so had to leave him with the other officers. Anyway, while I was driving home I was on the road out of town when I had to stop. I thought it was a car coming towards me. I flashed my car lights because his lights were so bright. But they weren't two lights like an ordinary car. First of all there was a beautiful orange light. Then it grew and became three, four, and then they changed colour!

I thought, 'what is going on here?', so I switched my police lights on. I thought, 'it's someone making fun of me'. Then the lights rose above me and I could see it. It had a smooth round base like a mirror. I could see the lights changing colour on it and then realised it was the blue and red lights on the top of my car. Then suddenly, it flew off, and all I remember is a metal disc with a triangular shape across it. That was the second time I'd seen that blue triangle that day.

Listening 12.1

One

A fascinating new theory suggests that Britain was once connected to the rest of Europe, by hills which rose above what is now the English Channel. Then, 300,000 years ago, a violent flood swept them away and the link disappeared. Within 24 hours the hills had vanished and Britain became an island. This explains why Britain remained uninhabited for such a long time. Even though men had been present they had left for warmer climates. Once this new barrier appeared, it most probably prevented Neanderthal man from returning to the island.

Two

While people say that weather forecasters are always getting it wrong the opposite is true. Yet it only takes one serious mistake for reputations to be affected, as shown by Britain's most infamous weather forecast. Britain had been preparing itself for storms, but on the evening of October 15th 1987, even though someone telephoned the television station saying she'd heard there would be a hurricane during the night, the country's most eminent weatherman, Michael Fish, said that the expected gales would not reach disastrous speeds. When, during the night, many parts of the country were devastated by incredibly high winds, everyone pointed the finger at poor Mr Fish, accusing him of failing to make the public aware of what was about to happen. It was the country's worst storm since the Great Storm of 1703.

Three

One of the biggest mysteries is the disappearance of the dinosaurs. For many decades scientists believed that they died out gradually due to climate change. Then the meteorite theory changed all that. A meteorite crashed into what is now the Gulf of Mexico and caused an immediate climate change, catastrophic to the dinosaurs, which simply vanished. However, in the last few years geologists have raised objections to this theory – claiming that the meteorite occurred well before the dinosaurs came on the scene, so that it can't have been the cause of their extinction.

Four

People are terrified of nuclear war, but the energy produced from a volcanic eruption can be even more catastrophic. Normally, there is plenty of warning and in 1902 Mount Pelée, on the island of Martinique, had been showing signs that it was about to explode. 'Why on earth didn't people leave the island?' you might ask. The answer is depressingly simple: even though the authorities should have evacuated the island's capital, St Pierre, they chose to ignore the signs because an election was going to be held. Twenty-eight thousand people were killed in the eruption. There were just two survivors: a shoemaker and a prisoner.

Five

In Roman times the southern part of the Mediterranean was known as 'the granary of the empire'. If the harvest failed it led to shortages and famine elsewhere. However, once the Romans left north Africa, nomads and their goats took over the area. One theory about desertification is that the goats kept on eating until nothing was left! However, we can't put all the blame on the nomads. Climate change and long periods of drought are probably as much to blame. And once fertile land is lost it is difficult to reverse the process.

Listening 12.2

Part A

Interviewer: Hurricanes have been more and more in the news over the last few decades. Hurricane Katrina, for example, in 2005, devastated the south-east of the United States. The flooding covered an area the size of the UK. With me today is weather expert Dr Kate Jackson, who is going to tell us about hurricanes. So, Kate, perhaps we could begin by asking what causes them.

Kate: Certainly, Jamie. It's all rather technical but I'll try my best. Let's start with where they appear, shall we? Basically, they form over the oceans in the warm zones we find either side of the equator.

Interviewer: OK. Why not over the equator itself?

Kate: Because over the equator the spin, the rotation of the earth, isn't great enough. It's the rotation of the earth which helps to generate the wind that is one of the main causes of hurricanes, you see.

Interviewer: Mm, I think so. Anyway, go on.

Kate: Well, what happens is that there is a temperature rise, and water vapour evaporates and forms clouds.

Interviewer: Just like for ordinary rain.

Kate: Exactly, except the wind, combined with the rise and fall of temperature, sets up a kind of chain reaction, which eventually creates a hurricane.

Interviewer: So when does a strong wind turn into a hurricane?

Kate: Well, officially when it reaches a speed of 120 kph, but some of those we've seen recently have been much more powerful. In Hurricane Katrina, winds got up to 280 kph!

Interviewer: Wow, I understand that the wind caused a lot of destruction, but the southern states were flooded too, weren't they?

Kate: Indeed, they were. This is due to the surge – the increase in the height of the level of the sea caused by the hurricane. And, before you ask, the highest recorded surge happened a hundred years ago in Australia. People found fish and even dolphins on the top of cliffs. Oh, and by the way, these cliff-tops were 15 metres above the usual level of the sea.

Interviewer: Wow. It's unbelievable. And what has been the most disastrous hurricane on record?

Kate: Economically, it was Katrina, but in terms of loss of life the worst so far was in Bangladesh in 1970. Half a million people died. Isn't that dreadful? With Katrina around 1,800 lives were lost.

Listening 12.3

Part B

Interviewer: One thousand eight hundred. How terrible. But what is the reason for the increased number of hurricanes these days? Is it tied up with global warming?

Kate: To my way of thinking, all the evidence points to that, but it is almost impossible to be one hundred per cent certain. There are other factors too. For instance, each three or four years there's a warm water current called El Niño, which appears in the eastern Pacific – El Niño is linked with increased hurricane activity.

Interviewer: OK – but going back to temperature levels, I know some people claim that the temperature of the oceans goes up and down naturally.

Kate: Mm, yes, there is some truth in that. In the early 1900s sea temperatures started to rise. But then they went down again only to rise again, and continue to rise from the 1970s.

Interviewer: So people who claim that rises and falls in temperature are natural have got a point?

Kate: Perhaps, but other scientists, myself included, think that atmospheric pollution was responsible for keeping temperatures down.

Interviewer: Atmospheric pollution?

Kate: Yes. Particles from factories actually helped to block out sunlight. But now, there is no question that world temperatures are rising all the time mostly because of CO_2 emissions. Burning fuels like coal and oil, the so-called 'fossil fuels' releases the carbon stored in them into the atmosphere.

Interviewer: Yes, I see that. So, how much CO_2 is actually in the atmosphere, then?

Kate: Well, there is 0.03 of a per cent. That's one part in 3300.

Interviewer: But that's absolutely minuscule. How can that possibly have any impact? I can't see what all the fuss is about.

Kate: Well, all I can say is that while it may seem very slight, just a tiny increase can have devastating consequences. If I had my way, I'd ban any car with a large engine.

Interviewer: Mm … if you say so. Right … and a couple of quick questions. First one: what is the difference between a hurricane and a typhoon?

Kate: Scientifically, none at all. They are just the names which have been used in different regions. Typhoon means, I think, 'big wind' in Japanese. We can also call them cyclones too. We shouldn't confuse them with tornadoes or twisters, because *they* happen over land.

Interviewer: Right, like in the mid-west in the United States. And is there a difference between hurricanes or typhoons in the northern and southern hemispheres?

Kate: Yes, they rotate differently. It's all rather complicated, but basically a hurricane in the northern hemisphere rotates anti-clockwise, and one in the southern hemisphere goes the other way round.

Interviewer: I see. OK, well, thanks for being with us today. And now for a weather update …

Listening 12.4

Speaker 1: It could be any number of things. We had some strong wind last night. It was blowing really hard and a tree fell down in my garden so it could have blown the corn over. Or maybe it was some kids playing around. We often get teenagers coming down from the city in the summer and they sleep out, so they could quite easily have done it. I also read that helicopters can make shapes like this, so it might have been as a result of some kind of flying machine. There's a military air force base about 50 miles away. Who knows? Perhaps a plane or something flew over last night.

Speaker 2: I'm absolutely certain that aliens did it. I mean, there have been lots of UFO sightings round here. A friend of mine saw lights in the sky only last week. This triangle of lights flew past his house, it was sort of metal, he said, and moving really quite quickly. Anyway, he saw them land in the distance. So it seems to me that any spaceship would leave a mark on the ground like that.

Speaker 3: Some crop circles are probably hoaxes and for fun, but in this case it would have been impossible for someone to make something this complex in the middle of the night. They couldn't have done it all in seven hours! The farmer said he'd been to the field in the evening and saw nothing and then the next morning it appeared. It must have been something more mysterious. I know that some people have seen UFOs around here.

Speaker 4: I can't believe all the fuss over this. In my opinion it's a complete hoax. For one thing, people are saying it's aliens. Well, aliens wouldn't come here and even if they did, why spend their time making circles in the corn? Surely they have better things to do! I think it's probably someone creating a story. It seems like the sort of thing a newspaper would set up, because we have loads of journalists visiting the village all of a sudden. In my opinion they should all go home – leave us alone.

Speaker 5: I can't seem to make my mind up on this. The fact is, it's there and it is very clever, very beautiful in a way. Whoever did it was very artistic. I have heard that there are groups of people who travel round the country making these circles. They do it as a kind of hobby. But I live nearby and I didn't hear anything so … I'm not really sure. Maybe it was aliens after all.

Listening 13.1

Newswoman: A new report on education published today says that the latest national test results are the worst in over 20 years. One ex-headmaster said the situation is appalling. That's the verdict on the spelling ability of school children in Great Britain after the results of last year's national tests were released. The report reveals that pupils who were tested, aged 11 and 14, made more spelling errors last year than they did four years ago. Some of the most common errors among half of the 11-year-olds were words such as 'change' and 'known', which were often spelled C-H-A-N-G and N-O-W-N'. In addition the word 'technique' caused problems for the majority of the 600,000 pupils taking the test! Well, we have Michael Bryant, our education correspondent, in the studio with us today. Michael, what are people saying about this report?

Michael: Well, one person who actually marked the tests told me that the report reveals that most errors had arisen because pupils had missed out letters, put the incorrect endings on words or used the wrong vowels altogether. The slip in spelling standards among 11- and 14-year-olds also comes as researchers found a decline in the ability to use basic punctuation correctly, such as capital letters, full stops and commas.

Newswoman: One thing that surprised me was that the government has been telling us that it has spent more money on education than any previous government. Given the results of the survey it's amazing that this can be the case. It would be interesting to know more about how the government has responded to all this criticism.

Michael: Well, I asked the Minister for Education what she thought some of the reasons were and she responded to the findings by suggesting that teachers may be at fault. She said she'd sent schools a list of 600 words all children should know in their first year at secondary school, at age 11, and another list of 700 words that pupils should have mastered by 14.

Newswoman: Really? And how have teachers reacted?

Michael: Well, the teachers' union said it would be commenting later in the day, once it had studied the report in more detail. In the past, the union has welcomed government initiatives, including the new-style English lessons which were introduced in schools last term, and where teachers begin each lesson with ten minutes of spelling. The idea is that every department plays a role. For example, maths teachers are meant to drill pupils in words connected with maths like 'geometrical', and sports teachers ensure pupils can spell 'athlete' and 'muscles', but the problem is that …

Listening 13.2

Channel 1

Interviewer: And if things weren't bad enough for the Prime Minister, today he came under fire again for his education policy. Heads of schools and teachers' associations issued a joint statement speaking out against what they see as a lack of interest and understanding in the future generations of the country. In the studio with me today is Michael Woods, chairman of the headmasters' association, who supported this statement. Mr Woods, good morning. What is the basis for this statement against the Prime Minister?

Woods: Well, it's quite simple. Year after year, this government has promised they would deliver on education but instead all we've seen is a cut in funding in both schools and resources.

Channel 2

Scientists at NASA are still monitoring a telecommunications satellite which has fallen out of orbit and is moving towards Earth. Problems with the satellite first became obvious when it stopped receiving signals about two months ago. Scientists had hoped it would burn up on entry into the Earth's atmosphere, but it looks as if larger parts of the satellite might reach the surface. The question now is: where exactly? With over two thirds of the Earth's surface being ocean, the chances of it hitting a populated area are low but not impossible.

Channel 3

I don't think anyone would argue that the economy has done well this year, but the outlook for next year is less predictable, and the government needs to think its strategy through very carefully. I'd predict a slow-down in house prices and I'd also expect inflation to rise by about half a per cent. The consumer will need to be a little more careful in the next 12 months and really start to watch their borrowing. Anyone with large credit card bills should pay them off as soon as possible, otherwise they could really get caught out.

Channel 4

This is a great week for you Leos, with good news at work – maybe a pay rise or a promotion. Romance might be coming your way. It's a good week to take up a sport or something healthy. Maybe you've been eating a little too much and it would be a good idea to go jogging or perhaps eat a little less. You get on well with the star sign Libra at this time of year, so spend some free time with them. Perhaps you should take a trip to the cinema and relax a little. You've been working hard and I think you need to reward yourself.

Channel 5

Well, the news coming from Hollywood is that they might be thinking of taking their friendship further. Rumours that Mel and Christina, who met on the set of their recent film, are to get married seem to be spreading across Los Angeles. We haven't been able to get an official response from the publicity office of either star but one close friend of the couple said they wouldn't be surprised and described the couple as 'very close in recent weeks'. This news comes very soon after Mel's much publicised break-up with his second wife.

Listening 14.1

One

Daughter: Come on, Dad, you can't possibly wear that old-fashioned suit – it's *so* 70s.

Father: What do you mean? I've had this for years … I'm proud I can still get into it.

Daughter: Yeah, but it looks as though you've just come out of an old TV programme. It's just so weird. Two buttons are out, three are in.

Father: Two buttons, three buttons – I couldn't care less, I'm not into fashion. Anyway, if I wait long enough two buttons will make a comeback.

Daughter: OK, but do you think you could change the shirt and tie. They don't go together at all. Those green stripes clash horribly with the pink.

Father: Do you really think so? Alright, if that makes you feel better, I will.

Two

Doctor: Yes, I perfectly understand, Hannah. In my opinion, the best way of losing weight is to follow a sensible balanced diet. Avoid fads like avoiding all carbohydrates or eliminating all fat from your diet. There are *no* miracle solutions. Take up some form of light exercise and then build up so that your body is getting a good workout for 20 minutes or so at least three times a week. Make sure you don't overdo it or you could get hurt, you know, tear a muscle or something like that. So avoid sports to start with which involve sharp violent movements, like football or even tennis.

Three

Melissa: Well, finally, here comes Lulu.

Raymond: And about time too. And oh my goodness! Look at her! She looks like an orange.

Melissa: Yes, and just look at that permanent smile.

Raymond: Mmm, she has had her face lifted at least three times. But gravity always wins in the end.

Melissa: And she should think about getting her eyes done, those bags look awful.

Lulu: Sorry I'm late. I've just been to the tanning salon.

Raymond: Don't worry, darling. We were just saying how gorgeous you look.

Four

You're on a tight budget; you don't have to wear expensive brands or designer labels to be stylish. Let the real you come through and develop your own look. Accessories such as scarves and brooches can give you that something extra with a bit of flair.

Five

One of the latest crazes is flash-mobbing. This is where a large group of young people, up to a couple of hundred, descend on a place they have agreed and decided on. They do something unexpected for a couple of minutes and then leave as quickly as they came. The meeting point is decided on the Internet. They gather and then they get a set of instructions to follow. Then they'll do things like invade a sofa shop and sit on the sofas for five minutes, or go to a bookshop and ask for a non-existent book.

Six

Well, when I think back to when I was a kid, you know when everyone smoked, there was nothing cooler than one of those petrol lighters … Zippos, that's it … a Zippo lighter. Anyway, I guess what I'm trying to say is that each generation has its own set of cult objects – it's normal. My lighter was a lot cheaper than an iPod, that's for sure. But these new objects, some *do* become classics in the end. And do you know, the other day in the shopping centre, I saw this place which was selling flying jackets – you know the type of thing airmen wore in the Second World War, with the fur collar and everything!? You can't get more retro than that, can you?

Seven

Well, here we go again. I know a lot of people will complain about it, because there are people living in poverty and dying of hunger, but people need to dream a little too, don't you think? To my way of thinking, there are a lot of other things which are far more unethical – like the arms trade, for instance. Fashion week doesn't hurt anyone. If anything it brightens up people's lives and makes them happier – and that can't be bad, can it?

Eight

Well, it certainly is a little bit behind the times, but it's a wonderful renovation project. And if a few things need doing to it then it will be a good investment. True, the kitchen and bathroom need to be modernised, but it has great potential. And it's an up-and-coming area; there are a few new and trendy restaurants starting to appear and I would say that in a couple of years this area will be as fashionable as Hampstead or Islington.

Listening 14.2

Philip: Is that you in that photograph, Florence?

Florence: Mm, yes, it is, Philip. It was the first time I'd worn my new school uniform. I was so proud of myself.

Damien: You look so cute with your hair in pigtails!

Florence: That's sweet of you, Damien. I'm in the summer uniform there. I've got a straw hat, see. But in the winter we had a coat with lots of buttons and a funny-looking hat. It was like a nightcap … you know, red with a long bit hanging down.

Philip: Oh no! You poor thing!

Florence: Yeah, people used to tease us … they called us 'Santa's little helpers'! It was complete misery. I don't know who thought the uniform up. I hated that hat, but we were made to wear it.

Damien: I know how you feel. We had to wear our school cap on the way to *and* from school. Things are a lot less strict nowadays!

Philip: I'm glad to hear it. I loathed wearing a uniform.

Damien: I didn't exactly like it either, but the great thing about a uniform is it's so easy. What I mean is you just get up and put it on.

Philip: Yes, but don't you think that kids should be allowed to wear what they want? After all it's a way of expressing themselves.

Damien: You say that, Philip, but kids end up putting on a kind of uniform of their own – you know, designer jeans and trainers. Don't you think that leads to a lot of unhealthy competitive dressing? *You* know … who is wearing the most *fashionable* brands, and so on.

Florence: Not to mention all the hours which are wasted gelling their hair to make it spiky or worrying about looking cool.

Philip: I suppose so, but I don't care what you say, that's still better than school uniform! You know, in the summer, we weren't allowed to take off our jackets! Our teachers didn't even let us take off our ties. It was torture.

Florence: I agree with you Philip. I don't see the point of making people uncomfortable. All the same, in a uniform at least everyone is the same. What I mean is there are no differences between the kids and it makes everyone look equal. It looks smart too.

Philip: Well, you say that, and at the beginning of the year it's true, but it soon gets scruffy – and when they grow they have a jacket which is far too small for them.

Damien: Philip has got a point. He's thought it through. When I was at school the uniform was really expensive so my family couldn't afford to let me have a new one every year. So my trousers always needed taking up for the first four months of the school year because they were too long, the next four months it was OK, but then for the last four months of the year they were too short and needed to be let down. In the end they looked awful!

Florence: All the same, I still think uniform is a good idea as it is much less trouble for parents.

Damien: I agree. After all, parents have enough stress as it is. Having their children complaining about not having *exactly* the perfect clothing for school and saying their friends have got better clothes than them is just more stress for them!

Philip: Maybe.

Listening 15.1

Speaker 1: And finally, guards at the Terracotta Army Museum in Xi'an, China, couldn't believe their eyes when they saw a man jump into the pit and disguise himself as one of the warriors. German art student, Paul Wendel, who was studying in China, decided to join the warriors he admired. These remarkable ancient terracotta soldiers are over 2,200 years old, and an important part of China's heritage. They were created to accompany their emperor in the afterlife. Wendel pretended he was one of them and stood as still as he could until the guards lifted him away. Apparently, he stayed frozen in his pose as the guards lifted him out.

Speaker 2: In Britain, November the 5th is 'Bonfire Night'. It celebrates the discovery of a plot to kill King James the 1st by blowing up the Houses of Parliament. Before Bonfire Night there's a tradition that children make a 'Guy' – a life-size doll of Guy Fawkes, the infamous conspirator. They'll take some old clothes and fill them up with newspaper. Then they'll make a head and draw a face on it, and perhaps stick on a beard. A few days before Bonfire Night, they'll display the Guy outside supermarkets and train stations saying 'A Penny for the Guy'. Of course, nowadays what they mean is 'at least 50p!'

Then they'll use this money to buy fireworks or sweets for the celebrations on the 5th.

Speaker 3: I enjoyed visiting well known sights such as Red Square in Moscow and going to the Hermitage museum in St Petersburg, but, to tell you the truth, the thing that most moved me was a short visit I made to Volgograd and seeing the absolutely awesome statue that some people call 'Mother Russia'. Volgograd used to be called Stalingrad and was the site of the terrible siege and historic battle which proved to be the turning point of the war. Anyway, the statue, which is made of concrete, stands outside Volgograd, overlooking the city. It is, for sure, the tallest statue in Europe and is a memorial which commemorates the struggle and sacrifices made by the people of Stalingrad and the Red Army.

Speaker 4: One of my favourite TV shows used to be with those rubber puppets. They were real works of art – you could immediately see who they were supposed to be. I used to like the way they made fun of politicians or famous or notorious personalities from show business and so on. And the actors who took them off sounded like the real thing. I don't know why they don't show it any more – I suppose they thought it was old-fashioned. The one thing I didn't appreciate, though, was the way they mocked the royal family – I mean, that's totally unfair, I think.

Speaker 5: Sometimes we should rely on our first impressions. For instance, the Getty Museum spent $10m on a fake statue which was supposed to come from ancient Greece. Now, everything about it seemed perfect, and museum officials managed to talk themselves into thinking it was real, but other experts knew the second that they looked at it that the statue was a fake. Years of examining hundreds of examples of the real thing simply told them that the Getty Museum had been taken in by a clever imitation.

Listening 15.2

Part A

Betty: So would you mind telling us how you got into these, the re-enactments?

Kelly: Well, basically, it was a way of getting to know people. I moved from London to this small town where I didn't know anyone. I hesitated a bit at first, 'cos I thought, you know, that there would be lots of weirdos, but I finally made up my mind to join and have been involved ever since.

Betty: Right, so basically you joined to make new friends, it wasn't because you were interested in history or anything like that?

Kelly: Actually, I wasn't that keen on history when I was at school. Mind you, since joining the society I have discovered a real love for history and our heritage.

Betty: And which side are you on?

Kelly: Well, I'm in a Royalist regiment, one which supports the king. You see, in the *real* war, in the 17th century, there was a local gentleman who established a regiment loyal to the king in my town. So the regiment I am in is a tribute to the original one. Anyway, I've always preferred the Cavaliers.

Betty: Me too. They had long hair, and lovely clothes and hats with feathers and all the rest. The Roundheads must have been a miserable-looking crowd, I think, in the brown and black they always wore! You can't imagine them having a good time, can you? So tell me, what happens in these re-enactments?

Kelly: Well, basically, we form a little army with other Royalist regiments, then we re-enact battles and other historic events against Roundhead regiments – of course the outcome of the battle is decided at the planning stage, so we just act the story out like a play on a large scale. We do try to keep the suspense going as much as possible for the spectators.

Betty: Goodness. So how many people can be involved?

Kelly: Well, sometimes there can be several hundred participants on each side, not counting the thousands of people who come along to watch.

Betty: And do you do this on a stage or somewhere like that?

Kelly: No, not at all. We travel to the original battlefields and camp there for the weekend of the re-enactment battle. We may have to travel hundreds of miles. There is usually a farmer who will let us park or put our tents up on his land.

Listening 15.3

Part B

Betty: I hope you don't mind my mentioning this, fighting isn't a very lady-like activity is it?

Kelly: Well, there are more lady-like roles. At first I was one of the women-folk. I was a cook. But when I realised that the soldiers were having more fun, I changed my mind and became a soldier too! Although this does mean dressing up as a man – there weren't women soldiers in those days as such.

Betty: So there's nothing to stop women from playing a full part in the fighting?

Kelly: No, anyone can wave a sword around. But I can't manage the pikes, those very long spears – well, they're five metres long and impossible for most of the women to handle! But there's nothing to stop a girl being a musketeer either, you know, firing a gun, or even joining the cavalry. Oh, and it almost slipped my mind, girls can be drummers too.

Betty: But isn't it dangerous? I mean taking part in a battle, even if it's a pretend one?

Kelly: No, not really, although people sometimes have small injuries. You have to mind where you stand – it hurts if a horse steps on your foot – it *really* hurts.

Betty: What was your first battle like?

Kelly: Great fun, although I did say to myself, 'you must be out of your mind, girl'. The noise and the smell of gunpowder are unimaginable.

Betty: Mm, goodness knows what the real thing must have been like. And what do you do other than this?

Kelly: Well, the social life is absolutely fantastic. You meet like-minded people from all walks of life and there are banquets … you know … *big* meals … for all the regiment. And dances! Every year we go to London to commemorate the execution of King Charles in 1649. There's a parade to where his head was cut off at the Mansion House.

Videoscripts

Unit 1   A match made in Africa

Narrator: Some friendships help us through hard times. In 2008, near Cape Town, in South Africa, a wild baby elephant is orphaned. The staff at nearby Shamwari game reserve is instantly worried about the calf. Elephant babies need milk for at least two years. Shamwari's resident filmmaker, Lyndal Davies, remembers that difficult time.

Lyndal Davies: We hoped one of the other elephants would adopt him, because they often will …

Narrator: Suffering from a drought, no herd females will nurse the calf. The Shamwari team moves in for a rescue.

Lyndal Davies: It's always dangerous when you dart an elephant, because the rest of the herd becomes very protective, and we knew that.

Narrator: The staff fears the dehydrated orphan may not make it through the rescue.

Dr Johan Joubert: I'm really concerned, this calf went down absolutely too quickly.

Narrator: But the skilled handlers retrieve him, and bring him back to Shamwari. The calf enters his new home and all are relieved he survived the trip, until he refuses to drink.

Lyndal Davies: Baby elephants are very emotional, a lot like human children, and if they're not happy everything shuts down. And of course this little one had lost his mum, so he was grieving, in a big way.

Narrator: He finally takes water, but no formula. The staff decides to give the orphan an animal companion. Soon after, Albert, a merino sheep from a neighbouring farm, arrives at Shamwari. The pair don't hit it off, exactly!

Lyndal Davies: Get the sheep an escape route, just close that door.

Narrator: The elephant's bluff charges send Albert into hiding. But within 24 hours awkward encounters turn playful, calm, even comfortable. The calf has a breakthrough.

Lyndal Davies: About three days after that he started to drink milk, which was a major victory. Within two weeks he was out having his first walk, with us and with Albert the sheep. They were learning to play together, they're even sleeping together, you'd see them lying down beside each other in the enclosure at night.

Narrator: As his chances for survival improve, the staff names the calf Temba, meaning 'hope'. The odd couple becomes inseparable.

Unit 3   Adventure

Narrator: New Zealand is a land of many beautiful and quiet natural places. Queenstown isn't one of them.

Bungee instructor: Diving out that way, here we go: five, four, three, two, one, push it out!

Narrator: People come from around the world to do adventure sports in Queenstown – especially bungee jumping.

Henry Van Asch: The gap there from the underside of that little silver jump pod out there is 134 metres, which is about 440 feet.

Narrator: That's a long way down! But the sport must be fun. There are many people waiting for a chance to do it. What do they feel like before a jump?

Bungee jumper 1: I'm so ready! Bring it on!

Bungee jumper 2: I'm getting excited actually, yeah.

Bungee instructor: Five, four, three, two, one …

Narrator: If you like exciting adventure sports, New Zealand is the place to do them.

Van Asch: New Zealand people have a very immediate lifestyle a lot of the time, and that's what people can experience when they come here.

Brendan Quill, jetboat driver: Hahaha! Nothing like it!

Narrator: Riding in a jetboat is a special experience. It's yet another New Zealand adventure invention. There's no propeller, so the boats can work in shallow water.

Brendan Quill: These machines … you can spin 'em on a dime!

Narrator: Jetboats were especially designed to get around New Zealand's shallow rivers, but they're also really good at giving customers a thrill.

Brendan Quill: Ha ha ha! Yee hee hee! This is one of the number-one pastimes of people coming to New Zealand … more importantly probably Queenstown.

Narrator: In New Zealand, it seems that nearly every day someone creates another adventure sport.

David Kennedy: You know we quite proudly call ourselves 'the adventure capital of the world'. There are so many adventure activities to do here. In fact, we worked it out that if you did one of every type of activity you'd be here for 60 days!

Graham Buxtom: OK, we're off.

Narrator: One of the newest adventures involves a five-hour hike up a mountain. The best part is, at the end of the hike, the hikers don't have to walk all the way down again.

Graham Buxtom: We'll stay up here for ten minutes or so … fifteen minutes. Then we'll jump in the helicopter and fly back to Queenstown.

Narrator: The helicopter turns the five-hour hike into a five-minute flight back to the city! These different adventure sports really help the tourism industry in New Zealand. They're also part of an adventurous culture that goes back to the birthplace of adventure tourism in New Zealand – the Kawarau Bridge. The bridge was the world's first commercial bungee-jumping site.

Bungee watcher: I think it's great – if someone else is doing it!

Narrator: High wire bungee and bridge bungee are both thrilling and slightly frightening sports.

Bungee instructor: Here we go Marlene, leaning forward: five, four, three, two, one!

Van Asch: The people who have to really try hard to jump are the ones that get the most out of it.

Narrator: At least that's what some people think.

Bungee instructor: How was that?

Marlene: I'm never bungee jumping again!

Narrator: Maybe for some people, jumping once is enough.

Bungee jumper 1: Cheers!

Bungee jumper 2: Ah, we deserve that.

Bungee jumper 1: That was a good one!

Narrator: Most jumpers are happy that they did it. Here in the land of adventure, the only question may be: what will they think of doing next? Whatever it is, someone here in the adventure capital of the world will be ready to give it a try!

Unit 5   Sleepy Hollow

Narrator: Nestled in the hills of New York's Hudson River Valley lies the town of Sleepy Hollow … a place where a spooky legend meets modern-day life. Dutch settlers came here in the 1600s to farm, trap, and fish. At this historic manor, you can still experience life as it was in the 17th and 18th centuries. It's a fun place to visit, but it's the tale of a gangly schoolmaster and a headless horseman that really put Sleepy Hollow on the map.

Jonathon Kruk: Now dwelling in these parts, in a tenant house, was a certain schoolmaster by the name of Ichabod Crane.

Narrator: American author, Washington Irving, visited this area as a boy, and is believed to have based *The Legend of Sleepy Hollow* on people and places right in this town. Bill Lent knows everything there is to know about the legend, showing tourists where the famous characters are buried.

Bill Lent: And when he was writing the book, he remembered the name on the stone, Katrina Van Tassel. Lead female character in *The Legend of Sleepy Hollow*.

Narrator: As the story goes, Ichabod Crane fled across this bridge … racing to escape the headless horseman close behind.

Jonathon Kruk: Ichabod urged his horse Gunpowder on, 'Come, come,' but the horse needed no further urging as it took off and headed down to get to that churchyard bridge.

Narrator: Every year Sal Tarantino plays the headless horseman in the town's Hallowe'en festival.

Sal Tarantino: The hardest problem is a real jack-o-lantern. We've tried that several times. A good-sized jack-o-lantern with the right candle in it weighs about 20 pounds and to hold that out on your arm and try to control the horse at 40 miles per hour in the dark doesn't work too well.

Narrator: Irving did not actually write the legend here in Sleepy Hollow. But he loved the area so much, he returned as an adult to live on this 24-acre estate right on the Hudson River. And nearly two centuries after Irving wrote *The Legend of Sleepy Hollow*, the history and landscape of this place still inspire. And the legend lives on.

Jonathon Kruk: If you listen, you'll hear the unmistakable clattering of hooves of the headless horseman … beware …

Unit 7   Solar cooking

Narrator: It's a cool, sunny day in Borrego Springs, California, and Eleanor Shimeall is preparing a meal. Unlike most people, she isn't using electricity, gas, charcoal, or wood to cook her food.

Eleanor Shimeall: I'm going to check on this chicken and rice and see how it's – whether it's cooking. Ah, it's doing a good job.

Narrator: Instead, Shimeall is using the sun to make her lunch, and she's done it almost every day for more than 20 years. In fact, she's made this entire delicious meal with solar power. A solar cooker needs only the light from the sun to cook meat, fish, grains, and vegetables – even if the air temperature isn't very hot. This method is becoming popular among people who are concerned about the environment. However, in developing countries, solar cookers can save lives.

Dr Bob Metcalf: With sunshine you have an alternative to fire. And that's important for two and a half billion people to learn about, because they're running out of traditional fuels.

Narrator: Dr Bob Metcalf is a microbiologist and a founding member of Solar Cookers International, or SCI for short. He, along with Eleanor Shimeall and her husband, helped to create the small nonprofit organisation 15 years ago. SCI has promoted solar cooking worldwide, especially in the developing countries of Africa. Their goals are to stop deforestation and to make women's lives easier.

Dr Bob Metcalf: They have to walk about two to three miles or so to collect wood. And then they have to tend the fire. And the smoke from that fire, it burns their eyes and chokes their lungs.

Narrator: According to the World Health Organization, this indoor pollution has been linked to the deaths of two million women and children each year. With help from other human aid groups, Solar Cookers International has already trained more than 22,000 families how to cook traditional foods with the sun.

Wendy: Oh, this is good. It's very good! The consistency is good; the texture is fine. No problem!

SCI Workshop Participant: We're all amazed that a cardboard box can cook.

Narrator: After each workshop, attendees are given their own portable solar 'cook kits'. They're expected to use the kits to help them with their daily tasks. The simple cookers cost about five dollars, last almost two years, and work exactly like the more costly kits.

Dr Bob Metcalf: Shiny things direct the sunshine onto a dark pot that then absorbs the sunshine, and changes that light energy into heat energy. And heat energy doesn't get out of the clear plastic bag; it doesn't get out of the window.

Narrator: SCI reports that solar cooking is also an effective way to make water pure and safe to drink.

Dr Bob Metcalf: Six thousand people a day are going to die of waterborne diseases in developing countries. If you heat water to 65° Celsius, 149° Fahrenheit, you can pasteurise water and make it safe to drink.

Narrator: Solar Cookers International has developed a useful measuring tool that helps people to know when water is safe to drink.

Dr Bob Metcalf: If the water gets hot enough to melt this wax, the water has reached pasteurisation temperatures.

Narrator: From Nepal to Nicaragua, solar cooking projects are helping people in nearly every country in the developing world. Some communities are even experimenting with solar cookers for large volumes of food. But SCI is not satisfied with just helping these people. Their goal is to increase the use of solar cookers everywhere.

Dr Bob Metcalf: Science is supposed to help and benefit all of mankind, and you've got something that is good science that could help two and a half billion people in the world. There's a great need for information that these things work.

SCI Workshop Participant: OK, solar cooker!

Unit 9   Oaxaca

Narrator: Let's travel to Mexico now, to the historic state of Oaxaca, a place that is famous for its traditions and its fantastic food. If you feel cold in winter, you can warm up in Oaxaca by enjoying its spicy chillies. Why not make the most of your time there by enjoying its beautiful dances and its lovely streets and buildings? When you come to Oaxaca, wonderful colours and fabulous smells are all around you. Oaxaca is one of the poorest states in Mexico, but it is rich in culture and Oaxacan food is famous around the world.

Susana Trilling: It's one of the best foods, it's very complex …

Narrator: Susana Trilling adores the chillies in Oaxacan food so she moved here fourteen years ago to start her own cooking school. Many foreigners have come to learn how to make authentic Oaxacan *mole* and other dishes. Susana's students heard about Oaxacan food in their own countries and they come here wanting to learn more about this amazing cuisine. People stay in Oaxaca and take cooking classes in the school. Oaxacan food developed a long time before European people came to America. Tradition is keeping Oaxacan food alive and Susana thinks it is as complicated to make as Thai or French food. It uses many different ingredients. The first step in cooking Oaxacan food is preparing a sauce called *mole*. This sensational sauce is made from chilli peppers, spices and various other ingredients. *Mole* is standard in many different Oaxacan dishes – people serve it with chicken and meat and everything else. But Oaxacan culture is more than just food – the state is also famous for its dancers. This dance is centuries old – it is called the *guelaguetza*. It tells about the culture, history and music of the Oaxacan people. Many of the magnificent buildings in the city are Mexican national treasures. This building is 500 years old and has fountains, gardens and archways. In the past, it was a government building. Today it has been transformed into a marvellous luxury hotel. Oaxacan people say that a healthy person is happy and loves to work and eat. After a short visit to Oaxaca you can see that that tradition is still true.

Unit 11   Secrets of Stonehenge

Narrator: Stonehenge has stood a silent watch over England's Salisbury Plain since the twenty-sixth century BC. It has withstood extensive remodelling, looting, and pilfering throughout the centuries. And while it certainly shows its age, in many ways this monument is timeless, it's mysterious … and it's a bit of an obsession for Michael Parker Pearson. Pearson is an archaeologist at Sheffield University and he's an expert in what is called the archaeology of death. He's been digging in and around Stonehenge since 1998, when he came up with a novel theory about the purpose of this ancient ring of stones. His idea is based on the fact that Stonehenge isn't an isolated monument.

Michael Parker Pearson: In 2006, we made a great discovery. We found a whole settlement – many houses, and these we think are the houses that were lived in by the people who built this thing here. We also think that it's part of a bigger complex – that Stonehenge wasn't here in isolation, sitting on Salisbury Plain, but was part of a much bigger group of monuments. And those houses are all clustered around a timber version of this thing.

Narrator: The second complex is called Woodhenge at a place called Durrington Walls.

Michael Parker Pearson: It's upstream that we found a number of large timber buildings, and some of these are houses – we've actually got some idea of where people lived when they came to celebrate and to actually build the timber and stone monuments.

Narrator: And Pearson believes that Durrington Walls was a very large community for its time. It's hardly recognisable now, but may have contained hundreds, perhaps thousands of homes. He also believes that the Durrington Walls site was where people lived. The temporary wood structures housed the living, according to Pearson, and the permanent stone structures were for the dead.

Michael Parker Pearson: It's our biggest cemetery from the third millennium – we estimate that there were about 240 cremation burials that were placed there.

Narrator: Pearson's theory is that Stonehenge isn't a lone, solitary monument at all, but rather just a small part of a larger community, where people buried their dead and their journey was recorded in the landscape and in the materials they used to build their homes and mortuaries. It's an elegant and compelling idea and one that suggests we're not all that different from our ancestors – it's just a matter of scale.

Unit 13   The greenhouse effect

Narrator: The past year's weather has been one of the most destructive in history.

Australia

The worst floods in four decades inundate the state of Queensland. The flood covers an area larger than France and Germany combined.

Russia

The hottest summer on record triggers drought and catastrophic wildfires, killing more than 50,000 people.

Pakistan

Extreme heat is followed by floods that cover one fifth of the country. 5,000 miles of roads and railways are washed away.

The United States

Record winter, cold and snow follow one of the warmest summers on record. In Chicago, this blizzard hits so hard and so fast it stops rush-hour traffic – dead in its tracks. Around the world, extreme weather is testing the limits of our endurance. And the cause of it all could not be more surprising, or more ordinary. At its core, the problem is all about water. Too much water.

Doctor Brian Soden teaches Meteorology and Oceanography at the University of Miami. He says the source of that heavy precipitation is all around us.

Doctor Brian Soden: You're wondering where all this extreme rainfall comes from. It starts here, at the ocean's surface. The ocean is a source of water in the atmosphere. And we can see it in various forms, in clouds, in rain, but it's the water we can't see, in the form of gases, water vapour, that has the most profound impact on weather and climate. Water vapour provides the source of fuel for storms, and it's a process that's occurring constantly, day after day.

Narrator: As the sun rises and warms the planet, billions of gallons of water evaporate from the surface of the oceans. Invisible to the eye, the sun transforms that water into a vapour that envelops the earth and nurtures life. More heat means more evaporation. And that means more energy builds up in the atmosphere – increasing the potential for more extreme and more destructive weather events.

Unit 15   Songlines of the Aborigines

Around 55,000 years ago, the Aborigines arrived in Australia. Their culture thrived for many thousands of years, until the large-scale arrival of the Europeans, which occurred in the nineteenth century. The culture survives today in remote pockets of the outback, and that's where we're going.

We're heading east now into Arnheim land in the northern territory of Australia. This is the cradle of what became one of the greatest civilisations in the history of humanity. Sadly, when European settlers arrived, that's not what they saw.

Adam McPhee, an Australian anthropologist, tells us that when Europeans first came to Australia they considered Aborigines as savages who lived on the land without exploiting it. In fact they missed out on one of the greatest philosophies of any culture on the planet.

European attempts to civilise the Aborigines had tragic results, and their numbers dwindled. By the mid-twentieth century nearly 90% of the population had perished.

We have now arrived at Ramingining which is a community that was probably established in the early seventies, when Aborigines were urged to move off the land. However, once people remained in places like Ramingining, they were suddenly separated from the very thing upon which the culture depended, the spiritual link to the landscape.

The Aborigines' beliefs are rooted in a deep respect for, and connection to, the land. It's no surprise that their rituals involved long walks tracing the footsteps of their ancestors, following the ancient pathways of the songlines.

Thousands of songlines form a network across the continent. Some are just a few miles long, others span hundreds of miles. Songlines have a practical purpose – they are vital for survival. They track the territory, indicating waterways, mountains, depressions.

They work as maps for finding food, and even map the borders between clans. But songlines also mark a spiritual journey. On their walks the Aborigines sing songs about the mythical stories of the 'dreaming', the time when the world as we know it was born.

When they sing the songs and follow their songlines, Aborigines return to that moment of creation, and each time they sing they ensure that the world is created all over again.

Information file

UNIT 4   page 45, exercise 9

> **Which of these animals do you think enjoys its life more?**

UNIT 7   page 70

World's worst ten inventions

1 weapons
2 mobile phones
3 cigarettes
4 cars
5 computers
6 TV
7 nuclear energy
8 plastic bags
9 fast food
10 car alarms

UNIT 7   page 74, exercise 6

STUDENT A

It was three o'clock one Icelandic morning and Rebekka Guoleifsdottir couldn't sleep. So she picked up her camera and drove to a lake outside her town. Standing in the lake with water up to her knees for an hour, she took picture after picture. Her final favourite image did not appear on an advertising billboard or in a gallery or magazine, but on the World Wide Web and her own homepage. Visitors who log on to her site just click on the photo they want and buy it online. She's recently been asked by the car maker Toyota to take photos. 'The web changes opportunities for all kinds of artists, like musicians,' said Guoleifsdottir. 'It's so much easier to get your stuff out there. Iceland is a small community of 300,000 people and it's hard to get recognised, but this way you can reach out everywhere.'

UNIT 7 page 74, exercise 6

STUDENT B

After three years of odd jobs like stacking shelves in a supermarket and setting up websites, it took a 21-year-old student a few minutes to come up with an idea which has made him more than one million dollars in four months. Alex Tew lay on his bed one night wondering how he could pay for his three-year degree course at university. The first thing he wrote on his notepad was, 'How can I become a millionaire?' Twenty minutes later, the Million Dollar Homepage idea was born. The idea was that Tew would sell pixels, the dots which make up a computer screen, as advertising space for a dollar a pixel. Anyone could buy pixels and post their logo so users would have a link to their website. Four months and 2,000 customers later Tew is about to sell the last 1,000 pixels having made a million.

UNIT 8 page 80, exercise 7

Bank robbery – ten years in prison
Computer hacking – probation for one year
Speeding – attend a talk by the police on how to drive safely
Shop lifting – do community service for 40 hours
Dropping litter – pay a fine of £100
Mugging – 18 months+ in prison

UNIT 8 page 83, exercise 9

[adapted from: The Week 22 July 2006 p14]
A prisoner who wanted to wish his girlfriend a happy birthday escaped from a jail in Montenegro. Dragan Boskovic, 26, escaped over a wall which was over ten-foot high, and went straight to his girlfriend's house, where he spent the evening. He finally explained his reasons to the police, to whom he turned himself in two hours later: 'I promised my girlfriend that I would say happy birthday, which I hadn't been able to do on the prison phone. I had no other option but to get the message to her personally.'

UNIT 10 page 100, exercise 2

YOU SCORED 18 OR ABOVE
You are a sensible shopper and don't overspend or buy things you don't need. You plan your purchases carefully rather than buying on a whim, and you put the work in to make sure you get a good deal. You might prefer to buy reliable brands, but you don't overspend on fashion items just because they have a designer logo.

YOU SCORED BETWEEN 11 AND 17
You are generally quite a careful shopper, but you can be tempted to make silly mistakes by bargains or special offers. Or perhaps you just have to have the latest mobile phone, or that designer handbag that you can't really afford! You need to plan your shopping more carefully – decide what you are going to buy, compare prices to find the best deal, and then make sure you stick to your decision.

YOU SCORED 10 OR BELOW
Your shopping habits could land you in big trouble! You probably have a wardrobe full of things you hardly ever wear. Discounts and bargains are great and can save you money, but you should decide what you need or want to buy before you head off for the sales, and shop around to find the best price before you buy. Set yourself a weekly or monthly budget and work hard at sticking to it.

CREDITS

Although every effort has been made to contact copyright holders before publication, this has not always been possible. If contacted, the publisher will undertake to rectify errors or omissions at the earliest opportunity

The publisher would like to thank the following sources for permission to reproduce their copyright protected images and videos:
Cover photo: Andrew Watson/Getty Images.
Inside photos: pp 10, 4.1 (Martin Barraud/Getty Images), 13 (Cengage Learning), 14 (Bob Pool/Photographer's Choice/Getty Images), 17 (Blend Images/Alamy), 18 (Caters News Agency Ltd/Rex Features), 20, 4.2 (OJO Images/Rex Features), 23 t&b (Adam Pacitti/Rex Features), 25 (Alliance/Shutterstock), 26 (kali9/Vetta/Getty Images), 30, 4.3 (Christie Goodwin/WireImage/Getty Images), 32 (TimoHartikainen/Rex Features), 33 ml (Seitsonen/Rex Features), 33 br (JEP Live Music/Alamy), 34 (VovaPomortzeff/Alamy), 36 t (Stephanie McGehee/Reuters), 36 b (LOOK Die Bildagentur der Fotografen GmbH/Alamy), 38 (Dmitry Naumov/Shutterstock), 39 (Jonathan Larsen/Diadem Images/Alamy), 40, 4.4 (Warren Photography), 42 (David Bagnall/Alamy), 43 (Nick Obank/Barcroft Media/Getty Images), 45 tl (Nick Obank/Barcroft Media/Getty Images), 45 ml (Dmitry Kalinovsky/Shutterstock), 46 tl (Blickwinkel/Alamy), 46 ml (Hannes Magerstaedt/Getty Images Entertainment/Getty Images), 50, 4.5 (Photos 12/Alamy), 52 (HBO/Everett/Rex Features Features), 53 (HBO/Everett/Rex Features Features), 58 (Buyenlarge/Moviepix/Getty Images), 60, 4.6 (Backyard Productions/Alamy), 65 (Beverly Joubert/National Geographic), 66 (Giovanni Mereghetti/Marka/Superstock Ltd), 70, 4.7 (PETER ESSICK/National Geographic), 71 (Reinhard Krause/Reuters), 72 (Pictorial Press Ltd./Alamy), 76 tl (Pumkinpie/Alamy), 76 bl (Microsoft Corporation), 78 (JoergBoethling/Alamy), 80, 4.8 (Flying Colours Ltd/Digital Vision/Getty Images), 82 (Jack Sullivan/Alamy), 83 (johnjohnson/Shutterstock), 84 (Alejandro Pagni/AFP/Getty Images), 85 (Cengage Learning), 86 (Mikadun/Shutterstock), 90, 6.9 (Dwight Eschliman/Stone/Getty Images), 91 mr (Dinnerinthesky/Solen/Rex Features Features), 91 br (Blaine Harrington III/Alamy), 93 (Erik Pendzich/Rex Features), 94 (Luo Wei/ChinaFotoPress/Getty Images), 96 (LOOK Die Bildagentur der Fotografen GmbH/Alamy), 97 (Fernando Madeira/Shutterstock), 98 (GlowImages/Alamy), 100, 6.10 (Blend Images/Alamy), 103 (garfotos/Alamy), 105 tr (Ron Niebrugge/Alamy), 105 br (Ian Townsley/Alamy), 107 (Minzayar/Reuters), 110, 6.11 (Mauricio Alanis/Getty Images), 111 (Karkas/Shutterstock), 112 tr (Glenn Hill/SSPL/Getty Images), 112 mr (Time & Life Pictures/Getty Images), 112 br (Bentley Archive/Popperfoto/Getty Images), 113 (Steve Alexander/Rex Features Features), 114 (Tom Bean/Alamy), 115 inset tl (mt1278/Shutterstock), 115 inset tr (Gelpi JM/Shutterstock), 115 inset ml (Coprid/Shutterstock), 115 inset mr (Pincarel/Shutterstock), 115 inset bl (Kekyalyaynen/Shutterstock), 115 inset br (Becky Stares/Shutterstock), 116 (Wavebreak Media ltd/Alamy), 118 (gary718/Shutterstock), 120, 6.12 (NavidBaraty/National Geographic), 121 (Patrick Mcfeeley/National Geographic), 122 tl (TanawatPontchour/Shutterstock), 122 tc (PiggingFoto/Shutterstock), 11 tr (ZeljkoRadojko/Shutterstock), 123 (Geospace/Science Photo Library), 124 (Mike Theiss/National Geographic/Getty Images), 125 (Creative Travel Projects/Shutterstock), 130, 6.13 (John Eder/The Image Bank/Getty Images), 133 (XPACIFICA/National Geographic), 134 tl (DreamPictures/The Image Bank/Getty Images), 134 tr (Realimage/Alamy), 134 ml (Cultura/Rex Features), 134 mr (Startraks Photo/Rex Features), 138 (Scott Olson/Getty Images News/Getty Images), 140, 6.14 (NielsPoulsen DK/Alamy), 143 (Aflo/Rex Features), 144 (John Martin/Alamy), 150, 6.15 (Jan Wlodarczyk/Alamy), 151 (O. Louis Mazzatenta/National Geographic), 152 (Fabio De Paola/Rex Features), 154 (Nikreates/Alamy), 157 (Mario Vazquez/AFP/Getty Images), 158 (Image Asset Management Ltd/Alamy), 159 (Robert Harding Picture Library/Superstock Ltd), 161 tl (The Photolibrary Wales/Alamy), 161tr (Bildbroker.de/Alamy), 161 bl (Barry Lewis/Alamy), 161 br (CandyBox Images/Shutterstock), 163 (Cengage Learning), 186 t (PhotoAlto/OdilonDimier/Getty Images), 186 b (Jim West/Alamy), 187 t (ep property/Alamy), 187 b (BUILT Images/Alamy), 238 t (photobar/Shutterstock), 238 b (HeroToZero/Shutterstock).

DVD videos: National Geographic (units 3, 5, 7, 9, 11, and 15); National Geographic Channel (units 1 and 13); Tom Dick and Debbie Productions (Speaking test).

Illustrations: 55 (Michael Perrin), 56 (Ilias Arahovitis/Beehive Illustration), 63 (Michael Perrin), 102 a-c (Michael Perrin), 104 a-f (Ilias Arahovitis/Beehive Illustration), 111 (Michael Perrin), 146 (Michael Perrin).

Text
We are grateful to the following for permission to reproduce copyright material:
Immediate Media Co. for an extract in Unit 1 from 'Soaps around the world' by Christopher Middleton, *BBC Radio Times*, 2007, copyright © Immediate Media Company Origin Limited; Mirrorpix for an extract in Unit 1 adapted from 'Gossip is good for you' by John Von Radowitz. *The Mirror*, 22 May 2006, Copyright © Mirrorpix 2006; Dennis for an extract in Unit 2 adapted from 'The Cinderellas of Hollywood' *The Week*, 27 July 2007, Copyright © The Week 2007; Adam Pacitti for information about himself in Unit 2. Reproduced with kind permission of Adam Pacitti, http://www.adampacitti.com/; Raleigh International for information in Unit 2 about Raleigh International, www.raleighinternational.org. Reproduced with permission; News UK for an extract in Unit 4 adapted from 'Bitten chef saved his life by snapping lethal spider' by Simon de Bruxelles, *The Times*, 27 April 2005, Copyright © News UK 2005, www.newssyndication.com; Telegraph Media Group Ltd for an extract in Unit 4 from 'The peacock and the petrol pump' by Richard Savill, copyright © Telegraph Media Group Limited, 2007; David Higham Associates Limited, Penguin Random House and Random House of Canada Limited for an extract in unit 5 from *In the Company of Cheerful Ladies: More from the No. 1 Ladies' Detective Agency* by Alexander McCall Smith, Birlinn, copyright © 2004, 2005 Alexander McCall Smith. Reproduced by permission of David Higham Associates Limited, Pantheon Books, an imprint of the Knopf Doubleday Publishing Group, a division of Random House LLC and Knopf Canada. All rights reserved; Workman Publishing Inc. for an extract in Unit 6 from '1,000 places to see before you die', copyright © 2003 by Patricia Schultz. Used by permission of Workman Publishing Co., Inc., New York. All Rights Reserved; Guardian News & Media Ltd for an extract in Unit 7 from 'Images of icy beauty come out of cold' by David Smith, copyright © Guardian News & Media Ltd 2005; Telegraph Media Group Ltd for an extract in Unit 8 from 'Dancing Robot Copies Human Moves' by Nic Flemin, copyright © Telegraph Media Group Limited, 2007; Dennis for an extract in Unit 8 adapted from 'Dragan Boskovic;, The Week, 22 July 2006, p.14, Copyright © The Week 2006; Telegraph Media Group Ltd for an extract in Unit 9 from 'All Mouth' by John Preston, copyright © Telegraph Media Group Limited, 2007; Toys Global Industry Analyst for an extract in Unit 11 from 'A Kids'-Eye View of Europe: Toys, Pocket Money and Spending' by Frédérique Tutt, copyright © The NPD Group – EuroToys Division; Immediate Media Co. for an extract in Unit 10 adapted from 'The Future of Food' by Hannah Devlin and Nic Fleming, *BBC Focus magazine*, June 2013, pp.52-59, copyright © Immediate Media Company Origin Limited; Solo Syndication for an extract in Unit 11 from : 'World's first 3-d crop circle found in English field' *The Daily Mail*, 11/06/2006, copyright © Solo Syndication, 2006; Guinness World Records Ltd for an extract in Unit 12 from 'The human lightning rod' from *The Guinness Book of Oddities*, p.142, copyright © Geoff Tibballs, 1995. Reproduced courtesy of Guinness World Records Limited; News UK for an extract in Unit 12 adapted from 'Climate Change Killed Golden Civilisations' by Michael Sheridan, *The Times*, January 2007, Copyright © News UK 2007, www.newssyndication.com; Spotlight Communications for details in Unit 13 adapted from 'Are you addicted to Social Media?', http://cdn2.business2commUnity.com/wp-content/uploads/2013/04/New-Social-Media-Addiction-Infographic.jpg, Spotlight Communications, www.spotlightcommunications.net. Reproduced with permission; and Guardian News & Media Ltd for an extract in Unit 15 from 'The master forger' by Mark Honigsbaum, copyright © Guardian News & Media Ltd 2005Z

In some instances we have been unable to trace the owners of copyright material and we would appreciate any information that would enable us to do so.